GLENCOE LANGUAGE ARTS

Grammar
AND
Composition
Handbook

GRADE 12

Glencoe
McGraw-Hill

New York, New York
Columbus, Ohio
Woodland Hills, California
Peoria, Illinois

Photo Credits
Cover Index Stock; **iii–xiv, 1** Amanita Pictures; **2–3** Amanita Pictures; **94** Amanita Pictures; **95** Laurence Dutton/Tony Stone Images; **438–439** Amanita Pictures; **530** Amanita Pictures; **531** Mark M. Lawrence/The Stock Market.

Printed in the United States of America.

Send all inquiries to:
Glencoe/McGraw-Hill
8787 Orion Place
Columbus, Ohio 43240

ISBN 0-07-825119-2

2 3 4 5 6 7 8 9 10   003   05 04 03 02 01

Table of Contents at a Glance

Table of Contents

Chapter 6   Subject-Verb Agreement   213

Chapter 12   Sentence Combining   370

CHAPTER 16   Research Paper Writing 478

CHAPTER 17   Business Writing 508

Table of Contents

Part One

• • • • • • • • • • • • • •

Ready Reference

The **Ready Reference** consists of three parts. The **Glossary of Terms** is a quick reference to language arts terms, defined and cross-referenced to relevant lessons. The **Usage Glossary** lists pairs of words that are easily confused and provides explanation for the correct usage of each word. The third part is **Abbreviations,** which consists of lists of many commonly used abbreviations.

GLOSSARY OF TERMS

abbreviation An abbreviation is a shortened form of a word. Abbreviations save space and time and prevent unnecessary wordiness. For instance, *M.D.* is more concise and easier to write than *Medical Doctor*. Most abbreviations have periods. If you are unsure of how to write an abbreviation, consult a dictionary (pages 86, 360).

EXAMPLE   Gerry left at 8:00 A.M.

EXAMPLE   Did she really leave at 8:00 A.M.?

absolute phrase An absolute phrase, also known as a nominative absolute, consists of a noun or a pronoun that is modified by a participle or a participial phrase. An absolute phrase has no grammatical relation to the rest of the sentence. An absolute phrase belongs neither to the complete subject nor to the complete predicate of a sentence. It stands "absolutely" by itself in relation to the rest of the sentence (page 156).

EXAMPLE   **Their throats parched by the searing heat,** the firefighters battled the blaze.

EXAMPLE   **The fire [being] out,** they coiled their hoses.

abstract noun An abstract noun names an idea, a quality, or a characteristic (page 97). *See concrete noun.*

EXAMPLES   **attitude   dignity   loyalty   sadness   temperature**

action verb An action verb tells what someone or something does. Some action verbs express physical action. Others express mental action (page 109).

EXAMPLE   Ted **waved** the signal flag. [physical action]

EXAMPLE   He **hoped** for success. [mental action]

active voice An action verb is in the active voice when the subject of the sentence performs the action (page 206). *See passive voice.*

EXAMPLE   The brown bear **caught** a salmon.

adjective An adjective is a word that modifies a noun or a pronoun by limiting its meaning. An adjective tells *what kind, which one, how many,* or *how much* (page 112).

EXAMPLES
red barn   **that** notebook   **cracked** pitcher

adjective clause An adjective clause is a subordinate clause that modifies a noun or a pronoun. An adjective clause may begin with a relative pronoun *(who, whom, whose, that,* or *which)* or the word *where* or *when.* An adjective clause normally follows the word it modifies (page 167).

EXAMPLE   Magazines **that inform** are best. [**The adjective clause tells *what kind* and modifies *Magazines*.**]

adjective phrase An adjective phrase is a prepositional phrase that modifies a noun or a pronoun (page 146).

EXAMPLE   Sally chose the sandwich **with cheese.** [**adjective phrase modifying a noun**]

adverb An adverb is a word that modifies a verb, an adjective, or another adverb (page 116).

EXAMPLES

modifying verbs   **Never** swim alone.
                                   verb

                               He has **seldom** complained.
                                  verb   verb

modifying adjectives   The movie was **very** scary and **too** long.
                                            adjective   adjective

modifying adverbs   She **almost** always waited **quite** patiently.
adverb   *adverb*

Adverbs modify by answering these questions:

EXAMPLES

When?   It should arrive **Saturday.**

Where?   Leave your coat **there.**

How?   He stacked the books **quickly** and **neatly.**

To what degree?   We were **very** sorry.

adverb clause An adverb clause is a subordinate clause that modifies a verb, an adjective, or another adverb in the main clause. It tells *when, where, how, why, to what extent,* or *under what conditions* (page 168).

EXAMPLE   **Before I took the test,** I studied for hours. **[The adverb clause tells *when* and modifies the verb *studied.*]**

adverb phrase An adverb phrase is a prepositional phrase that modifies a verb, an adjective, or another adverb (page 147).

EXAMPLE   Lynne works well **under pressure. [adverb phrase modifying the adverb *well.*]**

agreement Agreement is the match between grammatical forms. A verb must agree with its subject (page 215). A pronoun must agree with its antecedent (page 244).

EXAMPLE   The **freshmen** and **sophomores are debating** today. **[subject-verb agreement]**

EXAMPLE   **Lissa** thanked **her** brother for driving **her** to the dance. **[pronoun-antecedent agreement]**

antecedent An antecedent is the word or group of words to which a pronoun refers or that a pronoun replaces. All pronouns must agree with their antecedents in number, gender, and person (page 244).

EXAMPLE **Octavio Paz** is one of the greatest poets of **his** era. [singular masculine pronoun]

EXAMPLE **Emily Dickinson** wrote **her** poems on scrap paper. [singular feminine pronoun]

EXAMPLE **Walt Whitman** and **Emily Dickinson** are famous for **their** poetry. [plural pronoun]

apostrophe An apostrophe (') is a punctuation mark used in possessive nouns, possessive indefinite pronouns, and contractions. In contractions it shows that one or more letters have been left out (page 353).

EXAMPLE Leon didn't bring Celia's book, so she needs to borrow someone's.

appositive An appositive is a noun or a pronoun that is placed next to another noun or pronoun to identify it or give additional information about it (page 148).

EXAMPLE My friend **Ethan** works at a bookstore after school. [The appositive *Ethan* identifies the noun *friend*.]

appositive phrase An appositive phrase is an appositive plus any words that modify the appositive (page 148).

EXAMPLE He is saving money to travel to Bogotá, **the capital of Colombia.** [The appositive phrase, in blue type, identifies *Bogotá*.]

article Articles are the adjectives *a, an,* and *the. A* and *an* are called **indefinite articles**. They can refer to any one of a kind of person, place, or thing. *A* is used before consonant sounds, and *an* is used before vowel sounds. *The* is the **definite article.** It refers to a specific person, place, or thing (page 115).

EXAMPLES

indefinite He found **a** ring.   I ate **an** egg.

I have **a** used computer.   It's been almost **an** hour since he left.

| definite | He found **the** ring. | I ate **the** egg. |
| | I have **the** used computer. | It's almost **the** hour for lunch. |

auxiliary verb The most common auxiliary verbs are forms of *be* and *have*. They help the main verb express time by forming the various tenses (page 111).

EXAMPLE   We **will** weed the vegetable garden this morning.

EXAMPLE   Sandra **has** already weeded the peppers and the tomatoes.

EXAMPLE   We **were** weeding the flower beds when the rain started.

The other auxiliary verbs are not used primarily to express time. They are often used to emphasize meaning.

EXAMPLE   I **should be** leaving.

EXAMPLE   **Could** he **have** forgotten?

EXAMPLE   Marisa **may** already **be** finished.

B

brackets Use brackets ([ ]) to enclose information that you have inserted into a quotation for clarity. Use brackets to enclose a parenthetical phrase that already appears within parentheses (page 343).

EXAMPLE   We cannot be free until they [all Americans] are.

—James Baldwin

EXAMPLE   The name *Oregon* comes from the French word *oura-gan* (which means "hurricane" [referring to the Columbia River]).

C

case Personal pronouns have three cases, or forms. The three cases are called **nominative, objective,** and **possessive.**

The case of a personal pronoun depends on the pronoun's function in a sentence—that is, whether it's a subject, a complement, an object of a preposition, or a replacement for a possessive noun (page 234).

PERSONAL PRONOUNS

CASE	SINGULAR PRONOUNS	PLURAL PRONOUNS	FUNCTION IN SENTENCE
nominative	I, you, she, he, it	we, you, they	subject or predicate nominative
objective	me, you, her, him, it	us, you, them	direct object, indirect object, or object of preposition
possessive	my, mine, your, yours, her, hers, his, its	our, ours, your, yours, their, theirs	replacement for possessive noun(s)

clause A clause is a group of words that has a subject and a predicate (verb). A clause can function as a sentence by itself or as part of a sentence (page 163).

EXAMPLE   The curtain rose.

closing A closing is a way to end a letter. It begins with a capital letter and is followed by a comma (pages 300, 335).

EXAMPLES   Yours truly,   Sincerely,   Your friend,

collective noun A collective noun is singular in form but names a group (pages 100, 220).

EXAMPLES

family	herd	company	band	team
audience	troop	committee	jury	flock

colon A colon (:) is a punctuation mark. It's used to introduce a list and to separate the hour and the minutes when you write the time of day. It's also used after the salutation of a business letter (page 321).

EXAMPLE We need these ingredients: milk, eggs, raisins, and chopped pecans.

EXAMPLE The race will start at exactly 2:15 P.M.

EXAMPLE Dear Senator Mathers:

comma A comma (,) is a punctuation mark that's used to separate items or to set them off from the rest of a sentence (page 326).

EXAMPLE You'll find spoons, forks, and knives in that drawer.

EXAMPLE The clowns, who had crammed themselves into the tiny car, all jumped out at once.

comma splice One type of run-on sentence, a comma splice, occurs when two main clauses are joined by a comma only (page 177).

EXAMPLE

comma splice   It rained the entire time the boys were on vacation, they still enjoyed the trip.

correct   It rained the entire time the boys were on vacation. They still enjoyed the trip.

correct   It rained the entire time the boys were on vacation, but they still enjoyed the trip.

correct   It rained the entire time the boys were on vacation; they still enjoyed the trip.

common noun A common noun is the general—not the particular—name of a person, place, thing, or idea (page 99). *See proper noun.*

person	artist, uncle, poet
place	country, lake, park
thing	shuttle, vehicle, play
idea	era, religion, movement

comparative degree The comparative degree of an adjective or adverb is the form that shows two things being compared (page 258).

EXAMPLE Kim's dog is **smaller** than my dog. **[adjective]**

EXAMPLE My dog ran **more swiftly** than the cat. **[adverb]**

complement A complement is a word or a group of words that completes the meaning of a verb (page 138). *See also direct objects, indirect objects,* and *subject complements (predicate nominatives* and *predicate adjectives).*

EXAMPLE Carlos served **dinner.**

EXAMPLE Maria admires **him** deeply.

complete predicate The complete predicate consists of the simple predicate, or verb, and all the words that modify it or complete its meaning (page 133).

EXAMPLE The team **will be going from Illinois to Rhode Island by way of Cedar Point in Sandusky, Ohio.**

complete subject The complete subject consists of the simple subject and all the words that modify it (page 133).

EXAMPLE **The small black kitten in the top cage** is the one for me.

complex sentence A complex sentence has one main clause and one or more subordinate clauses (page 174).

Main Clause

EXAMPLE I like Toni Cade Bambara's stories
S V

Subordinate Clause   Subordinate Clause

because they have characters I can believe in.
S   V   S V   V

EXAMPLE When I read her stories, I enjoy them
            S V   S V

Subordinate Clause

because they are realistic.
          S V

compound-complex sentence A compound-complex sentence has two or more main clauses and at least one subordinate clause (page 174).

Main Clause   Subordinate Clause

EXAMPLE I read *Frankenstein*, which Mary Shelley wrote,
        S V   S   V

Main Clause

and I reported on it.
    S   V

compound predicate A compound predicate (or compound verb) is made up of two or more verbs or verb phrases that are joined by a conjunction and have the same subject (page 135).

EXAMPLE Maria **opened** her book, **grabbed** a pencil, and **started** her homework.

EXAMPLE Seagulls **will glide** or **swoop** down to the ocean.

compound preposition A compound preposition is a preposition that is made up of more than one word (page 120).

EXAMPLES

according to	because of	next to
ahead of	by means of	instead of
along with	except for	on account of

compound sentence A compound sentence contains two or more main clauses (page 173).

Main Clause

EXAMPLE Stories about the Old West are entertaining, **and**
        S   V

Main Clause

stories set in foreign countries are interesting.
   S   V

| | Main Clause | | Main Clause | |

EXAMPLE Stories entertain me, **and** riddles amuse me, **but**
S   V   S   V

Main Clause

poems are my favorite.
S   V

Main Clause

EXAMPLE Comedies delight us;
S   V

Main Clause

tragedies often teach us something.
S   V

compound subject A compound subject is made up of two or more simple subjects that are joined by a conjunction and have the same verb (page 134).

EXAMPLE **Tomatoes** and **carrots** are colorful vegetables.

EXAMPLE **Tomatoes** or **carrots** would add color to the salad.

EXAMPLE **Tomatoes, carrots,** and **peppers** are healthful.

compound verb *See compound predicate.*

concrete noun A concrete noun names an object that occupies space or can be recognized by any of the senses (sight, smell, hearing, taste, and touch) (page 97). *See abstract noun.*

EXAMPLES   air   melody   stone   aroma   heat

conjunction A conjunction is a word that joins single words or groups of words (page 122). *See coordinating conjunction, correlative conjunction, and subordinating conjunction.*

conjunctive adverb A conjunctive adverb is used to clarify the relationship between clauses of equal weight in a sentence. Conjunctive adverbs are preceded by semicolons and followed by commas (page 125).

EXAMPLES

to replace *and*	also, besides, furthermore, moreover
to replace *but*	however, nevertheless, nonetheless, still, though
to state a result	accordingly, consequently, then, therefore, thus
to state equality	equally, indeed, likewise, similarly

EXAMPLE   Janine is not very organized; **accordingly,** she carries a day planner and consults it often.

contraction   A contraction is a single word made up of two words that have been combined by omitting letters. Common contractions combine a subject and a verb or a verb and the word *not* (page 355).

EXAMPLES

you'd	*is formed from*	you had, you would
you're		you are
who's		who is, who has

coordinating conjunction   A coordinating conjunction joins words or groups of words that have equal grammatical weight in a sentence (page 122).

| and | but | or | so | nor | yet | for |

EXAMPLE   One **and** six are seven. **[two nouns]**

EXAMPLE   Merlin was smart **but** irresponsible. **[two adjectives]**

EXAMPLE   Let's put the note on the TV **or** on the refrigerator. **[two prepositional phrases]**

EXAMPLE   I wanted a new sun hat, **so** I bought one. **[two complete thoughts]**

EXAMPLE   He did not complain, **nor** did he object to our plan. **[two complete thoughts]**

EXAMPLE Lightning struck the barn, **yet** no fire started. [**two complete thoughts**]

EXAMPLE We didn't explore the summit that night, **for** the climb had exhausted us. [**two complete thoughts**]

correlative conjunction Correlative conjunctions work in pairs to join words and groups of words of equal grammatical weight in a sentence (page 123).

both . . . and	just as . . . so	not only . . . but (also)
either . . . or	neither . . . nor	whether . . . or

EXAMPLE **Both** he **and** I were there.

EXAMPLE **Either** she will sew new curtains, **or** I will put up the old blinds.

EXAMPLE I **not only** scrubbed **but also** waxed the floor.

dangling modifier Dangling modifiers seem logically to modify no word at all. To correct a sentence that has a dangling modifier, you must supply a word that the dangling modifier can sensibly modify (page 270).

EXAMPLES

dangling **Working all night long,** the fire was extinguished. [**participial phrase logically modifying no word in the sentence**]

clear **Working all night long,** the firefighters extinguished the fire. [**participial phrase modifying *firefighters***]

dangling **Sleeping soundly,** my dream was interrupted by the alarm. [**participial phrase logically modifying no word in the sentence**]

clear **Sleeping soundly,** I had my dream interrupted by the alarm. [**participial phrase modifying *I***]

dash A dash (—) is a punctuation mark. It's usually used in pairs to set off a sudden break or change in thought or speech (page 339).

EXAMPLE   Lionel Washington—he was my Boy Scout troop
           leader—is running for city council.

declarative sentence A declarative sentence makes a statement. A declarative sentence usually ends with a period but can end with an exclamation mark. This type of sentence is the most frequently used in speaking and writing (page 170).

EXAMPLE   I have four pets.

EXAMPLE   Two of my pets are dogs.

EXAMPLE   That's the cutest puppy I've ever seen!

demonstrative adjective A demonstrative adjective modifies a noun and points out something by answering the question *which one?* or *which ones? This, that, these,* and *those* are demonstrative adjectives when they modify nouns (page 113).

EXAMPLE   Bring **this** ticket with you.

EXAMPLE   Give **that** ticket to a friend.

EXAMPLE   We'll need **these** props for the show.

EXAMPLE   The director wrote **those** notes.

demonstrative pronoun A demonstrative pronoun points out specific persons, places, things, or ideas (page 105).

DEMONSTRATIVE PRONOUNS

singular	this	that
plural	these	those

EXAMPLE   Bring **this** with you.

EXAMPLE   Give **that** to a friend.

EXAMPLE   We'll need **these** for the show.

EXAMPLE   The director wrote **those.**

dependent clause *See subordinate clause.*

direct address Direct address is a name used in speaking directly to a person. Direct address may also be a word or phrase used in place of a name. Words used in direct address are set off by commas (page 335).

EXAMPLE **Christie,** do you like my haircut?

EXAMPLE You can't park here, **buddy.**

direct object A direct object answers the question *what?* or *whom?* after an action verb (page 138).

EXAMPLE Carlos served **dinner.**

EXAMPLE Paula called **Carlos** on the telephone.

direct quotation A direct quotation gives the speaker's exact words. It is preceded and followed by quotation marks (page 298).

EXAMPLE My little brother asked, **"Why can't I go too?"**

double comparison Don't use both *-er* and *more.* Don't use both *-est* and *most.* To do so would be an error called a double comparison (page 262).

EXAMPLES

incorrect A redwood grows more taller than an oak.

correct A redwood grows **taller** than an oak.

incorrect Aunt Ellie is my most kindest aunt.

correct Aunt Ellie is my **kindest** aunt.

double negative A double negative is two or more negative words used to express the same idea. Use only one negative word to express a negative idea (page 267).

incorrect	I don't have no stereo equipment.
correct	I do**n't** have **any** stereo equipment.
correct	I have **no** stereo equipment.

incorrect	We haven't seen no concerts this year.
correct	We have**n't** seen **any** concerts this year.
correct	We have seen **no** concerts this year.

ellipsis points Use a series of three spaced points, called ellipsis points (**. . .**), to indicate the omission of material from a quotation. Use three spaced points if the omission occurs at the beginning of a sentence. If the omission occurs in the middle or at the end of a sentence, use any necessary punctuation (for instance, a comma, a semicolon, or a period) plus the three spaced points. When it is necessary to use a period, do not leave any space between the last word and the first point, which is the period (page 344).

EXAMPLE   "Listen, my children, and you shall hear**. . . .**"

—Henry Wadsworth Longfellow

emphatic forms of a verb The present tense and the past tense have additional forms, called emphatic forms, that add special force, or emphasis, to the verb. You make the emphatic forms by using *do, does,* or *did* with the base form of the verb (page 204).

EXAMPLES

present emphatic	I **do hope** the train is on time.
	Tom **does have** a plane to catch.
past emphatic	He **did miss** his plane the last time because of a late train.

end mark An end mark is a punctuation mark used at the end of a sentence. Periods, question marks, and exclamation points are end marks (pages 319–320).

EXAMPLE   Here is your clean laundry.

EXAMPLE   Did you forget your jacket?

EXAMPLE   What a gorgeous salad that is!

essential clause Some adjective clauses are necessary to make the meaning of a sentence clear. Such an adjective clause is called an *essential clause,* or a *restrictive clause.* Do not set off an essential clause with commas (page 167).

EXAMPLE   Magazines **that have no substance** bore me.

EXAMPLE   Many writers **whose works have become famous** began their writing careers at the *New Yorker* magazine.

exclamation point An exclamation point (!) is a punctuation mark used to end a sentence that shows strong feeling (exclamatory). It's also used after strong interjections (page 320).

EXAMPLES   Yikes! We'll be late!

exclamatory sentence An exclamatory sentence expresses strong emotion and ends with an exclamation mark. Note that exclamatory sentences can be declarative (first example), imperative (second example), or interrogative (third example) while expressing strong emotion. In writing, exclamatory sentences should be used sparingly so as not to detract from their effectiveness (page 171).

EXAMPLE   She is such a beautiful dog!

EXAMPLE   Don't chew on that!

EXAMPLE   What do you think you are doing!

future perfect tense Use the future perfect tense to express one future action or condition that will begin *and* end before another future event starts.

You form the future perfect tense by using *will have* or *shall have* with the past participle of a verb: *will have practiced, shall have flown* (page 200).

EXAMPLE   By September I **will have saved** fifty dollars. [The money will be saved by the time another future event, the arrival of September, occurs.]

future tense Use the future tense to express an action or a condition that will occur in the future (page 196).

EXAMPLE   Robby **will order** the supplies.

EXAMPLE   I **will pack** the car in the morning.

G

gender The gender of a noun may be masculine (male), feminine (female), or neuter (referring to things) (page 244).

EXAMPLES   **man** (masculine)   **aunt** (feminine)   **notebook** (neuter)

gender-neutral language Language that does not assume the gender of a noun is called gender-neutral language. Use gender-neutral language when the gender is unknown or could be either masculine or feminine (pages 245, 452–453).

EXAMPLE   An *author* must capture **his or her** readers' interest.

EXAMPLE   *Authors* must capture **their** readers' interest.

EXAMPLE   *Authors* must capture readers' interest.

gerund A gerund is a verb form that ends in *-ing* and is used in the same ways a noun is used (page 152).

EXAMPLE **Cooking** is an enjoyable activity. **[gerund as subject]**

EXAMPLE My younger sister likes **swimming. [gerund as direct object]**

gerund phrase A gerund phrase contains a gerund plus any complements and modifiers (page 152).

EXAMPLE **Cross-country skiing** is good exercise.

EXAMPLE **Billie Holiday's soulful singing** delighted many audiences.

helping verb *See auxiliary verb.*

hyphen A hyphen (-) is a punctuation mark that's used in compound words (page 357).

EXAMPLE Luis's great-grandfather hung twenty-one bird feeders.

imperative mood The imperative mood expresses a command or makes a request (page 207).

EXAMPLE **Take** the express train home.

EXAMPLE Please **don't slam** the door.

imperative sentence An imperative sentence gives a command or makes request. An imperative sentence usually ends with a period but can end with an exclamation mark. In imperative sentences, the subject *you* is understood (page 171).

EXAMPLE Get off the table**.**

EXAMPLE Duck**!**

indefinite pronoun An indefinite pronoun refers to persons, places, things, or ideas in a more general way than a noun does (page 107).

INDEFINITE PRONOUNS

always singular			
another	either	neither	other
anybody	everybody	no one	somebody
anyone	everyone	nobody	someone
anything	everything	nothing	something
each	much	one	

always plural				
both	few	many	others	several

singular or plural					
all	any	enough	most	none	some

EXAMPLE **Everybody** needs food. [The indefinite pronoun *Everybody* refers to people in general.]

EXAMPLE Did you get **enough** to eat? [The indefinite pronoun *enough* refers to a general, not a specific, amount.]

EXAMPLE After two bowls of chili, I did not want **another**. [The indefinite pronoun *another* has the antecedent *bowls (of chili)*.]

independent clause An independent clause has a subject and a predicate and expresses a complete thought. It is the only type of clause that can stand alone as a sentence. An independent clause is also called a **main clause** (page 163).

EXAMPLE **The curtain rose.**

EXAMPLE **The cast bowed,** and **the audience applauded.**

EXAMPLE **The curtains closed for several minutes,** but **the applause continued.**

indicative mood The indicative mood, the one used far more often than the imperative mood or the subjunctive mood, makes a statement or asks a question (page 207).

EXAMPLE He **takes** the express train home.

EXAMPLE She **doesn't slam** the door.

indirect object An indirect object answers the question *to whom? for whom? to what?* or *for what?* after an action verb (page 139).

EXAMPLE   Tyrone served his **sisters** dinner.

EXAMPLE   Kim saved **Rosa** and **Manuel** seats.

indirect quotation An indirect quotation paraphrases a speaker's words and should not be capitalized or enclosed in quotation marks (page 298). *See direct quotation.*

EXAMPLE   My brother asked **why** he couldn't go.

EXAMPLE   She said **that** she wanted to leave early.

infinitive An infinitive is a verb form that is usually pre-ceded by the word *to* and is used as a noun, an adjective, or an adverb (page 153).

EXAMPLE   His goal is **to graduate. [infinitive as predicate nominative]**

EXAMPLE   They have the desire **to win. [infinitive as adjective]**

infinitive phrase An infinitive phrase contains an infinitive plus any complements and modifiers (page 154).

EXAMPLE   We stopped **to look at the beautiful scenery.**

EXAMPLE   **To be a good friend** is my goal.

intensive pronoun An intensive pronoun ends with *-self* or *-selves* and is used to draw special attention to a noun or a pronoun already named (pages 104–105, 240).

EXAMPLE   He **himself** delivered the flowers.

EXAMPLE   You must sign the application **yourself.**

EXAMPLE   Mariko **herself** made the bridesmaids' dresses.

interjection An interjection is a word or phrase that expresses emotion or exclamation. An interjection has no grammatical connection to other words (page 127).

EXAMPLE **Oh, my!** What is that?

EXAMPLE **Ouch,** it's hot!

EXAMPLE **Yikes,** I'll be late!

EXAMPLE **Ah,** that's better.

interrogative pronoun An interrogative pronoun is used to form questions (page 106).

| who | whom | what | which | whose |
| whoever | whomever | whatever | whichever | |

EXAMPLE **Who** is at the door?

EXAMPLE **Whom** would you prefer?

EXAMPLE **Whose** is this plaid coat?

EXAMPLE **Whatever** is that odd noise?

interrogative sentence An interrogative sentence asks a question. It usually ends with a question mark but can end with an exclamation point if it expresses strong emotion (page 171).

EXAMPLE How many pets do you have**?**

EXAMPLE What in the world were you thinking**!**

intransitive verb An intransitive verb is *not* followed by a word that answers the question *what?* or *whom?* (page 109). *See transitive verb.*

EXAMPLE The batter **swung** wildly. **[The verb is followed by a word that tells *how*.]**

inverted order A sentence written in inverted order, in which the predicate comes before the subject, serves to add emphasis to the subject (pages 137, 226).

PREDICATE	SUBJECT
Across the field **galloped**	the three **horses.**
In the distance **flowed**	a **river.**

irregular verb An irregular verb forms its past and past participle in some way other than by adding *-ed* or *-d* to the base form (page 187).

EXAMPLES

BASE FORM	PAST FORM	PAST PARTICIPLE
be, am, are, is	was, were	been
swim	swam	swum
put	put	put
write	wrote	written
lie	lay	lain

italics Italics are printed letters that slant to the right. *This sentence is printed in italic type.* Italics are used for the titles of certain kinds of published works, works of art, foreign terms, and other situations. In handwriting, underlining is a substitute for italics (page 350).

EXAMPLE   This *Newsweek* magazine has an article about Picasso's painting *Guernica.*

EXAMPLE   Cicero's saying *Omnia praeclara rara* can be translated as "All excellent things are scarce."

linking verb A linking verb links, or joins, the subject of a sentence (often a noun or a pronoun) with a noun, a pronoun, or an adjective that identifies or describes the subject. A linking verb does not show action. *Be* in all its forms—

am, is, are, was, were—is the most commonly used linking verb (page 110).

(page 110)

EXAMPLE The person behind the mask **was** you.

EXAMPLE The players **are** ready.

EXAMPLE Archery **is** an outdoor sport.

EXAMPLE They **were** sports fans.

Several other verbs besides *be* can act as linking verbs.

OTHER VERBS THAT CAN BE LINKING VERBS

appear	grow	seem	stay
become	look	sound	taste
feel	remain	smell	turn

EXAMPLE This salad **tastes** good.

EXAMPLE The sun **feels** warm on my shoulders.

EXAMPLE You **look** comfortable.

EXAMPLE The leaves **turned** brown.

main clause A main clause has a subject and a predicate and expresses a complete thought. It is the only type of clause that can stand alone as a sentence. A main clause is also called an **independent clause** (page 163).

(page 163)

EXAMPLE **The curtain rose.**

EXAMPLE **The cast bowed,** and **the audience applauded.**

EXAMPLE **The curtains closed for several minutes,** but **the applause continued.**

main verb A main verb is the last word in a verb phrase. If a verb stands alone, it's a main verb (page 111).

(page 111)

EXAMPLE The band members have been **selling** light bulbs for a month.

EXAMPLE One band member **sold** two cases of light bulbs.

misplaced modifier Misplaced modifiers modify the wrong word, or they seem to modify more than one word in a sentence. To correct a sentence that has a misplaced modifier, move the modifier as close as possible to the word it modifies (page 269).

EXAMPLE

misplaced **Soaring over the edge of the cliff,** the photographer captured an image of the eagle. **[participial phrase incorrectly modifying *photographer*]**

clear The photographer captured an image of the eagle **soaring over the edge of the cliff. [participial phrase correctly modifying *eagle*]**

mood of verbs Along with expressing tense and voice, verbs also express mood. A verb expresses one of three moods: the indicative mood, the imperative mood, or the subjunctive mood (page 207). *See indicative mood, imperative mood, and subjunctive mood.*

nominative case Use the nominative case for a pronoun that is a subject or a predicate nominative (page 234).

EXAMPLE **We** have raised enough money.

EXAMPLE The lead soprano will be **she.**

nonessential clause An adjective clause that adds information to a sentence but is not necessary to make the meaning of the sentence clear is called a *nonessential clause* or a *nonrestrictive clause.* Always use commas to set off a nonessential clause (pages 167–168, 329).

EXAMPLE James Thurber, **who was a famous humorist,** wrote for the *New Yorker.*

EXAMPLE His stories, **which include humorous incidents from his childhood in Ohio,** make funny and interesting reading.

nonrestrictive clause *See nonessential clause.*

noun A noun is a word that names a person, a place, a thing, or an idea (page 97).

EXAMPLES

person	uncle, doctor, baby, Luisa, son-in-law
place	kitchen, mountain, Web site, West Virginia
thing	apple, tulip, continent, seagull, amplifier
idea	respect, pride, love, appreciation, century

noun clause A noun clause is a subordinate clause that is used as a noun within the main clause of a sentence. You can use a noun clause as a subject, a direct object, an indirect object, an object of a preposition, or a predicate nominative (page 169).

EXAMPLE **Whoever wins the election** will speak. [noun clause as subject]

number Number refers to the form of a word that indicates whether it is singular or plural. A verb must agree with its subject in number (page 215).

EXAMPLES

SINGULAR	PLURAL
The **athlete exercises.**	The **athletes exercise.**
The **cat scratches.**	The **cats scratch.**

object complement An object complement answers the question *what?* after a direct object. That is, it *completes* the meaning of the direct object by identifying or describing it (page 139).

EXAMPLE   Residents find the park **peaceful. [adjective]**

EXAMPLE   Maya appointed me **spokesperson** and **treasurer. [nouns]**

EXAMPLE   My grandmother considers the property **hers. [pronoun]**

object of a preposition   An object of a preposition is the noun or pronoun that ends a prepositional phrase (page 121).

EXAMPLE   The diamonds in the **vault** are priceless. **[In shows the relationship between the diamonds and the object of the preposition, vault.]**

objective case   Use the objective case for a pronoun that is a direct object, an indirect object, or an object of a preposition (page 234).

EXAMPLE   The coach trained **her. [direct object]**

EXAMPLE   The prompter gave **me** my cues. **[indirect object]**

EXAMPLE   Third prize was split between **him** and **me. [object of preposition]**

parentheses   Parentheses ( ) are punctuation marks used to set off words that define or explain another word (page 341).

EXAMPLE   Myanmar **(**formerly Burma**)** is on the Bay of Bengal.

parenthetical expression   Parenthetical expressions are side thoughts that add information. Parenthetical expressions should be set off by commas, dashes, or parentheses (pages 331, 339, 341).

EXAMPLES   in fact   on the other hand   on the contrary

EXAMPLES   by the way   to be exact   after all

EXAMPLE   **By the way,** did Mom call today?

EXAMPLE   I'm responsible for about a hundred tickets—**to be exact,** 106.

participial phrase A participial phrase contains a participle plus any complements and modifiers (page 151).

EXAMPLE   The dog saw many ducks **swimming in the lake.**

EXAMPLE   **Barking loudly,** the dog approached the water.

participle A participle is a verb form that can function as an adjective (pages 113, 150).

EXAMPLE   A **moving** van is parked on our street. **[present participle]**

EXAMPLE   The dogs watched the **striped** cat. **[past participle]**

passive voice An action verb is in the passive voice when its action is performed on the subject (page 206). *See active voice.*

EXAMPLE   A salmon **was caught** by the brown bear.

past perfect tense Use the past perfect tense to indicate that one past action or condition began *and* ended before another past action or condition started. You form the past perfect tense by using the auxiliary verb *had* with the past participle of a verb: *had praised, had written* (page 199).

EXAMPLE

PAST   **PAST PERFECT**

Pat **dedicated** her play to the drama teacher who **had encouraged** her long ago. **[First the drama teacher encouraged Pat; then years later Patricia acknowledged her teacher's support.]**

past tense Use the past tense to express an action or a condition that was started and completed in the past (page 196).

EXAMPLE   The track meet **went** well.

EXAMPLE   Nan **set** a new school record for the shot put.

period A period (.) is a punctuation mark used to end a sentence that makes a statement (declarative) or gives a command (imperative). It's also used at the end of many abbreviations (pages 319, 360).

EXAMPLE I can't tell whether this recipe specifies "1 tsp." or "1 tbsp." of cinnamon. **[declarative]**

EXAMPLE Please mail a check to Dr. Benson. **[imperative]**

personal pronoun A personal pronoun refers to a specific person, place, thing, or idea by indicating the person speaking (the first person), the person being spoken to (the second person), or any other person, place, thing, or idea being discussed (the third person). Like a noun, a personal pronoun expresses number; that is, it can be singular or plural (pages 102, 234).

	PERSONAL PRONOUNS	
	SINGULAR	PLURAL
first person	I, me	we, us
second person	you	you
third person	he, him, she, her, it	they, them

EXAMPLES

first person	The song was dedicated to **me**. [*Me* **refers to the person speaking.**]
second person	Sam will copy the document for **you**. [*You* **refers to the person being spoken to.**]
third person	**She** gave **him** the good news. [*She* **and** *him* **refer to the people being talked about.**]

phrase A phrase is a group of words that acts in a sentence as a single part of speech (page 146).

positive degree The positive degree of an adjective or adverb is the form that cannot be used to make a comparison. This form appears as the entry word in a dictionary (page 258).

EXAMPLE My dog is **small**.

EXAMPLE The cat ran **swiftly**.

possessive pronoun A possessive pronoun takes the place of the possessive form of a noun (page 103).

POSSESSIVE PRONOUNS

	SINGULAR	PLURAL
first person	my, mine	our, ours
second person	your, yours	your, yours
third person	his, her, hers, its	their, theirs

predicate The predicate is the part of the sentence that says something about the subject (page 131).

EXAMPLE   Garth Brooks **will perform.**

predicate adjective A predicate adjective follows a linking verb and points back to the subject and further describes it (page 141).

EXAMPLE   Firefighters are **brave.**

EXAMPLE   Firefighters must be extremely **careful.**

predicate nominative A predicate nominative is a noun or a pronoun that follows a linking verb and points back to the subject to rename it or to identify it further (page 140).

EXAMPLE   Sopranos are **singers.**

EXAMPLE   Many current opera stars are **Italians** or **Spaniards.**

EXAMPLE   Fiona became both a **musician** and an **architect.**

preposition A preposition is a word that shows the relationship of a noun or a pronoun to another word in a sentence (page 119).

aboard	beneath	in	regarding
about	beside	inside	respecting

EXAMPLE   I read **to** Carlito **from** the new book.

prepositional phrase A prepositional phrase is a group of words that begins with a preposition and ends with a noun or a pronoun that is called the object of the preposition (page 146).

EXAMPLE   The diamonds **in the vault** are priceless. [*In* shows the relationship between *the diamonds* and the object of the preposition, *vault*.]

EXAMPLE   The telephone rang four times **during dinner.** [*During* shows the relationship between *rang* and the object of the preposition, *dinner*.]

EXAMPLE   Here is a gift **for you.** [*For* relates *gift* to the object of the preposition, *you*.]

present perfect tense Use the present perfect tense to express an action or a condition that occurred at some *indefinite time* in the past. You form the present perfect tense by using *has* or *have* with the past participle of a verb: *has permitted, have cut* (page 198).

EXAMPLE   The living-room clock **has stopped.**

EXAMPLE   They **have brought** the new couch a day early.

present tense The present tense expresses a constant, repeated, or habitual action or condition. It can also express a general truth or an action or a condition that exists only now. It is sometimes used in historical writing to express past events and, more often, in poetry, fiction, and journalism (especially in sports writing) to convey to the reader a sense of being there. This usage is sometimes called the *historical present tense* (page 193).

EXAMPLE   Isaac **likes** the taste of tea with honey in it. [not just this cup of tea but every cup of tea; a repeated action]

EXAMPLE   Emily **bakes** wonderful spice cookies. [always; a habitual action]

EXAMPLE   Gold **is** valuable. [a general truth]

EXAMPLE   I **see** a hummingbird at the feeder. [at this very moment]

EXAMPLE   The goalie **throws** her body across the opening and **blocks** the shot in the final seconds of the game. [historical present]

principal parts of verbs   All verbs have four principal parts: a *base form*, a *present participle*, a *simple past form*, and a *past participle*. All the verb tenses are formed from these principal parts (page 185).

EXAMPLES

PRINCIPAL PARTS OF VERBS

BASE FORM	PRESENT PARTICIPLE	PAST FORM	PAST PARTICIPLE
carry	carrying	carried	carried
play	playing	played	played
sing	singing	sang	sung

progressive forms of a verb   Each of the six tenses has a progressive form that expresses a continuing action. You make the progressive forms by using the appropriate tense of the verb *be* with the present participle of the main verb (page 204).

EXAMPLE

present progressive	They *are* **traveling.**
past progressive	They *were* **traveling.**
future progressive	They *will be* **traveling.**
present perfect progressive	They *have been* **traveling.**
past perfect progressive	They *had been* **traveling.**
future perfect progressive	They *will have been* **traveling.**

pronoun   A pronoun is a word that takes the place of a noun, a group of words acting as a noun, or another pronoun. The word or group of words to which a pronoun refers is called its antecedent (page 101).

EXAMPLE Though Georgia O'Keeffe was born in Wisconsin, **she** grew to love the landscape of the American Southwest. **[The pronoun *she* takes the place of its proper noun antecedent, *Georgia O'Keeffe*.]**

EXAMPLE When Georgia O'Keeffe and Alfred Stieglitz were married in 1924, **both** were famous artists. **[The pronoun *both* takes the place of the nouns *Georgia O'Keeffe* and *Alfred Stieglitz*.]**

EXAMPLE Though O'Keeffe **herself** was a painter, **her** husband was a photographer. **[The pronouns *herself* and *her* take the place of the nouns *O'Keeffe* and *O'Keeffe's*.]**

proper adjective A proper adjective is formed from a proper noun. It begins with a capital letter (page 115).

EXAMPLE Vancouver is a **Canadian** city.

EXAMPLE We visited the **London** Zoo.

proper noun A proper noun is the name of a particular person, place, thing, or idea (page 99). *See common noun.*

EXAMPLES

PROPER NOUNS

person	Michelangelo, Uncle Louis, Maya Angelou
place	Mexico, Lake Superior, Yellowstone National Park
thing	*Challenger*, Jeep, *Romeo and Juliet*
idea	Industrial Age, Judaism, Romanticism

Q

question mark A question mark (**?**) is a punctuation mark used to end a sentence that asks a question (interrogative) (page 320).

EXAMPLE Can you imagine what life would be like without television**?**

READY REFERENCE

Glossary of Terms **35**

quotation marks Quotation marks (" ") are punctuation marks used to enclose the exact words of a speaker. They're also used for titles of certain published works (page 349).

EXAMPLE "Let's record ourselves reading aloud," said Lou, "and give the tape to the children's hospital."

EXAMPLE They decided on something a bit more cheerful than "The Pit and the Pendulum."

reflexive pronoun A reflexive pronoun always ends with *-self* or *-selves* and refers, or reflects back, to the subject of the clause, indicating that the same person or thing is involved. A reflexive pronoun always adds information to a sentence (pages 104–105, 240).

EXAMPLE Jim uses a stopwatch to time **himself** on the track.

EXAMPLE She taught **herself** to play the piano.

EXAMPLE We imagined **ourselves** dancing in a forest glade.

regular verb A regular verb forms its past and past participle by adding *-ed* or *-d* to the base form (page 187).

EXAMPLES

REGULAR VERBS

BASE FORM	PAST FORM	PAST PARTICIPLE
climb	climbed	climbed
skate	skated	skated
trot	trotted	trotted

relative pronoun A relative pronoun is used to begin a subordinate clause (page 107).

RELATIVE PRONOUNS

who	whoever	which	that
whom	whomever	whichever	what
	whose	whatever	

EXAMPLE   The driver **who** arrived last parked over there. **[The relative pronoun *who* begins the subordinate clause *who arrived last.*]**

EXAMPLE   The meal **that** you prepared was delicious. **[The relative pronoun *that* begins the subordinate clause *that you prepared.*]**

restrictive clause *See essential clause.*

run-on sentence A run-on sentence is two or more complete sentences written as though they were one sentence (page 177). *See comma splice.*

EXAMPLE

run-on   It rained the entire time the boys were on vacation they still enjoyed the trip.

run-on   It rained the entire time the boys were on vacation but they still enjoyed the trip.

run-on   It rained the entire time the boys were on vacation, they still enjoyed the trip.

correct   It rained the entire time the boys were on vacation. **T**hey still enjoyed the trip.

correct   It rained the entire time the boys were on vacation, **but** they still enjoyed the trip.

correct   It rained the entire time the boys were on vacation; they still enjoyed the trip.

salutation A salutation is the greeting in a letter. The first word and any proper nouns in a salutation should be capitalized. In a friendly letter, the salutation ends with a comma; in a business letter, the salutation ends with a colon (pages 300, 323, 335).

EXAMPLE   **My** dear cousin **Nancy,**   **Dear Councilwoman Ramos:**

semicolon A semicolon (;) is a punctuation mark used to join the main clauses of a compound sentence (page 324).

EXAMPLE   Juliana will sing the melody; Maurice and Lee will harmonize.

sentence A sentence is a group of words that expresses a complete thought (page 131).

EXAMPLE   Hector Hugh Munro wrote stories using the pseudonym Saki.

sentence fragment A sentence fragment is an error that occurs when an incomplete sentence is punctuated as though it were complete (page 176).

EXAMPLE

fragment   **The two weary hikers walking for hours. [lacks complete predicate]**

complete sentence   The two weary hikers had been walking for hours.

simple predicate The simple predicate is the verb or verb phrase that expresses an action or a state of being about the subject of the sentence (page 132).

EXAMPLE   The team **will be going** from Illinois to Rhode Island by way of Cedar Point in Sandusky, Ohio.

simple sentence A simple sentence contains only one main clause and no subordinate clauses (page 172).

EXAMPLE Stories entertain.

EXAMPLE Long, complicated, fantastic stories with aliens, space travelers, and happy endings entertain and educate men, women, and children all over the world.

simple subject The simple subject is the key noun or pronoun (or word or word group acting as a noun) that tells what the sentence is about (page 132).

EXAMPLE The small black **kitten** in the top cage is the one I want.

subject The subject is the part of the sentence that names whom or what the sentence is about (page 131).

EXAMPLE **Dogs** were barking.

EXAMPLE Last in line was **he.**

subject complement A subject complement follows a subject and a linking verb and identifies or describes the subject (page 140). *See predicate nominative and predicate adjective.*

EXAMPLE Sopranos are **singers.**

EXAMPLE The star of the opera was **she.**

EXAMPLE The singer grew **hoarse.**

subjunctive mood The subjunctive mood is often replaced by the indicative mood in informal English. The subjunctive mood does, however, have two important uses in modern formal English (page 208). First, the subjunctive mood expresses, although indirectly, a demand, recommendation, suggestion, or statement of necessity.

EXAMPLE We demand [*or* recommend *or* suggest] that she **set** her alarm clock for 6:30 A.M. **[To form the subjunctive mood, drop the –s from the third-person singular.]**

EXAMPLE   It is necessary that she **be** on time for school. **[The subjunctive mood uses *be* instead of *am, is,* or *are.*]**

Second, the subjunctive mood is used to state a condition or a wish that is contrary to fact. Notice that this use of the subjunctive always requires the past tense.

EXAMPLE   If she **were** to oversleep, she would miss her ride to school. **[The subjunctive mood uses *were,* not *was.*]**

EXAMPLE   I wish (that) I **were** in San Antonio.

EXAMPLE   You are speaking to me as if I **were** a child.

PEANUTS reprinted by permission of United Feature Syndicate, Inc.

subordinate clause   A subordinate clause, also called a dependent clause, has a subject and a predicate but does not express a complete thought. It cannot stand alone as a sentence (page 164).

EXAMPLE   **When I was young,** dolls **that spoke** were my favorites.

EXAMPLE   **Whoever joins the circus** will travel across the country.

subordinating conjunction   A subordinating conjunction joins two clauses, or ideas, in such a way as to make one grammatically dependent on the other. The idea, or clause, that a subordinating conjunction introduces is said to be "subordinate," or dependent, because it cannot stand by itself as a complete sentence (page 124).

after	as though	since	until
although	because	so long as	when
as	before	so (that)	whenever

EXAMPLE   We can skate on the pond **when** the ice is thicker.

EXAMPLE   We can't skate **until** the ice is thicker.

EXAMPLE   **Because** the ice is still too thin, we must wait for a hard freeze.

superlative degree The superlative degree of an adjective or adverb is the form that shows three or more things being compared (page 258).

EXAMPLE   Of the three dogs, Ray's dog is the **smallest** one.

EXAMPLE   The squirrel ran **most swiftly** of all.

syllable When a word must be divided at the end of a line, it is generally divided between syllables or pronounceable parts. Because it is often difficult to decide where a word should be divided, consult a dictionary. In general, if a word contains two consonants occurring between two vowels or if it contains double consonants, divide the word between the two consonants (page 359).

EXAMPLES   foun-tain   struc-ture   lin-ger

tense Tenses are the forms of a verb that help to show time. There are six tenses in English: *present, past, future, present perfect, past perfect*, and *future perfect* (page 193).

EXAMPLE

present tense	I **sing.**
past tense	I **sang.**
future tense	I **shall** (*or* **will**) **sing.**
present perfect tense	I **have sung.**
past perfect tense	I **had sung.**
future perfect tense	I **shall** (*or* **will**) **have sung.**

transitive verb A transitive verb is an action verb followed by a word or words that answer the question *what?* or *whom?* (page 109). *See intransitive verb.*

EXAMPLE   The batter **swung** the bat confidently. [The action verb *swung* is followed by the noun *bat*, which answers the question *swung what?*]

verb A verb is a word that expresses action or a state of being and is necessary to make a statement (page 108).

EXAMPLE   The bicyclist **grinned.**

EXAMPLE   The riders **seem** enthusiastic.

verbal A verbal is a verb form that functions in a sentence as a noun, an adjective, or an adverb. Verbals are *participles, gerunds,* and *infinitives.* Each of these can be expanded into phrases (page 150).

EXAMPLE   **Exhausted,** the team headed for the locker room. **[past participle]**

EXAMPLE   **Swimming** is my sport. **[gerund]**

EXAMPLE   I want **to win. [infinitive]**

verb phrase A verb phrase consists of a main verb and all its auxiliary, or helping, verbs (page 111). The most common auxiliary verbs are forms of *be* and *have.* They help the main verb express time by forming the various tenses.

EXAMPLE   We **will weed** the vegetable garden this morning.

EXAMPLE   Sandra **has** already **weeded** the peppers and the tomatoes.

EXAMPLE   We **were weeding** the flowerbeds when the rain started.

The other auxiliary verbs are not used primarily to express time. They are often used to emphasize meaning.

EXAMPLE   I **should be leaving.**

EXAMPLE   **Could** he **have forgotten?**

EXAMPLE   Marisa **may** already **be finished.**

verbal phrase A verbal phrase is a verbal plus any complements and modifiers (page 150).

EXAMPLE   **Frightened by the barking dogs,** the kittens ran to their mother. **[participial phrase]**

EXAMPLE   **Swimming twenty laps a day** is my goal. **[gerund phrase]**

EXAMPLE   I like **to sing the fight song. [infinitive phrase]**

voice Voice is the form a verb takes to explain whether the subject performs the action or the action is performed upon the subject. An action verb is in the active voice when the subject of the sentence performs the action. An action verb is in the passive voice when its action is performed on the subject (page 206).

EXAMPLE   The brown bear **caught** a salmon. **[active voice]**

EXAMPLE   A salmon **was caught** by the brown bear. **[passive voice]**

USAGE GLOSSARY

This glossary presents some particularly troublesome matters of usage. The glossary will guide you in choosing between words that are often confused. It will also alert you to certain words and expressions you should avoid when you speak or write for school or business.

a, an Use *a* before words that begin with a consonant sound. Use *an* before words that begin with a vowel sound.

EXAMPLES **a** poem, **a** house, **a** yacht, **a** union, **a** one-track mind

EXAMPLES **an** apple, **an** icicle, **an** honor, **an** umbrella, **an** only child

accede, exceed *Accede* means "to agree." *Exceed* means "to go beyond."

EXAMPLE I **acceded** to Mom's wishes.

EXAMPLE Don't **exceed** the speed limit.

accept, except *Accept* is a verb that means "to receive" or "to agree to." *Except* is usually a preposition meaning "but." *Except* may also be a verb that means "to leave out or exclude."

EXAMPLE Will you **accept** our thanks?

EXAMPLE The president **accepted** the terms of the treaty.

EXAMPLE Everyone will be there **except** you. **[preposition]**

EXAMPLE The government **excepts** people with very low incomes from paying taxes. **[verb]**

access, excess *Access* means "admittance." An *excess* is a surplus.

EXAMPLE The thief gained **access** to the building with a stolen key.

EXAMPLE We have an **excess** of musical talent in our class.

adapt, adopt *Adapt* means "to change to meet new requirements" or "to adjust." *Adopt* means "to accept and take as one's own."

EXAMPLE I can **adapt** to new surroundings easily.

EXAMPLE We can **adapt** this old bathrobe for a Roman senator's costume.

EXAMPLE I think that dog has **adopted** you.

advice, advise *Advice*, a noun, means "an opinion offered as guidance." *Advise*, a verb, means "to give advice" or "to counsel."

EXAMPLE Why should I **advise** you when you never accept my **advice**?

affect, effect *Affect* is a verb that means "to cause a change in" or "to influence the emotions of." *Effect* may be a noun or a verb. As a noun, it means "result." As a verb, it means "to bring about or accomplish."

EXAMPLE The mayor's policies have **affected** every city agency.

EXAMPLE The mayor's policies have had a positive **effect** on every city agency. **[noun]**

EXAMPLE The mayor has **effected** positive changes in every city agency. **[verb]**

aggravate, annoy To aggravate something is to make it graver or more serious. Things that can be aggravated are, for example, illnesses and crimes. In informal speaking and writing, *aggravate* has another meaning: "to annoy, to irritate." When you are writing or speaking formally, don't use *aggravate* when *annoy* or *irritate* would be correct.

EXAMPLE Donna's asthma was **aggravated** by the wind-blown pollen.

EXAMPLE Now here's another letter from that same company; I think they want to **annoy [*not* aggravate]** me to death!

ain't *Ain't* is unacceptable in speaking and writing unless you're quoting someone's exact words or writing dialogue. Use *I'm not; you, we,* or *they aren't; he, she,* or *it isn't.*

all ready, already *All ready* means "completely ready." *Already* is an adverb that means "before" or "by this time."

EXAMPLE   The band was **all ready** to play its last number, but the fans were **already** leaving the stadium.

all right, alright The spelling *alright* is not acceptable in formal writing. Use *all right.*

EXAMPLE   Don't worry; everything will be **all right**.

all the farther, all the faster These expressions are not acceptable in formal speech and writing. Use *as far as* and *as fast as.*

EXAMPLE   Five hundred miles was **as far as** [*not* **all the farther**] we could drive in a single day.

EXAMPLE   This is **as fast as** [*not* **all the faster**] I can pedal.

all together, altogether Use *all together* to mean "in a group." Use *altogether* to mean "completely" or "in all."

EXAMPLE   Let's cheer **all together**.

EXAMPLE   You are being **altogether** silly.

EXAMPLE   I have three dollars in quarters and two dollars in dimes; that's five dollars **altogether**.

allusion, illusion An *allusion* is an indirect reference. An *illusion* is a false idea or appearance.

EXAMPLE   Her speech included an **allusion** to one of Robert Frost's poems.

EXAMPLE   The shimmering heat produced an **illusion** of water on the road.

almost, most Don't use *most* in place of *almost.*

EXAMPLE   Marty **almost** [*not* most] always makes the honor roll.

a lot, alot, allot *A lot* should always be written as two words. It means "a large number or amount." Avoid using *a lot* in formal writing; be specific. The verb *allot* means "to assign or set aside" or "to distribute."

EXAMPLE   **A lot** [*not* Alot] of snow fell last night.

   [*Better:* A great deal of snow fell last night.]

EXAMPLE   The legislature will **allot** funds for a new capitol.

altar, alter An *altar* is a raised structure at which religious ceremonies are performed. *Alter* means "to change."

EXAMPLE   The bride and groom approached the **altar**.

EXAMPLE   The wardrobe manager **altered** some of the costumes to fit the new cast members.

among, between In general use *among* to show a relationship in which more than two persons or things are considered as a group.

EXAMPLE   The committee will distribute the used clothing **among** the poor families in the community.

EXAMPLE   There was confusion **among** the players on the field.

   In general, use *between* to show a relationship involving two persons or things, to compare one person or thing with an entire group, or to compare more than two items within a group.

EXAMPLE   Mr. and Mrs. Ito live halfway **between** Seattle and Portland. **[relationship involving two places]**

EXAMPLE   What was the difference **between** Frank Sinatra and other vocalists of the twentieth century? **[one person compared with a group]**

EXAMPLE   Emilio could not decide **between** the collie, the cocker spaniel, and the beagle. **[items within a group]**

amount, number *Amount* and *number* both refer to quantity. Use *amount* for things that can't be counted. Use *number* for things that can be counted.

EXAMPLE   Fort Knox contains a vast **amount** of gold.

EXAMPLE   Fort Knox contains a large **number** of gold bars.

and/or This expression, once common in legal language, should be avoided in general writing. Change *and/or* to "this *or* that *or both*."

EXAMPLE   We'll go hiking **or** skiing **or both.** [*not* We'll go hiking **and/or skiing.**]

anxious, eager *Anxious* comes from *anxiety;* therefore, it implies uneasiness or apprehension. It is not a synonym for *eager,* which means "filled with enthusiasm."

EXAMPLE   Jean was **anxious** about her test results.

EXAMPLE   She was **eager** [*not* **anxious**] to begin college.

anyways, anywheres, everywheres, nowheres, somewheres Write and speak these words without the final *s: anyway, anywhere, everywhere, nowhere, somewhere.*

ascent, assent An *ascent* is a rise or an act of climbing. *Assent* as a verb means "to agree or consent"; as a noun, it means "agreement" or "consent."

EXAMPLE   We watched the **ascent** of the balloon.

EXAMPLE   Will your parents **assent** to our plans? **[verb]**

EXAMPLE   They were happy to give their **assent** to the plans. **[noun]**

a while, awhile Use *a while* after a preposition. Use *awhile* as an adverb.

EXAMPLE   She read for **a while**.

EXAMPLE   She read **awhile**.

bad, badly *Bad* is an adjective; use it before nouns and after linking verbs to modify the subject. *Badly* is an adverb; use it to modify action verbs.

EXAMPLE   Clara felt **bad** about the broken vase.

EXAMPLE   The team performed **badly** in the first half.

bare, bear *Bare* means "naked." A *bear* is an animal.

EXAMPLE   Don't expose your **bare** skin to the sun.

EXAMPLE   There are many **bears** in Yellowstone National Park.

base, bass One meaning of *base* is "a part on which something rests or stands." *Bass* pronounced to rhyme with *face* is a type of voice. When *bass* is pronounced to rhyme with *glass*, it's a kind of fish.

EXAMPLE   Who is playing first **base**?

EXAMPLE   We need a **bass** singer for the part.

EXAMPLE   We caught several **bass** on our fishing trip.

because of, due to Use *because of* with action verbs. Use *due to* with linking verbs.

EXAMPLE   The game was canceled **because of** rain.

EXAMPLE   The cancellation was **due to** rain.

being as, being that Some people use these expressions instead of *because* in informal conversation. In formal speaking and writing, use *because.*

EXAMPLE   **Because [*not* Being as]** their car broke down, they were late.

EXAMPLE   They were late **because [*not* being that]** their car broke down.

beside, besides *Beside* means "at the side of" or "next to." *Besides* means "in addition to."

EXAMPLE Katrina sat **beside** her brother at the table.

EXAMPLE **Besides** yogurt and fruit, the lunchroom serves muffins and bagels.

blew, blue *Blue* is the color of a clear sky. *Blew* is the past tense of *blow.*

EXAMPLE She wore a **blue** shirt.

EXAMPLE The dead leaves **blew** along the driveway.

boar, bore A *boar* is a male pig. *Bore* means "to tire out with dullness"; it can also mean "a dull person."

EXAMPLE Wild **boars** are common in parts of Africa.

EXAMPLE Please don't **bore** me with your silly jokes.

born, borne *Born* means "given life." *Borne* means "carried" or "endured."

EXAMPLE The baby was **born** at three o'clock in the morning.

EXAMPLE Migrant workers have **borne** many hardships over the years.

borrow, lend, loan *Borrow* means "to take something with the understanding that it will be returned." *Lend* means "to give something with the understanding it will be returned." *Borrow* and *lend* are verbs. *Loan* is a noun. Some people use *loan* as a verb, but most authorities prefer *lend.*

EXAMPLE May I **borrow** your bicycle for an hour?

EXAMPLE Will you **lend** me five dollars? **[verb]**

EXAMPLE I'll repay the **loan** on Friday. **[noun]**

bow When *bow* is pronounced to rhyme with *low,* it means "a knot with two loops." When *bow* rhymes with *how,* it means "to bend at the waist."

EXAMPLE   Can you tie a good **bow**?

EXAMPLE   Actors **bow** at the end of a play.

brake, break   As a noun, a *brake* is a device for stopping something or slowing it down. As a verb, *brake* means "to stop or slow down"; its principal parts are *brake, braking, braked,* and *braked.* The noun *break* has several meanings: "the result of breaking," "a fortunate chance," or "a short rest." The verb *break* also has many meanings. A few are "to smash or shatter," "to destroy or disrupt," "to force a way through or into," or "to surpass or excel." Its principal parts are *break, breaking, broke,* and *broken.*

EXAMPLE   Rachel, please put a **brake** on your enthusiasm. **[noun]**

EXAMPLE   He couldn't **brake** the car in time to avoid the accident. **[verb]**

EXAMPLE   To fix the **break** in the drainpipe will cost a great deal of money. **[noun]**

EXAMPLE   Don't **break** my concentration while I'm studying. **[verb]**

bring, take   *Bring* means "to carry from a distant place to a closer one." *Take* means "to carry from a nearby place to a more distant one."

EXAMPLE   Will you **bring** me some perfume when you return from Paris?

EXAMPLE   Remember to **take** your passport when you go to Europe.

bust, busted   Don't use these words in place of *break, broke, broken,* or *burst.*

EXAMPLE   Don't **break** [*not* bust] that vase!

EXAMPLE   Who **broke** [*not* busted] this vase?

EXAMPLE   Someone has **broken** [*not* busted] this vase.

EXAMPLE   The balloon **burst** [*not* **busted**] with a loud pop.

EXAMPLE   The child **burst** [*not* **busted**] into tears.

buy, by   *Buy* is a verb. *By* is a preposition.

EXAMPLE   I'll **buy** the gift tomorrow.

EXAMPLE   Stand **by** me.

can, may   *Can* indicates ability. *May* expresses permission or possibility.

EXAMPLE   I **can** tie six kinds of knots.

EXAMPLE   "You **may** be excused," said Dad. **[permission]**

EXAMPLE   Luanna **may** take some college classes during her senior year. **[possibility]**

can't hardly, can't scarcely   These phrases are considered double negatives. Don't use *hardly* or *scarcely* with *not* or the contraction *n't*.

EXAMPLE   I **can** [*not* **can't**] **hardly** lift this box.

EXAMPLE   The driver **can** [*not* **can't**] **scarcely** see through the thick fog.

capital, capitol   A *capital* is a city that is the seat of a government. *Capital* can also mean "money or property." As an adjective, capital can mean "involving execution" or "referring to an uppercase letter." *Capitol,* on the other hand, refers only to a building in which a legislature meets.

EXAMPLE   What is the **capital** of Vermont?

EXAMPLE   Anyone starting a business needs **capital**.

EXAMPLE   **Capital** punishment is not used in this state.

EXAMPLE   Hester Prynne embroidered a **capital** *A* on her dress.

EXAMPLE   The **capitol** has a gold dome.

carat, caret, carrot, karat A *carat* is a unit of weight for measuring gems. (A similar word, *karat*, is a measure for expressing the fineness of gold.) A *caret* is a proofreader's mark indicating an insertion. A *carrot* is a vegetable.

EXAMPLE   She was wearing a one-**carat** diamond set in a ring of eighteen-**karat** gold.

EXAMPLE   Draw a **caret** at the point where you want to insert a word.

EXAMPLE   Lottie fed her horse a **carrot**.

cent, scent, sent A *cent* is a penny. A *scent* is an odor. *Sent* is the past and past participle of *send*.

EXAMPLE   I haven't got one **cent** in my pocket.

EXAMPLE   The **scent** of a skunk is unpleasant.

EXAMPLE   I **sent** my grandma a birthday card.

choose, chose *Choose* is the base form; *chose* is the past tense. The principal parts are *choose, choosing, chose,* and *chosen*.

EXAMPLE   Please **choose** a poem to recite in class.

EXAMPLE   Brian **chose** to recite "The Charge of the Light Brigade."

cite, sight, site To *cite* is to quote or refer to. *Cite* can also mean "to summon to appear in a court of law." As a noun, *sight* means "vision." As a verb, *sight* means "to see." As a noun, a *site* is a place or a location; as a verb, *site* means "to place or locate."

EXAMPLE   Consuela **cited** three sources of information in her report.

EXAMPLE   The officer **cited** the driver for speeding.

EXAMPLE   My **sight** is perfect. **[noun]**

EXAMPLE   We **sighted** a scarlet tanager on our hike. **[verb]**

EXAMPLE   The board of education has chosen a **site** for the new high school. **[noun]**

EXAMPLE   The school will be **sited** on Meadow Boulevard. **[verb]**

clothes, cloths   *Clothes* are what you wear. *Cloths* are pieces of fabric.

EXAMPLE   Please hang all your **clothes** in your closet.

EXAMPLE   Use these **cloths** to wash the car.

coarse, course   *Coarse* means "rough," "crude," "not fine," "of poor quality." *Course* can mean "a school subject," "a path or way," "order or development," or "part of a meal." *Course* is also used in the phrase *of course*.

EXAMPLE   To begin, I will need some **coarse** sandpaper.

EXAMPLE   Mrs. Baldwin won't tolerate **coarse** language.

EXAMPLE   Are you taking any math **courses** this year?

EXAMPLE   The hikers chose a difficult **course** through the mountains.

complement, complementary; compliment, complimentary   As a noun, *complement* means "something that completes"; as a verb, it means "to complete." As a noun, *compliment* means "a flattering remark"; as a verb, it means "to praise." *Complementary* and *complimentary* are the adjective forms of the words.

EXAMPLE   This flowered scarf will be the perfect **complement** for your outfit. **[noun]**

EXAMPLE   This flowered scarf **complements** your outfit perfectly. **[verb]**

EXAMPLE   Phyllis received many **compliments** on her speech. **[noun]**

EXAMPLE   Many people **complimented** Phyllis on her speech. **[verb]**

EXAMPLE   Either hat would be **complementary** to that outfit.
            [adjective]

EXAMPLE   The hostess was especially **complimentary** to Phyllis.
            [adjective]

compose, comprise *Compose* means "to make up." *Comprise*
means "to include."

EXAMPLE   The mayor, the superintendent of schools, and the
            police chief **compose** the committee.

EXAMPLE   The committee **comprises** the mayor, the superinten-
            dent of schools, and the police chief.

consul; council, councilor; counsel, counselor A *consul* is a government official living in a foreign city to protect his or her
country's interests and citizens. A *council* is a group of
people gathered for the purpose of giving advice. A *councilor* is one who serves on a council. As a noun, *counsel*
means "advice" or "an attorney." As a verb, *counsel* means
"to give advice." A *counselor* is one who gives counsel.

EXAMPLE   The **consul** protested to the foreign government about
            the treatment of her fellow citizens.

EXAMPLE   The city **council** met to discuss the lack of parking
            facilities at the sports field.

EXAMPLE   The defendant received **counsel** from his **counsel**.
            [nouns]

EXAMPLE   The attorney **counseled** his client to plead innocent.
            [verb]

continual, continually; continuous, continuously *Continual*
describes action that occurs over and over but with pauses
between occurrences. *Continuous* describes an action that
continues with no interruption. *Continually* and *continuously* are the adverb forms of the adjectives.

EXAMPLE I could not concentrate because of the **continual** banging of the screen door and the **continuous** blare of the radio.

EXAMPLE This television ad is aired **continually**; I've seen it six times tonight.

EXAMPLE The rain fell **continuously**.

could of, might of, must of, should of, would of After the words *could, might, must, should,* and *would,* use the helping verb *have* or its contraction, *'ve,* not the word *of.*

EXAMPLE **Could** you **have** prevented the accident?

EXAMPLE You **might have** swerved to avoid the other car.

EXAMPLE You **must have** seen it coming.

EXAMPLE I **should've** warned you.

dear, deer *Dear* is a word of affection and is used to begin a letter. It can also mean "expensive." A *deer* is an animal.

EXAMPLE Talia is my **dear** friend.

EXAMPLE We saw a **deer** at the edge of the woods.

desert, dessert *Desert* has two meanings. As a noun, it means "dry, arid land" and is accented on the first syllable. As a verb, it means "to leave" or "to abandon" and is accented on the second syllable. A *dessert* is something sweet eaten after a meal.

EXAMPLE This photograph shows a sandstorm in the **desert**. [noun]

EXAMPLE I won't **desert** you in your time of need. [verb]

EXAMPLE Strawberry shortcake was served for **dessert**.

different from, different than In most cases, *different from* is the correct choice. Use *different than* only if *than* introduces a subordinate clause.

EXAMPLE   Square dancing is **different from** ballroom dancing.

EXAMPLE   I felt **different than** I had felt before.

diner, dinner   A *diner* is someone who dines or a place to eat. A *dinner* is a meal.

EXAMPLE   The **diners** at the corner **diner** enjoy the corned beef hash.

EXAMPLE   **Dinner** will be served at eight.

discover, invent   *Discover* means "to come upon something for the first time." *Invent* means "to produce something original."

EXAMPLE   Marie Curie **discovered** radium.

EXAMPLE   Eli Whitney **invented** the cotton gin.

discreet, discrete   These two adjectives have identical pronunciations but very different meanings. *Discreet* means "having good judgment," "prudent," or "unobtrusive." *Discrete* means "disconnected," "separate," or "individual."

EXAMPLE   The actor's agent read the reporters a brief, **discreet** statement that did not satisfy their curiosity.

EXAMPLE   The detective followed his subject at a **discreet** distance.

EXAMPLE   This floor, which looks like one piece of stone, is actually made of thousands of tiny **discrete** pieces glued together.

doe, dough   A *doe* is a female deer. *Dough* is a mixture of flour and a liquid.

EXAMPLE   A **doe** and a stag were visible among the trees.

EXAMPLE   Knead the **dough** for three minutes.

doesn't, don't   *Doesn't* is a contraction of *does not.* It is used with *he, she, it,* and all singular nouns. *Don't* is a contraction of *do not*. It is used with *I, you, we, they,* and all plural nouns.

EXAMPLE She **doesn't** know the answer to your question.

EXAMPLE The twins **don't** like broccoli.

emigrate, immigrate Use *emigrate* to mean "to leave one country and go to another to live." Use *immigrate* to mean "to come to a country to settle there." Use the preposition *from* with *emigrate*. Use *to* or *into* with *immigrate*.

EXAMPLE Karl **emigrated** from Germany.

EXAMPLE He **immigrated** to the United States.

eye, I An *eye* is what you see with; it's also a small opening in a needle. *I* is a personal pronoun.

EXAMPLE **I** have something in my **eye**.

farther, further Use *farther* in referring to physical distance. Use *further* in all other situations.

EXAMPLE San Antonio is **farther** south than Dallas.

EXAMPLE We have nothing **further** to discuss.

fewer, less Use *fewer* with nouns that can be counted. Use *less* with nouns that can't be counted. *Less* may also be used with numbers that are considered as single amounts or single quantities.

EXAMPLE There are **fewer** students in my math class than in my physics class.

EXAMPLE I used **less** sugar than the recipe recommended.

EXAMPLE David had **less** than two dollars in his pocket.
[*Two dollars* **is treated as a single sum, not as individual dollars.**]

EXAMPLE I can be there in **less** than thirty minutes. [*Thirty minutes* **is treated as a single period of time, not as individual minutes.**]

figuratively, literally *Figuratively* means "not truly or actually but in a symbolic way." *Literally* means "truly" or "actually."

EXAMPLE Dad hit the ceiling, **figuratively** speaking.

EXAMPLE You can't take him **literally** when he talks about the fish he's caught.

flaunt, flout *Flaunt* means "to make a showy display." *Flout* means "to defy."

EXAMPLE Enrique **flaunted** his knowledge of computer science at every opportunity.

EXAMPLE Darla **flouted** the law by jaywalking.

flour, flower *Flour* is used to bake bread. A *flower* grows in a garden.

EXAMPLE Sift two cups of **flour** into a bowl.

EXAMPLE A daisy is a **flower**.

for, four *For* is a preposition. *Four* is a number.

EXAMPLE Wait **for** me.

EXAMPLE I have **four** grandparents.

formally, formerly *Formally* is the adverb form of *formal*, which has several meanings: "according to custom, rule, or etiquette"; "requiring special ceremony or fancy clothing"; or "official." *Formerly* means "previously."

EXAMPLE   The class officers will be **formally** installed on Thursday.

EXAMPLE   Ed was **formerly** employed by Kwik Kar Kleen.

go, say Don't use forms of *go* in place of forms of *say*.

EXAMPLE   I tell her the answer, and she **says** [*not* goes], "I don't believe you."

EXAMPLE   I told her the news, and she **said** [*not* went], "Are you serious?"

good, well *Good* is an adjective; use it before nouns and after linking verbs to modify the subject. *Well* is an adverb; use it to modify action verbs. *Well* may also be an adjective meaning "in good health."

EXAMPLE   You look **good** in that costume.

EXAMPLE   Joby plays the piano **well**.

EXAMPLE   You're looking **well** in spite of your cold.

grate, great A *grate* is a framework of bars set over an opening. *Grate* also means "to shred by rubbing against a rough surface." *Great* means "wonderful" or "large."

EXAMPLE   The little girl dropped her lollipop through the **grate**.

EXAMPLE   Will you **grate** this cheese for me?

EXAMPLE   You did a **great** job!

had of Don't use *of* between *had* and a past participle.

EXAMPLE   I wish I **had known** [*not* had of known] about this sooner.

had ought, hadn't ought, shouldn't ought *Ought* never needs a helping verb. Use *ought* by itself.

EXAMPLE   You **ought** to win the match easily.

EXAMPLE   You **ought** not to blame yourself. *or* You **shouldn't** blame yourself.

hanged, hung Use *hanged* when you mean "put to death by hanging." Use *hung* in all other instances.

EXAMPLE   This state **hanged** three convicts between 1900 and 1950.

EXAMPLE   We **hung** Yoko's painting over the fireplace.

healthful, healthy *Healthful* means "favorable to one's health," or "wholesome." *Healthy* means "in good health."

EXAMPLE   We chose **healthful** picnic foods: whole-grain breads, juices, cheese, and fresh fruits.

EXAMPLE   A **healthy** person is likely to live longer than an unhealthy one.

hear, here *Hear* is a verb meaning "to be aware of sound by means of the ear." *Here* is an adverb meaning "in or at this place."

EXAMPLE   I can **hear** you perfectly well.

EXAMPLE   Please put your books **here**.

he, she, it, they Don't use a pronoun subject immediately after a noun subject.

EXAMPLE   The girls baked the cookies. [*not* **The girls they baked the cookies.**]

holey, holy, wholly *Holey* means "having holes." *Holy* means "sacred." *Wholly* means "completely."

EXAMPLE   I hate wearing **holey** socks.

EXAMPLE   Religious travelers make pilgrimages to **holy** places.

EXAMPLE   That dog is **wholly** devoted to you.

how come In formal speech and writing, use *why* instead of *how come.*

EXAMPLE **Why** weren't you at the meeting? [*not* **How come you weren't at the meeting?**]

imply, infer *Imply* means "to suggest." *Infer* means "to draw a conclusion from something."

EXAMPLE The baby's crying **implied** that he was hungry.

EXAMPLE I **inferred** from the baby's crying that he was hungry.

in, into, in to Use *in* to mean "inside" or "within." Use *into* to show movement from the outside to a point within. Don't write *into* when you mean *in to*.

EXAMPLE Jeanine was sitting outdoors **in** a lawn chair.

EXAMPLE When it got too hot, she went **into** the house.

EXAMPLE She went **in to** get out of the heat.

ingenious, ingenuous *Ingenious* means "clever," "inventive," "imaginative." *Ingenuous* means "innocent," "childlike," "sincere."

EXAMPLE What an **ingenious** plan you have dreamed up!

EXAMPLE Her **ingenuous** enthusiasm for the cafeteria food made us smile.

inside of Don't use *of* after the preposition *inside*.

EXAMPLE **Inside** [*not* **inside of**] the cupboard were several old photograph albums.

irregardless, regardless Use *regardless*. Both the prefix *ir-* and the suffix *-less* have negative meanings; therefore, *irregardless* is a double negative, which is incorrect.

EXAMPLE **Regardless** [*not* **Irregardless**] of what the critics said, I liked that movie.

its, it's *Its* is the possessive form of *it*. *It's* is a contraction of *it is* or *it has*.

EXAMPLE   The dishwasher has finished **its** cycle.

EXAMPLE   **It's [It is]** raining again.

EXAMPLE   **It's [It has]** been a pleasure to meet you, Ms. Donatello.

kind of, sort of Don't use these expressions as adverbs. Use *somewhat* or *rather* instead.

EXAMPLE   We were **rather** sorry to see him go. [*not* We were kind of sorry to see him go.]

kind of a, sort of a, type of a Omit the word *a*.

EXAMPLE   What **kind of** dog is that? [*not* What kind of a dog is that?]

knead, need *Knead* means "to mix or work into a uniform mass." As a noun, a *need* is a requirement. As a verb, *need* means "to require."

EXAMPLE   **Knead** the clay to make it soft.

EXAMPLE   I **need** a new jacket.

knight, night A *knight* was a warrior of the Middle Ages. *Night* is the time of day during which it is dark.

EXAMPLE   A handsome **knight** rescued the fair maiden.

EXAMPLE   **Night** fell, and the moon rose.

last, latest When you are speaking or writing of an author and say, "This is her latest book," you're understood to mean that she has written some books and that this is the most recent one. If, however, you had said, "This is her last book," then two meanings are possible. One is the same as in the first sentence; the other is that this is the last book that author will ever write. To be clear, get into the habit of saying *last* only when you mean "last" and saying *latest* instead when it's appropriate.

EXAMPLE   In her **last** poem, my sister explained why she is giving up writing poetry forever.

EXAMPLE   In her **latest** poem, my sister explained a family incident that happened only last weekend.

later, latter *Later* is the comparative form of *late*. *Latter* means "the second of two."

EXAMPLE   They will arrive on a **later** flight.

EXAMPLE   He arrived **later** than usual.

EXAMPLE   Both Scott and Sabrina are running for class president; I'm voting for the **latter**.

lay, lie *Lay* means "to put" or "to place." Its principal parts are *lay, laying, laid,* and *laid*. Forms of *lay* are usually followed by a direct object. *Lie* means "to rest or recline" or "to be positioned." Its principal parts are *lie, lying, lay,* and *lain*. Forms of *lie* are never followed by a direct object.

EXAMPLE   **Lay** your coat on the bed.

EXAMPLE   The children are **laying** their beach towels in the sun to dry.

EXAMPLE   Dad **laid** the baby in her crib.

EXAMPLE   Myrna had **laid** the book beside her purse.

EXAMPLE   **Lie** down for a few minutes.

EXAMPLE   The lake **lies** to the north.

EXAMPLE   The dog is **lying** on the back porch.

EXAMPLE   This morning I **lay** in bed listening to the birds.

EXAMPLE   You have **lain** on the couch for an hour.

lead, led As a noun, *lead* has two pronunciations and several meanings. When it's pronounced to rhyme with *head*, it means "a metallic element." When it's pronounced to rhyme with *bead*, it can mean "position of being in first place in a race or contest," "example," "clue," "leash," or "the main role in a play."

EXAMPLE **Lead** is no longer allowed as an ingredient in paint.

EXAMPLE Jason took the **lead** as the runners entered the stadium.

EXAMPLE Follow my **lead**.

EXAMPLE The detective had no **leads** in the case.

EXAMPLE Only dogs on **leads** are permitted in the park.

EXAMPLE Who will win the **lead** in this year's musical production?

As a verb, *lead* means "to show the way," "to guide or conduct," "to be first." Its principal parts are *lead, leading, led,* and *led.*

EXAMPLE Ms. Bachman **leads** the orchestra.

EXAMPLE The trainer was **leading** the horse around the track.

EXAMPLE An usher **led** us to our seats.

EXAMPLE Gray has **led** the league in hitting for two years.

learn, teach *Learn* means "to receive knowledge." *Teach* means "to give knowledge."

EXAMPLE Manny began to **learn** to play the piano at the age of six.

EXAMPLE Ms. Guerrero **teaches** American history.

leave, let *Leave* means "to go away." *Let* means "to allow to."

EXAMPLE I'll miss you when you **leave**.

EXAMPLE **Let** me help you with those heavy bags.

like, as, as if, as though *Like* can be a verb or a preposition. It should not be used as a subordinating conjunction. Use *as, as if,* or *as though* to introduce a subordinate clause.

EXAMPLE   I **like** piano music. **[verb]**

EXAMPLE   Teresa plays the piano **like** a professional. **[preposition]**

EXAMPLE   Moira plays **as** [*not* **like**] her teacher taught her to play.

EXAMPLE   He looked at me **as if** [*not* **like**] he'd never seen me before.

EXAMPLE   You sound **as though** [*not* **like**] you disagree.

like, say   Don't use the word *like* in place of forms of *say*.

EXAMPLE   I tell him to scroll down, and **he says** [*not* **he's like**], "What's scrolling down?"

EXAMPLE   I told her to turn left, and **she said** [*not* **she was like**], "Left!"

loath, loathe   *Loath* means "reluctant or unwilling." *Loathe* means "to hate."

EXAMPLE   Jeanine was **loath** to accept the responsibility.

EXAMPLE   Leonardo **loathes** sports.

loose, lose   The adjective *loose* means "free," "not firmly attached," or "not fitting tightly." The verb *lose* means "to misplace" or "to fail to win."

EXAMPLE   Don't **lose** that **loose** button on your shirt.

EXAMPLE   If we **lose** this game, we'll be out of the tournament.

mail, male   *Mail* is what turns up in your mailbox. A *male* is a man.

EXAMPLE   We received four pieces of **mail** today.

EXAMPLE   The **males** in the chorus wore red ties.

main, mane   *Main* means "most important." A *mane* is the long hair on a horse's neck.

EXAMPLE   What is your **main** job around the house?

EXAMPLE   The horse's **mane** was braided with colorful ribbons.

marshal, Marshall, martial, marital The first three words are pronounced the same. A *marshal* is a military official or a law officer. *Marshall* refers to the Marshall Islands in the Pacific Ocean. The adjective *martial* means "pertaining to war" or "pertaining to military life." The adjective *marital*, however, is pronounced with three syllables and means "pertaining to marriage."

EXAMPLE   The actor playing the town **marshal** walked onto the set carrying his Stetson.

EXAMPLE   Carol and her parents often spend the summer in the **Marshalls**, where they have relatives.

EXAMPLE   Roberto is a **martial** arts student.

EXAMPLE   The bride and groom wrote their own **marital** vows.

masterful, masterly *Masterful* means "strong," "bossy," or "domineering." *Masterly* means "like a master" or "showing great skill."

EXAMPLE   The overlord made a **masterful** gesture, and all the people bowed.

EXAMPLE   My violin teacher played a **masterly** solo at the end of our recital.

mean, medium, average The *mean* of a set of numbers is a middle point. To get the arithmetic mean, you add up all the items in the set and divide by the number of items. The *medium* is the middle number when the items are arranged in order of size. The *average*, a noun, is the same as the arithmetic mean; as an adjective, *average* is "usual" or "typical."

EXAMPLE The **mean** value of houses in a neighborhood is found by adding together all their selling prices and dividing the sum by the number of houses.

EXAMPLE We lined up all the ponies from smallest to biggest, and Taminka chose the **medium** one, the one in the center of the row.

EXAMPLE Let's figure out the **average** of all our test scores; then we can tell whether as a class we've improved.

EXAMPLE This crop of tomatoes is nothing unusual; it's pretty **average**.

meat, meet *Meat* is food from an animal. Some meanings of *meet* are "to come face to face with," "to make the acquaintance of," and "to keep an appointment."

EXAMPLE Some people don't eat **meat**.

EXAMPLE **Meet** me at the library at three o'clock.

miner, minor *Miner* is a noun that means "one who works in a mine." *Minor* can be a noun or an adjective. As a noun, it means "a person under legal age." As an adjective, it means "small in importance."

EXAMPLE Coal **miners** often suffer from a disease known as black lung.

EXAMPLE **Minors** are restricted by law from certain activities.

EXAMPLE Several well-known actors had **minor** roles in the film.

minute When *minute* is pronounced min′it, it means "sixty seconds" or "a short period of time." When *minute* is pronounced mī nōōt′, it means "very small."

EXAMPLE I'll be with you in a **minute**.

EXAMPLE Don't bother me with **minute** details.

moral, morale As a noun, a *moral* is a lesson taught by a fable or a story. As an adjective, *moral* means "decent," "right," "proper." *Morale* means "mental attitude."

EXAMPLE   Did you understand the **moral** of that story?

EXAMPLE   Jackson has strong **moral** principles.

EXAMPLE   The team's **morale** would be improved by a win.

nauseated, nauseous *Nauseated* means "feeling nausea" or "experiencing nausea, as in sea-sickness." *Nauseous,* on the other hand, means "causing nausea" or "sickening."

EXAMPLE   My **nauseated** family could not stand to look any longer at the **nauseous** dish of scrambled eggs and left-overs I had placed in front of them.

object *Object* is stressed on the first syllable when it means "a thing." *Object* is stressed on the second syllable when it means "oppose."

EXAMPLE   Have you ever seen an unidentified flying **object**?

EXAMPLE   Mom **objected** to the proposal.

off Don't use *off* in place of *from.*

EXAMPLE   I'll borrow some money **from [*not* off]** my brother.

off of Don't use *of* after the preposition *off.*

EXAMPLE   He fell **off [*not* off of]** the ladder, but he didn't hurt himself.

ordinance, ordnance An *ordinance* is a law. *Ordnance* is a word for military weapons and equipment.

EXAMPLE   Our town has an **ordinance** against lying on the sidewalk.

EXAMPLE   Private Malloy was assigned to guard the **ordnance**.

ought to of Don't use *of* in place of *have* after *ought to.*

EXAMPLE You **ought to have** [*not* ought to of] known better.

outside of Don't use *of* after the preposition *outside.*

EXAMPLE I'll meet you **outside** [*not* outside of] the library.

overlook, oversee Overlook can mean "to look past or miss" and "to look down at from above." *Oversee* means "to supervise workers or work."

EXAMPLE Lynn calculated the net profit we made from the car wash, but she had **overlooked** the cost of the lemonade and snacks provided for the workers.

EXAMPLE The ridgetop cabin **overlooks** the whole valley.

EXAMPLE Part of the caretaker's job is to **oversee** the garden staff, the groundskeeping staff, and the security staff.

pair, pare, pear A *pair* is two. *Pare* means "to peel." A *pear* is a fruit.

EXAMPLE I bought a new **pair** of socks.

EXAMPLE **Pare** the potatoes and cut them in quarters.

EXAMPLE Would you like a **pear** or a banana?

passed, past *Passed* is the past form and the past participle of the verb *pass. Past* can be an adjective, a preposition, an adverb, or a noun.

EXAMPLE We **passed** your house on the way to school. **[verb]**

EXAMPLE The **past** week has been a busy one for me. **[adjective]**

EXAMPLE We drove **past** your house. **[preposition]**

EXAMPLE At what time did you drive **past**? **[adverb]**

EXAMPLE I love Great-grandma's stories about the **past**. **[noun]**

pause, paws A *pause* is a short space of time. *Pause* also means "to wait for a short time." *Paws* are animal feet.

EXAMPLE We **pause** now for station identification.

EXAMPLE I wiped the dog's muddy **paws**.

peace, piece *Peace* means "calmness" or "the absence of conflict." A *piece* is a part of something.

EXAMPLE We enjoy the **peace** of the countryside.

EXAMPLE The two nations have finally made **peace**.

EXAMPLE May I have another **piece** of pie?

persecute, prosecute *Persecute* means "to torment." *Prosecute* means "to bring legal action against."

EXAMPLE Bullies sometimes **persecute** younger, weaker children.

EXAMPLE The government **prosecuted** Al Capone for tax evasion.

personal, personnel *Personal* means "private" or "individual." *Personnel* are employees.

EXAMPLE Employees should not make **personal** telephone calls during working hours.

EXAMPLE All **personnel** will receive a bonus in July.

plain, plane *Plain* means "not fancy," "clear," or "a large area of flat land." A *plane* is an airplane or a device for smoothing wood; it can also mean "a flat surface."

EXAMPLE He wore a **plain** blue tie.

EXAMPLE The solution is perfectly **plain** to me.

EXAMPLE Buffalo once roamed the **plains**.

EXAMPLE We took a **plane** to Chicago.

EXAMPLE Jeff used a **plane** to smooth the rough wood.

EXAMPLE The two metal surfaces of this machine must be perfect **planes**.

precede, proceed *Precede* means "to go before" or "to come before." *Proceed* means "to continue" or "to move along."

EXAMPLE   Our band **preceded** the homecoming floats as the parade **proceeded** through town.

precedence, precedents *Precedence* means "superiority of rank or position." *Precedents* are previous events that serve as examples for future actions or decisions.

EXAMPLE   Doing your schoolwork has **precedence** over playing computer games.

EXAMPLE   The legal **precedents** for the decision were clear and numerous.

principal, principle As a noun, *principal* means "head of a school"; it can also mean "a sum of money borrowed or invested." As an adjective, *principal* means "main" or "chief." *Principle* is a noun meaning "basic truth or belief" or "rule of conduct."

EXAMPLE   Mr. Washington, our **principal**, will speak at the morning assembly. **[noun]**

EXAMPLE   What was your **principal** reason for joining the club? **[adjective]**

EXAMPLE   The **principle** of fair play is important in sports.

quiet, quit, quite The adjective *quiet* means "silent" or "motionless." The verb *quit* means "to stop" or "to give up or resign." The adverb *quite* means "very" or "completely."

EXAMPLE   Please be **quiet** so I can think.

EXAMPLE   Shirelle has **quit** the swim team.

EXAMPLE   We were **quite** sorry to lose her.

raise, rise *Raise* means "to cause to move upward." It can also mean "to breed or grow" and "to bring up or rear." Its principal parts are *raise, raising, raised,* and *raised.* Forms of *raise* are usually followed by a direct object. *Rise* means "to move upward." Its principal parts are *rise, rising, rose,* and *risen.* Forms of *rise* are never followed by a direct object.

EXAMPLE **Raise** your hand if you know the answer.

EXAMPLE My uncle is **raising** chickens.

EXAMPLE Grandma and Grandpa Schwartz **raised** nine children.

EXAMPLE Steam **rises** from boiling water.

EXAMPLE The sun is **rising**.

EXAMPLE The children **rose** from their seats when the principal entered the room.

EXAMPLE In a short time, Loretta **had risen** to the rank of captain.

rap, wrap *Rap* means "to knock." *Wrap* means "to cover."

EXAMPLE **Rap** on the door.

EXAMPLE **Wrap** the presents.

rational, rationale *Rational*, an adjective, means "sensible," "sane." A *rationale* is a reason for doing something. *Rationale* is a noun.

EXAMPLE Melody always behaves in a **rational** manner.

EXAMPLE I didn't understand Clive's **rationale** for quitting his job.

read, reed *Read* means "to understand the meaning of something written." A *reed* is a stalk of tall grass.

EXAMPLE Will you **read** Jimmy a story?

EXAMPLE We found a frog in the **reeds** beside the lake.

real, really *Real* is an adjective; use it before nouns and after linking verbs to modify the subject. *Really* is an adverb; use it to modify action verbs, adjectives, and other adverbs.

EXAMPLE Winona has **real** musical talent.

EXAMPLE She is **really** talented.

real, reel *Real* means "actual." A *reel* is a spool to wind something on, such as a fishing line.

EXAMPLE I have a **real** four-leaf clover.

EXAMPLE My dad bought me a new fishing **reel**.

reason is because Don't use *because* after *reason is.* Use *that* after *reason is,* or use *because* alone.

EXAMPLE The **reason** I'm tired **is that** I didn't sleep well last night.

EXAMPLE I'm tired **because** I didn't sleep well last night.

respectfully, respectively *Respectfully* means "with respect." *Respectively* means "in the order named."

EXAMPLE The audience listened **respectfully** as the poet read his latest work.

EXAMPLE Sue, Jerry, and Chad will be president, secretary, and treasurer, **respectively**.

root, rout, route, en route A *root* is a part of a plant. As a verb, *rout* means "to defeat"; as a noun, it means "a defeat." A *route* is a road or way for travel. *En route* means "on the way."

EXAMPLE A carrot is a **root**.

EXAMPLE The Tigers **routed** the Bears in last week's game. **[verb]**

EXAMPLE The game ended in a **rout** for the Bears. **[noun]**

EXAMPLE Let's take the **route** that runs along the river.

EXAMPLE We stopped for lunch **en route**.

row When *row* is pronounced to rhyme with *low*, it means "a series of things arranged in a line" or "to move a boat by using oars." When *row* is pronounced to rhyme with *how*, it means "a noisy quarrel."

EXAMPLE   We sat in the last **row** of the theater.

EXAMPLE   Let's **row** across the lake.

EXAMPLE   My sister and I had a serious **row** yesterday, but today we've forgotten about it.

said, says *Said* is the past form and the past participle of *say*. *Says* is used in the present tense with *he*, *she*, *it*, and all singular nouns. Don't use *says* when you should use *said*.

EXAMPLE   At dinner last night, Neil **said** he wasn't hungry.

EXAMPLE   He always **says** that, but he eats everything anyway.

sail, sale A *sail* is part of a boat. It also means "to travel in a boat." A *sale* is a transfer of ownership in exchange for money.

EXAMPLE   As the boat **sails** away, the crew raise the **sail**.

EXAMPLE   The **sale** of the house was completed on Friday.

sea, see A *sea* is a body of water. *See* means "to be aware of with the eyes."

EXAMPLE   The **sea** is rough today.

EXAMPLE   I can **see** you.

set, sit *Set* means "to place" or "to put." Its principal parts are *set, setting, set,* and *set*. Forms of *set* are usually followed by a direct object. *Sit* means "to place oneself in a seated position" or "to be in a seated position." Its principal parts are *sit, sitting, sat,* and *sat*. Forms of *sit* are not followed by a direct object.

Set is an intransitive verb when it's used with *sun* to mean "the sun is going down" or "the sun is sinking below the horizon." When *set* is used in this way, it is not followed by a direct object.

EXAMPLE   Lani **sets** the pots on the stove after the sun **sets**.

EXAMPLE   The children **sit** quietly at the table.

sew, sow   *Sew* means "to work with needle and thread." When *sow* is pronounced to rhyme with *how*, it means "a female pig." When *sow* is pronounced to rhyme with *low*, it means "to plant."

EXAMPLE   Can you **sew** a button on a shirt?

EXAMPLE   The **sow** has five piglets.

EXAMPLE   Some farmers **sow** corn in their fields.

shear, sheer   *Shear* has to do with cutting or breaking off. *Sheer* can mean "thin and fine," "utter or complete," or "steep."

EXAMPLE   It's time to **shear** the sheep.

EXAMPLE   He decided to **shear** off his beard.

EXAMPLE   The bride's veil was made of a **sheer** fabric.

EXAMPLE   You are talking **sheer** nonsense.

EXAMPLE   It was a **sheer** drop from the top of the cliff.

shined, shone, shown   Both *shined* and *shone* are past tense forms and past participles of *shine*. Use *shined* when you mean "polished"; use *shone* in all other instances.

EXAMPLE   Clete **shined** his shoes.

EXAMPLE   The sun **shone** brightly.

EXAMPLE   Her face **shone** with happiness.

Shown is the past participle of *show;* its principal parts are *show, showing, showed,* and *shown*.

EXAMPLE You **showed** me these photographs yesterday.

EXAMPLE You have **shown** me these photographs before.

slow, slowly *Slow* may be used as an adverb only in such expressions as *Go slow* or *Drive slow.* In other instances where an adverb is needed, *slowly* should be used. You can't go wrong if you always use *slow* as an adjective and *slowly* as an adverb.

EXAMPLE We took a **slow** ferry to the island.

EXAMPLE The ferry moved **slowly** through the water.

some, somewhat Don't use *some* as an adverb in place of *somewhat.*

EXAMPLE The team has improved **somewhat [*not* some]** since last season.

son, sun A *son* is a male child. A *sun* is a star.

EXAMPLE Kino is Mr. and Mrs. Akawa's **son**.

EXAMPLE We watched as the **sun** rose over the horizon.

stationary, stationery *Stationary* means "fixed" or "unmoving." *Stationery* is writing paper.

EXAMPLE This classroom has **stationary** desks.

EXAMPLE Rhonda likes to write letters on pretty **stationery**.

straight, strait *Straight* means "not crooked or curved"; it can also mean "direct" or "directly." A *strait* is a narrow waterway connecting two larger bodies of water. In the plural, it can also mean "difficulties" or "distress."

EXAMPLE Can you draw a **straight** line without a ruler?

EXAMPLE We drove **straight** to the airport.

EXAMPLE The **Strait** of Gibraltar connects the Mediterranean Sea and the Atlantic Ocean.

EXAMPLE   People who don't control their spending often find themselves in financial **straits**.

suit, suite To distinguish these similar-looking nouns, focus on what constitutes them. For instance, *suit* is usually used in the phrases "a suit of clothes" and "a suit of cards." *Suite*, on the other hand, is usually used in the phrases "a suite of furniture" and "a suite of rooms." To further distinguish them, *suit* rhymes with *boot*, and *suite* is pronounced *sweet*.

EXAMPLE   David bought himself a new **suit** for his interview.

EXAMPLE   After the cards were dealt, I saw that I held in my hand cards from every **suit** except diamonds.

EXAMPLE   The Pattersons bought a **suite** of maple living-room furniture.

EXAMPLE   The hotel offered the large family a **suite** of interconnecting rooms.

sure, surely *Sure* is an adjective; use it before nouns and after linking verbs to modify the subject. *Surely* is an adverb; use it to modify action verbs, adjectives, and other adverbs.

EXAMPLE   Are you **sure** about that answer?

EXAMPLE   You are **surely** smart.

tail, tale A *tail* is what a dog wags. A *tale* is a story.

EXAMPLE   The dog's **tail** curled over its back.

EXAMPLE   Everyone knows the **tale** of Goldilocks and the three bears.

tear When *tear* is pronounced to rhyme with *ear*, it's a drop of fluid from the eye. When *tear* is pronounced to rhyme with *bear*, it means "a rip" or "to rip."

EXAMPLE A **tear** fell from the child's eye.

EXAMPLE **Tear** this rag in half.

than, then *Than* is a conjunction used to introduce the second part of a comparison.

EXAMPLE LaTrisha is taller **than** LaToya.

EXAMPLE Ted ordered more food **than** he could eat.

Then has several related meanings that have to do with time: "at that time," "soon afterward," "the time mentioned," "at another time." *Then* can also mean "for that reason" or "in that case."

EXAMPLE My grandmother was a young girl **then**.

EXAMPLE We ate lunch and **then** washed the dishes.

EXAMPLE I look forward to seeing you **then**.

EXAMPLE Sometimes I feel completely confident; **then** I feel totally incompetent.

EXAMPLE "It's raining," said Joy.
"**Then** we can't go," wailed her brother.

that there, this here Don't use *there* or *here* after *that, this, those,* or *these.*

EXAMPLE I can't decide whether to read **this** [*not* this here] magazine or **that** [*not* that there] book.

EXAMPLE Fold **these** [*not* these here] towels and hang **those** [*not* those there] shirts in the closet.

that, which, who *That* may refer to people or things. *Which* refers only to things. *Who* refers only to people.

EXAMPLE The poet **that** wrote *Leaves of Grass* is Walt Whitman.

EXAMPLE I have already seen the movie **that** is playing at the Bijou.

EXAMPLE   The new play, **which** closed after a week, received poor reviews.

EXAMPLE   Students **who** do well on the test will receive scholarships.

their, there, they're   *Their* is a possessive form of *they;* it's used to modify nouns. *There* means "in or at that place." *They're* is a contraction of *they are.*

EXAMPLE   A hurricane damaged **their** house.

EXAMPLE   Put your books **there**.

EXAMPLE   **They're** our next-door neighbors.

theirs, there's   *Theirs* is a possessive form of *they* used as a pronoun. *There's* is a contraction of *there is.*

EXAMPLE   **Theirs** is the white house with the green shutters.

EXAMPLE   **There's** your friend Chad.

them   Don't use *them* as an adjective in place of *those.*

EXAMPLE   I'll take one of **those [*not* them]** hamburgers.

this kind, these kinds   Use the singular forms *this* and *that* with the singular nouns *kind, sort,* and *type.* Use the plural forms *these* and *those* with the plural nouns *kinds, sorts,* and *types.*

EXAMPLE   Use **this kind** of lightbulb in your lamp.

EXAMPLE   Do you like **these kinds** of lamps?

EXAMPLE   Many Pakistani restaurants serve **that sort** of food.

EXAMPLE   **Those sorts** of foods are nutritious.

EXAMPLE   **This type** of dog makes a good pet.

EXAMPLE   **These types** of dogs are good with children.

thorough, through, threw *Thorough* means "complete." *Through* is a preposition meaning "into at one side and out at another." *Through* can also mean "finished." *Threw* is the past tense of *throw.*

EXAMPLE   We gave the bedrooms a **thorough** cleaning.

EXAMPLE   A breeze blew **through** the house.

EXAMPLE   At last I'm **through** with my homework.

EXAMPLE   Lacey **threw** the ball.

to, too, two *To* means "in the direction of"; it is also part of the infinitive form of a verb. *Too* means "very" or "also." *Two* is the number after *one.*

EXAMPLE   Jaleela walks **to** school.

EXAMPLE   She likes **to** study.

EXAMPLE   The soup is **too** salty.

EXAMPLE   May I go **too**?

EXAMPLE   We have **two** kittens.

toward, towards People in Great Britain use *towards,* but the preferred form in the United States is *toward.*

EXAMPLE   Smiling, she walked **toward** me.

try and Use *try to.*

EXAMPLE   Please **try to** [*not* try and] be on time.

type, type of Don't use *type* as an adjective.

EXAMPLE   What **type of** music [*not* what type music] do you like?

uninterested, disinterested *Uninterested* means "not interested," "unenthusiastic," and "indifferent." *Disinterested* means "impartial," "unbiased, not favoring either side in a dispute."

EXAMPLE I threw the collie a biscuit, but, supremely **uninterested**, he let it lie where it fell.

EXAMPLE The judge listened carefully to all the witnesses in that tangled case before handing down her **disinterested** and even-handed decision.

unless, without Don't use *without* in place of *unless.*

EXAMPLE **Unless [*not* Without]** I earn some money, I can't go to camp.

used to, use to The correct form is *used to.*

EXAMPLE We **used to [*not* use to]** live in Cleveland, Ohio.

waist, waste Your *waist* is where you wear your belt. As a noun, *waste* means "careless or unnecessary spending" or "trash." As a verb, it means "to spend or use carelessly or unnecessarily."

EXAMPLE She tied a colorful scarf around her **waist**.

EXAMPLE Buying those skis was a **waste** of money.

EXAMPLE Put your **waste** in the dumpster.

EXAMPLE Don't **waste** time worrying.

wait, weight *Wait* means "to stay or remain." *Weight* is a measurement.

EXAMPLE   **Wait** right here.

EXAMPLE   Her **weight** is 110 pounds.

wait for, wait on *Wait for* means "to remain in a place in anticipation of something expected." *Wait on* means "to act as a server."

EXAMPLE   **Wait for** me at the bus stop.

EXAMPLE   Nat and Tammy **wait on** diners at The Golden Griddle.

way, ways Use *way*, not *ways*, in referring to distance.

EXAMPLE   It's a long **way** [*not* ways] to Tipperary.

weak, week *Weak* means "feeble" or "not strong." A *week* is seven days.

EXAMPLE   She felt **weak** for a **week** after the operation.

weather, whether *Weather* is the condition of the atmosphere. *Whether* means "if"; it is also used to introduce the first of two choices.

EXAMPLE   The **weather** in Portland is mild and rainy.

EXAMPLE   Tell me **whether** you can go.

EXAMPLE   I can't decide **whether** to fly or drive.

when, where Don't use *when* or *where* incorrectly in writing a definition.

EXAMPLE   A simile is a comparison using *like* or *as*. [*not* **A simile is when you compare two things using *like* or *as*.**]

EXAMPLE   A watercolor wash is a thin coat of paint applied to paper that has been dampened with water. [*not* **A watercolor wash is where you dampen the paper before applying paint.**]

where Don't use *where* in place of *that*.

EXAMPLE   I see **that [*not* where]** the Cubs are in the basement again.

where . . . at Don't use *at* after *where*.

EXAMPLE   **Where** is your mother? [*not* **Where is your mother at?**]

who, whom *Who* is in the nominative case. Use it for subjects and predicate nominatives. *Whom* is in the objective case. Use it for direct objects, indirect objects, and objects of prepositions.

EXAMPLE   **Who** is that woman with the red umbrella?

EXAMPLE   **Whom** did you see at the mall?

who's, whose *Who's* is a contraction of *who is* or *who has*. *Whose* is the possessive form of *who*.

EXAMPLE   **Who's [Who is]** conducting the orchestra?

EXAMPLE   **Who's [Who has]** read this book?

EXAMPLE   **Whose** umbrella is this?

wind When *wind* rhymes with *finned*, it means "moving air." When *wind* rhymes with *fined*, it means "to wrap around."

EXAMPLE   The **wind** is strong today.

EXAMPLE   **Wind** the bandage around your ankle.

wood, would *Wood* comes from trees. *Would* is a helping verb.

EXAMPLE   **Would** you prefer a **wood** bookcase or a metal one?

wound When *wound* is pronounced to rhyme with *sound,* it is the past tense of *wind.* When *wound* is pronounced wo͞ond, it means "an injury in which the skin is broken."

EXAMPLE   I **wound** the bandage around my ankle to cover the **wound**.

your, you're   *Your* is the possessive form of *you. You're* is a contraction of *you are.*

EXAMPLE   **Your** arguments are convincing.

EXAMPLE   **You're** doing a fine job.

ABBREVIATIONS

An abbreviation is a short way to write a word or a group of words. Abbreviations should be used sparingly in formal writing except for a few that are actually more appropriate than their longer forms. These are *Mr., Mrs.,* and *Dr. (doctor)* before names, A.M. and P.M., and B.C. and A.D.

Some abbreviations are written with capital letters and periods, and some with capital letters and no periods; some are written with lowercase letters and periods, and some with lowercase letters and no periods. A few may be written in any one of these four ways and still be acceptable. For example, to abbreviate *miles per hour,* you may write *MPH, M.P.H., mph,* or *m.p.h.*

Some abbreviations may be spelled in more than one way. For example, *Tuesday* may be abbreviated *Tues.* or *Tue. Thursday* may be written *Thurs.* or *Thu.* In the following lists, only the most common way of writing each abbreviation is given.

When you need information about an abbreviation, consult a dictionary. Some dictionaries list abbreviations in a special section in the back. Others list them in the main part of the book.

MONTHS

Jan.	January	none	July
Feb.	February	Aug.	August
Mar.	March	Sept.	September
Apr.	April	Oct.	October
none	May	Nov.	November
none	June	Dec.	December

DAYS

Sun.	Sunday	Thurs.	Thursday
Mon.	Monday	Fri.	Friday
Tues.	Tuesday	Sat.	Saturday
Wed.	Wednesday		

TIME AND DIRECTION

CDT	central daylight time	MST	mountain standard time
CST	central standard time	PDT	Pacific daylight time
DST	daylight saving time	PST	Pacific standard time
EDT	eastern daylight time	ST	standard time
		NE	northeast
EST	eastern standard time	NW	northwest
		SE	southeast
MDT	mountain daylight time	SW	southwest

A.D.	in the year of the Lord (Latin *anno Domini*)
B.C.	before Christ
B.C.E.	before the common era
C.E.	common era
A.M.	before noon (Latin *ante meridiem*)
P.M.	after noon (Latin *post meridiem*)

MEASUREMENT

The same abbreviation is used for both the singular and the plural meaning of measurements. Therefore, *ft.* stands for both *foot* and *feet,* and *in.* stands for both *inch* and *inches.* Note that abbreviations of metric measurements are commonly written without periods. U.S. measurements, on the other hand, are usually written with periods.

Metric System

Mass and Weight

t	metric ton
kg	kilogram
g	gram
cg	centigram
mg	milligram

Capacity

kl	kiloliter
l	liter
cl	centiliter
ml	milliliter

Length

km	kilometer
m	meter
cm	centimeter
mm	millimeter

U.S. Weights and Measures

Weight

wt.	weight
lb.	pound
oz.	ounce

Capacity

gal.	gallon
qt.	quart
pt.	pint
c.	cup
tbsp.	tablespoon
tsp.	teaspoon
fl. oz.	fluid ounce

Length

mi.	mile
rd.	rod
yd.	yard
ft.	foot
in.	inch

MISCELLANEOUS MEASUREMENTS

p.s.i.	pounds per square inch
MPH	miles per hour
MPG	miles per gallon
d.p.i.	dots per inch
rpm	revolutions per minute
C	Celsius, centigrade
F	Fahrenheit
K	kelvin
kn	knot
kW	kilowatt

COMPUTER AND INTERNET

CPU	central processing unit
CRT	cathode ray tube
DOS	disk operating system
e-mail	electronic mail
K	kilobyte
URL	uniform resource locator
DVD	digital video disc
d.p.i	dots per inch
WWW	World Wide Web
ISP	internet service provider
DNS	domain name system

UNITED STATES (U.S.)

In most cases, state names and street addresses should be spelled out. The postal abbreviations in the following lists should be used with ZIP codes in addressing envelopes. They may also be used with ZIP codes for return addresses and inside addresses in business letters. The traditional state abbreviations are seldom used nowadays, but occasionally it's helpful to know them.

State	Traditional	Postal
Alabama	Ala.	AL
Alaska	none	AK
Arizona	Ariz.	AZ
Arkansas	Ark.	AR
California	Calif.	CA
Colorado	Colo.	CO
Connecticut	Conn.	CT
Delaware	Del.	DE
District of Columbia	D.C.	DC
Florida	Fla.	FL
Georgia	Ga.	GA
Hawaii	none	HI
Idaho	none	ID
Illinois	Ill.	IL
Indiana	Ind.	IN
Iowa	none	IA
Kansas	Kans.	KS
Kentucky	Ky.	KY
Louisiana	La.	LA
Maine	none	ME
Maryland	Md.	MD
Massachusetts	Mass.	MA
Michigan	Mich.	MI
Minnesota	Minn.	MN
Mississippi	Miss.	MS

Missouri	Mo.	MO
Montana	Mont.	MT
Nebraska	Nebr.	NE
Nevada	Nev.	NV
New Hampshire	N.H.	NH
New Jersey	N.J.	NJ
New Mexico	N. Mex.	NM
New York	N.Y.	NY
North Carolina	N.C.	NC
North Dakota	N. Dak.	ND
Ohio	none	OH
Oklahoma	Okla.	OK
Oregon	Oreg.	OR
Pennsylvania	Pa.	PA
Rhode Island	R.I.	RI
South Carolina	S.C.	SC
South Dakota	S. Dak.	SD
Tennessee	Tenn.	TN
Texas	Tex.	TX
Utah	none	UT
Vermont	Vt.	VT
Virginia	Va.	VA
Washington	Wash.	WA
West Virginia	W. Va.	WV
Wisconsin	Wis.	WI
Wyoming	Wyo.	WY

Frank and Ernest

SPECIAL IMPORTED ALPHABET SOUP

IT'S IMPORTED FROM EASTERN EUROPE -- WATCH OUT FOR THE LUMPS OF CONSONANT CLUSTERS.

THAVES

© 1998 Thaves / Reprinted with permission. Newspaper dist. by NEA, Inc.

POSTAL ADDRESS ABBREVIATIONS

The following address abbreviations are recommended by the U.S. Postal Service to speed mailing. In most writing, these words should be spelled out.

Alley	ALY	North	N
Annex	ANX	Parkway	PKY
Avenue	AVE	Place	PL
Boulevard	BLVD	Plaza	PLZ
Center	CTR	River	RIV
Circle	CIR	Road	RD
Court	CT	South	S
Drive	DR	Square	SQ
East	E	Station	STA
Estates	EST	Street	ST
Expressway	EXPY	Terrace	TER
Heights	HTS	Trace	TRCE
Highway	HWY	Trail	TRL
Island	IS	Turnpike	TPKE
Lake	LK	Viaduct	VIA
Lane	LN	Village	VLG
Lodge	LDG	West	W
Mount	MT		

ADDITIONAL ABBREVIATIONS

ac	alternating current
dc	direct current
AM	amplitude modulation
FM	frequency modulation
RF	radio frequency
ASAP	as soon as possible
e.g.	for example (Latin *exempli gratia*)
etc.	and others, and so forth (Latin *et cetera*)
i.e.	that is (Latin *id est*)
Inc.	incorporated
ISBN	International Standard Book Number
lc	lowercase
misc.	miscellaneous
p.	page
pp.	pages
re	with regard to
R.S.V.P.	please reply (French *répondez s'il vous plaît*)
SOS	international distress signal
TM	trademark
uc	uppercase
vs.	versus
w/o	without

Part Two

• • • • • • • • • • • • •

Grammar, Usage, and Mechanics

Chapter 1

Parts of
Speech

● ● ● ● ● ● ● ● ● ● ● ● ● ●

PRETEST **Identifying Parts of Speech**

For each numbered word in the paragraph below, write one of these words to identify its part of speech: noun, pronoun, verb, adjective, adverb, preposition, conjunction, interjection.

Slowly[1] I walked[2] through[3] the forest.[4] Around[5] me,[6] ancient[7] trees reached[8] high[9] into[10] the sky. Mosses[11] cushioned my steps, but[12] pine needles crackled crisply[13] under[14] my feet. I[15] was entirely[16] alone,[17] except for small[18] brown squirrels, raucous ravens,[19] and[20] a solitary woodpecker. His noisy[21] pecking resounded[22] in[23] the still afternoon air. The stuttering rhythm was oddly calming. Oh,[24] this[25] was[26] the place I felt alive[27] yet[28] at[29] peace. This was my spiritual[30] home.

1.1 NOUNS

A **noun** is a word that names a person, a place, a thing, or an idea.

EXAMPLES	**PERSON**	aunt, ecologist, Rodrigo, father-in-law, child
EXAMPLES	**PLACE**	playground, city, living room, Arizona
EXAMPLES	**THING**	moon, whale, chipmunk, Empire State Building
EXAMPLES	**IDEA**	democracy, hope, century, impatience

CONCRETE AND ABSTRACT NOUNS

A **concrete noun** names an object that occupies space or can be recognized by any of the senses.

EXAMPLES	salt	whisper	thunder	sand	scent

An **abstract noun** names an idea, a quality, or a characteristic.

EXAMPLES	confusion	grief	patience	clarity	friendship

SINGULAR AND PLURAL NOUNS

Most **nouns** are singular or plural. A singular noun names one person, place, thing, or idea. A plural noun names more than one.

EXAMPLES	**SINGULAR**	boy, branch, story, hoof, woman
EXAMPLES	**PLURAL**	boys, branches, stories, hooves, women

PRACTICE Plural Nouns

Write the plural form of each noun. Consult a dictionary if you need help.

1. apple
2. horse
3. lady
4. child
5. tree

6. match
7. family
8. penny
9. life
10. foot

POSSESSIVE NOUNS

The possessive form of a noun can show possession, ownership, or the general relationship between two nouns. For instance, if we want to say "the chair of Lynn," we can say "**Lynn's** chair."

To form the possessive of a singular noun, even one that ends in *s*, add an apostrophe and an *s*.

EXAMPLES **Susie's** calculator   **Morris's** strobe light

To form the possessive of a plural noun that ends in *s*, add just an apostrophe.

EXAMPLES the **Wilsons'** newspaper   the **boys'** headaches

To form the possessive of a plural noun that doesn't end in *s*, add an apostrophe and an *s*.

EXAMPLES   the **women's** meeting

the **sheep's** noses

PRACTICE   **Possessive Form of Nouns**

Rewrite each phrase below, using the possessive form of the noun in parentheses.

1. the (hawk) wings
2. the (book) cover
3. (William) ability
4. (Elvis) guitar
5. the (king) crown
6. Mrs. (Jones) pet cat
7. the (girls) grandfather
8. (Liz) dreams
9. the (dresses) hems
10. the (bear) paws

COMPOUND NOUNS

A **compound noun** is a noun made up of two or more words. Compound nouns may be open, hyphenated, or closed.

EXAMPLES	**OPEN**	music box, press secretary, public defender
EXAMPLES	**HYPHENATED**	great-grandfather, good-bye, sister-in-law
EXAMPLES	**CLOSED**	bedroom, headache, mailbox

COMMON AND PROPER NOUNS

A **common noun** is the general—not the particular—name of a person, place, thing, or idea.

A **proper noun** is the name of a particular person, place, thing, or idea.

Proper nouns are capitalized. Common nouns are usually not capitalized.

PROPER NOUNS

EXAMPLES	PERSON	James Baldwin, Toni Morrison, Sandra Cisneros
EXAMPLES	PLACE	Chicago, Great Britain, Antarctica, Madison Square Garden
EXAMPLES	THING	Ford Motor Company, World Trade Center, *Tom Sawyer*
EXAMPLES	IDEA	Jazz Age, Buddhism, Industrial Revolution, Romanticism

PRACTICE Common and Proper Nouns

Identify each noun by writing common *or* proper. *If a noun is common, also write* concrete *or* abstract *to further identify it.*

1. Ms. Fulton played with her new collie puppy.
2. The first man to walk on the Moon was Neil Armstrong.
3. Some bats live in towers.
4. Washington and his troops faced great hardship at Valley Forge.
5. I saw Mark McGwire fill the stadium with excitement.

COLLECTIVE NOUNS

A **collective noun** is singular in form but names a group.

| EXAMPLES | family | class | crew | band | committee |
| | troop | jury | flock | swarm | audience |

A collective noun is sometimes considered singular and sometimes considered plural. If you're talking about a group as a whole acting together, consider the collective noun singular. If you're talking about the individual members of a group, consider the collective noun plural.

EXAMPLE SINGULAR The **band** *travels* in an old bus.

EXAMPLE PLURAL   The **band** *are going* to assemble here at noon.

PRACTICE **Collective Nouns**

Write each collective noun. Label it S if it's singular and P if it's plural.

1. The Girl Scout troop is taking a trip to Santa Fe.
2. The family disagree about who should do dishes.
3. The committee votes to approve the school budget.
4. Before halftime, the band stands at the end of the field.
5. The litter of tigers wander in all directions.
6. That corporation seems to buy out another company every other week.
7. Usually the cast scatter after the play is over.
8. The production team almost always makes its deadline.
9. The flock flew in a V formation.
10. The class can't make up their minds about Prom.

1.2 PRONOUNS

A **pronoun** is a word that takes the place of a noun, a group of words acting as a noun, or another pronoun. The word or group of words to which a pronoun refers is called its **antecedent**.

EXAMPLE When N. Scott Momaday wrote *The Way to Rainy Mountain,* **he** was retelling Kiowa legends. [**The pronoun *he* takes the place of the noun *N. Scott Momaday*.**]

EXAMPLE Langston Hughes and Arna Bontemps were major figures of the Harlem Renaissance. **Both** edited *The Book of Negro Folklore.* [**The pronoun *both* takes the place of the nouns *Langston Hughes* and *Arna Bontemps*.**]

EXAMPLE   Very **few** can still remember poems **they** memorized for class. **[The pronoun *they* takes the place of the pronoun *few*.]**

There are about seventy-five pronouns in English. Each pronoun belongs in one or more of these categories: personal and possessive pronouns, reflexive and intensive pronouns, demonstrative pronouns, interrogative pronouns, relative pronouns, and indefinite pronouns.

PERSONAL AND POSSESSIVE PRONOUNS

A **personal pronoun** refers to a specific person, place, thing, or idea by indicating the person speaking (the first person), the person or people being spoken to (the second person), or any other person, place, thing, or idea being talked about (the third person).

Personal pronouns express number—that is, they are either singular or plural.

PERSONAL PRONOUNS		
	SINGULAR	**PLURAL**
FIRST PERSON	I, me	we, us
SECOND PERSON	you	you
THIRD PERSON	he, him, she, her, it	they, them

EXAMPLE   **FIRST PERSON**   **We** will keep the pup with **us**. **[*We* and *us* refer to the people speaking.]**

EXAMPLE   **SECOND PERSON**   **You** may use the spell-checking program. **[*You* refers to the person or people being addressed.]**

THIRD PERSON   **They** accomplished all the tasks
assigned to **them**. [*They* and *them*
refer to persons being discussed.]

Third-person singular pronouns also express **gender**.
He and *him* are masculine; *she* and *her* are feminine; *it* is
neuter—that is, neither masculine nor feminine.

Among the personal pronouns are forms that show
possession or ownership. These are called **possessive
pronouns**, and they take the place of the possessive
forms of nouns.

POSSESSIVE PRONOUNS		
	SINGULAR	**PLURAL**
FIRST PERSON	my, mine	our, ours
SECOND PERSON	your, yours	your, yours
THIRD PERSON	his her, hers its	their, theirs

Some of the pronouns in the chart above are paired. In
the pairs, the first form can be used before a noun. The
second form in each pair can stand alone as a noun does.
His and *its* can be used in both ways.

EXAMPLE   **USED BEFORE A NOUN**   Is that **her** journal?

EXAMPLE   **USED ALONE**   That journal is **hers**.

Notice that possessive pronouns do not contain
apostrophes. Take particular note that the possessive
pronoun *its* has no apostrophe. It is a common error to
mistake *its* and the contraction *it's*.

EXAMPLE   The cat was eating **its** food. **[possessive pronoun]**

EXAMPLE   **It's** my mother's cat. **[contraction for *It is*]**

Write each pronoun. Identify it by writing first person, second person, *or* third person. *Then write* singular *or* plural. *If the pronoun is possessive, write* possessive.

1. We went to the store yesterday.
2. You have to give her the library book.
3. There were more of them than there were of us.
4. The brown pony, with its black mane and tail, looks different from the rest.
5. Please give me your tickets, children.
6. Allan Pinkerton founded his detective agency in 1850.
7. When my friends and I went to the movies, we had fun.
8. The cat licked its sore paw.
9. Sheila was too young, so she was not allowed to go to the movie alone.
10. He went to the library on Saturday to do his homework.

REFLEXIVE AND INTENSIVE PRONOUNS

To form the reflexive and intensive pronouns, add *–self* or *–selves* to certain personal and possessive pronouns.

REFLEXIVE AND INTENSIVE PRONOUNS

	SINGULAR	PLURAL
FIRST PERSON	myself	ourselves
SECOND PERSON	yourself	yourselves
THIRD PERSON	himself, herself, itself	themselves

Notice that there are no such words as *hisself, theirself,* or *theirselves.*

A **reflexive pronoun** refers back to the subject of the sentence or clause and indicates that the same person or thing is involved. A reflexive pronoun adds information to a sentence.

EXAMPLE   We considered **ourselves** lucky to have avoided the tornado.

EXAMPLE   In stage makeup, I don't even look like **myself**.

An **intensive pronoun** adds emphasis to another noun or pronoun. It does not add information to a sentence. If the intensive pronoun is omitted, the meaning of the sentence will still be the same.

EXAMPLE   You **yourself** decided not to rename the file.

An **intensive pronoun** is often placed directly after its antecedent. However, an intensive pronoun may appear anywhere in a sentence.

EXAMPLE   I **myself** balanced the checkbook.

EXAMPLE   I balanced the checkbook **myself**.

DEMONSTRATIVE PRONOUNS

A **demonstrative pronoun** points out specific persons, places, things, or ideas.

DEMONSTRATIVE PRONOUNS		
SINGULAR	this	that
PLURAL	these	those

EXAMPLE **This** is your new toothbrush.

EXAMPLE Let me do **that** for you.

EXAMPLE Are **these** the cookies you liked so well?

EXAMPLE I think I'll take **those**.

INTERROGATIVE AND RELATIVE PRONOUNS

An **interrogative pronoun** is used to form questions.

INTERROGATIVE PRONOUNS		
who?	whom?	whose?
whoever?	whomever?	whatever?
which?	whichever?	what?

EXAMPLE **Who** made this delicious salad dressing?

EXAMPLE **Whom** are you expecting?

EXAMPLE **Whose** are these cute earrings?

EXAMPLE **What** did she say?

EXAMPLE **Which** of the flavors is your favorite?

EXAMPLE **Whatever** were you thinking?

EXAMPLE **Whomever** are you calling at this time of night?

A **relative pronoun** is used to begin a special subject-verb word group called a subordinate clause. (See Chapter 4.)

RELATIVE PRONOUNS			
who	whoever	which	that
whom	whomever	whose	what
	whichever	whatever	

EXAMPLE Rhonda held out paper cups of water to the marathon runners, **who** grabbed them eagerly. [The relative pronoun *who* begins the subordinate clause *who grabbed them eagerly*.]

EXAMPLE The novel **that** she wrote is on the best-seller list. [The relative pronoun *that* begins the subordinate clause *that she wrote*.]

INDEFINITE PRONOUNS

An **indefinite pronoun** refers to a person, a place, a thing, or an idea in a more general way than a noun does.

EXAMPLE Do you know **anyone** in your class? [The indefinite pronoun *anyone* does not refer to a specific person.]

EXAMPLE **Several** have submitted applications for college. [The indefinite pronoun *Several* does not refer to a specific group of people.]

EXAMPLE The group responsible for posters reported that **none** were ready. [The indefinite pronoun *none* has the specific antecedent *posters*.]

SOME INDEFINITE PRONOUNS

all	both	everything	nobody	others
another	each	few	none	several
any	either	many	no one	some
anybody	enough	most	nothing	somebody
anyone	everybody	much	one	someone
anything	everyone	neither	other	something

PRACTICE Pronouns

Write each pronoun. Identify it by writing reflexive,
intensive, demonstrative, interrogative, relative, *or*
indefinite.

1. Two-year-olds often want to do everything themselves.
2. Chocolate is made from cocoa, but cocoa itself is quite
bitter.
3. Whoever thought of that must have been a genius!
4. As Latonya sneaked up to the cookies, Ms. Ross said,
"Don't touch those until after dinner."
5. In the future, someone may travel to Mars.
6. The dog that barked was Ralph's.
7. Whom was Joe debating?
8. Isaac found himself shopping for a new computer.
9. Whatever did Mr. Begay mean by that?
10. Al ended up with a brown jacket, which wasn't cheap.

1.3 VERBS

A **verb** is a word that expresses an action or a state
of being and is necessary to make a statement.

EXAMPLES The author **summarized** his story.

The artist **cleaned** her brushes.

The actor **winked** at the audience.

This banner **appears** dusty.

Verbs express time—present, past, and future—by means of various *tense* forms.

EXAMPLE **PRESENT TENSE** I **smell** the roses.

EXAMPLE **PAST TENSE** I **smelled** the roses.

EXAMPLE **FUTURE TENSE** I **will smell** the roses.

ACTION VERBS

An **action verb** tells what someone or something does.

Action verbs can express action that is either physical or mental.

EXAMPLE **PHYSICAL ACTION** The chorus **sang** the new song.

EXAMPLE **MENTAL ACTION** The chorus **liked** the new song.

A **transitive verb** is followed by a word or words that answer the question *what?* or *whom?*

The word or words that answer the question *what?* or *whom?* after a transitive verb are called the **direct object.** (See Chapter 2.)

EXAMPLE She **spoke** the words of the challenge. [**The verb *spoke* is followed by the noun *words*, which answers the question *spoke what?*]**

An **intransitive verb** is *not* followed by a word that answers the question *what?* or *whom?*

EXAMPLE She **spoke** clearly. [**The verb is followed by a word that tells *how*.]**

Write each verb. Identify it by writing transitive *or*
intransitive. *If it is transitive, write the word or words*
that answer the questions what? *or* whom?

1. My brother served in the army for four years.
2. Farmers harvest their crops in the fall.
3. The horse jumped the fence and raced down the road.
4. Mozart wrote his first symphony at the age of eight.
5. Tourists explore in Yellowstone National Park each year.
6. Carey clapped loudly for the actors.
7. Jason teased Noel on the playground after school.
8. The bus veered off the highway.
9. The traditional log cabin originally came from Sweden.
10. Many people swim at beaches in the summer.

LINKING VERBS

A **linking verb** links, or joins, the subject of a sentence
(often a noun or a pronoun) with a noun, a pronoun,
or an adjective that identifies or describes the subject.
A linking verb does not show action.

Be in all its forms is the most commonly used linking
verb. Forms of *be* include *am, is, are, was, were, will be,*
has been, and *was being.*

EXAMPLES   That tailor **is** an expert.

This spring **has been** rainy.

These rosebushes **are** rare.

Tomorrow **will be** a sunny day.

Several other verbs besides *be* can act as linking verbs.

OTHER VERBS THAT CAN BE LINKING VERBS

appear	grow	seem	stay
become	look	smell	taste
feel	remain	sound	turn

EXAMPLE   This lemonade **tastes** sour.

VERB PHRASES

The verb in a sentence may consist of more than one word. The words that accompany the main verb are called **auxiliary**, or helping, **verbs**.

A **verb phrase** consists of a main verb and all its auxiliary, or helping, verbs.

AUXILIARY VERBS			
FORMS OF BE	am, is, are, was, were, being, been		
FORMS OF HAVE	has, have, had, having		
OTHER AUXILIARIES	can, could do, does, did	may, might shall, should	must will, would

The most common auxiliary verbs are forms of *be* and *have*. They help the main verb express time by forming the various tenses.

EXAMPLE   We **had expected** the letter for days.

The other auxiliary verbs are not used primarily to express time. They are often used to emphasize meaning.

EXAMPLE   You **should exercise** daily.

Write each verb and verb phrase. Identify it by writing transitive, intransitive, *or* linking.

1. Giovanni will always be my best friend.
2. Reggie rode the broken bike for a few yards.
3. Andrew bought a yellow rose for Juanita.
4. Phillip was kicking a rock on his way to the bus stop.
5. I did not steal your wallet!
6. Susan must have run across the playground.
7. Leo is a good piano player.
8. At the end of his ride, Andrew immediately sat down.
9. From a distance, the Statue of Liberty seems small.
10. Stradivarius made remarkable violins.

1.4 ADJECTIVES

An **adjective** is a word that modifies a noun or a pronoun by limiting its meaning.

EXAMPLES	**three** dollars	**any** objections	**baby** ducks
	Chinese teacup	**purple** balloon	**no** parking

An adjective may describe a noun or pronoun by answering one of these questions: *What kind? Which one? How many? How much?*

EXAMPLES	*WHAT KIND?*	**blue** scarf	**artistic** license
EXAMPLES	*WHICH ONE?*	**that** attitude	**second** try
EXAMPLES	*HOW MANY?*	**thirty** pages	**several** improvements
EXAMPLES	*HOW MUCH?*	**any** trouble	**no** mayonnaise

Two verb forms can also act as adjectives: the present participle, which ends in *–ing,* and the past participle, which ends in *–ed* or is irregularly formed.

EXAMPLES a **dancing** hen   the **crumpled** paper   a **broken** dish

Pronouns can also serve as adjectives. For example, possessive pronouns (*my, our, your, his, her, its,* and *their*) act as adjectives when they modify nouns. Demonstrative pronouns (*this, that, these,* and *those*) can also be considered demonstrative adjectives when they modify nouns. Similarly, nouns can serve as adjectives. Possessive nouns, like possessive pronouns, can be used as adjectives. In fact, any noun that modifies another noun can be considered an adjective.

EXAMPLES   **my** kitten **[possessive adjective]**

those bicycles **[demonstrative adjective]**

Lucy's report **[possessive noun acting as adjective]**

leather shoes **[noun acting as adjective]**

An adjective's position in relation to the word it modifies may vary.

EXAMPLES   How **spicy** the *chili* is!

The **spicy** *chili* steamed in its kettle.

The *chili* is **spicy**.

Peppers make the *chili* **spicy**.

The *chili*, **spicy** as tamales, steamed in its kettle.

Spicy as tamales, the *chili* steamed in its kettle.

PRACTICE **Adjectives**

Write each adjective and the word it modifies.

  1. I saw a kite in the sky on a windy day.
  2. Don't let that vicious dog get out of the yard!

3. A cracked mirror may reflect distorted images.

4. Across a calm lake, they saw the dim light of campfires.

5. The silvery sheen of the vase reflected the yellow and gold flowers.

6. The furry brown stuffed bear sat on her white bedspread.

7. In the spring, most trees become green.

8. The largest state in the United States is Alaska.

9. Raffi feeds his pet snake daily.

10. The tall building across the street looks old.

FoxTrot

by Bill Amend

ADJECTIVES THAT COMPARE

Many adjectives have different forms to indicate their degree of comparison. The **positive form** indicates no comparison. The **comparative form** compares two nouns or pronouns. The **superlative form** compares more than two nouns or pronouns.

EXAMPLES

POSITIVE	COMPARATIVE	SUPERLATIVE
slow	slower	slowest
lucky	luckier	luckiest
strenuous	more strenuous	most strenuous
good, well	better	best
bad	worse	worst

Write the correct comparative or superlative form of the adjective in parentheses. Consult a dictionary if necessary.

1. Albert Einstein was probably the (famous) scientist of his time.
2. California is home to some of the world's (tall) trees.
3. I believe that Matt is (old) than Jason.
4. Some snakes can unhinge their jaws to swallow food (large) than their heads.
5. Australia is the (small) of the continents.
6. The (long) alphabet I know of is Cambodian, with seventy-four letters.
7. I think lilies are (beautiful) than daisies.
8. The world's (large) telescopes are in Hawaii.
9. Ted's art is colorful, but Kim's art is (intriguing).
10. That band just gave me the (bad) headache I've ever had.

ARTICLES

Articles are the adjectives *a, an,* and *the. A* and *an* are called **indefinite articles.** *A* is used before consonant sounds, and *an* is used before vowel sounds. *The* is called the **definite article.**

EXAMPLES

| INDEFINITE | I wrote **a** play. | Ernesto wrote **an** article. |
| DEFINITE | I wrote **the** play. | Ernesto wrote **the** article. |

PROPER ADJECTIVES

A **proper adjective** is formed from a proper noun and begins with a capital letter.

EXAMPLE We attended the **Shakespearean** Drama Festival.

EXAMPLE The **Texan** barbecue was a success.

EXAMPLE The **Victorian** Era in England lasted from 1837 to 1901.

The following suffixes, along with others, are often used to form proper adjectives: *-an, -ian, -n, -ese,* and *-ish.* Sometimes there are other changes as well. Check the spelling in a dictionary.

EXAMPLES

PROPER NOUNS	PROPER ADJECTIVES
America	American
China	Chinese
England	English
Brazil	Brazilian
Africa	African

PRACTICE Proper Adjectives

Rewrite each phrase, changing the noun in blue type into a proper adjective. Consult a dictionary if necessary.

1. writers of **Norway**
2. food of **Mexico**
3. polar bears of **Iceland**
4. the soldiers of **Rome**
5. the rain forests of **Brazil**
6. furniture of **Sweden**
7. singers of **Zambia**
8. trees of **Indonesia**
9. rugs of **India**
10. the mountains of **Kenya**

1.5 ADVERBS

An **adverb** is a word that modifies a verb, an adjective, or another adverb by making its meaning more specific.

The following sentences illustrate the use of adverbs to modify verbs, adjectives, and adverbs.

EXAMPLES	**MODIFYING VERBS**	She ran **quickly**.
		She has **often** won.
EXAMPLE	**MODIFYING ADJECTIVES**	She is **very** talented and **extremely** diligent.
EXAMPLE	**MODIFYING ADVERBS**	She **almost** always runs **quite** fast.

Adverbs tell *when, where, how,* and *to what degree*.

EXAMPLE	**WHEN**	I got your letter **yesterday**.
EXAMPLE	**WHERE**	The wagon train headed **west**.
EXAMPLE	**HOW**	Play this section **softly** and **sweetly**.
EXAMPLE	**TO WHAT DEGREE**	This railing is **dangerously** rickety.

POSITION OF ADVERBS

An adverb that is modifying a verb can sometimes be placed in different positions in relation to the verb. An adverb that modifies an adjective or another adverb, however, must immediately precede the word it modifies.

EXAMPLES

MODIFYING A VERB   **Generally** we *eat* at six.

We **generally** *eat* at six.

We *eat* at six **generally**.

MODIFYING AN ADJECTIVE   The soup was **definitely** *lukewarm*.

MODIFYING AN ADVERB   We **almost** *never* have dessert.

NEGATIVE WORDS AS ADVERBS

The word *not* and the contraction *n't* are adverbs. Certain adverbs of time, place, and degree also have negative meanings.

EXAMPLES The color did**n't** fade.

That dye **hardly ever** fades.

EXAMPLES If correctly set, this dye **never** fades.

The tints can **barely** be distinguished.

EXAMPLES There are **no** undyed patches.

We can**not** complain about the color.

PRACTICE Adverbs

Write each adverb and what it modifies. Then tell whether what is modified is a verb, *an* adjective, *or another* adverb.

1. Greg slept too soundly to be awakened by the storm.
2. The wolf ate the food hungrily.
3. The squirrel stored the nuts haphazardly.
4. The bowling ball was unusually heavy.
5. Norman almost always brought his lunch to school.
6. Jasmine walked hurriedly toward the library.
7. Reluctantly Carlos asked a question.
8. The play began fairly awkwardly.
9. Krista hit the ball hard, and it soared easily over the fence.
10. I almost never wake before seven o'clock.

ADVERBS THAT COMPARE

Some adverbs, like adjectives, have different forms to indicate the degree of comparison.

POSITIVE	COMPARATIVE	SUPERLATIVE
sat **near**	sat **nearer**	sat **nearest**
talks **slowly**	talks **more slowly**	talks **most slowly**
dances **well**	dances **better**	dances **best**
writes **badly**	writes **worse**	writes **worst**
draws **beautifully**	draws **more beautifully**	draws **most beautifully**
looks **far**	looks **farther**	looks **farthest**
left **early**	left **earlier**	left **earliest**

PRACTICE   **Adverbs That Compare**

Write the comparative and superlative forms of each adverb. Consult a dictionary if necessary.

1. powerfully
2. late
3. calmly
4. hungrily
5. light

6. often
7. gladly
8. quietly
9. hard
10. smooth

1.6 PREPOSITIONS

A **preposition** is a word that shows the relationship of a noun or a pronoun to another word in a sentence.

EXAMPLE   The mother **of** the kittens lives here. [*Of* shows the relationship of *mother* to *kittens*.]

EXAMPLE   I will see you **after** lunch. [*After* expresses the time relationship between *lunch* and when I *will see* you.]

EXAMPLE   She sang her song **for** them. [*For* relates the verb *sang* to the pronoun *them*.]

GRAMMAR/USAGE/MECHANICS

COMMONLY USED PREPOSITIONS

aboard	beneath	in	regarding
about	beside	inside	respecting
above	besides	into	since
across	between	like	through
after	beyond	near	throughout
against	but (meaning *except*)	of	to
along	by	off	toward
amid	concerning	on	under
among	despite	onto	underneath
around	down	opposite	until
as	during	out	up
at	except	outside	upon
before	excepting	over	with
behind	for	past	within
below	from	pending	without

A **compound preposition** is a preposition that is made up of more than one word.

COMPOUND PREPOSITIONS

according to	because of	instead of
ahead of	by means of	next to
along with	except for	on account of
apart from	in addition to	on top of
aside from	in front of	out of
as to	in spite of	owing to

A **prepositional phrase** is a group of words that begins with a preposition and ends with a noun or a pronoun called the **object of the preposition**.

EXAMPLE   Jorge and Mei Ling went **to the fair**.

EXAMPLE   César rode **along with them**.

EXAMPLE   I met them **at the candied-apples stand**.

EXAMPLE   Everyone **but César** had a candied apple.

EXAMPLE   César satisfied his sweet tooth **with saltwater taffy**.

Some words may be used as either prepositions or adverbs. A word is used as a preposition if it has a noun or a pronoun as its object. A word is used as an adverb if it does not have an object.

WORD USED AS PREPOSITION	WORD USED AS ADVERB
EXAMPLE I left my boots **outside** the back door.	I left my boots **outside**.
EXAMPLE The bird flew **over** the fence.	The bird flew **over**.
EXAMPLE Everyone came **aboard** the boat.	Everyone came **aboard**.

PRACTICE   Prepositional Phrases

Write each prepositional phrase. Underline the preposition and draw a circle around the object of the preposition.

1. The jewelry store is around the corner and down the street.
2. According to the map my dad gave me, Tulsa is east of Oklahoma City.
3. Alex found his pen under the chair cushion and two quarters between the couch cushions.
4. Without any hope of victory, Ralph prepared his concession speech.
5. Chewing gum in class is forbidden.

6. It is often said that the grass is greener on the other side of the fence.

7. Ernest Hemingway wrote about the lost generation.

8. The ocean contains most of all the plant life on the planet.

9. A typical tree receives only 10 percent of its nutrition from the soil.

10. After the long movie, John finally headed home.

1.7 CONJUNCTIONS

A **conjunction** is a word that joins single words or groups of words.

COORDINATING CONJUNCTIONS

A **coordinating conjunction** joins words or groups of words that have equal grammatical weight in a sentence.

COORDINATING CONJUNCTIONS						
and	but	or	so	nor	for	yet

EXAMPLE Their skit includes a rabbit **and** a bird.

EXAMPLE Ms. Fernandez dresses fashionably **but** tastefully.

EXAMPLE Hang the snowshoes in the mudroom **or** in the garage.

EXAMPLE Winter days are short, **so** houseplants may need extra light.

EXAMPLE We didn't stop to ask directions, **nor** did we even consult a map.

EXAMPLE I'm glad Andrea won first prize, **for** she deserves it.

EXAMPLE Joe claims Italian descent, **yet** he doesn't like pasta.

CORRELATIVE CONJUNCTIONS

Correlative conjunctions work in pairs to join words and groups of words of equal grammatical weight in a sentence.

CORRELATIVE CONJUNCTIONS		
both . . . and	just as . . . so	not only . . . but (also)
either . . . or	neither . . . nor	whether . . . or

Correlative conjunctions make the relationship between words or groups of words a little clearer than do coordinating conjunctions.

EXAMPLES

COORDINATING CONJUNCTIONS	CORRELATIVE CONJUNCTIONS
Kim **and** I must test the software.	**Both** Kim **and** I must test the software.
You **or** José can make the call.	**Either** you **or** José can make the call.
He spray painted the security camera **and** robbed the bank.	He **not only** spray painted the security camera **but also** robbed the bank.

PRACTICE Coordinating and Correlative Conjunctions

Write all conjunctions. Then identify them as either coordinating *or* correlative.

1. Frank wanted to go to either the movies or the arcade.
2. Mia's mom and dad keep family pictures on the piano.
3. Just as people dislike overcrowding, so do plants respond badly to it.
4. Pauline is not a writer, but she makes up stories.

5. Jason is the best basketball player on the team, so he is the captain.

6. Haley neither liked her broccoli nor ate it.

7. Surely Malcolm or Kay will help me with math.

8. He not only belongs to the track team at school, but also plays tennis on the weekends.

9. Mahatma Gandhi was both a lawyer and a religious leader.

10. The golf pro has been enormously successful, yet he remains approachable.

SUBORDINATING CONJUNCTIONS

A **subordinating conjunction** joins two clauses, or thoughts, in such a way as to make one grammatically dependent on the other.

The thought, or clause, that a subordinating conjunction introduces is said to be subordinate, or dependent, because it cannot stand by itself as a complete sentence.

EXAMPLE **Since** you learned to dance, you have become more graceful.

EXAMPLE **Whenever** I skate, I wear elbow and knee pads.

EXAMPLE The children may come along **provided that** they stay with us.

EXAMPLE We sat by the lake **while** the sun set.

COMMON SUBORDINATING CONJUNCTIONS

after	as though	provided (that)	unless
although	because	since	until
as	before	so long as	when
as far as	considering (that)	so (that)	whenever

as if	if	than	where
as long as	inasmuch as	though	whereas
as soon as	in order that	till	wherever
			while

PRACTICE   Subordinating Conjunctions

Write each subordinating conjunction.

1. After the rains fell, the crops were ruined by flooding.
2. Although she had a television, Andrea preferred to read.
3. Bill Bradley played professional basketball before he was a senator.
4. Greg fixed dinner because he was the best cook among us.
5. Considering that he had no experience, Mario did well.
6. Until the airplane was invented, balloons were used to take aerial photographs.
7. Jim ran laps while the rest of the team watched.
8. As soon as Sue finishes breakfast, we will go.
9. Jan works only when someone is watching her.
10. I acted as if I didn't know about it.

CONJUNCTIVE ADVERBS

A **conjunctive adverb** is used to clarify the relationship between clauses of equal grammatical weight in a sentence.

Conjunctive adverbs are usually stronger, more precise, and more formal than coordinating conjunctions. Notice that when a coordinating conjunction is used between clauses, a comma precedes the coordinating conjunction. When a conjunctive adverb is used between clauses, a semicolon precedes the conjunctive adverb, and a comma follows it.

EXAMPLES

COORDINATING CONJUNCTION	I don't mind bright green kitchen walls myself**, but** shouldn't we ask your mother?
CONJUNCTIVE ADVERB	I don't mind bright green kitchen walls myself**; still,** shouldn't we ask your mother?

Conjunctive adverbs have many uses, as the following examples show.

EXAMPLES TO REPLACE *AND*	also, besides, furthermore, moreover
EXAMPLES TO REPLACE *BUT*	however, nevertheless, nonetheless, still
EXAMPLES TO STATE A RESULT	accordingly, consequently, then, therefore, thus
EXAMPLES TO STATE EQUALITY	equally, likewise, similarly

PRACTICE Conjunctive Adverbs

Rewrite each sentence, changing coordinating conjunctions to conjunctive adverbs.

1. Bamboo grows very tall, and it may grow three feet in twenty-four hours.
2. Eric took a quick lead in the race, but he lost.
3. Liz may have wanted to go to medical school, but she became an architect.
4. Michele works at a fast food restaurant, and her best friend applied for a job at the same place.
5. I have to go to basketball practice, so I will miss the beginning of my favorite show.

6. I have tons of homework, but I will do my best to get to the party.

7. Joe likes his hamster, Sparks, and Jacque likes his potbellied pig, Pinky.

8. Samuel enjoys debating, and it was not surprising when he was voted captain of the debate team.

9. Manuel organized the school banquet, so he was offered a summer job.

10. Dan doesn't like dogs, but he walks the family dog every morning.

1.8 INTERJECTIONS

An **interjection** is a word or a phrase that expresses emotion or exclamation. An interjection has no grammatical connection to other words in the sentence and is set off from the other words by an exclamation point or a comma.

Different emotions are expressed by different interjections.

EXAMPLE	SURPRISE	**Oh, my!** I had no idea.
EXAMPLE	DELIGHT	**Ah**, that's good.
EXAMPLE	CONFUSION	**Good grief!** Is that true?
EXAMPLE	PAIN	**Ouch!** That hurts.
EXAMPLE	JOY	**Wow!** This is super!

Interjections are mainly used in speaking. Use them sparingly when you write.

PRACTICE Interjections

Identify each interjection.

1. Good grief! I've said this a thousand times.
2. Ha! I've heard you at least a million times.
3. Ouch! I stubbed my toe on that iron rabbit.

4. Poor baby! I just stepped on a real slug.
5. Goodness, that giant sequoia is tall!
6. Duh! That's why they call it a giant.
7. Brrr! It's as cold here as at the South Pole today.
8. Yikes! You're right. I just saw a penguin get on the Broadway bus.
9. Well, did you see that? That was the weirdest dog I've ever seen.
10. No wonder! It was a possum.

PRACTICE Parts of Speech

Use each word below in two sentences as two different parts of speech. You will write a total of twenty sentences. In each sentence, circle the word. After each sentence, give the word's part of speech.

EXAMPLE bow

She wore a (bow) in her hair. noun.

The dancers (bow) after each performance. verb

1. inside	**5.** watch	**9.** about
2. use	**6.** cloud	**10.** snake
3. concern	**7.** stalk	
4. those	**8.** orange	

PRACTICE Proofreading

Rewrite the following passage, correcting errors in spelling, capitalization, grammar, and usage. Add any missing punctuation. Write legibly to be sure one letter is not mistaken for another. There are ten mistakes.

Frances E. W. Harper

[1]The famous writer Frances Ellen Watkins Harper was born in 1825 in Maryland which was then a free state. [2]An orphan before she was three, she was brought up by her uncle, a teacher. [3]William Watkins held strong

political views, especially about abolishun, and his influence on young Frances was great. [4]She attended her uncle's School until 1839. [5]Her first book of poems, "Forest Leaves," was published in 1845, when she was twenty years old. [6]In 1850 Harper became the first woman teacher at union seminary in Wilberforce, Ohio, despite great protest. [7]Her next teaching position was in Pennsylvania, where she lived in a station of the famous Underground Railroad and experiensed much that would influence her later writing.

[8]In 1854 Harper found herself exiled from her birthplace, because of new laws. [9]These laws state that African Americans who came in through the northern border of the state could be enslaved and sold. [10]The writer then threw herself heart and sole into abolitionism. [11]As she traveled around the North and Canada speaking against enslaved people, she used her own poetry and prose in her presentations. [12]This writing of hers' became so popular that her second book was published "by popular demand."

POSTTEST   Identifying Parts of Speech

For each numbered word in the paragraph below, write one of these words to identify its part of speech: noun, pronoun, verb, adjective, adverb, preposition, conjunction, interjection.

What an experience![1] There[2] I stood[3] at[4] the edge[5] of the Grand Canyon. Above[6] me[7] stretched an amazingly[8] blue sky and below me was one[9] of the wonders[10] of the world. The size[11] of this geological[12] miracle[13] was not just impressive;[14] it was startling. Wherever[15] I looked, the colors[16] dazzled[17] my eyes, and[18] I found myself[19] searching for[20] a word[21] to describe the sight,[22] yet[23] I could not[24] find[25] it.[26] All[27] I could say[28] was,[29] "Wow!"[30]

Chapter 2

Parts of the Sentence

● ● ● ● ● ● ● ● ● ● ● ● ● ● ● ● ●

PRETEST **Identifying Subjects and Predicates**

Identify each underlined word or group of words in the paragraph by writing one of these labels: simple subject, complete subject, simple predicate, complete predicate.

I <u>can see the backyards on my block from my upstairs window</u>.[1] Behind them are <u>the garages</u>.[2] <u>A clean, wide alley</u>[3] <u>runs behind the garages</u>.[4] My neighbors <u>walk there from their cars to their apartments</u>.[5] Across the alley, I <u>see</u>[6] the backs of buildings one street over. <u>They</u>[7] all <u>have porches and stairways</u>.[8] <u>Some</u>[9] of the porches <u>are empty</u>.[10] <u>Some</u>[11] <u>are crowded with pots of flowers</u>.[12] Someday I[13] <u>will paint</u>[14] this view. I <u>will paint it in the pink light and purple shadows of sunset</u>.[15]

Identify each underlined word or group of words by writing one of these labels: direct object, indirect object, object complement, predicate nominative, predicate adjective.

Lake Quinault, Washington, is a remarkable <u>place</u>.[16] Low mountains surround a glacier-fed <u>lake.</u>[17] Five-hundred-year-old trees touch the <u>sky</u>.[18] The forest floor displays <u>ferns</u>[19] and mosses. Mushrooms dot the ground, and the trees that wear them are <u>lovely</u>.[20] These fungi, delicate as wild-flowers, make the brown and gray tree trunks <u>colorful</u>.[21] Clouds lie low above the lake and give <u>Earth</u>[22] their <u>bounty</u>.[23] This is <u>one</u>[24] of the few temperate rain forests in the world, and rainfall is <u>high</u>,[25] often measuring more than 150 inches in a year.

One can see <u>tourists</u>[26] from Germany, France, England, and Japan on the forest paths, enjoying one of America's wonders. Often the majesty of the trees renders <u>visitors</u>[27] <u>speechless</u>.[28] A writer living here could create <u>fairy tales</u>[29] and legends. The deep, beautiful, mysterious forest would give any <u>writer</u>[30] inspiration.

2.1 SIMPLE SUBJECTS AND SIMPLE PREDICATES

A **sentence** is a group of words that expresses a complete thought.

Every sentence has two basic parts, a *subject* and a *predicate*.

The **subject** is the part of the sentence that names whom or what the sentence is about.

The **predicate** is the part of the sentence that says something about the subject.

Both the subject and the predicate can consist of more than one word.

The **simple subject** is the key noun or pronoun that tells whom or what the sentence is about.

The **simple predicate** is the verb or verb phrase that expresses the action or state of being of the subject of the sentence.

Remember, a simple predicate that is a verb phrase consists of a verb and any auxiliary, or helping, verbs.

EXAMPLES

SIMPLE SUBJECT	SIMPLE PREDICATE
Nikki Giovanni	writes.
Everyone	will attend.
Cookies	were baking.
Traffic	slowed.

You find the simple subject by asking *who?* or *what?* about the verb. For example, in the first sentence above, the proper noun *Nikki Giovanni* answers the question *Who writes?*

Atlantic Feature © 1999 Mark Parisi

Write each simple subject and simple predicate. Underline the simple predicate.

1. The sixteenth president of the United States was Abraham Lincoln.
2. Oklahoma became a state in 1907.
3. The short red-haired girl with the bright blue shirt gave the visiting dignitary a bouquet of flowers.
4. Jennifer, the best athlete in the school, scored twenty points in one basketball game.
5. Not a soul stirred in the night.
6. According to this book, cranberry juice contains a number of important nutrients.
7. The largest mammal in the world is the blue whale.
8. Styrofoam cups can sit in landfills for millions of years.
9. Tennis player Venus Williams won the Wimbledon ladies' singles title in the year 2000.
10. The sign on top of the bookshelf reads Large Print.

GRAMMAR/USAGE/MECHANICS

2.2 COMPLETE SUBJECTS AND COMPLETE PREDICATES

In most sentences, the addition of other words and phrases to the simple subject and the simple predicate expands or modifies the meaning of the sentence.

The **complete subject** consists of the simple subject and all the words that modify it.

The **complete predicate** consists of the simple predicate (the verb or verb phrase) and all the words that modify it or complete its meaning.

EXAMPLES

COMPLETE SUBJECT	COMPLETE PREDICATE
The celebrated Nikki Giovanni	writes fantastic poetry.
Everyone in the French club	will attend the meeting.
Chocolate chip cookies	were baking in the oven.
The rush-hour traffic	slowed to a snail's pace.

PRACTICE **Complete Subjects and Complete Predicates**

Identify each underlined complete subject or complete predicate by writing CS *(complete subject) or* CP *(complete predicate).*

1. The Kremlin <u>is an ancient fortress in Russia</u>.
2. <u>One particularly ferocious animal</u> is the tiger.
3. <u>Zack and Drew</u> played baseball at the park all afternoon and into the evening.
4. <u>Two of the girls from my class</u> are competing in the city science fair tomorrow.
5. The television with a thirty-five inch screen <u>is my favorite</u>.
6. Wise gardeners <u>do not plant too early in the spring</u>.
7. <u>A queen termite</u> can give birth to half a billion new termites during her lifetime.
8. The Beatles <u>were arguably the best rock and roll band in the 1960s</u>.
9. <u>The world's oldest passenger train line</u> connected Manchester and Liverpool, England.
10. I <u>need to do the dishes and fold the laundry</u>.

2.3 COMPOUND SUBJECTS AND COMPOUND PREDICATES

A **compound subject** is made up of two or more simple subjects that are joined by a conjunction and have the same verb.

Coordinating and correlative conjunctions are commonly used to join the subjects in a compound subject.

EXAMPLE   **Books** and **magazines** are sold at the new store.

EXAMPLE   **Water** or **soda** will be served with dinner.

EXAMPLE   Neither the **bus** nor the **subway** goes there.

EXAMPLE   Both **experience** and adequate **training** are necessary.

When there are more than two subjects in the compound subject, the conjunction is usually used only between the last two words, and the words are separated by commas.

EXAMPLE   **Crimson, cerise,** and **vermilion** are shades of red.

Some sentences have more than one simple predicate.

A **compound predicate** (or **compound verb**) is made up of two or more verbs or verb phrases that are joined by a conjunction and have the same subject.

EXAMPLE   Artists **draw** and **paint**.

EXAMPLE   Yvette **sat** on a bench, **opened** her lunch box, and **ate** a sandwich.

In compound verbs that contain verb phrases, the auxiliary verb may or may not be repeated before the second verb.

EXAMPLE   Cats **will hiss** and **will scratch** when frightened.

EXAMPLE   Cats **will hiss** and **scratch** when frightened.

A sentence may have both a compound subject and a compound predicate.

EXAMPLE   **Comedians** and **musicians delight** and **entertain** audiences.

Compound Subjects and Compound Predicates

Write CS *if a sentence has a compound subject. Write* CP *if a sentence has a compound predicate. Then write each simple subject and simple predicate.*

1. The Mets and the Yankees are both New York City baseball teams.
2. Sara and Joan went to the mall after school.
3. Georgina tripped and fell over the new rug.
4. Some cloth makers spin, dye, and weave wool.
5. Fred Astaire and Ginger Rogers danced magnificently in a long series of entertaining movies.
6. Paul went to the party and met a couple of new friends.
7. My best friend, Andrew, pitches and plays the outfield.
8. Koalas and platypuses are found only in Australia.
9. Most of the audience in the theater laughed and cried during the play.
10. Jeanne's sleeping bag and her tent kept her warm on the coldest night in the woods.

2.4 ORDER OF SUBJECT AND PREDICATE

In English the subject comes before the verb in most sentences. Some exceptions to this normal word order are discussed below.

In **commands** and **requests**, the subject is usually not stated. The predicate is the entire sentence. The pronoun *you* is understood to be the subject.

EXAMPLES **[You] Listen!** **[You]** Please **see** me. **[You] Be** careful.

Questions frequently begin with a verb or a helping verb or the words *who, whom, what, when, where, why,* or *how.*

EXAMPLE   **Did** he reply?

EXAMPLE   **Have** you **read** Nikki Giovanni's poetry?

EXAMPLE   **What** do they sing?

In these cases, the subject generally follows the verb or helping verb. To find the subject of a question, rearrange the words to form a statement.

	SUBJECT	PREDICATE
EXAMPLE	He	did reply.
EXAMPLE	You	have read Nikki Giovanni's poetry.
EXAMPLE	They	do sing what.

A sentence written in **inverted order**, in which the predicate comes before the subject, serves to add emphasis to the subject.

	PREDICATE	SUBJECT
EXAMPLE	Under the moonlight **sat**	the old cypress **tree.**
EXAMPLE	Above the forest **circled**	three **hawks.**

Remember, a word in a prepositional phrase is never the subject.

When the word *there* or *here* begins a sentence and is followed by a form of the verb *to be*, the subject follows the verb. The word *there* or *here* is almost never the subject of a sentence.

	PREDICATE	SUBJECT
EXAMPLE	Here **are**	the **quilts** from my grandma.
EXAMPLE	There **is**	the **book** on the table.

PRACTICE   Simple Subjects and Simple Predicates

Write each simple subject and simple predicate. If a subject is understood, write (You).

1. Please stop that noise.

2. Up the river, a waterfall tumbles over the rocks.

3. How much wool can one sheep produce?

4. All the way around the bases ran our best power hitter.

5. Here is the rabbit hole.

6. Over the fence and into the weeds flew the ball.

7. Wait for me, Sally.

8. Our dinner tasted delicious after our long hike.

9. Save me one piece of watermelon, please.

10. Is this the way to San Francisco?

2.5 COMPLEMENTS

A **complement** is a word or a group of words that completes the meaning of a verb.

There are four kinds of complements: *direct objects, indirect objects, object complements,* and *subject complements.*

DIRECT OBJECTS

A **direct object** answers the question *what?* or *whom?* after an action verb.

The subject of a sentence usually performs the action indicated by the verb. That action may be directed toward or received by someone or something—the direct object. Direct objects are nouns, pronouns, or words acting as nouns, and they may be compound. Only transitive verbs have direct objects.

EXAMPLE   Estella sold her **computer**. [Estella sold *what?*]

EXAMPLE   Tamara watched the **professor**. [Tamara watched *whom?*]

EXAMPLE   Estella sold her **computer** and **radio**. [Estella sold *what?*]

INDIRECT OBJECTS

An **indirect object** answers the question *to whom? for whom? to what?* or *for what?* after an action verb.

A sentence can have an indirect object only if it has a direct object. Two clues can help you identify indirect objects. First, an indirect object always comes between the verb and the direct object.

EXAMPLE   The owner gave **us** a discount. **[The owner gave a discount *to whom?*]**

EXAMPLE   Ahmad bought **Jeremy** and **Sean** candy. **[Ahmad bought candy *for whom?*]**

Second, if you add the word *to* or *for* in front of an indirect object, the sentence will still make sense.

EXAMPLE   Rami left Jennifer a message.

Rami left a message for Jennifer.

Notice that in the second sentence, the proper noun *Jennifer* is no longer an indirect object. It has become the object of a preposition. (See Chapter 1.)

OBJECT COMPLEMENTS

An **object complement** answers the question *what?* after a direct object. That is, it *completes* the meaning of the direct object by identifying or describing it.

Object complements occur only in sentences with direct objects and only in those sentences with the following action verbs or with similar verbs that have the general meaning of "make" or "consider":

appoint	consider	make	render
call	elect	name	think
choose	find	prove	vote

An object complement usually follows a direct object. It may be an adjective, a noun, or a pronoun.

EXAMPLE   The bonus made Susan **happy**. [adjective]

EXAMPLE   I named my dog **Sadie**. [proper noun]

EXAMPLE   Our cat considers that pillow **hers**. [pronoun]

SUBJECT COMPLEMENTS (PREDICATE NOMINATIVES, PREDICATE ADJECTIVES)

A **subject complement** follows a subject and a linking verb and identifies or describes the subject.

There are two kinds of subject complements: *predicate nominatives* and *predicate adjectives*.

A **predicate nominative** is a noun or a pronoun that follows a linking verb and points back to the subject to rename it or to identify it further.

EXAMPLE   Cellists are **musicians**.

EXAMPLE   The soloist for this concert is **someone** from Dallas.

EXAMPLE   My favorite singer is **he**.

Predicate nominatives are usually found in sentences that contain forms of the linking verb *be*. A few other linking verbs as well (for example, *become* and *remain*) can be followed by a predicate nominative.

EXAMPLE   Alexis remains an **admirer** and a **friend**.

EXAMPLE   That class became a **challenge** for me.

A **predicate adjective** is an adjective that follows a linking verb and points back to the subject and further describes it.

EXAMPLE   My sister is **generous**.

EXAMPLE   Some doctors are **compassionate**.

Predicate adjectives may follow any linking verb.

EXAMPLE   I feel very **insecure**.

EXAMPLE   The coffee shop looked **busy**.

EXAMPLE   The author seemed **intelligent** and **thoughtful**.

EXAMPLE   Lori's tale sounded **preposterous** to me.

EXAMPLE   The boy appeared **happy**.

EXAMPLE   Dinner smells **delicious**.

EXAMPLE   The milk tastes **sour**.

GRAMMAR/USAGE/MECHANICS

PRACTICE Complements

Write each complement and identify it by writing DO *for a direct object,* IO *for an indirect object,* OC *for an object complement,* PN *for a predicate nominative, or* PA *for a predicate adjective.*

1. Leo Tolstoy wrote *War and Peace*.
2. Trisha gave her sister her old bicycle.
3. After the game, Pauline considered herself lucky.
4. Paul Bunyan was a very large man.
5. We watched a good movie last night.
6. I wished Jack good luck in the track meet.
7. *Gone with the Wind* remains popular with all ages after all these years.

8. Xavier judged the municipal government guilty of irresponsibility in the matter of the waste site.
9. Isaac wrote Jan and Paul a letter from Europe.
10. William Shakespeare may have been England's greatest playwright.

PRACTICE Proofreading

Rewrite the following passage, correcting errors in spelling, capitalization, grammar, and usage. Add any missing punctuation. Write legibly to be sure one letter is not mistaken for another. There are ten mistakes.

Edna Ferber

[1]One of the great American writers, Edna Ferber was born in 1887 in Kalamazoo, Michigan. [2]Her father was a hungarian-born Jewish storekeeper and her mother an American-born Jewish housewife. [3]When Edna was twelve the family moved to Wisconsin. [4]When she graduated from High School, she was offered a job on the *Appleton Daily Crescent*. [5]Since her family's finances would not allow her to go to college, she took the job. [6]Later she moved to the *Milwaukee Journal*.

[7]Ferber worked so hard at the *Journal,* that she collapsed from exhaustion. [8]While she were resting up, she wrote her first short story, and in 1911 her first novel appeared. [9]It was about a newspaperwoman in Milwaukee. [10]She then wrote a series of stories about a traveling saleswoman Emma McChesney. [11]The stories were so popular that Edna Ferber became nationally famous, and based a play on them. [12]She later collaborated on a number of plays with famous playwright George S. Kaufman but it is for her novels that she is best known.

[13]In 1925 Ferber won a pulitzer prize for her novel *So Big,* which told the story of a woman bringing up a child on a farm outside Chicago. [14]Some of her other important books include *Cimarron, Giant,* and *Showboat,* which was made into a musical classic, it is still performed today.

POSTTEST   Identifying Subjects and Predicates

Identify each underlined word or group of words in the paragraph by writing one of these labels: simple subject, complete subject, simple predicate, complete predicate.

Beads <u>are made everywhere</u>.[1] <u>These miniature artworks</u>[2] <u>are fashioned from various substances</u>.[3] <u>Czechoslovakia</u>[4] <u>is famous for glass beads</u>.[5] <u>From many parts of Africa come</u>[6] <u>brightly colored pottery beads fashioned by hand</u>.[7] <u>Silver beads from India</u>[8] <u>are</u>[9] beautiful. <u>The Philippines</u>[10] <u>offers uniquely shaped coil beads</u>.[11] <u>Their size and fascinating beauty</u>[12] make beads ideal for barter. Today, <u>collectors</u>[13] <u>may pay</u>[14] thousands of dollars for one bead. <u>Imagine that!</u>[15]

POSTTEST   Identifying Complements

Identify each underlined word or group of words by writing one of these labels: direct object, indirect object, object complement, predicate nominative, predicate adjective.

Generally, birds do not possess much <u>intelligence</u>.[16] Mammals far exceed <u>birds</u>[17] in the ability to think and learn. One reason for this is birds' low brain-surface to body-weight <u>ratio</u>.[18] Birds simply have very small <u>brains</u>.[19] Crows and ravens are <u>exceptions</u>,[20] to some degree. They are unusually <u>smart</u>[21] for birds. Scarecrows seldom scare <u>crows</u>.[22] In captivity a raven can learn many <u>skills</u>,[23] such as how to respond to a name. This intelligence may explain the <u>position</u>[24] of ravens in Native American folklore. Many tribes consider <u>ravens</u>[25] "<u>tricksters</u>"[26] and tell of their cleverness.

Chickens, on the other hand, are <u>dumb</u>.[27] Owls give <u>us</u>[28] the <u>impression</u>[29] of wisdom because of their large and keen eyes, but owls are only a little <u>smarter</u>[30] than chickens.

Phrases

● ● ● ● ● ● ● ● ● ● ● ● ● ● ●

PRETEST **Identifying Prepositional Phrases**

There are ten prepositional phrases in the paragraph below. Write the prepositional phrases. For each, write the word or words modified by the phrase. Then write ADJ *(adjective) or* ADV *(adverb) to identify the type of phrase.*

A tiny stuffed bear sits on Maisie's computer. Beside him is a turtle with a purple head. In the light from the window, they look a little shabby. They droop over the monitor. Why should anyone value these bits of cloth? Perhaps they are reminders of humor and nonsense in a world filled with beige metal and gigabytes.

PRETEST **Identifying Verbals and Appositives**

Identify each italicized word by writing one of these labels: participle, gerund, infinitive, appositive.

11. *Sleeping* at his friend's house, Augie woke up early.
12. The pitcher, *Ryan,* threw a no-hitter.

13. Before *going* out, should I change clothes?

14. *Mourning* his pet, Mr. Thomas picked up the dog's toys.

15. I went into town, hoping *to find* Mark.

16. May, *a girl from my hometown,* was the most talented entrant in the contest.

17. The band marched across the bridge *spanning* the creek.

18. How often have you gotten in trouble for *talking* in class?

19. The great novelist *Thomas Hardy* was actually most interested in poetry.

20. I found a broken bowl in the kitchen and went *to look* for my brother's cat.

Identify each italicized group of words by writing one of these labels: prepositional phrase, appositive phrase, participial phrase, infinitive phrase, gerund phrase, absolute phrase.

21. The sense you have *of your voice* is usually wrong.

22. *Listening to yourself on a tape recorder* can be a shock.

23. Everyone will recognize your voice *except you*.

24. Experts *trained in this field* say that people throughout the world reject the sound of their own voices.

25. The main reason for this is *the functioning of our speech apparatus.*

26. Speech vibrations begin in the larynx, *the voice box.*

27. *The vibrations being softened by your skull and its contents,* you hear your voice with certain qualities.

28. Your friends, on the other hand, hear the vibrations *traveling to them through the air.*

29. *For that reason,* your voice sounds higher and sharper to your friends than to you.

30. *To hear your own voice as it really sounds,* you must hear it recorded in some way.

3.1 PREPOSITIONAL PHRASES

A **phrase** is a group of words that acts in a sentence as a single part of speech.

A **prepositional phrase** is a group of words that begins with a preposition and ends with a noun or a pronoun, which is called the **object of the preposition.**

EXAMPLE The new picture hangs **on the wall.**
[*Wall* **is the object of the preposition** *on.*]

EXAMPLE The room **beside the kitchen** is empty.
[*Kitchen* **is the object of the preposition** *beside.*]

EXAMPLE That puzzle is too difficult **for me.**
[*Me* **is the object of the preposition** *for.*]

For a list of common prepositions, see page 120.

Be careful to distinguish between the preposition *to* (*to the house, to Tucson*) and the *to* that marks an infinitive (*to read, to jog*). See pages 153–154 for more about infinitives.

Adjectives and other modifiers may be placed between a preposition and its object. Also, a preposition may have more than one object.

EXAMPLE He looked **across the broad, serene river.**
[adjectives added]

EXAMPLE The view was **to the east and the south.** [two objects]

Prepositional phrases may also occur in a sequence of two or more.

EXAMPLE The bird **at the top of that tree** is chirping.

A prepositional phrase usually functions as an adjective or an adverb. When it is used as an adjective, it modifies a noun or a pronoun and is called an *adjective phrase.* An adjective phrase always follows the word it modifies.

EXAMPLE I pressed the button **on the right.**
[adjective phrase modifying the noun *button*]

EXAMPLE Which **of the buttons** starts the engine?
[adjective phrase modifying the pronoun *which*]

When a prepositional phrase is used as an adverb, it modifies a verb, an adjective, or an adverb and is called an *adverb phrase.*

EXAMPLE **After work** I returned the shirt **to the store.**
[adverb phrases modifying the verb *returned*]

EXAMPLE This bus will be convenient **for you.**
[adverb phrase modifying the adjective *convenient*]

EXAMPLE This lawnmower works well **for its age.**
[adverb phrase modifying the adverb *well*]

An adverb phrase that modifies a verb may appear in different positions in a sentence.

EXAMPLE She wore a beautiful diamond ring **on her finger.**
[adverb phrase modifying *wore*]

EXAMPLE She wore **on her finger** a beautiful diamond ring.
[adverb phrase modifying *wore*]

EXAMPLE **On her finger,** she wore a beautiful diamond ring.
[adverb phrase modifying *wore*]

Writing Tip

Place adjective and adverb phrases exactly where they belong.
A misplaced phrase can be confusing. See page 269 for more about
misplaced modifiers.

PRACTICE **Prepositional Phrases**

Write the prepositional phrases. For each, write the word or words modified by the phrase. Then write ADJ (adjective) or ADV (adverb) to identify the type of phrase.

1. Josephine walked right past the door.
2. If you don't pick the ripe apples, they will fall off the apple tree.
3. Althea moved the chair to the living room.
4. The library is on the way to my friend's house.
5. Chess is a game with many tactics.
6. I saw *Citizen Kane* yesterday for the first time.
7. The cat ran up the tree.
8. There are six servings in this cereal box.
9. If you get hungry this afternoon, you can find fruits and vegetables in the refrigerator.
10. My dog often sleeps under the kitchen table.

3.2 APPOSITIVES AND APPOSITIVE PHRASES

An **appositive** is a noun or a pronoun that is placed next to another noun or pronoun to identify it or give additional information about it.

EXAMPLE   My sister **Jodi** works at the hospital. [**The appositive Jodi identifies the noun *sister*.**]

An **appositive phrase** is an appositive plus any words that modify the appositive.

EXAMPLE   She works with Dr. Martin, **an award-winning pediatrician.** [**The appositive phrase, in blue type, identifies *Dr. Martin*.**]

Use commas to set off any appositive or appositive phrase that is not essential to the meaning of the sentence.

EXAMPLE   Jodi's coworker **Emma** has five children. **[The appositive**
Emma is essential because Jodi has more than one
coworker.]

EXAMPLE   Emma's husband, **Phil,** is a carpenter. **[The appositive**
Phil is not essential because Emma has only one husband.]

Usually an appositive or an appositive phrase follows the noun or pronoun it identifies or explains. Occasionally an appositive phrase precedes the noun or pronoun.

EXAMPLE   **A compassionate person,** Jodi helps many patients.

PRACTICE   Appositives and Appositive Phrases

Write each appositive or appositive phrase and the noun or pronoun that is identified or explained by the appositive.

1. Williams, my sister's college, has a great sports program.
2. Chicago, the largest city in Illinois, has the biggest Polish population of any city other than Warsaw.
3. Math, Erin's favorite class, was cancelled because of the assembly.
4. Tracy's grandmother, the world's greatest cook, invited me to dinner.
5. The game was tied after the ninth inning, the final scheduled inning.
6. The speaker was Baseball Hall of Famer Ted Williams.
7. Oren's best friend, Miles, is going to move.
8. The world's largest desert, the Sahara, is in Africa.
9. Eamon de Valera, a president of the Republic of Ireland, was born in New York City.
10. The first woman in the House of Representatives, Jeanette Rankin, was elected in 1916.

3.3 VERBALS AND VERBAL PHRASES

A **verbal** is a verb form that functions in a sentence as a noun, an adjective, or an adverb.

A **verbal phrase** is a verbal plus any complements and modifiers.

Verbals are *participles, gerunds,* and *infinitives.* Each of these can be expanded into phrases.

PARTICIPLES AND PARTICIPIAL PHRASES

A **participle** is a verb form that can function as an adjective.

Present participles always end in *-ing (losing).* Past participles often end in *-ed (winded),* but some are irregularly formed *(broken).* Many commonly used adjectives are actually participles.

EXAMPLE   The baseball team is on a **losing** streak.
[present participle as an adjective]

EXAMPLE   The **winded** runner stopped to rest.
[past participle as an adjective]

EXAMPLE   The **fallen** trees were remnants of a **devastating** storm. **[irregular past participle and present participle as adjectives]**

When a participle is part of a verb phrase, the participle is not functioning as an adjective.

EXAMPLES

PARTICIPLE AS AN ADJECTIVE   The **lost** package was never recovered.

PARTICIPLE IN A VERB PHRASE   The warehouse **had lost** my shipment

A **participial phrase** contains a participle plus any complements and modifiers.

Participial phrases can be placed in various positions in a sentence. They always act as adjectives.

EXAMPLE **Preparing for the lunar eclipse,** we set our alarm clocks.

EXAMPLE The full moon, **suspended in the sky,** was brilliant.

EXAMPLE **Badly needing sleep** but **delighted by the spectacle,** we maintained our vigil.

A participial phrase at the beginning of a sentence is usually followed by a comma.

A past participle may be used with the present participle of the auxiliary verb *have* or *be*.

EXAMPLE **Having read about the eclipse,** we were anxious to see it.

EXAMPLE We watched the moon **being consumed by shadow.**

PRACTICE **Participles and Participial Phrases**

Write the participles and participial phrases. Then write the word or words each participle or participial phrase modifies.

1. I'm afraid I spilled cranberry juice on the freshly ironed tablecloth.

2. For her new bedroom, Sara prefers painted wooden furniture.

3. Their walls were the color of a peeled banana.

4. Elizabethan plays, printed without an author's name, were often credited to the wrong person.

5. Writing as a teenager, Phyllis Wheatley became the second American woman ever to publish a book.

6. Some burrowing animal dug holes all over our lawn.

7. A dirty old sign warned of falling rocks.
8. Broken promises are the legacy of the U. S. government's relationship with Native Americans.
9. A fast moving object lit up the night sky.
10. Rowing quickly, we tried to make it to shore before the leak in the boat got larger.

GERUNDS AND GERUND PHRASES

A **gerund** is a verb form that ends in *-ing* and is used in the same way a noun is used.

EXAMPLE **Training** is essential. [gerund as subject]

EXAMPLE My aunt enjoys **golfing.** [gerund as direct object]

EXAMPLE We should give **communicating** more attention. [gerund as indirect object]

EXAMPLE Do we get credit for **trying?** [gerund as object of preposition]

EXAMPLE His passion was **sailing.** [gerund as predicate nominative]

EXAMPLE My favorite sports, **boxing** and **wrestling,** require strength and agility. [gerunds as appositives]

A **gerund phrase** contains a gerund plus any complements and modifiers.

EXAMPLE **Climbing the mountain** was a challenging activity.

EXAMPLE I enjoy my grandma's **down-home cooking.**

Although both a gerund and a present participle end in *-ing,* they function as different parts of speech. A gerund is used as a noun, whereas a present participle is used as part of a verb phrase or as an adjective.

EXAMPLES

PARTICIPLE IN A VERB PHRASE **I am sewing** this hem. [present participle functioning as main verb]

| PARTICIPLE AS AN ADJECTIVE | **Sewing a button on her shirt,** Beth pricked her finger. [present participle in participial phrase modifying *Beth*] |
| GERUND | **Sewing** is Beth's favorite pastime. [gerund functioning as subject] |

PRACTICE Gerunds and Gerund Phrases

Write the gerunds and gerund phrases. Identify the way each is used by writing one of these labels: subject, direct object, indirect object, object of a preposition, predicate nominative, appositive.

1. He thinks he's special for being in a yacht club.
2. Feeling bad won't help anything unless the problem is fixed and stays fixed.
3. Since we moved, the sport I like best is skiing.
4. Living in Seattle has many benefits, as well as some disadvantages.
5. Going to Oklahoma to visit their grandparents is a great Thanksgiving tradition, according to the Daley children.
6. The best thing that happened to me today was seeing you.
7. Morning is a good time for watering the lawn.
8. Helena could not stop laughing.
9. Walking is a good exercise for most people.
10. I usually enjoy bicycling in the mountains.

INFINITIVES AND INFINITIVE PHRASES

An **infinitive** is a verb form that is usually preceded by the word *to* and is used as a noun, an adjective, or an adverb.

When you use the word *to* before the base form of a verb, *to* is not a preposition but part of the infinitive form of the verb.

EXAMPLE **To volunteer** is rewarding. [infinitive as subject]

EXAMPLE No one wants **to leave.** [infinitive as direct object]

EXAMPLE Their decision was **to merge.** [infinitive as predicate nominative]

EXAMPLE I felt the need **to call.** [infinitive as adjective]

EXAMPLE Everyone was prepared **to sacrifice.** [infinitive as adverb]

An **infinitive phrase** contains an infinitive plus any complements and modifiers.

EXAMPLE Would you prefer **to sleep until noon?**

EXAMPLE **To speak slowly and clearly** is important.

EXAMPLE We plan **to work safely and effectively.**

Occasionally, an infinitive phrase may have its own subject.

EXAMPLE Our neighbor encourages **the dog to bark.** [*Dog* is the subject of the infinitive *to bark.* The entire infinitive phrase *the dog to bark* acts as the direct object of the sentence.]

EXAMPLE The teacher asked **Maria to give a speech.** [*Maria* is the subject of the infinitive *to give.* The entire infinitive phrase *Maria to give a speech* acts as the direct object of the sentence.]

Note that the subject of the infinitive phrase comes between the main verb and the infinitive. The subject of an infinitive phrase always follows an action verb.

Sometimes the word *to* is dropped before an infinitive.

EXAMPLE Let me **[to] do the dishes.**

EXAMPLE We could have heard **a pin [to] drop.**

Write the infinitives and infinitive phrases. For each, write noun, adjective, *or* adverb *to tell how the infinitive or infinitive phrase is being used.*

1. Jenny left to play baseball.
2. As the storm approached, Sally began to worry.
3. I am convinced that Agnes's only purpose in life is to make others happy.
4. I feel the need to buy a baseball glove.
5. Watching Tiger Woods makes me want to play golf.
6. Will you help plant the community garden?
7. The new puppy likes to hide in the hamper.
8. The first woman to win the Nobel Peace Prize was Jane Addams, in 1931.
9. I don't want to hear another word out of you!
10. Since the party, my desire to eat marshmallows is gone.

PRACTICE Verbals and Appositives

Identify each italicized word by writing one of these labels: participle, gerund, infinitive, appositive.

1. *Driving* fast can be awfully dangerous.
2. President Eisenhower's favorite pastime, *golf,* benefitted from the attention he brought to it.
3. I'm sorry, but I simply can't imagine *living* at the Arctic Circle, much less the Antarctic.
4. The largest elephant weighs no more than a newly *born* blue whale.
5. The people on the jury were not allowed *to leave* the hotel room.
6. *Trying* mightily, Stephen was able to move the boulder a few inches.

7. The drowning boy was saved by Rusty, *the wonder dog.*

8. I can't forget *seeing* that blue heron at dawn.

9. *Swimming* against the current in the river, I got tired.

10. Joe helped *to fix* the sprinkler.

3.4 ABSOLUTE PHRASES

An **absolute phrase,** also known as a nominative absolute, consists of a noun or a pronoun that is modified by a participle or a participial phrase. An absolute phrase has no grammatical relation to the rest of the sentence.

An absolute phrase belongs neither to the complete subject nor to the complete predicate of a sentence. It stands "absolutely" by itself in relation to the rest of the sentence.

EXAMPLE   **Its wings badly damaged in the storm,** the aircraft crashed.

EXAMPLE   We departed on schedule, **the weather [being] perfect.**

PRACTICE   Absolute Phrases

Write each absolute phrase.

1. Its stem snapped by a playful puppy, the day lily fell sadly to the ground.

2. We slid across the gymnasium floor, the surface slick from a fresh waxing.

3. The water being icy cold, we were unable to go swimming.

4. The ladder, its rungs broken, stood useless in the garage.
5. The dress, its sequins glittering in the light, was an amazing sight.
6. Great arms spanning the wide screen, the creature loomed over the audience.
7. We sat around the campfire, its flames darting up into the night.
8. My arms aching, I put the last box of books into the moving van.
9. I sat, my glasses shattered, in front of a pile of new mystery novels.
10. Her computer in for repairs, Wilda tried to write by hand.

PRACTICE Phrases

Identify each italicized group of words by writing one of these labels: participial phrase, infinitive phrase, gerund phrase, appositive phrase, absolute phrase, prepositional phrase.

1. Emily Dickinson wrote *about deep personal feelings.*
2. One flower, *a giant water lily,* has leaves large enough to support a child.
3. *Lacking wheels,* the car sat in the side yard.
4. The crew's mission is *to go boldly where no one has gone before.*
5. I feel a strong need *to work in the garden for a while.*
6. A typical tree receives ten percent *of its nutrition* from the soil.
7. It can be difficult *to forgive cruel people.*
8. Finn, *standing in the cold stream,* didn't catch one fish.
9. *My head swimming,* I got groggily to my feet and brushed off my pants.
10. I hate *feeling lost.*

Rewrite the following passage, correcting errors in spelling, capitalization, grammar, and usage. Add any missing punctuation. Write legibly to be sure one letter is not mistaken for another. There are ten mistakes.

Jane Austen

[1]Considered by many to be Englands finest novelist, Jane Austen was born in 1775 in Hampshire, England, to a quiet middle-class family. [2]She begun writing as a teenager and sold her first book when she was twenty-eight years old. [3]The publisher she sold it to put it away on the shelf, and did not issue it. [4]In 1811, *Sense and Sensibility* was published, it was soon followed by *Pride and Prejudice*. [5]both books had actually been written years earlier, but no publisher had been willing to take a chance on such unusual novels.

[6]Jane Austen's books were unusual simply because they dealt with the ordinary events of daily life among middle-class people. [7]Until Austen, novels involved king's and battles and great romances, or they dealt with tragedy and desperate poverty.

[8]Austen's greatness was not reconized during her lifetime. [9]Still, their were some who saw her genius. [10]The writers Coleridge, Tennyson Macaulay, and Scott all admired her. [11]Today her books are required reading for anyone who want to know the best of Western culture.

Write the prepositional phrases. For each, write the word or words modified by the phrase. Then write ADJ (adjective) or ADV (adverb) to identify the type of phrase.

1. Nagaland is one of the smallest states in India.
2. The state is named for the local inhabitants, the Nagas, or "Hill People."

3. It is located along the border with Burma.
4. The Naga Hills, reaching a height of 12,600 feet, run through the state.
5. Sixteen separate tribes live together in the state of Nagaland.
6. Each tribe expresses its identity through dialect, customs, and traditional costumes.
7. In a largely Hindu country, seventy-five percent of the Nagas are Christian.
8. Nagaland has a strong movement for independence.
9. For many years, the Indian government banned outsiders from entering Nagaland.
10. Today tourists explore the beauties of this remote state.

POSTTEST **Identifying Verbals and Appositives**

Identify each italicized word by writing one of these labels: participle, gerund, infinitive, appositive.

11. One of the most interesting animals *living* in the American West is the brown bear.
12. *Seeing* a brown bear is one of the joys of Yellowstone.
13. *Varying* in weight from three hundred pounds to more than five hundred pounds, the adult brown bear usually lives alone.
14. A mother bear, however, keeps her *growing* cubs with her for more than a year.
15. Oddly, brown bears do not have *to be* brown.
16. These appealing animals, b*rown bears,* can be gray, silver-blue, beige, or even black.
17. One of the largest brown bears, the *grizzly,* can be up to eight feet long!
18. It would be terrifying *to see* such an animal in the wild.
19. *Being* afraid would be quite natural too.
20. An *angered* bear can be incredibly dangerous.

Identify each italicized group of words by writing one of these labels: participial phrase, infinitive phrase, gerund phrase, appositive phrase, absolute phrase, prepositional phrase.

21. George Washington, *first president of the United States,* is known to have had false teeth.

22. *Myths about presidents being common,* many people have said that Washington's teeth were made of wood.

23. Was he the first person *to use false teeth?*

24. No, some Egyptian mummies from seven thousand years ago have been found *to have them.*

25. *Carved from ivory,* false teeth were a common sight among wealthy Romans of the first century A.D.

26. In more modern times, *making artificial teeth from porcelain* was the usual practice.

27. Today most false teeth are made from a synthetic material, *a plastic.*

28. That material has the advantage of *lasting for a long time.*

29. *With improved dental hygiene,* the need for complete sets of false teeth is not so great.

30. *Worrying about getting a splinter from your teeth* is a thing of the past.

Chapter 4

Clauses and Sentence Structure

● ● ● ● ● ● ● ● ● ● ● ● ● ●

PRETEST   **Identifying Main Clauses and Subordinate Clauses**

Copy each sentence. Underline each main clause once and each subordinate clause twice.

  1. Bring water because today will be hot.
  2. If you throw something in the air, it will come down, unless it gets caught somewhere.
  3. Tiger Woods, whom I admire, won the tournament.

4. It is important that you come home for the holidays.

5. Antonio certainly enjoys what he does.

6. After the votes were counted, we all waited for the big announcement.

7. When Al was a sophomore in high school, he played on the hockey team.

8. *A Farewell to Arms,* which was written by Ernest Hemingway, is set during World War I.

9. When I sleep until noon, I feel that my day is half gone.

10. I met Maya Angelou, who is a famous author.

PRETEST Identifying Simple, Compound, Complex, and Compound-Complex Sentences

Identify each sentence by writing S for simple, C for compound, CX for complex, or CC for compound-complex.

11. Before I leave, I'll check the flashlight batteries.

12. Our school's mascot is a wildcat; our rival's mascot is a panda.

13. If Lena isn't going to the dance, then I'm not going, either.

14. Always wear a seatbelt when you're in a car.

15. Larry and his friends from down the block always like to roller-blade through the park in the middle of town.

16. Rhona's team plays for the championship tonight, but she can't be at the game.

17. When my cousin plays with blocks, she usually builds castles, but sometimes she builds ordinary houses.

18. The Beatles' song "In My Life" is one of the greatest songs ever written, according to my brother.

19. I wear a big, floppy hat in the sun.

20. Tell me your answer, and I'll tell you whether you're right.

Identify each of the following groups of words by writing F for fragment, R for run-on sentence, or S for sentence.

21. Go home, don't stop anywhere on the way.
22. Hardly even seeing me as I passed under her nose.
23. Rescuers are working quickly, they'll save the dog.
24. Running, jumping, and singing, she hardly even noticed that she'd gone a mile.
25. Because of the weather.
26. The chair was uncomfortably hard I sat in it anyway.
27. Those scissors cut anything, they're brand new.
28. If Prinna is going to Paris, I hope she takes pictures.
29. Watch your step.
30. The pitter-patter of the rain on the tin roof.

4.1 MAIN CLAUSES

A **clause** is a group of words that has a subject and a predicate and functions as part of a sentence or as a whole sentence.

Clauses fall into two categories: *main clauses,* which are also called *independent clauses,* and *subordinate clauses,* which are also called *dependent clauses.*

A **main clause** has a subject and a predicate and expresses a complete thought. It is the only type of clause that can stand alone as a sentence.

Every sentence must have at least one main clause. A coordinating conjunction is not part of a main clause.

Main Clause

EXAMPLE Lori walked the dog.
　　　　　 S　　 V

EXAMPLE

	Main Clause		Main Clause

Lori took her dog to the store, and she bought him treats.
  S V   S V

Both the subject and the predicate of a main clause may be compound.

EXAMPLE

	Main Clause		Main Clause

Lori and Zeke walk to the park, and Zeke runs and plays.
  S   S V   S V   V

"The paper and ink content is within acceptable norms, but the contract itself appears to have too many clauses."

© 1996 Ted Goff

4.2 SUBORDINATE CLAUSES

A **subordinate clause** has a subject and a predicate but does not express a complete thought, so it cannot stand alone as a sentence.

There are three types of subordinate clauses: **adjective clauses,** which modify nouns or pronouns; **adverb clauses,** which modify verbs, adjectives, or adverbs; and **noun clauses,** which function as nouns.

A subordinate clause is dependent on the rest of the sentence because a subordinate clause does not make sense by itself. A subordinating conjunction or a relative pronoun usually introduces a subordinate clause.

(See page 124 for a list of common subordinating conjunctions and page 107 for a list of relative pronouns.) Note that unlike a coordinating conjunction connecting two main clauses, a subordinating conjunction or a relative pronoun is part of the subordinate clause.

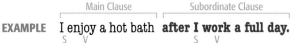

EXAMPLE I enjoy a hot bath **after I work a full day.**

In some cases, the relative pronoun can also function as the subject of a subordinate clause.

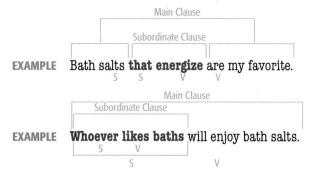

EXAMPLE Bath salts **that energize** are my favorite.

EXAMPLE **Whoever likes baths** will enjoy bath salts.

In the first example, the subordinating conjunction *after* placed before *I work a full day* creates a word group—*after I work a full day*—that cannot stand alone as a main clause. Although the clause has a subject and a predicate, it does not express a complete thought.

In the second example, the relative pronoun *that* begins a subordinate clause that comes between the subject and the verb of the main clause. *That* also serves as the subject of the subordinate clause, and *energize* is its verb. *That energize* cannot, however, stand alone.

In the third example, the subordinate clause functions as the subject of the sentence. *Whoever* functions as the subject of the subordinate clause, *whoever likes baths. Likes* is the verb, and *baths* is the direct object. *Whoever likes baths* cannot, however, stand alone.

PRACTICE Subordinate Clauses

Write the subordinate clause or clauses from each sentence.

1. The test will be on what we have studied this month.
2. If Scout hadn't been such a lovable character, then *To Kill a Mockingbird* might not have been so popular.
3. That is the park where we saw the enormous dog.
4. I hope that we can see each other before you have to leave.
5. When Phil went sledding, he borrowed my gloves.
6. The committee that purchases equipment voted for the proposal.
7. After the circus left town, many people were disappointed because they hadn't gone to see it.
8. When the sun rises, the sidewalk heats up and the day begins.
9. Wash your hands before you come to the table.
10. That kind is good, but do you think that it's the best?

PRACTICE Main Clauses and Subordinate Clauses

Copy the sentences. Underline the main clauses once and the subordinate clauses twice.

1. Do you know if the French and Indian War was fought between the French and the Indians?
2. My favorite shirt is the one that my grandmother brought me from Nigeria.
3. Fernando, who wants to be the best gymnast, trains every day.
4. If I could, I would eat raspberries all day long.
5. Give the bat to whoever is up next.
6. Many people who live in Mexico City use public transportation.
7. The bus was twenty minutes late because an accident blocked the road.

8. Li's coach watched eagerly as Li walked to the high dive.

9. The *New York Times,* which I love to read, is one of the most respected publications in the nation.

10. Something tells me that you miss your friends.

4.3 ADJECTIVE CLAUSES

An **adjective clause** is a subordinate clause that modifies a noun or a pronoun.

An adjective clause may begin with a relative pronoun (*who, whom, whose, that,* and *which*) or *where* or *when.* An adjective clause normally follows the word it modifies.

EXAMPLE   Athletes **who perform in the Olympics** must spend years in training.

EXAMPLE   Cities **that host the Olympics** need many athletic facilities.

EXAMPLE   The city **where the 1996 Summer Olympics took place** was Atlanta.

Sometimes the relative pronoun is dropped from the beginning of an adjective clause.

EXAMPLE   The mug **I use most often** came from those Olympics. **[The relative pronoun *that* has been omitted.]**

Some adjective clauses are needed to make the meaning of a sentence clear. Such an adjective clause is called an *essential clause,* or a *restrictive clause.* It must not be set off with commas.

EXAMPLE   Tourists **who travel to the games** stay in hotels.

EXAMPLE   The living area **that is designated for the athletes** is called the Olympic Village.

An adjective clause that adds information to a sentence but is not necessary to make the meaning of the sentence clear is called a *nonessential clause,* or a *nonrestrictive clause.* Always use commas to set off a nonessential clause.

EXAMPLE   The Columbia Broadcasting System, **which televised the 1998 Winter Olympics,** set up a Web site for the athletes.

EXAMPLE   The athletes, **who received thousands of messages,** appreciated this service.

When choosing between *that* and *which* to introduce an adjective clause, use *that* to begin an essential clause and *which* to begin a nonessential clause.

EXAMPLE   Millions watched the 1998 Winter Olympics, **which took place in Nagano.**

EXAMPLE   Other competitions **that include similar events** are less publicized.

4.4 ADVERB CLAUSES

An **adverb clause** is a subordinate clause that modifies a verb, an adjective, or an adverb. It tells *when, where, how, why, to what extent,* or *under what conditions.*

Adverb clauses begin with subordinating conjunctions. An adverb clause can come either before or after the main clause. When the adverb clause comes first, separate it from the main clause with a comma. (See Lesson 11.6.)

EXAMPLE   **Before winter began,** I planted bulbs. **[The adverb clause tells *when* and modifies the verb *planted.*]**

EXAMPLE   Bulbs usually do well **if you use fertilizer. [The adverb clause tells *under what conditions* and modifies the adverb *well.*]**

EXAMPLE   The flowers are beautiful **because the winter was mild. [The adverb clause tells *why* and modifies the adjective *beautiful.*]**

Elliptical adverb clauses have words left out of them. You can easily supply the omitted words because they are understood or implied.

EXAMPLE   The hyacinths are more fragrant **than the tulips [are fragrant].**

EXAMPLE   **While [I am] gardening,** I always take time to enjoy the flowers.

4.5 NOUN CLAUSES

A **noun clause** is a subordinate clause that is used as a noun within the main clause of a sentence.

You can use a noun clause as a subject, a direct object, an indirect object, an object of a preposition, or a predicate nominative.

EXAMPLE   **Whatever you can learn about computers** will prove useful in the workplace. **[noun clause as subject]**

EXAMPLE   You should take **whichever computer classes are offered. [noun clause as direct object]**

EXAMPLE   The instructor gave **whoever was available** word-processing lessons. **[noun clause as indirect object]**

EXAMPLE   You can get by on **what you learn in this class.** **[noun clause as object of the preposition]**

EXAMPLE   The basics of computers is **what you must learn.** **[noun clause as predicate nominative]**

The following are some words that can be used to introduce noun clauses.

how	whatever	which	whose
however	when	whichever	why
if	where	who, whom	
that	wherever	whoever	
what	whether	whomever	

Sometimes the introductory word is dropped from a noun clause.

EXAMPLE I think **computers will be even more important in the future.** [*That* **has been omitted from the beginning of the clause.**]

PRACTICE **Subordinate Clauses**

Write the subordinate clause from each sentence. Then write ADJ if it's an adjective clause, ADV if it's an adverb clause, or N if it's a noun clause.

1. I can hardly keep my eyes open today because I was too excited to sleep last night.
2. You can have whatever you want.
3. Joanna, who volunteers at the hospital, writes a column in the school newspaper.
4. We drove five hundred miles before we stopped for the night.
5. It's hard to write a paragraph that has no adjectives.
6. What we hoped would happen never did happen.
7. When it fell from the pillow, the wedding ring rolled down the aisle.
8. Williams College is where I hope to go to school.
9. That is the restaurant where we had my party.
10. After I vacuum the rug, my room will be spotless!

4.6 FOUR KINDS OF SENTENCES

Sentences are often classified according to their purpose. There are four purposes that sentences may have: to make a statement, to give an order or make a request, to ask a question, and to express strong emotion.

A **declarative sentence** makes a statement.

EXAMPLE Andrew moved to Miami.

EXAMPLE He has lived there since January.

A declarative sentence usually ends with a period but can end with an exclamation mark. This type of sentence is the most frequently used in speaking and writing.

An **imperative sentence** gives a command or makes a request.

EXAMPLE Write me a letter.

EXAMPLE Andrew, please send your address.

An imperative sentence usually ends with a period but can end with an exclamation mark. In imperative sentences, the subject *you* is understood.

An **interrogative sentence** asks a question.

EXAMPLE Do you like the weather?

EXAMPLE What do you do after work?

An interrogative sentence usually ends with a question mark but can end with an exclamation mark if it expresses strong emotion.

An **exclamatory sentence** expresses strong emotion.

EXAMPLE I can't believe you moved!

EXAMPLE Call me soon!

EXAMPLE What were you thinking!

An exclamatory sentence ends with an exclamation mark. Note that sentences are not exclusively exclamatory but can be declarative (first example), imperative (second example), or interrogative (third example) while expressing strong emotion. In writing, exclamatory sentences should be used sparingly so as not to detract from their effectiveness.

Identify each sentence by writing D *for declarative,* IT *for interrogative,* IM *for imperative, or* E *for exclamatory.*

1. Have you ever been to the top of the Sears Tower?
2. I would love to go to Sea World!
3. When Christy told me the news, I was shocked.
4. How much should I pay you for those apples?
5. Jeremy, play nicely with your brother.
6. I'm allergic to pollen, so flowers make me sneeze.
7. Move that candle away from the curtains!
8. Did you take a ring from my jewelry box?
9. Share the crayons.
10. The marathon runner collapsed at the finish line.

4.7 SIMPLE AND COMPOUND SENTENCES

Sentences are sometimes classified by their structure. Sentence structures are *simple, compound, complex,* and *compound-complex.*

A **simple sentence** contains only one main clause and no subordinate clauses.

A simple sentence may contain a compound subject or a compound predicate or both. The subject and the predicate can be expanded with adjectives, adverbs, prepositional phrases, appositives, and verbal phrases.

EXAMPLE   Musicians perform. **[simple sentence]**

EXAMPLE   Musicians and singers travel and perform. **[simple sentence with compound subject and compound predicate]**

EXAMPLE   Musicians in popular bands give performances frequently. **[simple sentence including a prepositional phrase, a direct object, and an adverb]**

A **compound sentence** contains two or more main clauses.

The main clauses in a compound sentence are usually joined by a comma and a coordinating conjunction (*and, but, or, nor, yet, for, so*).

EXAMPLE   Many popular bands play rock and roll, but others play rhythm and blues.

EXAMPLE   Sting sings rock and roll, and Puff Daddy raps, but they performed together at the MTV Video Music Awards.

Main clauses in a compound sentence may be joined by a semicolon used alone or by a semicolon and a conjunctive adverb (such as *however, therefore, nevertheless*) or by a semicolon and an expression such as *for example.*

EXAMPLE   Different types of music can be fused together; ska combines rock and reggae.

EXAMPLE   People often have set opinions about music; **nevertheless,** one should keep an open mind.

EXAMPLE   Different styles of music influence one another; **for example,** rock and roll developed from jazz.

GRAMMAR/USAGE/MECHANICS

PRACTICE   **Simple and Compound Sentences**

Identify each sentence by writing S *for a simple sentence or* C *for a compound sentence.*

1. I hope to be the winner, but I don't think I will be.
2. The baseball broke the window, set off the alarm, and was chased by the dog.
3. My alarm rang at six o'clock, but I didn't get up until eight.
4. Watching the clouds pass, we thought about the storm.
5. I fell down the stairs and bruised my foot.

6. The Red Sox won the game, so we all got free slices of pizza at the local pizzeria.

7. Manny will bring the coleslaw; Rupert will bring the potato salad.

8. I bought new slacks and a new shirt.

9. Regina's binoculars were quite expensive; nevertheless, she let us all try them.

10. The horse, jumping over the fence, ran freely through the meadow.

4.8 COMPLEX AND COMPOUND-COMPLEX SENTENCES

A **complex sentence** has one main clause and one or more subordinate clauses.

Subordinate Clause | Main Clause

EXAMPLE If you study the development of music, you will learn

Subordinate Clause

that music has been heavily influenced by society.

Subordinate Clause

EXAMPLE When you listen to a song,

Main Clause | Subordinate Clause

you should think about the culture that influenced it.

A **compound-complex sentence** has two or more main clauses and at least one subordinate clause.

Main Clause

Subordinate Clause

EXAMPLE Billie Holiday, who lived from 1915 to 1959, grew up in

Main Clause

a poor family, and she became a famous jazz singer.

Complex and Compound-Complex Sentences

Identify each sentence by writing CX *for complex sentence or* CC *for compound-complex sentence. Then write the subordinate clause from each sentence.*

1. While Mark drives home from work, he often listens to jazz, but sometimes he listens to news radio.
2. Affordable medical care is a major issue in politics because there are so many people without health insurance.
3. Agatha Christie, who wrote detective mysteries, is one of my favorite authors.
4. Our city newspaper wrote about the scandal before anyone else knew about it; however, the paper wasn't acknowledged for exposing it.
5. I assume that the teacher will tell us our grades.
6. I will give you money for whatever you want to buy, but you have to share it with your sister.
7. Ann can't find the pen that she uses for writing letters.
8. After she lifted weights, Ami's back was sore and tight.
9. The hotel where Sue stayed on her vacation was hit by a tornado three months later, but now it's been rebuilt.
10. Mary Jane, who will attend college next year, lives in Boston, but she will not be going to school in Boston.

Simple, Compound, Complex, and Compound-Complex Sentences

Copy the following sentences. Identify each sentence by writing S *for simple,* C *for compound,* CX *for complex, and* CC *for compound-complex. Underline each main clause once and each subordinate clause twice.*

1. The yearbook, which we worked on for months, is one of the school's best.
2. Our team won the game, and then we all celebrated.

3. Dealing with political and moral issues, that radio program was controversial.
4. After you finish the bike ride, make sure that you lock up.
5. My aunt had a baby, and when she returned from the hospital, the whole family pitched in to help her.
6. Our old car needs new brakes; however, my parents will not repair the car because new brakes are too expensive.
7. The deer, running quickly through the woods, tried to escape from the predator.
8. My uncle bought a shower curtain with bass on it because he loves to fish.
9. My watch started to irritate my wrist, so my dad bought me a new one.
10. Steve wrote a letter to his senator, whom he had always admired, and the senator wrote him a personal response.

4.9 SENTENCE FRAGMENTS

A **sentence fragment** is an error that occurs when an incomplete sentence is punctuated as though it were complete.

There are three things you should look for when you review your work for sentence fragments. First, look for a group of words without a subject. Then, look for a group of words without a complete predicate, especially a group that contains a verbal or a verbal phrase. Finally, be sure you haven't punctuated a subordinate clause as if it were a complete sentence.

Many times, you can correct a sentence fragment by attaching it to a main clause. Other times, you may need to add words to make the sentence complete.

EXAMPLE

FRAGMENT	COMPLETE SENTENCE
Danielle is on the basketball team. **Played for fun as a child.** [lacks subject]	Danielle is on the basketball team. She played for fun as a child.
Danielle scoring more points than any other player. [lacks complete predicate]	Danielle was scoring more points than any other player.
The injured Danielle. [lacks complete predicate and contains verbal]	The injured Danielle was taken to the emergency room.
Because she was taken out of the game. The opposing team won. [subordinate clause]	Because she was taken out of the game, the opposing team won.

Sentence fragments can be used to produce special effects, such as adding emphasis or conveying realistic dialogue. Remember that professional writers use sentence fragments carefully and intentionally. In most of the writing you do, including your writing for school, you should avoid sentence fragments.

4.10 RUN-ON SENTENCES

A **run-on sentence** is two or more complete sentences written as though they were one sentence.

There are two types of run-on sentences. The first occurs when two main clauses are joined by a comma only. This is called a *comma splice.*

EXAMPLE **RUN-ON** Meteorology is fascinating to me, I watch the Weather Channel every day.

The second type of run-on sentence occurs when two main clauses have no punctuation separating them. This can occur with or without a conjunction.

EXAMPLE **RUN-ON** Meteorology is fascinating to me I watch the Weather Channel every day.

EXAMPLE **RUN-ON** Meteorology is fascinating to me and I watch the Weather Channel every day.

You can correct a run-on sentence in several ways. The method you choose in correcting your writing will depend on the relationship you want to convey between the two clauses.

METHOD OF CORRECTING RUN-ON	COMPLETE SENTENCE
Add end punctuation between the clauses and make two sentences.	Meteorology is fascinating to me. **I** watch the Weather Channel every day.
Separate the clauses with both a comma and a coordinating conjunction.	Meteorology is fascinating to me, **and** I watch the Weather Channel every day.
Separate the clauses with a semicolon.	Meteorology is fascinating to me; I watch the Weather Channel every day.
Add a semicolon and a conjunctive adverb between the clauses.	Meteorology is fascinating to me; **therefore,** I watch the Weather Channel every day.
Change one of the main clauses to a subordinate clause. Separate the two clauses with a comma if appropriate.	**Because** meteorology is fascinating to me, I watch the Weather Channel every day. I watch the Weather Channel every day **because** meteorology is fascinating to me.

PRACTICE Fragments and Run-on Sentences

Identify each numbered item by writing F *for fragment or* R *for run-on sentence. Then rewrite each item, correcting the error.*

1. Martin's dog under the porch of the big, old house.
2. Someday I'll be just like Dorothy Sayers, I'll write good mysteries.

3. Pass the glue stick to me it's mine.
4. Sometimes underestimating the power of a determined teenager.
5. What an absolutely fabulous anchor leg of the race!
6. I can't believe it, my college application got lost in the mail!
7. Pen in hand and ready to write.
8. Works well, is a great value, and is very attractive.
9. The room is hot, will you turn up the fan?
10. Please leave me alone, I'm not in a good mood.

PRACTICE Proofreading

Rewrite the following passage, correcting errors in spelling, capitalization, grammar, and usage. Add any missing punctuation. Write legibly to be sure one letter is not mistaken for another. There are ten mistakes.

José Martí

[1]Cuban writer and revolutionery José Martí was born in Havana in 1853. [2]At the age of seventeen, the government exiled him to Spain because of his efforts to fight for Cuban independence from that nation. [3]After earning a law degree in Spain, Martí went to Mexico City, and worked as a journalist. [4]There, and in Guatemala, he continued to promote the cause of liberty which did not make him popular with those countries governments. [5]Returned to Cuba in 1878 with his wife, the daughter of another exiled Cuban.

[6]Martí did not stop fighting for Cuba's freedom so he was again exiled. [7]This time, he stayed only briefly in Spain, then he went to the United States and settled in New York City. [8]In New York, he wrote newspaper articles essays, poems, and stories and worked constantly for the cause of Cuban independence.

[9]In 1895, José Martí went to Cuba to join the war for independence from Spain he died in one of the early battles. [10]His deeply felt, personal, and original writings, which reflect both kindness and an intense love of liberty, made him one of the most important Hispanic writers.

Identify each boldface, numbered clause as M for main or S for subordinate. Then identify each subordinate clause as adjective (ADJ), adverb (ADV), or noun (N).

When you walk through here,[1] **try not to break anything.**[2]
Why do you care[3] about what I'm reading?
I hope **that you get my letter**[4] before it is too late.[5]
Stop worrying about me[6]; I'll be fine.[7]
The rose bloomed[8] before my birthday.
If you climb too high in the tree,[9] you may not be able to get down.
Rudy's friend, **who is moving to Alabama,**[10] is sad because he's leaving everyone behind.

Identify each sentence by writing S for simple, C for compound, CX for complex, or CC for compound-complex.

11. Mr. Cummins avoided squashing any petunias in the garden.

12. Rachel played the mother, Rob played the father, and Jordan played the son.

13. Ms. Maloney, who was my brother's favorite teacher, transferred to a different school.

14. This meal was both tasty and healthy.

15. *The Invisible Man* is one of my favorite books, but my brother thought that it was too long and confusing.

16. Brian took his time on the test, but I rushed.

17. If I accidentally broke a vase, would you be angry?

18. That game is purely luck; moreover, it is not the least bit interesting.
19. The woman who sells flowers on the corner is very friendly; I like to talk to her.
20. When I get home, I'm going to take a hot bath.

Identifying Fragments, Run-on Sentences, and Sentences

Identify each numbered item by writing F *for fragment,* R *for run-on sentence, or* S *for sentence.*

21. My homework, sitting on the table untouched.
22. I want to walk across the country, but I don't think I would make it.
23. That bed is too soft, this one is just right.
24. If you give me the key and really trust me.
25. Stop staring at me!
26. Frequent stops at the little gas station down the road.
27. The mail came we brought it inside.
28. The wait here is too long, let's go somewhere else.
29. I picked up the pennies that had spilled and put them back in the jar.
30. At the top of the hill, our little house in the shadows of the large trees.

Chapter 5

Verb Tenses and Voice

● ● ● ● ● ● ● ● ● ● ● ● ● ● ● ●

PRETEST **Identifying the Correct Verb Form**

Read each sentence. Then write the correct form of the verb in parentheses.

1. Yesterday Susan (begin) her three-day journey to the West Coast to visit her sister.
2. Earlier a mosquito (bite) me on the arm.
3. Gillian might have (run) around the corner like that just to scare me.
4. Samantha must have (blow) up the balloons this morning, before anyone else got here.
5. Richard (break) his brand-new camera a couple of days ago, and it isn't fixed yet.
6. Earth (revolve) around the Sun.

7. Chester (bring) his delicious chicken salad to my graduation party last week.
8. Samuel went to Lisette's for dinner and (come) home with a bad cold.
9. Hank could have (come) to the baseball game even though he's no longer on the team.
10. The sun (rise) in the east every day.
11. By the time I returned, Joeleen had (draw) a tiger standing in high grass.
12. At my last party, Tony and Franklin (eat) just about all the potato chips between them.
13. In the golf tournament I (see) today, Tiger Woods hit a drive all the way to the green.
14. Everyone believed that the murder victim had accidentally (fall) over the cliff.
15. Alexandra begged her parents until they finally (get) her a puppy from the Humane Society.
16. JoMarie has never (go) to the opera before.
17. Sylvia will have (receive) a fine education by the time she graduates.
18. When my mom gets home, she will (make) herself some coffee and then read the newspaper.
19. All last summer, my brother and I (keep) the lawn mowed and the garden watered.
20. My family went to a dude ranch last year, and I (ride) horses every day.

PRETEST **Identifying the Verb Tense 1**

Identify the italicized verb tense by writing one of these labels: present, past, future, present perfect, past perfect, future perfect.

21. All whales *give* birth underwater.
22. As of today, Gilad *will have attended* every baseball game the team has played.

23. The fan *has worked* well for keeping us cool today.
24. In 1872 Mark Twain *invented* a self-pasting scrapbook that contained blank pages covered with a type of gum.
25. The New York Public Library *adds* more than a half-million items to its collection every year.
26. Eric *has stayed* home from school often this year.
27. I'm sure Gino *will take* the children to the zoo next week.
28. When I turned around, my baby brother Jake *had crawled* through the house.
29. Jeremy *circled* the bases in his home-run trot.
30. Mel hit a home run with the bat he *had carved* by hand.

PRETEST **Identifying the Verb Tense 2**

Identify the italicized verb form by writing one of these labels: present progressive, past progressive, future progressive, present perfect progressive, past perfect progressive, future perfect progressive, present emphatic, past emphatic.

31. Joseph *is walking* quickly to school because it is cold today.
32. Camille *was fishing* all last weekend.
33. Jared *did have* an operation last week.
34. On March 6, Jessie *will have been driving* for two years.
35. Yolanda *has been working* here for years.
36. I *have been reading* a book while watching television.
37. If conditions don't improve, I *will be quitting* this job.
38. Over the summer, *are* you *forgetting* everything you learned in school?
39. Very well, if you *do make* the coffee, I'll make the toast.
40. I *had been looking* out the window for a glimpse of a hummingbird before you arrived.

Rewrite each sentence. Correct verbs in the wrong tense, or change verbs in passive voice to active voice.

41. The stunned castaways were discovered by the rescue boat.

42. Would you rather have gone out to eat or stay at home?

43. If you load peanut butter and raisins on celery, you had a snack called ants on a log.

44. I liked most modern music, but I prefer oldies.

45. When my mom gets home, we had dinner.

46. The boxes were stacked by the produce assistant.

47. Jasmine had ridden horses for three years before she takes lessons.

48. Jackie walks to the store and bought a rolling pin.

49. My teeth were cleaned by the dental hygienist.

50. Andie has been excited about the play, but now she was just bored by the long rehearsals.

5.1 PRINCIPAL PARTS OF VERBS

All verbs have four **principal parts: a base form, a present participle, a simple past form,** and a **past participle.** All the verb tenses are formed from these principal parts.

Principal Parts of Verbs

Base Form	Present Participle	Past Form	Past Participle
open	opening	opened	opened
fall	falling	fell	fallen
cry	crying	cried	cried
speak	speaking	spoke	spoken
be	being	was, were	been

You can use the base form (except the base form of *be*) and the past form by themselves as main verbs. To function as the simple predicate in a sentence, the present participle and the past participle must always be preceded by one or more auxiliary verbs.

EXAMPLE Doors **open.** [base or present form]

EXAMPLE Doors **opened.** [past form]

EXAMPLE Doors **are opening.** [present participle with the auxiliary verb *are*]

EXAMPLE Doors **have opened.** [past participle with the auxiliary verb *have*]

PRACTICE **Principal Parts of Verbs**

Write the correct form of the principal part of the verb described in parentheses.

1. John Adams (past form of *serve*) as the second president of the United States.

2. Allison is (present participle of *announce*) the winner at the awards dinner.

3. They (base form of *try*) harder than the other groups.

4. Sherry (present participle of *work* preceded by the auxiliary verbs *had been*) on the set for hours.

5. Jarvis (past participle of *ask* preceded by the auxiliary verb *was*) to join the school orchestra.

6. By next week, Dolores (past participle of *complete* preceded by the auxiliary verbs *will have*) her driver's training.

7. Bernard (past form of *think*) the game was over.

8. Frank will probably (present participle of *move* preceded by the auxiliary verb *be*) to Portland at the end of the school year.

9. Before yesterday, Kostya (past participle of *see* preceded by the auxiliary verb *had*) only one play.

10. The gravel road (past participle of *put* preceded by the auxiliary verb *has*) a lot of wear on my tires.

5.2 REGULAR AND IRREGULAR VERBS

A **regular verb** forms its past and past participle by adding –*ed* or –*d* to the base form.

REGULAR VERBS		
BASE FORM	**PAST FORM**	**PAST PARTICIPLE**
laugh	laughed	laughed
talk	talked	talked
like	liked	liked

Some regular verbs undergo spelling changes when a suffix that begins with a vowel is added.

EXAMPLE   fry + **-ed** = fri**ed**

EXAMPLE   stop + **-ed** = stop**ped**

An **irregular verb** forms its past and past participle in some way other than by adding –*ed* or –*d* to the base form.

COMMON IRREGULAR VERBS		
BASE FORM	**PAST FORM**	**PAST PARTICIPLE**
be, am, are, is	was, were	been
bear	bore	borne
beat	beat	beaten *or* beat
become	became	become

Common Irregular Verbs, continued

BASE FORM	PAST FORM	PAST PARTICIPLE
begin	began	begun
bite	bit	bitten *or* bit
blow	blew	blown
break	broke	broken
bring	brought	brought
burst	burst	burst
buy	bought	bought
cast	cast	cast
catch	caught	caught
choose	chose	chosen
come	came	come
creep	crept	crept
cut	cut	cut
dive	dived *or* dove	dived
do	did	done
draw	drew	drawn
drink	drank	drunk
drive	drove	driven
eat	ate	eaten
fall	fell	fallen
feel	felt	felt
find	found	found
fling	flung	flung
fly	flew	flown

GRAMMAR/USAGE/MECHANICS

Common Irregular Verbs, continued

BASE FORM	PAST FORM	PAST PARTICIPLE
freeze	froze	frozen
get	got	got *or* gotten
give	gave	given
go	went	gone
grow	grew	grown
hang	hung *or* hanged**	hung *or* hanged**
have	had	had
hit	hit	hit
hold	held	held
keep	kept	kept
know	knew	known
lay*	laid	laid
lead	led	led
leave	left	left
lend	lent	lent
let	let	let
lie*	lay	lain
lose	lost	lost
make	made	made
pay	paid	paid
put	put	put
read	read	read
ride	rode	ridden
ring	rang	rung

Common Irregular Verbs, continued

BASE FORM	PAST FORM	PAST PARTICIPLE
rise*	rose	risen
run	ran	run
say	said	said
see	saw	seen
seek	sought	sought
sell	sold	sold
set*	set	set
shake	shook	shaken
shine	shone *or* shined***	shone *or* shined***
shrink	shrank *or* shrunk	shrunk *or* shrunken
sing	sang	sung
sink	sank	sunk
sit*	sat	sat
sleep	slept	slept
speak	spoke	spoken
spend	spent	spent
spring	sprang *or* sprung	sprung
steal	stole	stolen
sting	stung	stung
swear	swore	sworn
swim	swam	swum
swing	swung	swung
take	took	taken
teach	taught	taught

Common Irregular Verbs, continued

BASE FORM	PAST FORM	PAST PARTICIPLE
tear	tore	torn
tell	told	told
think	thought	thought
throw	threw	thrown
wear	wore	worn
weave	wove	woven
win	won	won
write	wrote	written

*For more detailed instruction on *lay* versus *lie* and *rise* versus *raise*, see Usage Glossary pages 64 and 73.

*For more detailed instruction on *sit* versus *set*, see Usage Glossary page 75.

**Use *hanged* only when referring to death by hanging.

***Shone is intransitive. (The sun *shone*.) *Shined* is transitive. (I *shined* my shoes.)

GRAMMAR/USAGE/MECHANICS

PRACTICE   Past and Past Participle Forms of Verbs

Copy and complete the chart. Make sure that you have spelled each form correctly.

BASE FORM	PAST FORM	PAST PARTICIPLE
1. lead		
2. freeze		
3. teach		

Practice, Past and Past Participle Forms of Verbs, continued

BASE FORM	PAST FORM	PAST PARTICIPLE
4. make		
5. hang		
6. fly		
7. arrive		
8. sink		
9. buy		
10. tell		
11. sit		
12. eat		
13. know		
14. draw		
15. die		
16. ride		
17. throw		
18. speak		
19. lose		
20. get		
21. blow		
22. cast		
23. go		
24. fling		
25. seek		

Write the correct form of the verb in parentheses.

1. Anthea will (ride) her horse tomorrow in the field near Ridgeton Road.
2. The church bell has (ring) for every birth in the town for a century.
3. Benita (lend) her favorite dress to Daphne for the dance at the school.
4. I should have (know) he would be late.
5. He had (grow) so much during the summer I could hardly recognize him.
6. The tiger has (become) almost extinct.
7. Yesterday Ian (forget) the cooler.
8. Before I could warn her that it was dangerous, Ishi had (drive) her car over the bridge.
9. By tonight, Chester will have (write) a three-page paper on rabbits.
10. Mora (run) to the store during last night's rain.

5.3 TENSE OF VERBS

The **tenses** of a verb are the forms that help to show time.

There are six tenses in English: **present, past, future, present perfect, past perfect,** and **future perfect.**

PRESENT TENSE

The present-tense form of a verb is the same as the verb's base form, except for the third-person singular, which adds *–s* or *–es*. Exceptions are the verbs *be* and *have*.

PRESENT TENSE OF THE VERB *PAINT*

	SINGULAR	PLURAL
FIRST PERSON	I **paint**.	We **paint**.
SECOND PERSON	You **paint**.	You **paint**.
THIRD PERSON	She, he, or it **paints**.	They **paint**.
	Kris **paints**.	The artists **paint**.

PRESENT TENSE OF THE VERB *BE*

	SINGULAR	PLURAL
FIRST PERSON	I **am** honest.	We **are** honest.
SECOND PERSON	You **are** honest.	You **are** honest.
THIRD PERSON	She, he, or it **is** honest.	They **are** honest.
	Tomás **is** honest.	The girls **are** honest.

PRESENT TENSE OF THE VERB *HAS*

	SINGULAR	PLURAL
FIRST PERSON	I **have** a dog.	We **have** a dog.
SECOND PERSON	You **have** a dog.	You **have** a dog.
THIRD PERSON	She, he, or it **has** a dog.	They **have** a dog.
	Danny **has** a dog.	The Smiths **have** a dog.

The **present tense** expresses a constant, repeated, or habitual action or condition. It can also express a general truth.

EXAMPLE   Molly **puts** horseradish on ham sandwiches. **[not just *this* ham sandwich but every ham sandwich; a repeated action]**

EXAMPLE   The Yazoo River **flows** into the Mississippi River. **[always; a habitual action]**

EXAMPLE   Ice **melts** at thirty-two degrees Fahrenheit. **[a general truth]**

The **present tense** can also express an action or a condition that exists only now.

EXAMPLE   Mindy **has** a headache. **[not always but just now]**

EXAMPLE   The fireplace wall **feels** dangerously hot. **[at this very moment]**

The **present tense** is sometimes used in historical writing to express past events and, more often, in poetry, fiction, and journalism (especially in sports writing) to convey to the reader a sense of "being there." This usage is sometimes called the *historical present tense*.

EXAMPLE   Though he **is** aware of the danger, Benjamin Franklin **decides** to risk electrocution to verify his theory.

EXAMPLE   The runner on first base **inches** toward second.

PRACTICE   Present Tense

Write a sentence using each of the following verb forms. The content of your sentence should express the kind of present tense indicated in parentheses.

1. equals (generally true)
2. works (a repeated or habitual action)

3. see (at this very moment)
4. walk (a repeated or habitual action)
5. have (generally true)
6. feels (not always, but just now)
7. begins (an event in history)
8. wears (a constant action)
9. is (at this very moment)
10. plays (a repeated or habitual action)

PAST TENSE

Use the **past tense** to express an action or a condition that was started and completed in the past.

EXAMPLE   General Lee **shook** General Grant's hand.

EXAMPLE   The Confederate troops **unloaded** their supplies.

Nearly all regular and irregular verbs (except *be*) have just one past-tense form, such as *climbed* or *ran*. The verb *be* has two past-tense forms, *was* and *were*.

PAST TENSE OF THE VERB *BE*

	SINGULAR	PLURAL
FIRST PERSON	I **was** glad.	We **were** glad.
SECOND PERSON	You **were** glad.	You **were** glad.
THIRD PERSON	She, he, or it **was** glad.	They **were** glad.
	Bob **was** glad.	The girls **were** glad.

FUTURE TENSE

Use the **future tense** to express an action or a condition that will occur in the future.

You form the future tense of any verb by using the auxiliary verb *shall* or *will* with the base form: *I shall wait; you will telephone.* Note: In modern American English, *shall* is very seldom used except for questions in which *I* or *we* is the subject: *Shall I meet you there? Shall we have lunch now?*

EXAMPLE   Ignacio **will mask** the woodwork.

EXAMPLE   Elaine **will paint** the room.

There are three other ways to express future time besides using the future tense. They are as follows:

1. Use *going to* with the present tense of *be* and the base form of a verb.

EXAMPLE   Ignacio **is *going to* mask** the woodwork.

2. Use *about to* with the present tense of *be* and the base form of a verb.

EXAMPLE   Ignacio **is *about to* mask** the woodwork.

3. Use the present tense with an adverb or an adverb phrase that shows future time.

EXAMPLE   Elaine **paints** the room ***tomorrow.***

EXAMPLE   Elaine **paints** the room ***next Tuesday morning.***

Reprinted with special permission of King Features Syndicate.

Rewrite each sentence so that the verb expresses the future tense in the four ways taught in this lesson.

1. Marcia removed the pictures from the wall.
2. Our dog ate all her dinner.
3. Janet climbed to the top of the hill.
4. We studied together for the history test.
5. Mathilda replaced Felipe as pitcher.

Identify the italicized verb tense by writing one of these labels: present, past, future.

1. The slow turning of the ceiling fan *cools* the room almost as well as an air conditioner.
2. Gerry *ran* down the sidewalk to greet his dad.
3. Helen *hopes* the comment she made to the group wasn't misunderstood.
4. To whom *shall* I give this extra ticket to the game?
5. Wally *walked* over to Cecilia's house after school to do homework.
6. With courage and pride, John Hancock *signed* the Declaration of Independence.
7. I *like* to watch baseball on television.
8. In volleyball a team *needs* a two-point lead to win.
9. In August we *will kayak* down the Colorado River.
10. Tomorrow Dominic *will meet* his match.

5.4 PERFECT TENSES

PRESENT PERFECT TENSE

Use the **present perfect tense** to express an action or a condition that occurred at some *indefinite time* in the past.

Do not be confused by the word *present* in the name of the present perfect tense. This tense expresses past time. The word *present* refers to the tense of the auxiliary verb *has* or *have*.

You form the present perfect tense by using *has* or *have* with the past participle of a verb: *has studied, have known.*

EXAMPLE   The cake **has fallen** in the oven.

EXAMPLE   I **have promised** to bring cakes for the bake sale.

The present perfect tense can refer to completed action in past time only in an indefinite way. Adverbs such as *yesterday* cannot be added to make the time more specific.

EXAMPLE   We **have seen** this movie.

EXAMPLE   The beans **have grown** taller.

To be specific about completed past time, you would normally use the simple past tense.

EXAMPLE   We **saw** this movie during spring break.

EXAMPLE   The beans **grew** a foot taller over the weekend.

The present perfect tense can also be used to express the idea that an action or a condition *began in the past and is still happening*. To communicate this idea, you would normally add adverbs (or adverb phrases or clauses) of time.

EXAMPLE   Lionel **has studied** ballet **for two years.**

EXAMPLE   Beth Ann **has hit** three home runs **in a row.**

PAST PERFECT TENSE

Use the **past perfect tense** to indicate that one past action or condition began *and* ended before another past action or condition started.

You form the past perfect tense by using the auxiliary verb *had* with the past participle of a verb: *had painted, had sung*.

EXAMPLE
Past
Frank **won** the race in the car whose carburetor

Past Perfect
he **had rebuilt**. [First Frank rebuilt the carburetor; the rebuilding was complete; then he won the race.]

EXAMPLE
Past Perfect
LaVerne **had perfected** her dance routine before she

Past
entered the contest. [She practiced until her routine was perfect; the perfecting was complete; then she entered the dance contest.]

FUTURE PERFECT TENSE

Use the **future perfect tense** to express one future action or condition that will begin *and* end before another future event starts.

You form the future perfect tense by using *will have* or *shall have* with the past participle of a verb: *will have rested, shall have won*.

EXAMPLE
By August you **will have learned** how to swim. [Learning how to swim will be complete by the time another future event, the arrival of August, happens.]

EXAMPLE
Before she has paid all her debts, she **will have paid** hundreds of dollars in interest. [The interest will already have been paid by the time another future event, the paying of all her debts, is reached.]

Read the verb in parentheses. Then write the tense indicated in brackets.

EXAMPLE This problem would not be facing us if you (do) the work. **[past perfect]**

Answer: had done

1. We (be) to Yellowstone three times in the past five years. **[present perfect]**

2. Mabel (sit) down to dinner when the phone rang. **[past perfect]**

3. By Tuesday, I (finish) the project. **[future perfect]**

4. Moira (play) the oboe in the school band for two years. **[present perfect]**

5. Phil (perform) that concerto at the music school recital before I did. **[past perfect]**

6. Peggy (earn) her masters degree before she joins the Peace Corps. **[future perfect]**

7. The mayor (invite) the winners of the essay contest to dinner this evening. **[present perfect]**

8. Before this evening, Amy (fix) the porch swing. **[future perfect]**

9. Leandra (play) soccer for a long time. **[present perfect]**

10. Sherry (work) on the garden for hours when she stopped for the night. **[past perfect]**

PRACTICE **Tense of Verbs**

Identify the italicized verb tense by writing one of these labels: present, past, future, present perfect, past perfect, future perfect.

1. Raoul *has given up* on making the team.

2. Lauren *had fallen* off the porch.

GRAMMAR/USAGE/MECHANICS

3. This means that in just three years Marlene *will have changed* schools twice.

4. Richard *ran* all the way home.

5. Danielle and her sister Sue always *fight* over who is the better swimmer.

6. Fran *will finish* the dishes later.

7. My nephews *have* always *looked* forward to playing in the creek near their grandparents' house.

8. In 1869 Myra Bradwell *became* the first female lawyer in the state of Illinois.

9. *Will* anyone *take* my place on the committee?

10. Joey *had shaken* his head sadly at the remark.

PRACTICE **The Six Tenses**

Write two paragraphs in which you use each of the six tenses. Try to use at least three of the irregular verbs from the chart that begins on page 187. Be sure that each verb agrees with its subject in number. (See page 215 for more information about subject-verb agreement.)

Frank and Ernest

© 1992 Thaves / Reprinted with permission. Newspaper dist. by NEA, Inc.

VERB TENSE TIME LINE

FUTURE

NOW

PAST

FUTURE
- action or condition will occur in the future

I **will finish** my work tonight.

FUTURE PERFECT
- future action or condition will begin *and* end before another starts

I **will have finished** my work before I leave.

PRESENT
- action or condition exists only now
- constant, repeated, or habitual action or condition
- a general truth

I **finish** my work on time.

PRESENT PERFECT
- action or condition that occurred at an *indefinite* past time
- action began in the past and still occurs now

I **have finished** my work.

PAST PERFECT
- past action or condition began *and* ended before another past action or condition started

I **had finished** my work before I left.

PAST
- action or condition was started and completed in the past

I **finished** my work.

5.5 PROGRESSIVE AND EMPHATIC FORMS

Each of the six tenses has a **progressive** form that expresses a continuing action.

You make the progressive forms by using the appropriate tense of the verb *be* with the present participle of the main verb.

PRESENT PROGRESSIVE	They *are* **studying.**
PAST PROGRESSIVE	They *were* **studying.**
FUTURE PROGRESSIVE	They *will be* **studying.**
PRESENT PERFECT PROGRESSIVE	They *have been* **studying.**
PAST PERFECT PROGRESSIVE	They *had been* **studying.**
FUTURE PERFECT PROGRESSIVE	They *will have been* **studying.**

The present tense and the past tense have additional forms, called **emphatic forms,** that add special force, or emphasis, to the verb.

You make the emphatic forms by using *do, does,* or *did* with the base form of the verb.

PRESENT EMPHATIC	We **do have** enough money for lunch.
	Cindy **does have** her umbrella with her.
PAST EMPHATIC	We **did leave** a large tip.

PRACTICE Progressive and Emphatic Forms

Identify the italicized verb form by writing one of these labels: present progressive, past progressive, future progressive, present perfect progressive, past perfect progressive, future perfect progressive, present emphatic, past emphatic.

1. My cousin Katie *has been working* at the library for at least two years.

2. Tony *is buying* a used car for delivering pizzas.

3. In just two minutes, Anthony *will have been running* for three hours.

4. Tarik and Tanya *did have* enough money to buy bus tickets home.

5. Aaron *will be flying* to France tomorrow afternoon.

6. Timmy *has been looking* all over Central Park for a goose.

7. Mike *was buying* groceries at the new supermarket by the highway.

8. The group *had been calling* every hotel in Rome for reservations.

9. The ocean tides *are rising*.

10. Yes, Joselina and Janet *do go* to the movies at the mall every weekend.

5.6 CONSISTENCY OF TENSES

Don't shift, or change, tenses when two or more events occur at the same time.

EXAMPLE   **INCORRECT**   The dogs **caught** sight of the cat, and at once they **chase** it. **[The tense needlessly shifts from the past to the present.]**

EXAMPLE   **CORRECT**   The dogs **caught** sight of the cat, and at once they **chased** it. **[Now it is clear that both events happened at nearly the same time.]**

Do shift tenses to show that one event precedes or follows another.

EXAMPLE   **INCORRECT**   By the time the omelet **was** ready, I **set** the table. **[The two past-tense verbs give the mistaken impression that both events—the omelet's cooking and the setting of the table—happened at the same time.]**

EXAMPLE   **CORRECT**   By the time the omelet **was** ready, I **had set** the table. [**The shift from the past tense** *(was)* **to the past perfect tense** *(had set)* **clearly shows that the setting of the table happened before the omelet was cooked.**]

Keep a statement about a general truth in the present tense even if other verbs are in the past tense.

We **learned** that water **expands** when it **freezes.**

5.7 VOICE OF VERBS

An action verb is in the **active voice** when the subject of the sentence performs the action.

EXAMPLE   The new student **threw** a wicked fastball.

An action verb is in the **passive voice** when its action is performed on the subject.

EXAMPLE   A wicked fastball **was thrown** by the new student.

Generally the active voice is stronger, but at times the passive voice is preferable or even necessary. If you don't want to call attention to the performer of the action or don't know who the performer is, use the passive voice.

EXAMPLE   Doorbells up and down the street **were rung.** [**You may not want to identify the culprit.**]

EXAMPLE   The tires **were slit.** [**You may not know who the culprit is.**]

You form the passive voice by using a form of the auxiliary verb *be* with the past participle of the verb. The tense of a passive verb is determined by the tense of the auxiliary verb.

EXAMPLE   The gift **is wrapped** in pretty paper. [**present tense, passive voice**]

EXAMPLE   The gift **was wrapped** in pretty paper. [**past tense, passive voice**]

EXAMPLE   The gift **will be wrapped** in pretty paper. **[future tense, passive voice]**

PRACTICE   Voice of Verbs

Rewrite each sentence, changing active verbs to passive and passive verbs to active.

EXAMPLE   To the fans' dismay, the umpire called a strike.

    Answer: To the fan's dismay, a strike was called by
             the umpire.

1. Ice cream cones were invented by a street vendor.
2. The barbed-wire fence tamed the American West.
3. Without her hit, the game would have been lost by us.
4. The beavers built a large dam on the stream.
5. Lisa was missed by everyone at the party.
6. The vase was broken by my butterfingered brother.
7. Mara met Alain at the bus station in town.
8. A book store was opened by Adam in the center of town.
9. Rain pelted the forest in a steady downpour.
10. The Greek astronomer Eratosthenes first calculated the circumference of the Earth.

5.8 MOOD OF VERBS

Along with expressing tense and voice, verbs also express mood.

A verb expresses one of three **moods:** the **indicative mood,** the **imperative mood,** or the **subjunctive mood.**

The indicative mood—the one most frequently used—makes a statement or asks a question. The imperative mood expresses a command or makes a request.

EXAMPLE   **INDICATIVE MOOD**   She **sets** her alarm clock for 6:30 A.M.

EXAMPLE   **IMPERATIVE MOOD**   **Set** your alarm clock for 6:30 A.M.

The subjunctive mood is often replaced by the indicative mood in informal English. The subjunctive mood does, however, have two important uses in modern formal English.

1. The subjunctive mood expresses, although indirectly, a demand, recommendation, suggestion, or statement of necessity.

EXAMPLE We demand [*or* **recommend** *or* **suggest**] that she **set** her alarm clock for 6:30 A.M. [**To form the subjunctive mood, drop the** *–s* **from the third-person singular.**]

EXAMPLE It is necessary that she **be** on time for school. [**The subjunctive mood uses** *be* **instead of** *am, is,* **or** *are.*]

2. The subjunctive mood is used to state a condition or a wish that is contrary to fact. Notice that this use of the subjunctive always requires the past tense.

EXAMPLE If she **were** to oversleep, she would miss her ride to school. [**The subjunctive mood uses** *were,* **not** *was.*]

EXAMPLE I wish (that) I **were** a genius.

EXAMPLE You are speaking to me as if I **were** a child.

PRACTICE Mood of Verbs

Identify the mood of each italicized verb by writing indicative, imperative, *or* subjunctive.

1. Mozart's music *strikes* me as delightful.
2. I wish I *were* in a better mood today.
3. Before tomorrow morning, *give* me a list of all the supplies you will need.
4. I suggest that you *turn off* the water before you leave.
5. Lisa *will turn* sixteen in January.
6. It is crucial to me that my dog *learn* basic obedience.
7. Please *let* me take care of that.

8. Maggie *laughed* in the rudest possible way at the broken-down old car.

9. He acts as if he *were* the boss.

10. *Go* right at the next corner and down two blocks.

PRACTICE Proofreading

Rewrite the passage, correcting errors in spelling, capitalization, grammar, and usage. Write legibly to be sure one letter is not mistaken for another. There are ten mistakes. (For this exercise, no sentences should be in the historical present.)

Margaret Fuller

¹Margaret Fuller was the first American woman ever to be a foreign correspondent. ²Born on May 23, 1810, in Cambridgeport, Massachusetts. ³She was educated in her own home by her father, who was a lawyer. ⁴When she was ten years old, she was already reading latin. ⁵Later she goes to a school in Groton, Connecticut. ⁶Then she was hired by Bronson Alcott, the father of Louisa May Alcott, to teach in his school.

⁷In 1839 Fuller returned to Boston and beginned holding seminars in her home. ⁸Many famous men and women payed to hear her talk about a variety of subjects. ⁹Speaking in "public" for pay was banned for women at the time, these seminars were technically illegal. ¹⁰Fuller also become a member of the Transcendental Club, joining other intellectuals such as Ralph Waldo Emerson.

¹¹Fuller wrote book reviews, essays, and books. ¹²Then in 1846 Horace Greeley made her a foriegn correspondent for his newspaper, the *New York Tribune*. ¹³She traveled to europe and sent home articles about life on that continent. ¹⁴Before long she became as well known in Europe as in the United States. ¹⁵She dies, with her husband and son, in a shipwreck off the coast of New York during a voyage back to the United States.

Write the correct form of the verb in parentheses.

1. After graduation yesterday, most of the senior class (swim) across the lake to celebrate.
2. Those two girls have (fight) for years, but they're still good friends.
3. Jake (buy) Karen dinner for her birthday last week.
4. Each week Samantha is (pay) ten dollars to mow Ms. Cohen's lawn.
5. Unfortunately for all of us, Koto had (forget) to bring the picnic basket.
6. If nothing is done, thousands of species will have (become) extinct by the end of the decade.
7. To my great relief, the painting had (dry) before the exhibit opened.
8. Has anyone (take) her place on the committee yet?
9. The white pebbles on the path (shine) in the moonlight.
10. Leah should have (know) she could trust Vi.
11. Virginia (lend) her skis to Orah last weekend.
12. To his grandparents' surprise, Adler had (grow) a great deal during the school year.
13. The school fire alarm has been (ring) only once so far this year.
14. I had no idea Eartha had (ride) horses for so long.
15. I saw a flock of Canada geese as they (fly) south for the winter.
16. Last season the team (hit) eighty-seven home runs.
17. Despite its name, the nocturnal jackal is often (see) in the daytime.
18. If you aren't there and ready by three, you will have (make) a big mistake.
19. His face (fall) as he saw the size of his opponent.
20. While her father parked the car, Aleta (run) across the lawn to greet her mother.

Identify the italicized verb tense by writing one of these labels: present, past, future, present perfect, past perfect, future perfect.

21. By Tuesday, we *will have learned* all we need to know about the proposed budget.

22. One white daisy *looks* much like another.

23. The book *fell* off the shelf by itself.

24. She *has driven* this road many times.

25. *Will* anyone *lend* me a sweater?

26. Geri *had* never *bought* a pair of high heels before.

27. *Will* Allison *be* completely ready for the academic triathlon by next week?

28. Keisha *has wanted* that set of golf clubs for months.

29. Arthur *walks* three miles every day.

30. A hummingbird *drank* at the feeder for three or four minutes.

Identify the italicized verb form by writing one of these labels: present progressive, past progressive, future progressive, present perfect progressive, past perfect progressive, future perfect progressive, present emphatic, past emphatic.

31. I *did leave* my wallet in Jackie's car after all.

32. *Will* Taylor *be leaving* for school before we get back from vacation?

33. Nan *had been looking* forward to the class picnic.

34. The cereal box *was sitting* on the table where you put it.

35. Nicole *does bear* a certain resemblance to her mother, I tell you.

36. *Is* Lars *going* to the speech tournament next month?

GRAMMAR/USAGE/MECHANICS

37. Jamie *has been practicing* her violin since three o'clock this afternoon.

38. I don't care what you say; I *do have* naturally curly hair.

39. Quinn and Meredith *are collecting* for children's charities right now.

40. Lewis *will have been waiting* for you for an hour.

POSTTEST **Correcting Verb Tense and Changing Voice**

Rewrite each sentence. Correct verbs in the wrong tense, or change verbs in passive voice to active voice.

41. Library cards are given out by the librarian.

42. *Pictures from an Exhibition* was written by Russian composer Modest Petrovich Mussorgsky.

43. By the time Jason finished the race, he drank sixty-four ounces of water.

44. That dress was made by Sula.

45. Jarvis and Cora have been walking in the park earlier this morning.

46. *Harpers Dictionary of Contemporary Usage* was used by the writer when she wanted an expert opinion on usage.

47. The cake is ruined because Caleb slams the oven door when he left.

48. By next year, Tomas has grown taller.

49. Bella did her research, outlined her report, and begins to write.

50. The channel was changed by Peter.

Chapter 6

Subject-Verb Agreement

• • • • • • • • • • • • • • • •

PRETEST   **Identifying the Simple Subject
and the Correct Verb Form**

*Write the simple subject of each sentence. Then write the
correct verb from the choices in parentheses.*

1. My favorite television show (comes, come) on after the
nightly news.

2. Why (does, do) the cat seem so scared?

3. The journalists who write for *Newsweek* (call, calls) ahead to set up an interview.

4. Matt's family always (goes, go) to Montana for a week in the summer.

5. The markings on a tiger's face (is, are) different for every tiger.

6. Neither Alice, who was the soloist, nor the choir members (was, were) familiar with the new piece of music.

7. All of the children (hopes, hope) that it will snow enough to cancel school.

8. Under what circumstances (is, are) William available to go with us?

9. Four renowned doctors, each an expert in his or her own field, (lectures, lecture) at the medical convention this weekend.

10. The end result (was, were) tremendous advantages for both of us.

11. *Gulliver's Travels* (is, are) still entertaining.

12. Buying products in bulk (saves, save) money.

13. Here at long last (is, are) the dozen vegetarian pizzas we ordered.

14. One of the contestants (is, are) eligible to win the big prize tonight.

15. Jim's poems about his experiences and feelings (was, were) a window into his heart.

16. Watering all the plants (is, are) a boring but necessary part of my job.

17. Three teaspoons (equals, equal) one tablespoon.

18. Gina's family (has, have) huge feet and, therefore, trouble finding shoes.

19. According to this brochure, the West Indies (is, are) warm in January.

20. Each boy and girl in the class (knows, know) how to play chess.

6.1 AGREEMENT OF SUBJECTS AND VERBS

Number refers to the form of a word that indicates whether it is singular or plural. A verb must agree with its subject in number.

Singular subjects indicate one and require a singular verb. Plural subjects indicate more than one and require a plural verb. With most regular verbs, add *–s* or *–es* to form the singular.

EXAMPLES **SINGULAR** The **author writes.** The **champion boxes.**

EXAMPLES **PLURAL** The **authors write.** The **champions box.**

An exception to the rule occurs with the pronouns *I* and *you.* Both take the plural form of a verb, even when *you* refers to one person. The only exception is *be;* when *I* is the subject, the verb form is *am.*

EXAMPLE **I eat** breakfast.

EXAMPLE **You prepare** dinner.

Whether functioning as main verbs or auxiliary verbs, *be, have,* and *do* change in form to show agreement. In fact, the number of a verb phrase is indicated by these auxiliary verbs. Notice in the verb phrases the main verbs do not change form.

EXAMPLES **SINGULAR** I **am** late.

He **is laughing.**

The applicant **has** experience.

She **has listened** intently.

Does he **need** help?

EXAMPLES **PLURAL** We **are** late.

We **are laughing.**

The applicants **have** experience.

They **have listened** intently.

Do they **need** help?

Write the correct verb from the choices in parentheses.

1. He (goes, go) to the park at least twice a week.
2. My earrings (is, are) silver and turquoise.
3. The plants (leans, lean) toward the light.
4. You (has, have) not seen anything, yet!
5. Omar (flies, fly) his kite in the park on breezy Sunday afternoons.
6. Every year, Sam (runs, run) in a 10k race to raise money for homeless cats.
7. Flutes (plays, play) beautiful music.
8. Jerome's brothers (works, work) for a big law firm.
9. Children (waits, wait) at the corner for the school bus.
10. (Does, do) the hamster need to be fed?

Frank and Ernest

© 1998 Thaves / Reprinted with permission. Newspaper dist. by NEA, Inc.

6.2 INTERVENING PHRASES AND CLAUSES

Don't mistake a word in an intervening phrase or clause for the subject of a sentence. The simple subject is never in a prepositional phrase. Make sure the verb agrees with the actual subject and not with the object of the preposition.

EXAMPLE   The **paper** in those boxes **is** for the copy machine. [The singular verb *is* agrees with the singular subject *paper,* not with the plural object of the preposition, *boxes*.]

EXAMPLE   The **dogs** in that class **are** well behaved. [The plural verb *are* agrees with the plural subject *dogs,* not with the object of the preposition, *class*.]

If a singular subject is linked to another noun by a phrase, the subject is still considered singular. Expressions such as *accompanied by, as well as, in addition to, plus,* and *together with* introduce phrases that modify the subject without changing its number. Although their meaning is similar to that of *and,* these expressions don't form compound subjects.

EXAMPLE   **Fried rice,** along with wonton soup, **makes** a delicious meal.

EXAMPLE   **Isaac,** accompanied by Jerome, **goes** to the movies on Saturday.

Appositives and adjective clauses give information about the subject but don't change its number. Make sure you don't mistake a word in an appositive or an adjective clause for the subject of the sentence.

APPOSITIVES

EXAMPLE   **Emma,** one of my good friends, **visits** Australia every year.

EXAMPLE   Four well-known **writers,** all very skilled at their craft, **lecture** at the seminar.

ADJECTIVE CLAUSES

EXAMPLE   **Virginia Woolf,** who was one of the Bloomsbury Group members, **expresses** emotion in her writing.

EXAMPLE   The **rivers** that bordered Mesopotamia **are** the Tigris and the Euphrates.

GRAMMAR/USAGE/MECHANICS

Most of the following sentences contain an error in subject-verb agreement. For each sentence, write the subject and the corrected verb. If a sentence is already correct, write C.

1. The pages of the book is decorated with drawings.
2. The wallaby, together with the kangaroo, are native to Australia.
3. Ms. Hunter, who was one of my first soccer coaches, wants to open a soccer camp.
4. Tornadoes, a frequent danger in the spring, causes fear among residents of "Tornado Alley."
5. The mountains in New Mexico spans the state from the north to the south.
6. The cat, who is getting on my nerves, wants to be petted.
7. The junction of the Mississippi and Missouri Rivers lie just north of St. Louis.
8. Tamika, in addition to the other students, ride the train.
9. The horse, as well as the cows, like that pasture best.
10. Pyramids, one of the seven wonders of the world, amazes tourists.

6.3 AGREEMENT WITH COMPOUND SUBJECTS

A compound subject that is joined by *and* or *both . . . and* is plural unless its parts belong to one unit or they both refer to the same person or thing.

EXAMPLES **PLURAL** The **Tigris** and the **Euphrates flow** through southwestern Asia.

Both **rivers** and **streams provide** irrigation for farmland.

| EXAMPLES | SINGULAR | **Toast** and **tea is** my favorite breakfast. [one unit] |
| | | Her **friend** and **companion is** George. [one person] |

With compound subjects joined by *or* or *nor* (or by *either . . . or* or *neither . . . nor*), the verb agrees with the subject closer to it.

EXAMPLES	SINGULAR	Either the **tortoise** or the **hare wins** the race.
		Raisins or an **apple makes** a good snack.
EXAMPLES	PLURAL	Neither **Kara** nor her **friends like** winter.
		Neither **foxes** nor **dogs eat** only meat.

PRACTICE   **Agreement with Compound Subjects**

Write the complete subject of each sentence. Then write the correct verb form from the choices in parentheses.

1. Neither Kansas nor the Dakotas (borders, border) the Gulf of Mexico.
2. Macaroni and cheese really (hits, hit) the spot.
3. Both Thanksgiving and New Year's Day (falls, fall) on Thursday this year.
4. Either the five boys or she (gets, get) to use the dressing room first.
5. Neither Sally nor the Nelsons (appears, appear) to be having a very good time.
6. My brother and friend (is, are) Yoshiya.
7. Records and cassette tapes (has been replaced, have been replaced) in many homes by compact discs.
8. David and Romie (gets, get) married on Saturday.
9. Bacon and eggs (is, are) my favorite breakfast.
10. Both my sisters and my cousin (reads, read) Dickens.

6.4 AGREEMENT WITH SPECIAL SUBJECTS

COLLECTIVE NOUNS

A **collective noun** names a group of persons, things, or animals.

When a collective noun refers to a group as a whole, it requires a singular verb. When a collective noun refers to each member of a group individually, it requires a plural verb.

EXAMPLE **SINGULAR**   The **chorus sings** beautifully.

EXAMPLE **PLURAL**   The **chorus have** separate parts to learn.

When deciding the number of the verb needed for a collective noun, it is helpful to look for the pronouns *its* and *their.* When a collective noun is referred to by *its,* the collective noun requires a singular verb. When a collective noun is referred to by *their,* the collective noun needs a plural verb.

EXAMPLE **SINGULAR**   The **litter** of kittens **stays** in *its* cage.

EXAMPLE **PLURAL**   The **litter follow** *their* mother in a single-file line.

SPECIAL NOUNS

Certain nouns that end in *s,* such as *mathematics, molasses,* and *news,* require singular verbs.

EXAMPLE   **Molasses is** the key ingredient in my pecan pie.

EXAMPLE   The **news arrives** later here.

Certain other nouns that end in *s,* such as *scissors, pants, binoculars,* and *eyeglasses,* require plural verbs.

EXAMPLE   The **scissors are** in the drawer.

EXAMPLE   **Binoculars are** handy for bird-watching.

Many other nouns that end in *s*, such as *mumps, measles, ethics, statistics,* and *politics,* depending on the meaning, may require either a singular or a plural verb. In general, if the noun refers to a whole, such as a disease or a science, it requires a singular verb. If it is referring to qualities, activities, or individual items, it requires a plural verb.

EXAMPLE   SINGULAR   **Mumps is** contagious.

EXAMPLE   PLURAL   **Mumps are** itchy.

EXAMPLE   SINGULAR   **Statistics is** one of my favorite courses.

EXAMPLE   PLURAL   **Statistics are** the basis for many reports.

MANY A, EVERY, AND EACH

When *many a, every,* or *each* precedes a subject, whether simple or compound, the subject is considered singular.

EXAMPLE   *Many a* **decision was made.**

EXAMPLE   *Many a* **joke** and **cartoon was included.**

EXAMPLE   *Every* **dog has** a distinct personality.

EXAMPLE   *Every* **restaurant** and **diner serves** sandwiches.

EXAMPLE   *Each* **author writes** differently.

EXAMPLE   *Each* **penny** and **dime was counted.**

NOUNS OF AMOUNT

When a plural noun of amount refers to one unit, it acts as a singular subject. When it refers to individual units, it acts as a plural subject.

EXAMPLE   SINGULAR   Eight **dollars is** the cost of the ticket.

EXAMPLE   PLURAL   Eight **dollars lie** on the table.

When a fraction or a percentage refers to a singular word, it requires a singular verb. When it refers to a plural word, it requires a plural verb.

EXAMPLE **SINGULAR** Sixty **percent** of the *money* **was spent** on food.

EXAMPLE **PLURAL** Sixty **percent** of our *resources* **were used.**

Units of measurement usually require singular verbs.

EXAMPLE **Sixteen by twenty inches is** a standard size for a picture frame.

EXAMPLE **Ten millimeters equals** one centimeter.

TITLES

A title of a creative work always acts as a singular subject, even if a noun within the title is plural.

EXAMPLE ***All the King's Men* was** the 1947 Pulitzer Prize winner.

EXAMPLE **"Giant Steps" is** one of John Coltrane's masterworks.

COUNTRIES AND CITIES

Names of countries and cities require singular verbs.

EXAMPLE The **United States has** a democratic government.

EXAMPLE **Los Angeles is** in California.

PRACTICE **Agreement with Special Subjects**

Write the correct verb form from the choices in parentheses.

1. Many an insect and reptile species (is discovered, are discovered) every year.

2. The wolf pack (hunts, hunt) for its food.

3. *Little Women* (is, are) popular among boys and girls.
4. Mathematics (is, are) so logical!
5. Five hours (passes, pass) without a sign of the culprit.
6. Forty-seven feet (is, are) my best distance so far this year in the shot put.
7. Colorado Springs (sits, sit) at the foot of Pike's Peak in the Rocky Mountains.
8. Molasses (drips, drip) slowly from the spoon.
9. Each story and poem (deals, deal) with the coming of spring.
10. The group (disagrees, disagree) about what salad dressing they should buy.

6.5 INDEFINITE PRONOUNS AS SUBJECTS

Some indefinite pronouns are always singular, some are always plural, and others may be singular or plural, depending on their use.

INDEFINITE PRONOUNS	
SINGULAR	another, anyone, anybody, anything, each, either, everybody, everyone, everything, neither, nobody, no one, nothing, one, other, somebody, someone, something
PLURAL	both, few, many, others, several
SINGULAR OR PLURAL	all, any, enough, most, much, none, some

Singular indefinite pronouns require singular verbs. Plural indefinite pronouns require plural verbs.

EXAMPLES **SINGULAR** **Everyone is** welcome.

Someone gives me the number.

EXAMPLES **PLURAL** **Both are** able to play.

Few are coming to the party.

The number of the pronouns in the last row of the chart depends on the words to which they refer. If the pronoun refers to a singular word, then it requires a singular verb. If the pronoun refers to a plural word, then it requires a plural verb.

EXAMPLE SINGULAR **None** of the candy **was left.** [*none* refers to *candy,* a singular noun]

EXAMPLE PLURAL **None** of the sweets **were left.** [*none* refers to *sweets,* a plural noun]

PRACTICE Indefinite Pronouns as Subjects 1

Write the correct verb from the choices in parentheses for each sentence.

1. The boys are exhausted, and several (is, are) just about ready to give up.
2. Allen and Rosie hurry, but both (trips, trip) while rounding the corner.
3. Enough of the flowers (remains, remain) to make quite a lovely bouquet.
4. Much of the fruit (has, have) spoiled.
5. Most of the cars are sporty, but few (is, are) very powerful.
6. (Is, are) each of the winners going to be at the assembly?
7. Either of the choices (solves, solve) our problem.
8. When I sit down too quickly, everything (falls, fall) from my pocket.
9. Some of the teachers (agrees, agree) with me.
10. At this point, everyone (wants, want) another chance.

PRACTICE Indefinite Pronouns as Subjects 2

From the chart in this lesson, choose five indefinite pronouns that are always singular and write sentences using each as a subject. Then do the same for five that are always plural and five that can be either singular or plural. Underline the verb in each sentence and be ready to explain why you used that verb form.

6.6 PHRASES AND CLAUSES AS SUBJECTS

Whenever a phrase or a clause acts as a subject, the verb must be singular.

EXAMPLE **Swimming laps is** good exercise. [The gerund phrase *swimming laps* functions as the subject and agrees with the singular verb *is*.]

EXAMPLE **To eat three pies is** gluttonous. [The infinitive phrase *to eat three pies* functions as the subject and agrees with the singular verb *is*.]

EXAMPLE **Whoever receives the most votes wins** the election. [The noun clause *whoever receives the most votes* functions as the subject and agrees with the singular verb *wins*.]

GRAMMAR/USAGE/MECHANICS

PRACTICE **Phrases and Clauses as Subjects**

Write the correct verb from the choices in parentheses for each sentence.

1. Reading enjoyable books (is, are) mind expanding.
2. Whoever finds the most listed items (gets, get) a valuable prize.
3. To follow in the footsteps of great thinkers (is, are) an honorable goal.
4. Frequent arguing with coworkers (leads, lead) to bad working conditions.
5. At this point, to sleep eight hours (is, are) impossible.

6. Whatever statements those people have made (is, are) completely untrue.

7. Mountain climbing with friends (builds, build) trust.

8. To finish a book long before your flight is over (makes, make) for a boring last hour.

9. Picking cherries (requires, require) a tall ladder.

10. What you think of your neighbors (is, are) not really any business of mine.

6.7 AGREEMENT IN INVERTED SENTENCES

In an **inverted sentence** the subject follows the verb.

Inverted sentences often begin with prepositional phrases. Don't mistake the object of the preposition for the subject.

EXAMPLE   **SINGULAR**   By the tables **sits** the **student.**

EXAMPLE   **PLURAL**   At the table **sit** the **students.**

In sentences beginning with *there* or *here,* the subject follows the verb. The words *there* and *here* almost never function as the subject of a sentence.

EXAMPLE   **SINGULAR**   Here **is** the **map.**

                    There **is no one** available.

EXAMPLE   **PLURAL**   Here **are** the **maps.**

                    There **are** no **volunteers** available.

In a question, an auxiliary verb usually comes before the subject. Look for the subject between the auxiliary verb and the main verb.

EXAMPLE   **SINGULAR**   **Does Katy like** pizza?

EXAMPLE   **PLURAL**   **Do they like** pizza?

Most of the following sentences contain an error in subject-verb agreement. For each sentence, write the incorrect verb and the correct verb. If a sentence is correct, write C.

1. On the clotheslines hang the laundry.
2. Here is the albums I promised you.
3. Into the clearing walks the moose and the calf.
4. Why is the dogs acting so strange?
5. Beneath a rock hide the insects.
6. There goes my mom and dad.
7. Here is your missing documents.
8. Between the columns and across the marble floor walks the group of tourists.
9. Which boy are you going to ask for a date?
10. Under the steps live a family of raccoons.

Write the subject of each sentence. Then write the correct verb from the choices in parentheses.

1. On top of the shelves (lies, lie) the hat.
2. Everyone (finishes, finish) together.
3. The team (plays, play) its last game today.
4. How many books (is, are) Juana going to read before the end of the year?
5. There (was, were) more noisy people in the park this year than last.
6. All of the advice (concerns, concern) your problem.
7. Each flower and plant (needs, need) to be watered.
8. Playing golf and tennis (relaxes, relax) Tse Hoe's mother.
9. In one of those envelopes (is, are) the million dollar prize.
10. However you want to answer the questions (is, are) fine with me.

6.8 AGREEMENT WITH SUBJECT, NOT PREDICATE NOMINATIVE

Don't be confused by a predicate nominative that is different in number from the subject. Only the subject affects the number of the linking verb.

EXAMPLE Her great **joy was** Japanese gardens. [The singular verb *was* agrees with the singular subject *joy,* not with the plural predicate nominative *gardens.*]

EXAMPLE Japanese **gardens were** her great joy. [The plural verb *were* agrees with the plural subject *gardens,* not with the singular predicate nominative *joy.*]

PRACTICE Agreement with Subject, Not Predicate Nominative

Write the subject of each sentence. Then write the correct verb from the choices in parentheses.

1. Pianos (is, are) a member of the stringed instrument group.
2. The mountains in the northern part of the state (is, are) a popular tourist destination.
3. The main problem with the paper (was, were) too many misspellings.
4. The successful parties (was, were) the result of intense planning.
5. My favorite food (is, are) sandwiches.
6. Reunion T-shirts (was, were) your responsibility.
7. Fruits (is, are) a major source of vitamin C.
8. The special on tonight's menu (is, are) pork chops.
9. The singers (was, were) the last act of the show.
10. The children's lunch (was, were) toasted cheese sandwiches.

6.9 AGREEMENT IN ADJECTIVE CLAUSES

When the subject of an adjective clause is a relative pronoun, the verb in the clause must agree with the word to which the relative pronoun refers.

If the relative pronoun is the subject of the clause and it refers to a singular word, the verb in the adjective clause must be singular.

EXAMPLE   The **man who teaches** my yoga class dresses in white.

If the relative pronoun is the subject of the clause and it refers to a plural word, then the verb in the adjective clause must be plural.

EXAMPLE   **Classrooms that have** computers are convenient.

If an adjective clause is preceded by *one of (plural word)*, then the relative pronoun will refer to the plural word, and the verb in the clause must be plural.

EXAMPLE   *Sanctuary* is one of my favorite **books that were** written by Faulkner. [**The relative clause refers to** *books* **because all of the books are written by Faulkner.**]

If an adjective clause is preceded by *the only one of (plural word)*, the relative pronoun will refer to the word *one*, and the verb in the clause must be singular.

EXAMPLE   Pedro is the only **one** of the Fernandez children **who owns** a car. [**The relative clause refers to** *one* **because only one person owns a car.**]

PRACTICE   **Agreement with Relative Pronouns**

Write the relative pronoun and the word to which it refers. Then write the correct verb from the choices in parentheses.

1. The man who (wants, want) to meet the president is waiting outside.
2. This is one of the rooms in the house that (has, have) fireplaces.
3. My aunts who (lives, live) in San Diego are visiting.

4. Most action movies that (stars, star) Will Smith are a lot of fun.
5. The grilled chicken is the only one of the choices that (is, are) low in fat.
6. Those phones that (does, do) not have cords are convenient.
7. The dog that (wins, win) the dog show will be on the cover of the club's magazine.
8. I support the only one of the candidates who (has answered, have answered) reporters' questions directly.
9. Bill and Casper, oddly enough, are both towns that (is, are) in Wyoming.
10. The basement entrance is the only one that (has, have) an alarm.

PRACTICE Proofreading

Rewrite the following passage, correcting errors in spelling, capitalization, grammar, and usage. Add any missing punctuation. Write legibly to be sure one letter is not mistaken for another. There are ten mistakes.

A Special Place

[1]During the second half of the nineteenth century, African Americans in the South was persecuted by Jim Crow laws. [2]Josephine Allensworth and her husband, Allen, moved to Los Angeles in the hope of finding more freedom. [3]They were disappointed, and decided to found a Town for African Americans. [4]They wanted a place, where black people could live "free from the restrictions of race." [5]They also wanted to give a home to African American soldiers who had served their country.

[6]In 1908 the town of Allensworth was born in Tulare County, California. [7]By the time four years had past, it has two general stores and a number of small businesses. [8]The president of the school board, librarian, and sponsor of the Women's Improvement Association were Josephine Allensworth. [9]The town lasted until the 1950s. [10]Only one of hundreds of similar towns in this country. [11]Today, the history of these towns remind us that African Americans have always fought persecution.

Write the simple subject of each sentence. Then write the correct verb from the choices in parentheses.

1. Here (is, are) the newspapers that need to be delivered.

2. His backpack, plus a raincoat, (was, were) all he took.

3. Monkeys (uses, use) their prehensile tails.

4. Inside the beautifully wrapped packages (was, were) absolutely nothing.

5. All summer long, fishing and rowing a boat (is, are) Paul's greatest joy.

6. Help, in the form of firefighters, (needs, need) to arrive soon.

7. Min and her mother (walks, walk) every day.

8. To be precise (is, are) not necessarily the most important thing.

9. Somebody (wants, want) to hear me sing.

10. Many a fish and crab (washes, wash) up on the beach.

11. The thousands of lakes in Minnesota's beautiful lake region (provides, provide) recreation for millions.

12. Statistics (is, are) not always reliable.

13. My dream destination for a long vacation (is, are) the Himalayas.

14. Bickering with coworkers (is, are) not productive.

15. Neither he, a novice, nor she, an experienced skier, (wants, want) to risk skiing under these conditions.

16. Twelve dollars (was, were) too much to pay for one pair of socks.

17. Her boyfriend and mixed-doubles partner (was, were) Rodrigo.

18. Some of us (knows, know) how to behave.

19. Inside the safe (lies, lie) the treasure maps.

20. Next week, the Youth Explorer group (receives, receive) their merit badges.

GRAMMAR/USAGE/MECHANICS

Using Pronouns Correctly

● ● ● ● ● ● ● ● ● ● ● ● ● ●

PRETEST **Identifying the Correct Pronoun**

For each sentence, write the correct pronoun from the choices in parentheses.

1. The play was a real eye-opener for Jacqui and (I, me).
2. Bette and (they, them) made up the pep squad.
3. Melinda was far faster than (I, me) in the relay.
4. If the party was ruined, the fault was (theirs, their's).
5. (Who, Whom) do you think could be responsible for this big mess?
6. (Who, Whom) do you want to give the first speech at the assembly?

7. Both of us were more than a little eager to see (them, they) before we left.

8. Mr. Jenkins and (her, she), the lone survivors of the game, continued with only one chair left.

9. The shortstop tagged both runners, Tad and (I, me), as we stood together on second base.

10. He was sure that (whoever, whomever) had taken his book was still around.

11. (We, Us) students were the ones who missed school the most.

12. Do you really think Joe and (I, myself) knew that?

13. They served (theirselves, themselves) and then sat on the bench to eat.

14. We helped (ourself, ourselves) to extra pieces of pie because it was Thanksgiving.

15. Between you and (I, me), I feel that I should have won the match.

16. Since the dog is really my father's, she obeys him better than (I, me).

17. Their aunt visits Marla and (she, her) at college once in the fall and once in the spring.

18. A prospective doctor must spend many years studying before receiving (his or her, their) degree.

19. The star of the television show, (who, whom) I can't stand, is leaving at the end of the season.

20. Those are the characters about (who, whom) my story is written.

21. Herb and (she, her) are the last ones to care what other people think.

22. (Who, Whom) can I get to drive Aunt Joy to the doctor's office this morning?

23. Neither of (we, us) thought the new horror movie was all that horrifying.

24. My parents thought (they, them) should screen the porch.

25. Here come Nat and (she, her) to warm up.

7.1 CASE OF PERSONAL PRONOUNS

Pronouns that refer to persons or things are called **personal** pronouns.

Personal pronouns have three **cases,** or forms. The three cases are called **nominative, objective,** and **possessive.** The case of a personal pronoun depends on the pronoun's function in a sentence—that is, whether it is a subject, a complement, an object of a preposition, or a replacement for a possessive noun.

		PERSONAL PRONOUNS	
CASE	**SINGULAR PRONOUNS**	**PLURAL PRONOUNS**	**FUNCTION IN SENTENCE**
NOMINATIVE	I, you, she, he, it	we, you, they	subject or predicate nominative
OBJECTIVE	me, you, her, him, it	us, you, them	direct object, indirect object, or object of preposition
POSSESSIVE	my, mine, your, yours, her, hers, his, its	our, ours, your, yours, their, theirs	replacement for possessive noun(s)

Use these rules to avoid errors with the case of personal pronouns:

1. Use the nominative case for a personal pronoun in a compound subject.

EXAMPLE Dorothy and **I** planted the perennials.

EXAMPLE **She** and Luke planted the annuals.

EXAMPLE **He** and **I** designed the drip irrigation system.

2. Use the objective case for a personal pronoun in a compound object.

EXAMPLE Lana brought Dorothy and **them** some lemonade.

EXAMPLE For Luke and **me,** there was iced tea.

Hint: When you are choosing a pronoun for a sentence that has a compound subject or a compound object, try saying the sentence to yourself without the conjunction and the other subject or object.

EXAMPLE The sprinkler sprayed [Dorothy and] **me.**

Note: It is considered courteous to place the pronoun *I* or *me* last in a series.

EXAMPLE **Kris, Rick,** and **I** transplanted this rosebush.
[nominative case]

EXAMPLE The tiller was rented by **Edmund** and **me.**
[objective case]

3. Use the nominative case for a personal pronoun after a linking verb.

EXAMPLE The best garden designer was **he.**

EXAMPLE The most careful weeders are **we.**

EXAMPLE The creakiest in the knees am **I!**

This rule is changing. In informal speech, people often use the objective case after a linking verb; they say, *It's me, It was him.* Some authorities even recommend using the objective case in informal writing to avoid sounding pretentious. To be strictly correct, however, use the nominative case after a linking verb, especially in formal writing.

4. Never spell possessive personal pronouns with apostrophes.

EXAMPLE This shovel is **hers.**
The pitchforks are **theirs.**
This is **yours.**

It's is a contraction for *it is* or *it has.* Don't confuse *it's* with the possessive pronoun *its.*

EXAMPLE **It's** time to thin the carrots. Please bring me the kneeler and **its** cushion.

5. Use possessive pronouns before gerunds (-*ing* forms used as nouns).

EXAMPLE **Your** mowing the lawn was a big help.

EXAMPLE **His** eating all the ripe berries was to be expected.

EXAMPLE We are glad of **their** lending us the wheelbarrow.

PRACTICE **Personal Pronouns**

Write the correct personal pronoun from the choices in parentheses.

1. (We, Us) grandchildren often visit our grandparents.
2. Our teacher and (she, her) want to see the academic quiz team after school.
3. The horse has (its, it's) tail braided.
4. I can't stand (his, him) complaining all the time.
5. The best project at the math fair was (their's, theirs)
6. Talk to Pia and (he, him) first; I can wait.
7. The best muralists in the school are Al and (she, her).
8. Joley's bike is just like (her's, hers)
9. (They, Them) and (we, us) are playing bridge tonight.
10. I keep forgetting that (its, it's) Wednesday.

7.2 PRONOUNS WITH AND AS APPOSITIVES

Use the nominative case for a pronoun that is an appositive to a subject or a predicate nominative.

EXAMPLE The ringmasters, **Keri and she,** had a difficult task.
[*Ringmasters* is the subject of the sentence.]

EXAMPLE The stars of the show were two brothers, **Ananda** and **he**. [***Brothers*** **is a predicate nominative.**]

Use the objective case for a pronoun that is an appositive to a direct object, an indirect object, or an object of a preposition.

EXAMPLE The crowd applauded the jugglers, **Reed** and **him**. [***Jugglers*** **is a direct object.**]

EXAMPLE The strongest acrobats gave the climbers, **Kate** and **her,** boosts to help them climb. [***Climbers*** **is an indirect object.**]

EXAMPLE The best costumes were worn by the tightrope walkers, **Leeza** and **him**. [***Walkers*** **is the object of the preposition** ***by.***]

It is considered courteous to place the pronoun *I* or *me* last in a pair or series of appositives.

EXAMPLE The jugglers, **William, Abeni,** and **I,** performed our routines perfectly. [**nominative case**]

EXAMPLE The audience gave the unicycle riders, **Cai** and **me,** a special prize. [**objective case**]

When a pronoun is followed by an appositive, choose the case of the pronoun that would be correct if the appositive were omitted.

EXAMPLE **We performers** were pleased with the circus we had organized. [***We,*** **which is in the nominative case, is correct because** ***we*** **is the subject of the sentence.**]

EXAMPLE   The circus earned money for the local hospital and for **us students.** [*Us*, which is in the objective case, is correct because *us* is the object of the preposition *for*.]

Hint: When you are choosing the correct pronoun, it is often helpful to say the sentence to yourself leaving out the appositive.

EXAMPLE   **We** were pleased with the circus we had organized.

EXAMPLE   The circus earned money for the local hospital and for **us.**

PRACTICE   Pronouns with and as Appositives

Write the correct pronoun from the choices in parentheses.

1. As time passed, it began to look bad for our team, Aunt Sara and (I, me).

2. The older pair of bridge players, Mrs. Ving and (he, him), beat us.

3. The entire group, Ms. Matthews, the principal, and (he, him), met before school.

4. (We, Us) researchers finally discovered that a traveling preacher had met the young couple, Aaron and (her, she), in El Paso.

5. The worst batters on the team are the Lewis brothers, Clyde and (he, him).

6. With great patience, the wrangler showed (we, us) greenhorns the ropes.

7. Ian came with Jack's buddies, Meghan and (him, he) to my opening at the gallery.

8. Our last best chance, Rita and (she, her), had failed to come through for us.

9. Let's give the final dancers, Jason and (she, her), better lighting so that the costume designers, Patsy and (I, me), can have our work appreciated.

10. Despite what has been written, (we, us) teenagers are just as concerned as anyone else.

"Stop referring to you and me as 'we'!"

7.3 PRONOUNS AFTER THAN AND AS

When words are left out of an adverb clause that begins with *than* or *as,* choose the case of the pronoun that you would use if the missing words were fully expressed.

EXAMPLE You skate more skillfully than **I.** [That is, . . . ***than I skate.*** **The nominative pronoun *I* is the subject of the adverb clause *than I skate.*]**

EXAMPLE The crash startled Becca as much as **me.** [That is, . . . ***as much as it startled me.*** **The objective pronoun *me* is the direct object in the adverb clause *as much as it startled me.*]**

Some sentences can be completed with either a nominative or an objective pronoun, depending on the meaning intended by the speaker or writer.

EXAMPLE The manager respects the director more than **I [respect the director].**

EXAMPLE The manager respects the director more than **[the manager respects] me.**

PRACTICE **Pronouns After *Than* and *As***

Rewrite each sentence, choosing the correct pronoun from the choices in parentheses and adding the necessary words to complete the comparison.

EXAMPLE That little dog is much braver than (I, me).

   Answer: That little dog is much braver than I am brave.

 1. There is no one else in the class as talented as (he, him).
 2. The haunted house scared the kids more than (I, me).
 3. At fifteen, Lu was taller than her mother or (he, him).
 4 Elephants have smaller appetites than (I, me).
 5. Mozart was a better composer than (they, them).
 6. Pizza makes Jake as happy as (her, she).
 7. Zack likes fishing more than (I, me).
 8. John has always been faster than (she, her).
 9. She didn't find the dog as frightening as (I, me).
10. My grandparents always do better at any kind of board games than (I, me).

7.4 REFLEXIVE AND INTENSIVE PRONOUNS

Observe the following rules when you use reflexive and intensive pronouns.

Don't use *hisself, theirself,* or *theirselves.* All three are incorrect forms. Use *himself* and *themselves.*

EXAMPLE Billy pruned the apple tree **himself.**

EXAMPLE My sisters **themselves** put the family budget on the computer.

Use a reflexive pronoun when a pronoun refers to the subject of the sentence.

EXAMPLE **INCORRECT** I made me a tuna sandwich.

CORRECT I made **myself** a tuna sandwich.

EXAMPLE **INCORRECT** We found us a new house.

CORRECT We found **ourselves** a new house.

Don't use a reflexive pronoun unnecessarily. Remember that a reflexive pronoun must refer to the subject, but it must not take the place of the subject.

EXAMPLE **INCORRECT** Deliver the papers to Mr. Morton or myself, please.

CORRECT Deliver the papers to Mr. Morton or **me,** please.

EXAMPLE **INCORRECT** Tam and yourself have done good work.

CORRECT Tam and **you** have done good work.

PRACTICE Reflexive and Intensive Pronouns

Most of the sentences below contain errors in pronoun use. Rewrite the incorrect sentences, correcting the errors by replacing the incorrect pronouns. If a sentence is already correct, write C.

EXAMPLE Give the bill to either Jed or myself.

Answer: Give the bill to either Jed or me.

1. Ally and I did the project ourself.
2. Dave tripped hisself with the rake.

3. Alice stacked a half cord of firewood by herself.
4. I found me a good summer job.
5. Upon studying the photograph, I realized that I was looking at a picture of myself.
6. Jimbo and she had caught theirselves a dozen fish.
7. Raye was hungry, so she bought her and me sandwiches.
8. George and yourself can get that project done easily if you really try.
9. The troll lived by himself under the bridge.
10. By late in the afternoon, the number of contestants had been reduced to just herself and myself.

7.5 *WHO* AND *WHOM* IN QUESTIONS AND SUBORDINATE CLAUSES

In questions use the nominative pronoun *who* for subjects and the objective pronoun *whom* for direct and indirect objects and for objects of a preposition.

EXAMPLE **Who** needs a ride home? [*Who* **is the subject of the verb** *needs.*]

EXAMPLE **Whom** did you call? [*Whom* **is the direct object of the verb** *did call.*]

EXAMPLE **Whom** did they send a telegram? [*Whom* **is the indirect object of the verb** *did send.*]

EXAMPLE **For whom** is this bouquet of roses? [*Whom* **is the object of the preposition** *for.*]

In questions that have an interrupting expression (such as *did you say* or *do you think*), it often helps to drop the interrupting phrase to make it easier to decide whether to use *who* or *whom.*

EXAMPLE **Who** do you think broke the window? [**Think, "***Who* **broke the window?"** *Who* **is the subject of the verb** *broke.*]

In subordinate clauses, use the nominative pronouns *who* and *whoever* for subjects and predicate nominatives.

EXAMPLE   Ask them **who** will be home for dinner. [***Who** is the subject of the noun clause **who will be home for dinner**.*]

EXAMPLE   They know **who** her supervisor is. [***Who** is the predicate nominative of the noun clause **who her supervisor is**.*]

EXAMPLE   The winner of the Miss Congeniality Award will be **whoever** deserves it. [***Whoever** is the subject of the noun clause **whoever deserves it**.*]

In subordinate clauses, use the objective pronouns *whom* and *whomever* for direct and indirect objects and for the objects of prepositions.

EXAMPLE   They told her **whom** she could call. [***Whom** is the direct object of the verb **could call** in the noun clause **whom she could call**.*]

EXAMPLE   Rembrandt is a painter about **whom** I have read quite a bit. [***Whom** is the object of the preposition **about** in the adjective clause **about whom I have read quite a bit**.*]

EXAMPLE   The new president will be **whomever** the voters elect. [***Whomever** is the direct object of the verb **elect** in the noun clause **whomever the voters elect**.*]

In informal speech, many people generally use *who* in place of *whom* in sentences such as *Who did you vote for?* In writing and in formal speaking situations, however, make the distinctions between *who* and *whom*.

When the pronouns *who* and *whom* are used in questions, they are called **interrogative pronouns;** when *who/whoever* and *whom/whomever* are used to introduce subordinate clauses, they are called **relative pronouns.**

For each sentence, write the correct pronoun from the choices in parentheses.

1. (Who, Whom) do you think will want to come to my party?
2. The bell tolls for (whoever, whomever) rings it.
3. Mom and Dad told me (who, whom) I could invite to my sleepover.
4. For (who, whom) is the package on the hall table intended?
5. (Who, Whom) did the coach say is starting in the game today?
6. (Whoever, Whomever) did you have in mind for that particular job?
7. The mayor, (who, whom) was just here, is looking for you.
8. I can choose (whoever, whomever) I like for the role.
9. (Who, Whom) baked this bread?
10. (Whoever, Whomever) broke this dish will pay for it.

7.6 PRONOUN-ANTECEDENT AGREEMENT

An **antecedent** is the noun or pronoun to which a pronoun refers or that a pronoun replaces. All pronouns must agree with their antecedents in **number** (singular or plural), **gender** (masculine, feminine, or neuter), and **person** (first, second, or third).

A pronoun's antecedent may be a noun, another pronoun, or a phrase or a clause acting as a noun. In the following examples, the pronouns appear in blue type and their antecedents appear in blue italic type. Notice that they agree in both number and gender.

EXAMPLE *Samuel Clemens* used Mark Twain as **his** pseudonym. [singular masculine pronoun]

EXAMPLE *Mary Anne Evans* used George Eliot as **her** pseudonym. [singular feminine pronoun]

EXAMPLE Dogwood *blossoms* are admired for **their** beauty. [plural pronoun]

EXAMPLE I subscribe to this *magazine* for **its** monthly column on writing. [singular neuter pronoun]

Traditionally, a masculine pronoun was used when the gender of an antecedent was not known or might be either masculine or feminine. When you are reading literature written before the 1970s, remember that *his* may mean *his,* it may mean *her,* or it may mean *his or her.*

EXAMPLE A careful *diver* checks **his** equipment before each dive.

This usage has changed, however. Many people now feel that the use of masculine pronouns excludes half of humanity.

Use gender-neutral language when the gender is unknown or could be either masculine or feminine. Here are three ways to avoid using a masculine pronoun when the antecedent may be feminine:

1. Use *his or her, he or she,* and so on.
2. Make the antecedent plural and use a plural pronoun.
3. Eliminate the pronoun.

EXAMPLE A careful *diver* checks **his or her** equipment before each dive.

EXAMPLE Careful *divers* check **their** equipment before each dive.

EXAMPLE A careful *diver* checks **the** equipment before each dive. [no pronoun]

Gender-Neutral Pronoun-Antecedent Agreement

Rewrite each sentence in three different ways, using gender-neutral language.

EXAMPLE A writer must work to express his ideas well.

Answer: A writer must work to express his or her ideas well.

Writers must work to express their ideas well.

A writer must work to express ideas well.

1. A coach must earn his team's respect.
2. A good teacher often spends hours preparing to teach her class.
3. A doctor must gain his patients' trust.
4. Does every senator do favors for his contributors?
5. A game warden must keep his eye out for poachers.

When the antecedent of a pronoun is a **collective noun,** the number of the pronoun depends on whether the collective noun is meant to be singular or plural.

EXAMPLE The ***team*** plays **its** last game of the season. **[The collective noun *team* conveys the singular sense of one unit. Therefore, the singular pronoun *its* is used.]**

EXAMPLE The ***team*** argue among **themselves** about **their** batting order. **[The collective noun *team* conveys the plural sense of several people with different opinions. Therefore, the plural reflexive pronoun *themselves* and the plural personal pronoun *their* are used.]**

EXAMPLE The ***orchestra*** play **their** instruments with passion. **[The collective noun *orchestra* is being used in the plural sense of several people performing separate actions. Therefore, the plural pronoun *their* is used.]**

EXAMPLE The **orchestra** gives **its** best performance of the year.
[The collective noun *orchestra* is being used in the singular sense of one single group working together. Therefore, the singular pronoun *its* is used.]

PRACTICE Agreement with Collective Nouns

Write the correct pronoun from the choices in parentheses. Then write the collective noun that is the subject of each sentence and tell whether it is singular or plural in the sentence.

EXAMPLE The jury is always accompanied by a bailiff on (its, their) way to the courtroom.

Answer: its, jury, singular

1. My group always disagree about where to eat (its, their) lunches.
2. The all-star team from my hometown lost (its, their) will to win before the final game of the tournament.
3. The Supreme Court handed down (its, their) opinion on the last day of the session.
4. The city council voted (its, their) consciences.
5. The flock of geese found (its, their) way south.

A pronoun must agree in **person** (first, second, or third person) with its antecedent.

Don't use *you*, a second-person pronoun, to refer to an antecedent in the third person. Either change *you* to an appropriate third-person pronoun or replace it with a suitable noun.

EXAMPLE **POOR** Linda and Soo will visit Spain, where **you** can see Arabic architecture.

BETTER Linda and Soo will visit Spain, where **they** can see Arabic architecture.

| BETTER | Linda and Soo will visit Spain, where **visitors** can see Arabic architecture. |

When the antecedent of a pronoun is another pronoun, be sure that the two pronouns agree in person. Avoid unnecessary shifts from *they* to *you, I* to *you,* or *one* to *you.*

EXAMPLE	POOR	**They** love to walk the forest trails, where **you** can hear the birds singing.
	BETTER	**They** love to walk the forest trails, where **they** can hear the birds singing.
EXAMPLE	POOR	**I** visited the coast of Maine, where **you** can go on a whale watch.
	BETTER	**I** visited the coast of Maine, where **I** was able to go on a whale watch.
EXAMPLE	POOR	When **one** teaches something to a child, **you** can learn a lot.
	BETTER	When **one** teaches something to a child, **one** can learn a lot.
	BETTER	When **you** teach something to a child, **you** can learn a lot.

PRACTICE Agreement in Person

Rewrite each item, correcting the inappropriate use of you *by substituting a third-person pronoun or a suitable noun.*

EXAMPLE   Amateur chefs can take cooking classes, where you can learn professional techniques.

       Answer: Amateur chefs can take cooking classes, where they can learn professional techniques.

1. He watches the kind of shows that make you double over with laughter.

2. Ms. Horner likes to go to the corner diner, where you can get a great plum pie.

3. I went to a resort where you can play golf and tennis.
4. If one has determination, you can do great things.
5. I love to get up early because you can get so much done before leaving for school.

An **indefinite pronoun** must agree with its antecedent in **number.** Use a singular personal pronoun when the antecedent is a singular indefinite pronoun. Use a plural personal pronoun when the antecedent is a plural indefinite pronoun.

INDEFINITE PRONOUNS

ALWAYS SINGULAR	another anybody anyone anything each	either everybody everyone everything much	neither no one nobody nothing one	other somebody someone something
ALWAYS PLURAL	both	few	many	others	several
SINGULAR OR PLURAL	all	any	enough	most	none	some

EXAMPLE   *Each* of the women had to put **her** suitcase in storage.

EXAMPLE   *One* of the men brought **his** antique abacus.

EXAMPLE   *Many* of the dentists have **their** own X-ray equipment.

Note that the plural nouns in the prepositional phrases—*of the women, of the men*—don't affect the number of the personal pronouns. *Her* and *his* are singular because *each* and *one*, their antecedents, are singular.

When no gender is specified, use gender-neutral wording.

EXAMPLE   **Everyone** must bring **his or her** own lunch.

GRAMMAR/USAGE/MECHANICS

If you find the preceding sentence a bit awkward, the best solution may be to reword the sentence. You might use a plural indefinite pronoun or a suitable noun (such as *people*) to replace the singular indefinite pronoun. You might even eliminate the personal pronoun entirely.

EXAMPLE   ***All*** must bring **their** own lunches.

EXAMPLE   ***People*** must bring **their** own lunches.

EXAMPLE   ***Everyone*** must bring **a** lunch. **[no pronoun]**

PRACTICE   **Gender-Neutral Agreement with Indefinite Pronoun Antecedents**

Rewrite each sentence in three ways, using gender-neutral language.

EXAMPLE   Each student must identify his topic.

Answer: Each student must identify his or her topic.
All students must identify their topics.
Each student must identify a topic.

1. Anyone who lost his backpack should check the office.
2. Everybody raised his hand.
3. Each of the workers has to turn in his timesheet.
4. Everyone should train his dog to behave properly.
5. Will someone volunteer to demonstrate his project?

7.7 CLEAR PRONOUN REFERENCE

Make sure that the antecedent of a pronoun is clearly stated. Make sure that a pronoun cannot possibly refer to more than one antecedent.

VAGUE PRONOUN REFERENCE

To avoid a **vague pronoun reference,** don't use the pronoun *this, that, which, it, any,* or *one* without a clearly stated antecedent.

EXAMPLE **VAGUE** Gwendolyn Brooks was a creative and gifted writer, and **this** is apparent from her poetry. **[What is apparent from Brooks's poetry? Her talent is apparent, but *talent* is not specifically mentioned in the sentence.]**

CLEAR Gwendolyn Brooks was a creative and gifted writer, and **her talent** is apparent from her poetry.

EXAMPLE **VAGUE** In 1906 many buildings in San Francisco burned, **which** was caused by the great earthquake of April 18. **[What was caused by the earthquake? A fire was caused, but the word *fire* does not appear in the sentence.]**

CLEAR In 1906 a fire, **which** was caused by the great earthquake of April 18, burned many buildings in San Francisco.

PRACTICE Clear Pronoun Reference

Rewrite each item, replacing vague pronouns with specific words.

1. I wrote to complain about the product, but the company never answered it.
2. People should read poetry before they try to get one published.
3. The Eccentric Professor Bookshop had a big sale the other day, but I didn't need any.

4. The other team was much bigger than our team, which made us nervous.

5. Nageen was a traditional folk singer; it was beautiful to hear.

UNCLEAR AND INDEFINITE PRONOUN REFERENCE

If a pronoun seems to refer to more than one antecedent, either reword the sentence to make the antecedent clear or eliminate the pronoun.

EXAMPLE	UNCLEAR ANTECEDENT	When Mrs. Baines told Lisa not to drive to school again, **she** was upset. [Which word is the antecedent of *she*? Is Mrs. Baines upset or is Lisa?]
	CLEAR ANTECEDENT	Mrs. Baines was upset when **she** told Lisa not to drive to school again.
	NO PRONOUN	When Mrs. Baines told Lisa not to drive to school again, **Mrs. Baines** was upset.

The pronouns *it, you,* and *they* should not be used as if they were indefinite pronouns. Instead, you should name the performer of the action. In some cases, you may be able to reword the sentence in such a way that you do not name the performer of the action and you do not use a pronoun.

EXAMPLE	INDEFINITE	In college **you** learn to be independent.
	CLEAR	In college **students** learn to be independent.
EXAMPLE	INDEFINITE	In some neighborhoods, **they** pick up the garbage twice a week.
	CLEAR	In some neighborhoods, the garbage **is picked up** twice a week.

EXAMPLE **INDEFINITE** In *Healthy Teen* magazine, **it** suggests eating more than four servings of vegetables each day.

CLEAR ***Healthy Teen*** magazine suggests eating more than four servings of vegetables each day.

PRACTICE Correcting Unclear and Indefinite Pronoun Reference

Rewrite each sentence, correcting any unclear or indefinite pronoun references.

EXAMPLE On most airplanes and trains, you cannot play loud music.

Answer: On most airplanes and trains, people cannot play loud music.

1. My brother looks like Michael Jordan, except that he has a shaved head.

2. Lena told Ms. Hahm that she didn't understand math.

3. To get out rust stains, you can use lemon juice.

4. Where I come from, they don't believe in wearing ties to dinner.

5. On the other side of the fence stood a horse; it was made of old wooden planks.

PRACTICE Proofreading

Rewrite the following passage, correcting errors in spelling, capitalization, grammar, and usage. Add any missing punctuation. Write legibly to be sure one letter is not mistaken for another. There are ten mistakes.

Frida Kahlo

[1]Frida Kahlo was born in a suburb of Mexico City. [2]Her grandfather was from Hungary, but her grandmother and him lived in Mexico. [3]As a

young child Frida came down with polio. ⁴Then during her teenage years, she was criticly injured in a bus accident. ⁵Illness and injuries cause you to spend many years in bed. ⁶During her recovery, she spent a great deal of time painting, and they were remarkable.

⁷Frida married Diego Rivera one of Mexico's most famous painters. ⁸They say that there were few people at that time who were as important to Mexico's artistic and cultural life as Diego and her. ⁹Frida sold few of her paintings, choosing instead to give it to friends. ¹⁰Recently Frida Kahlo's paintings have become popular. ¹¹Today, many years after her death, one painting may sell for as much as a million dollars. ¹²More importantly, Frida Kahlo has become a symbol of strength and freedom for Hispanics, women, and whomever loves art anywhere in the world.

POSTTEST   Identifying the Correct Pronoun

For each sentence, write the correct pronoun from the choices in parentheses.

1. The car stopped before it ran over Sid and (I, me).
2. He and (they, them) met at the convenience store after school.
3. My friends and (she, her) tried to get us to agree.
4. (We, Us) artists enjoy our lives even though we don't have much money.
5. (Who, Whom) is going to the baseball game with the youth group?
6. Lucilla is a far better driver than (I, me).
7. Everyone needs to make sure (his or her, their) permission slip is signed.
8. The game pleased Rocco as much as it depressed Danny and (I, me).
9. The judge ordered both defendants, Phoebe and (he, him), to perform community service.
10. Although I expected Carlos to be late, (him, his) arriving after the game completely surprised me.

11. The director demanded that (we, us) actors learn our lines before the first rehearsal.

12. Is that message meant for Ricardo or (me, myself)?

13. Katie and Kitty wanted to do it by (theirselves, themselves) this time.

14. Except for you and (I, me), there is nobody that can carry a tune in the play.

15. The best person for the job is (she, her).

16. You wanted to know who bought the flowers; well, it was (I, me).

17. I like getting the newsletter because I'm interested in (its, their) articles.

18. His dad wants George and (she, her) to work in the family hardware store on the weekends.

19. The people coming to the picnic should bring (his or her, their) own food.

20. From (who, whom) did you receive that beautiful necklace of dandelions?

21. Are you sure that both (he and she, him and her) are coming?

22. (Who, Whom) is going with (who, whom)?

23. Either of (we, us) two could be the one that you are looking for.

24. Our neighbors have a much larger garage than (we, us).

25. I think I'm going to go get (me, myself) another one of those baked potatoes.

Chapter 8

Using Modifiers Correctly

• • • • • • • • • • • • • • • •

PRETEST **Using Modifiers Correctly**

For each sentence, write the correct word or words from the choices in parentheses.

1. I like both of the frozen yogurt flavors in the cafeteria, but I like the chocolate (better, best).
2. The car Tommy always wants to drive is the (fast, faster, fastest) of our two cars.
3. All my friends are smart, but I'd have to say that Joan is (smarter, smartest).
4. It is (far, farther, further) to Lake Tahoe than to Reno.
5. The (bad, worse, worst) movie I ever saw was *Isadora*.
6. My mother always says that I should be careful not to behave (bad, badly) in public.

7. Sheila says that helping flood victims was the (more rewarding, most rewarding) experience of her life.

8. As the youngest of the four children, Madeleine was also the (littler, littlest).

9. This poem is a (more perfect, more nearly perfect) example of the sonnet form than the other.

10. Many primates use tools (good, well).

11. That is truly the (most smelly, smelliest) pair of socks I've ever come across!

12. Sam was the (less, least) agile gymnast on the twelve-person team.

13. Of the Mississippi and the Amazon, which is the (more long, longer) river?

14. Of the three puppies, Inga thought the spotted one was (cuter, cutest).

15. The right side of the table is (more weak, weaker) than the left.

PRETEST **Correcting Incomplete Comparisons, Double Negatives, and Misplaced and Dangling Modifiers**

Rewrite each sentence, correcting any errors.

16. Simon was the most happiest kid in the entire class this morning.

17. Gliding smoothly through the air, the crowd watched the balloon.

18. It really don't make no difference to me.

19. Ripe plums are more softer than unripe ones.

20. A border collie is smarter than any dog.

21. My aunt Sylvania is more reserved than anyone in the world.

22. He's mean, and I don't want nothing to do with him.

23. The pilot only talks on the loudspeaker when there's a problem.

24. The house next door is larger than across the street.

25. The trailer flew up in the air propelled by the tornado.

26. The woman took the cell phone from her bag because it was ringing.

27. Ovid's mother told him when he was out to be polite.

28. There isn't no way I'm going near that cave.

29. Nicely browned and dripping with juices, we found the turkey irresistible.

30. A horse's back is stronger than a man.

8.1 THE THREE DEGREES OF COMPARISON

Most adjectives and adverbs have three degrees: the positive, or base, form; the comparative form; and the superlative form.

The **positive** form of a modifier cannot be used to make a comparison. (This form appears as the entry word in a dictionary.)

The **comparative** form of a modifier shows two things being compared.

The **superlative** form of a modifier shows three or more things being compared.

EXAMPLES	POSITIVE	This computer is **fast.**
		I ran **slowly.**
EXAMPLES	COMPARATIVE	This computer is **faster** than that one.
		I ran **more slowly** than my friend.
EXAMPLES	SUPERLATIVE	Of these three computers, this one is the **fastest** machine.
		I ran **most slowly** of all.

In general, for one-syllable modifiers, add -*er* to form the comparative and -*est* to form the superlative.

EXAMPLE small, small**er,** small**est**
My cousin's room is **smaller** than mine.
That is the **smallest** dog I have ever seen.

For some words, adding -er and -est requires spelling changes.

EXAMPLE   late, lat**er,** lat**est**

EXAMPLE   flat, fla**tter,** fla**ttest**

EXAMPLE   merry, merr**ier,** merr**iest**

With some one-syllable modifiers, it may sound more natural to use *more* and *most* instead of -er and -est.

EXAMPLE   apt, **more** apt, **most** apt

EXAMPLE   I am **more apt** to drink diet soda than you are.

For most two-syllable adjectives, add -er to form the comparative and -est to form the superlative.

EXAMPLE   friendly, friendl**ier,** friendl**iest**

That parrot is **friendlier** than this one.

This cockatoo is the **friendliest** bird here.

If -er and -est sound awkward with a two-syllable adjective, use *more* and *most* instead.

EXAMPLE   prudent, **more** prudent, **most** prudent

My father's new business plan is **more prudent** than his old plan.

In general, for adverbs ending in -ly, use *more* and *most* to form the comparative and superlative degrees.

EXAMPLE   sweetly, **more** sweetly, **most** sweetly

Of my three friends, I think Jane sings **most sweetly.**

For modifiers of three or more syllables, always use *more* and *most* to form the comparative and superlative degrees.

EXAMPLE   significant, **more** significant, **most** significant

These data are the **most significant** ones for our future research.

Less and *least,* the opposite of *more* and *most,* can also be used with most modifiers to show comparison.

EXAMPLE   You used to be **less thoughtful** than you are now.

EXAMPLE   This salad is the **least fattening** thing on the menu.

Less and *least* are used before modifiers that have any number of syllables.

Some adjectives, such as *unique, perfect, final, dead,* and *square,* cannot logically be compared because they describe an absolute condition. For instance, something is or is not perfect, so it would be impossible for a thing to be more perfect than another thing. However, you can sometimes use *more nearly* and *most nearly* with absolute modifiers.

EXAMPLE   Clara's rug is **more nearly square** than Paula's.

EXAMPLE   The form of that sonnet is the **most nearly perfect** one I have ever seen.

PRACTICE   **The Three Degrees of Comparison**

Rewrite each sentence to correct the error in comparison. If the sentence is already correct, write C.

1. Between Ronald and Frank, I think Ronald is the most polite boy.
2. Peter is worser at typing than I am.
3. I've been changing my mind, but now I've made my most final decision.
4. Among gorillas, the alpha male is usually strongest than the others.

5. Juan has a unique way of looking at things.

6. Malika is the most perfect person I know.

7. The sun shone warmlier today than yesterday.

8. My essay is longer than yours.

9. Julio was the older of the three brothers.

10. Wei is the intelligentest person in his class.

8.2 IRREGULAR COMPARISONS

A few modifiers form their comparative and superlative degrees irregularly. It is most helpful simply to memorize their forms.

MODIFIERS WITH IRREGULAR FORMS OF COMPARISON

POSITIVE	COMPARATIVE	SUPERLATIVE
good	better	best
well	better	best
bad	worse	worst
badly	worse	worst
ill	worse	worst
far (distance)	farther	farthest
far (degree, time)	further	furthest
little (amount)	less	least
many	more	most
much	more	most

Write the correct comparison from the choices in parentheses.

1. He speaks (less, littler) than any other candidate.
2. When I disappointed my father, I felt (worse, worst) than I ever have.
3. Go no (further, farther) along that road.
4. The prematurely born baby is doing much (better, best).
5. Of steak and chicken, Harold likes steak (less, least).
6. The Crusades happened (farther, further) back in time than the Enlightenment.
7. Of all our sodas, people buy the orange one (more, most) often.
8. Some days Tyler feels quite ill; other days he feels (weller, better).
9. There are many types of birds and even (more, much) types of insects.
10. The concert I saw last night was performed (badder, worse) than the last one.

8.3 CORRECTING DOUBLE COMPARISONS

Don't use both *-er* and *more.* Don't use both *-est* and *most.* To do so would be an error called a **double comparison.**

EXAMPLE	INCORRECT	Chimpanzees are more smaller than gorillas.
	CORRECT	Chimpanzees are **smaller** than gorillas.
EXAMPLE	INCORRECT	That is the most saddest song on the album.
	CORRECT	That is the **saddest** song on the album.
EXAMPLE	INCORRECT	She is the most attractivest girl in school.
	CORRECT	She is the **most attractive** girl in school.

Rewrite each sentence to correct the error in comparison. If the sentence is already correct, write C.

1. The sky today is the most brightest I have ever seen.
2. Hector knew that he was more quicker than Jason.
3. Everyone who caught the virus felt ill, but Mickey felt most worst.
4. The electric guitar was the most loudest instrument in the band.
5. Amy thought that Zelda was more prettier than Eliza.
6. This film is more frightening than the last one I saw.
7. June 21 is the most longest day of the year.
8. Mount Rushmore is more bigger than most other sculptures.
9. That type is the more abundant of the two wildflowers.
10. This work is the most hardest I've ever done.

8.4 CORRECTING INCOMPLETE COMPARISONS

Do not make an incomplete or unclear comparison by omitting the word *other* or the word *else* when you compare a person or thing with its group.

EXAMPLE	UNCLEAR	New York City has more skyscrapers than any city in the United States. [*Any city* includes *New York City*.]
	CLEAR	New York City has more skyscrapers than any **other** city in the United States.
EXAMPLE	UNCLEAR	Juanita received more gifts than anyone. [*Anyone* includes *Juanita*.]
	CLEAR	Juanita received more gifts than anyone **else.**

Be sure your comparisons are between like things—that is, similar things.

EXAMPLE	UNCLEAR	The salary of a teacher is lower than a lawyer. **[The salary of a teacher is being compared illogically with a person, namely, a lawyer.]**
	CLEAR	The salary of a teacher is lower than **that of a lawyer.**
	CLEAR	The salary of a teacher is lower than **the salary of a lawyer.**
	CLEAR	A teacher's salary is lower than **a lawyer's.** **[The word *salary* is understood after *lawyer's.*]**

PRACTICE Correcting Incomplete Comparisons

Rewrite each sentence, correcting the error in comparison. If a sentence is already correct, write C.

1. Over a short distance, the speed of a quarter horse exceeds a thoroughbred.
2. My dog's fur is thicker than my cat.
3. Saturn has more rings than any planet in our solar system.
4. The number buttons on my telephone are easier to see than yours.
5. A cow's stomach is much larger than a horse.
6. You can see that our house is smaller than any other in our neighborhood.
7. The color of your shoes is different from your socks.
8. Sherpas are better mountain climbers than anyone.
9. Lhasa is at a higher elevation than any other city in the world.
10. Do you agree that the ermine has prettier fur than any animal?

GRAMMAR/USAGE/MECHANICS

Rewrite each sentence, correcting the error in comparison. If a sentence is already correct, write C. *Consult a dictionary if necessary.*

1. I was more hungrier than I had ever been.
2. Mallory loved *Little Women* more than any book she had read.
3. The doctor was the best in the hospital.
4. My cousin Clara is the most bravest human being I've ever met.
5. The South Pole is farthest from civilization than any other place on earth.
6. My sister Wendy is much more short than her best friend, Gavin.
7. It's pretty clear that a fireman's job is more dangerous than a secretary.
8. Some mountains are higher than others.
9. I am more sleepier now than I ever was.
10. The North Star is the brighter star in the night sky.

8.5 *GOOD* OR *WELL; BAD* OR *BADLY*

Always use *good* as an adjective. *Well* may be used as an adverb of manner telling how ably or how adequately something is done. *Well* may also be used as an adjective meaning "in good health."

EXAMPLE   Jaleel is a **good** guitarist. [adjective]

EXAMPLE   Your new perfume smells **good**. [adjective after a linking verb]

EXAMPLE   I feel **good** when I hear our song. [adjective after a linking verb]

EXAMPLE Aziza plays the violin **well.** [adverb of manner]

EXAMPLE She isn't feeling **well.** [adjective meaning "in good health"]

Always use *bad* as an adjective. Use *badly* as an adverb.

EXAMPLE The quarterback made a **bad** throw. [adjective]

EXAMPLE That meat tastes **bad.** [adjective after a linking verb]

EXAMPLE I feel **bad** about my mistake. [adjective after a linking verb]

EXAMPLE This pitcher is leaking **badly.** [adverb after an action verb]

PRACTICE   *Good or Well; Bad or Badly*

Rewrite each sentence, correcting all errors in comparison. If a sentence is already correct, write C.

1. She planned the garden good, and it looks beautiful.
2. The gallery framed my painting very bad.
3. The ground squirrel has adapted quite well to living outside trees.
4. I'm afraid to ask my doctor what he thinks of my condition for fear that he'll say, "It looks badly."
5. You were awfully sick yesterday; are you sure you're feeling good today?
6. The cat was behaving bad around the kitten.
7. Lawrence looks really good in red, but yellow looks bad on him.
8. Whenever I ask Salvador how he is, he always replies, "I'm doing well."
9. The casserole Kerry made last night tasted well.
10. The cooked cabbage smelled badly.

Give the comparative and superlative forms of each modifier. Consult a dictionary if necessary.

1. slowly
2. badly
3. adequate
4. loud
5. exuberant

6. close
7. round
8. cloudy
9. well
10. gentle

Frank and Ernest

INSECT GRAMMAR

TERMITE TERMITIER TERMITIEST

© 1996 Thaves / Reprinted with permission. Newspaper dist. by NEA, Inc.

GRAMMAR/USAGE/MECHANICS

8.6 CORRECTING DOUBLE NEGATIVES

Don't use two or more negative words to express the same idea. To do so is an error called a **double negative.** Use only one negative word to express a negative idea.

EXAMPLE	**INCORRECT**	I didn't hear no thunder.
	CORRECT	I did**n't** hear **any** thunder.
	CORRECT	I heard **no** thunder.
EXAMPLE	**INCORRECT**	She hasn't had no visitors.
	CORRECT	She has**n't** had **any** visitors.
	CORRECT	She has had **no** visitors.

EXAMPLE	INCORRECT	He never eats no ice cream.
	CORRECT	He **never** eats **any** ice cream.
	CORRECT	He eats **no** ice cream.

The words *hardly* and *scarcely* are negative words. Don't use them with other negative words, such as *not*.

EXAMPLES	INCORRECT	I didn't hardly look at the map.
		There isn't scarcely enough time for lunch.
	CORRECT	I **hardly** looked at the map.
		There is **scarcely** enough time for lunch.

PRACTICE Correcting Double Negatives

Revise each sentence that has a double negative. When possible, show two or more correct revisions. If a sentence is already correct, write C.

1. I'm not going to eat no more of that cake.
2. Willa didn't hardly ever need to work to succeed.
3. All night long, Harvey hasn't scarcely looked at the algebra assignment.
4. I never told nobody about our secret.
5. Don't give me any more trouble, or you'll never hear the end of it.
6. Callandra didn't find no ring that fit her.
7. Napoleon was offered his choice of fruit, but he didn't want none.
8. I know scarcely anything at all about the situation.
9. I didn't have no time to get to the train.
10. Arthur never fails to listen to his elders; he is a good boy.

8.7 CORRECTING MISPLACED AND DANGLING MODIFIERS

Misplaced modifiers modify the wrong word, or they seem to modify more than one word in a sentence.

Place modifiers as close as possible to the words they modify in order to make the meaning of the sentence clear.

EXAMPLES

MISPLACED   At the last meeting, the mayor discussed the enormous cost of filling in the Westfields Gorge **with city council members.** [prepositional phrase incorrectly modifying *filling in*]

CLEAR   At the last meeting, the mayor discussed **with city council members** the enormous cost of filling in the Westfields Gorge. [prepositional phrase correctly modifying *discussed*]

MISPLACED   **Running smoothly and easily,** the crowd watched the marathoners. [participial phrase incorrectly modifying *crowd*]

CORRECT   The crowd watched the marathoners **running smoothly and easily.** [participial phrase correctly modifying *marathoners*]

Sometimes a misplaced modifier can be corrected by revising the sentence, for example, rephrasing the main clause or adding a subordinate clause.

EXAMPLE

MISPLACED   **Blowing from the north,** the pines were tossed by the wind. [participial phrase incorrectly modifying *pines*]

CLEAR	The pines were tossed by the wind, **which blew from the north.** [participial phrase recast as a subordinate clause correctly modifying *wind*]
CLEAR	**Blowing from the north,** the wind tossed the pines. [After the main clause has been recast, the participial phrase correctly modifies *wind*.]

Place the adverb *only* immediately before the word or group of words that it modifies.

If *only* is not positioned correctly in a sentence, the meaning of the sentence may be unclear.

EXAMPLE	UNCLEAR	Ainsley **only** has music class on Tuesday. [Does Ainsley have only one class on Tuesday, or does he have music class on no other day than Tuesday, or is Ainsley the only person (in a group) who has one class on Tuesday?]
	CLEAR	Ainsley has **only** music class on Tuesday. [He has no other class that day.]
	CLEAR	Ainsley has music class **only** on Tuesday. [He does not have music class on any other day.]
	CLEAR	**Only** Ainsley has music class on Tuesday. [No one else has music class on Tuesday.]

Dangling modifiers seem logically to modify no word at all. To correct a sentence that has a dangling modifier, you must supply a word that the dangling modifier can sensibly modify.

EXAMPLES	DANGLING	**Using high-powered binoculars,** the lost child was found. [participial phrase logically modifying no word in the sentence]

CLEAR	Using high-powered binoculars, the rescuers found the lost child. [participial phrase correctly modifying *rescuers*]
CLEAR	The rescuers found the lost child **because they used high-powered binoculars.** [subordinate clause modifying *found*]
DANGLING	**Celebrating my victory,** a dinner with my friends lasted till midnight. [participial phrase logically modifying no word in the sentence]
CLEAR	**Celebrating my victory,** my friends and I stayed at the dinner table till midnight. [participial phrase modifying *my friends and I*]

PRACTICE Correcting Misplaced and Dangling Modifiers

Rewrite each sentence, correcting the misplaced and dangling modifiers.

1. Not seeing the pothole, the skateboard went flying.
2. My cousin went on and on, describing the details of her wedding in the elevator.
3. The guide found the lion following its trail.
4. The trapeze artist only slipped once.
5. We saw the dinosaurs on a field trip to the natural history museum.
6. I jumped on a train that was going to Boston by mistake.
7. We only watched the first part of the movie.
8. Driving the old car, the brakes gave out.

9. Watching the documentary, the television went dead.

10. Realizing it was after 9:00, Mrs. Risen told her daughter that she should go to bed.

PRACTICE Proofreading

Rewrite the following passage, correcting errors in spelling, capitalization, grammar, and usage. Add any missing punctuation. Write legibly to be sure one letter is not mistaken for another. There are ten mistakes.

Stephen Sondheim

[1]Stephen Sondheim is one of the most famousest songwriters in American musical theater. [2]He was born in New York City in 1930. [3]At the age of ten, his parents divorced, and he went with his mother to live in Pennsylvania. [4]There he got to know Oscar Hammerstein II another great American songwriter. [5]Hammerstein taught him many basics of writing for the musical theater. [6]Sondheim graduated from Williams college and then studied in New York with the composer Milton Babbitt.

[7]In hardly no time, Sondheim was a major success. [8]At the age of twenty-five, he wrote the lyrics for West Side Story. [9]At once, he was one of the respectedest lyricists in town. [10]His songs are not like any other lyricist. [11]They express what people really feel and think. [12]His choice of words and his rhymes are interesting and complex, and so is his music.

[13]For many years now, Sondheim writes complete musicals. [14]He writes the music, the song lyrics, and the dialog for the characters. [15]He is surely one of the most greatest musical talents in modern times.

POSTTEST Using Modifiers Correctly

For each sentence, write the correct word or words from the choices in parentheses.

1. Fast food tastes good, but homemade food tastes (better, best).

2. Octavio is feeling (more worse, worse) now that his fever is higher.

3. Juanita and Cheryl are competing to see who is the (more, most) athletic.

4. The more cola that kid drinks, the (more silly, sillier) he gets.

5. Although you're sick, you don't look too (bad, badly).

6. This swimming pool is the (deeper, deepest) that I have ever seen.

7. Marabelle gets away with doing (less, the least) of all of us, while still getting (more, the most) allowance.

8. Athletes are pushing their bodies (further, furthest) than they did in the past.

9. Mandy's current artwork is (less, least) appealing than what she used to do.

10. Syd thinks that Ellis is the (more, most) accomplished poet of the three Buckner brothers.

11. Laser surgery is (more precise, most precise) than operating on someone with a scalpel.

12. What is the (most low, lowest) form of life?

13. Today, I feel really (well, good) about myself.

14. If Janet keeps working on her stamina, soon she will be able to run much (farther, further) than Mitzi can.

15. A new house is probably (more square, more nearly square) than an old one.

POSTTEST Correcting Incomplete Comparisons, Double Negatives, and Misplaced and Dangling Modifiers

Rewrite each sentence, correcting any errors.

16. Oswald and Hildegard found the flowers hiking up the mountain.

17. Donnel, who doesn't have no willpower, couldn't never stick to no budget.

18. Stitching the quilt, the pattern became obvious to me.

19. Stewart won't get scarcely any relief from this heat until he gets a fan.

20. I found my missing baseball glove cleaning my room.

21. I love my nephews and nieces more than anyone in the world.

22. A dolphin is smarter than any sea mammal.

23. Clattering in the wind, the storm broke the shutters off the house.

24. Tameka's dancing is better than a professional.

25. The hyenas ate the gazelle with long teeth shining in the African sun.

26. Don't try to pat the dog on the porch that is growling.

27. "I only have one other point to add," remarked the speaker.

28. The photojournalist took a picture of a demonstrator with a long lens camera.

29. If properly cooked, everyone will like this meal.

30. I can't hardly think of anything else to say.

Chapter 9

Diagraming Sentences

• • • • • • • • • • • • • •

PRETEST Diagraming Sentences

Diagram each sentence.

1. Dinner awaits.
2. Neither Frank nor Elsbeth works.
3. The older dog sleeps longer.
4. That question really stumped me.
5. Nehru was India's first prime minister.
6. The presidential candidate, a senator from Maine, is a Republican.
7. The policeman was both angry and suspicious.
8. While Joe rewound the video, we decided to fix some popcorn.
9. Skiing was hard for me.
10. Polishing the silver, Reginald prepared the heirloom.
11. A house pet may be a dog, or it may be a cat.
12. Whenever he is gone, we lose the game.
13. Everyone loves a baby who smiles and coos.
14. There are eleven players on a football team.

15. That everyone came for Sunday dinner pleased my mother.

16. Her knapsack heavily laden, Alana struggled up the steps.

17. This check is for whoever finishes the job.

18. The general moved the troops to safety while he could, and then he planned his next attack.

19. The principal asked when I planned to graduate.

20. Vito, canceling the next meeting is a bad idea.

9.1 DIAGRAMING SIMPLE AND COMPOUND SENTENCES

A **sentence diagram** shows how the various words and parts of a sentence function in the sentence and relate to the sentence as a whole.

It is vital to know the parts of a sentence before you begin diagraming. Diagraming just gives you a visual picture of how these parts relate to one another.

When writing a sentence in a diagram, retain the capitalization but leave out the punctuation.

SUBJECTS AND VERBS

Start your diagram with a horizontal line, called a baseline, bisected by a vertical line. Find the simple subject of the sentence and place it on the left of the vertical line; then place the simple predicate to the right of the vertical line.

EXAMPLE   Trees grow.

| Trees | grow |

A sentence with an understood subject is diagramed in the same way; however, the understood subject is placed in parentheses.

EXAMPLE   Hurry!

| (you) | Hurry |

Diagram each sentence.

1. Scatter!
2. Monkeys can climb.
3. Do you mind?
4. Grandpa has been skiing.
5. Henry shifted.

COMPOUND SUBJECTS AND COMPOUND VERBS

To diagram compound subjects and compound verbs, follow the example diagram. If a correlative conjunction, such as *both . . . and,* is used, place the introductory conjunction to the left of the dotted line and the second part to the right.

EXAMPLE   Both juries and judges evaluate and decide.

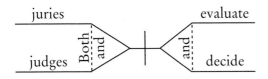

NOUNS OF DIRECT ADDRESS

To diagram nouns of direct address, follow the example diagram.

EXAMPLE   Felix, stay.

Felix

(you) | stay

Diagram each sentence.

1. Dan and Jean sing.
2. Harry, dive and swim!
3. Hurry, class.
4. Either the Democrat or the Republican could win.
5. Yells and screams unnerve and annoy.

ADJECTIVES AND ADVERBS

Both adjectives and adverbs are placed on slanted lines leading from the modified words. If an adverb modifies an adjective or another adverb, the adverb is placed on a slanted line parallel to the adjective or adverb and is connected with a straight line.

EXAMPLE   Young pine trees grow quite fast.

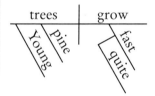

SENTENCES BEGINNING WITH *HERE* OR *THERE*

Here and *there* often function as adverbs when they begin a sentence.

EXAMPLE   Here comes the bus.

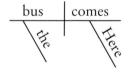

If *there* begins a sentence and does not modify the verb, then it functions as an expletive.

EXAMPLE   There is a new plan.

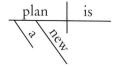

PRACTICE   **Diagraming Adjectives and Adverbs**

Diagram each sentence.

1. The disabled man stood slowly.
2. Misha and Kay bowed gratefully.
3. There is so little time.
4. Are you studying hard?
5. The beautiful, sunny day ended quite peacefully.

DIRECT OBJECTS AND INDIRECT OBJECTS

A direct object appears on the baseline to the right of the verb. The verb and the direct object are separated by a vertical line that does not cross the baseline. Indirect objects are placed on a horizontal line parallel to the baseline and are linked to the verb by a slanted line.

EXAMPLE   Jone gave her mother a gift.

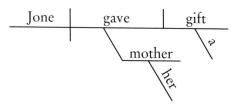

Diagram compound direct and indirect objects in the same way you diagram compound subjects.

EXAMPLE   Kris gave her dog and cat food and attention.

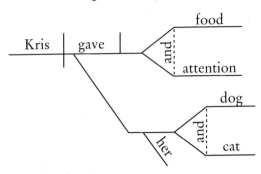

PRACTICE   **Diagraming Direct Objects and Indirect Objects**

Diagram each sentence.

1. Tillie made Alfie a milkshake.
2. Can Martin recite the whole poem?
3. Coach Harris gave Eloise and Deirdre the gym keys and the volleyball equipment.
4. Will you lend me the money?
5. The stylist braided my hair and arranged my new extensions.

SUBJECT COMPLEMENTS AND OBJECT COMPLEMENTS

Subject complements are placed on the baseline to the right of the verb. They are separated from the verb by a slanted line that does not cross the baseline.

EXAMPLE   Whales are mammals.

Whales | are \ mammals

Diagram compound subject complements in the same way you diagram compound subjects.

EXAMPLE Whales are both friendly and intelligent.

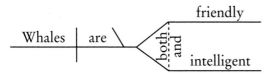

Object complements are diagramed the same way subject complements are, but a direct object comes between the verb and the object complement.

EXAMPLE Critics consider Woolf's books influential.

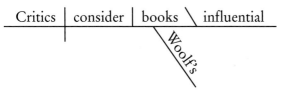

Diagram compound object complements the same way you diagram compound subjects.

EXAMPLE Biographers consider Woolf's life rich but tragic.

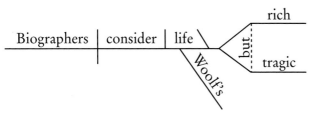

PRACTICE **Diagraming Subject Complements and Object Complements**

Diagram each sentence.

1. I found the play long and dull.
2. Olives are my favorite food.
3. Timothy considers practice important.
4. That attorney is a well-known defense lawyer.
5. The president is the nation's chief executive.

APPOSITIVES AND APPOSITIVE PHRASES

To diagram an appositive, simply place the word in parentheses beside the noun or pronoun it identifies. To diagram an appositive phrase, place the appositive in parentheses and place any modifying words on slanted lines directly beneath the appositive.

EXAMPLE William Shakespeare, the English playwright, was a commoner.

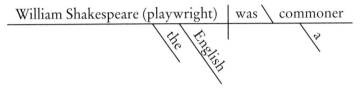

PRACTICE **Diagraming Appositives and Appositive Phrases**

Diagram each sentence.

1. My math teacher, Mr. DeSoto, also teaches shop.
2. Degas, a famous artist, often painted ballerinas.
3. The pack rat, a strange little North American animal, hoards miscellaneous items.
4. American money is green, my favorite color.
5. Darla makes the best éclairs, little custard-filled pastries.

PREPOSITIONAL PHRASES

To diagram prepositional phrases, follow the example diagram.

EXAMPLE Students of history study cultures of the past.

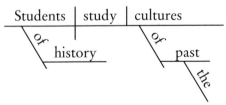

Diagram each sentence.

1. Over the hills, in the next county, lived an old farmer.
2. The little brown house in the forest smelled of gingerbread.
3. Tommy went across the street to the store on the corner.
4. Dogs are barking in all the yards in the neighborhood.
5. Napoleon was sent into exile on the island of Elba.

PARTICIPLES AND PARTICIPIAL PHRASES

To diagram participles and participial phrases, follow the example diagram.

EXAMPLE   Perplexed astronomers continue their work researching the origin of our galaxy.

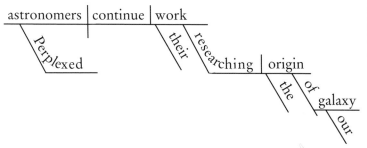

PRACTICE Diagraming Participles
and Participial Phrases

Diagram each sentence.

1. Standing on the cliff, I looked down into the ocean.
2. Frederick snacked throughout the morning, ruining his appetite for lunch.
3. Sneezing, I reached for a tissue.
4. Hector saw a plum falling from a tree.
5. Tired after a hard practice, the football team took a long time changing their clothes.

GRAMMAR/USAGE/MECHANICS

GERUNDS AND GERUND PHRASES

To diagram gerunds and gerund phrases, follow the example diagram.

EXAMPLE Establishing an alibi is one way of proving your innocence.

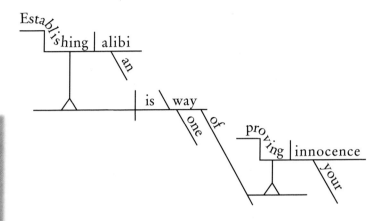

PRACTICE Diagraming Gerunds and Gerund Phrases

Diagram each sentence.

1. At times, I like watching TV.
2. For walking in the forest, boots work best.
3. Sometimes I cannot stop eating chips.
4. Tanning can be bad for your skin.
5. The cadet practiced marching daily.

INFINITIVES AND INFINITIVE PHRASES

If an infinitive or an infinitive phrase functions as an adverb or an adjective, diagram it as you would diagram a prepositional phrase. Infinitives and infinitive phrases functioning as nouns are also diagramed as prepositional phrases are; however, these are placed on stilts.

To restore a historical home is a worthwhile goal.

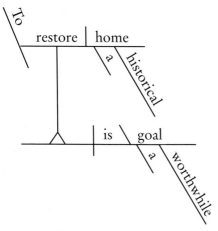

To diagram an infinitive phrase that has a subject, follow the example diagram.

EXAMPLE My father helped me restore my house.

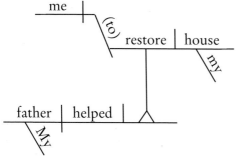

Even though *to* was omitted in the sentence, it is implied and, therefore, is included in the diagram. The parentheses signify the omission in the sentence.

PRACTICE **Diagraming Infinitives and Infinitive Phrases**

Diagram each sentence.

1. The librarian hoped to find all the books.
2. I needed to do something else first.

3. The principal helped the students organize the council elections.
4. Do you really want to go on that ride?
5. To have lunch with you today would be perfect.

ABSOLUTE PHRASES

An absolute phrase is placed above the rest of the sentence and is not connected to it in any way. Place the subject of the phrase on a horizontal line, and connect the participle and any modifiers to the subject of the phrase.

EXAMPLE   Its exterior freshly painted, the house looked almost new.

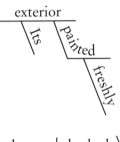

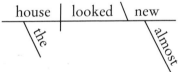

PRACTICE   **Diagraming Absolute Phrases**

Diagram each sentence.

1. The computer broken, George typed his entire term paper by hand.
2. The tree in the field, its old branches twisted, looked pathetic.
3. Mom returning soon, we rushed to rearrange the furniture in the family room.

4. Sally fell asleep on the couch, the cat sprawled happily across her stomach.

5. Dinner completely ruined, we went out to our favorite restaurant.

PRACTICE **Diagraming Phrases**

Diagram each sentence.

1. To photograph a hummingbird at rest was Pat's lifelong dream.

2. In the practice of acupuncture, small needles are stuck into the body of the patient.

3. The Amins invited the Smiths to a barbeque.

4. Walking through the woods, Rebecca and Ben talked.

5. Would you like to go to the beach with me?

6. Robert, my mother's cousin, loves to buy things cheaply.

7. Its surface recently repaired, the road was safer.

8. Waiting for Paige was Keeley's morning ritual.

9. Reaching a small ledge, I lingered awhile to gather energy for the rest of the climb.

10. Art signaled the teacher by putting his pencil down.

GRAMMAR/USAGE/MECHANICS

COMPOUND SENTENCES

A **compound sentence** is two or more simple sentences joined by either a semicolon, a colon, or a comma and a conjunction.

Diagram each main clause of a compound sentence separately. If the clauses are connected by a semicolon or a colon, use a dotted line to connect the verbs of each main clause. If the main clauses are connected by a conjunction, place the conjunction on a solid horizontal line, and connect it to the verbs of each main clause by dotted lines.

EXAMPLE Reading is my favorite pastime, for it is educational and enjoyable.

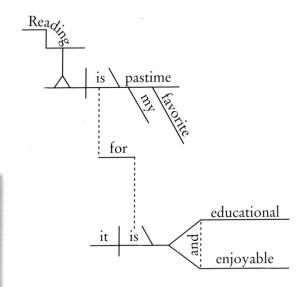

PRACTICE **Diagraming Compound Sentences**

Diagram each sentence.

1. Dogs are mammals, and canaries are birds.
2. This carrot cake tastes very good, but it has too much fat in it.
3. Most monkeys are experts at climbing trees, and they rarely fall.
4. Mrs. Lewis searched the rubble for her photo album, but the tornado had carried it away.
5. Monday of next week is good for me; Tuesday would be even better.

9.2 DIAGRAMING COMPLEX AND COMPOUND-COMPLEX SENTENCES

A **complex sentence** has one main clause and one or more subordinate clauses.

ADJECTIVE CLAUSES

To diagram a complex sentence containing an adjective clause, place the main clause in one diagram and the adjective clause in another diagram beneath it. Use a dotted line to connect the introductory word of the clause to the modified noun or pronoun in the main clause.

EXAMPLE   The author whom you like wrote a novel that is a best-seller.

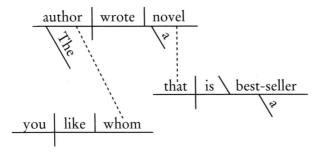

PRACTICE Diagraming Complex Sentences: Adjective Clauses

Diagram each sentence.

1. The baker who made those wonderful French pastries recently retired.
2. The elderly man who lives down the street always mows his own lawn.

3. Is this one of the roads that lead to Rome?

4. I ate the pizza, which had pineapple and ham on it.

5. Sierra phoned her brother, who was babysitting.

ADVERB CLAUSES

To diagram a complex sentence containing an adverb clause, place the adverb clause in a separate diagram beneath the main clause. Connect the two clauses with a diagonal dotted line, on which you will put the subordinating conjunction. The dotted line will connect the verb in the adverb clause to the modified word in the main clause.

EXAMPLE Before she bought her stereo, she researched the market.

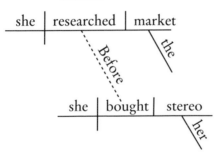

| PRACTICE | **Diagraming Complex Sentences: Adverb Clauses** |

Diagram each sentence.

1. Since I woke up, I have been wanting breakfast.

2. Whenever the children ran after the ball, their dog chased them.

3. The elephant disappeared into thin air while the audience watched in amazement.

4. I am playing ball as soon as I get home from school.

5. We will not rest until everyone has equal rights.

NOUN CLAUSES

Diagram the main clause and place the noun clause on a stilt in its appropriate position. You must identify the function of the introductory word of the noun clause. It may have a function within the noun clause, or it may simply connect the noun clause to the main clause. If the latter is the case, place the introductory word on a line of its own above the verb in the noun clause, connecting it to the verb with a dotted vertical line. If it has a function within the clause, diagram it appropriately.

Noun Clause as Subject

EXAMPLE   Whoever enjoys surfing will like this beach.

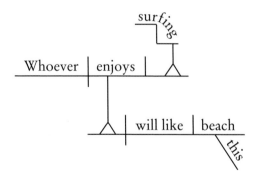

PRACTICE   **Diagraming Noun Clauses as Subjects**

Diagram each sentence.

1. Whatever you want is fine.
2. That I was winning the game wore on Sarah's nerves.

3. That guns do not belong in schools should be very obvious to everyone.
4. Where the asteroid will land is anyone's guess.
5. How the characters will resolve their conflict is still a mystery to me.

Noun Clause as Direct Object

EXAMPLE   I heard that Sheila is moving to Nebraska.

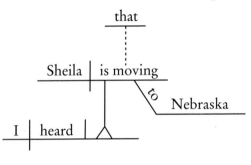

PRACTICE   **Diagraming Noun Clauses as Direct Objects**

Diagram each sentence.

1. Joanne discovered that Greg was in the yard.
2. I will believe whatever I want.
3. Nobody knows who left the door unlocked.
4. The manager will reward whoever makes the most sales during the next month.
5. Tomorrow the director will tell us who is cast in the school play.

Noun Clause as Object of a Preposition

EXAMPLE   This service provides meals for whoever needs them.

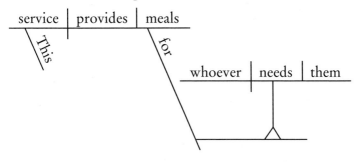

Diagram each sentence.

1. A good lifeguard watches for whoever is having trouble in the water.
2. The manager lectured employees about what she saw in the break room.
3. Mr. Roberts ran from whatever he saw in the cemetery.
4. The food was there for whoever became hungry during the meeting.
5. This story is about what happened to my grandfather during the war.

"I'm the bad grammar fairy. I've just broken all your infinitives and misplaced half your prepositions."

COMPOUND-COMPLEX SENTENCES

A **compound-complex sentence** has two or more main clauses and at least one subordinate clause.

Diagram a compound-complex sentence like you would diagram a compound sentence.

EXAMPLE People who train dogs for a living attend dog shows, and if they win, they receive money.

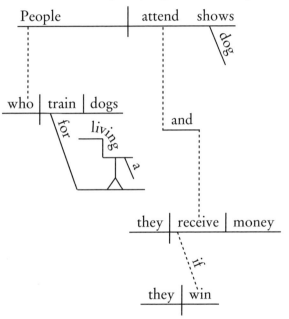

PRACTICE **Diagraming Compound-Complex Sentences**

Diagram each sentence.

1. I have been walking since I awoke this morning, and I am very tired.
2. The harvest mouse climbs slender wheat stalks to feast on the grains, and it uses the stalks to build its nest.

3. Walk after you dine, and aid your digestion.

4. Russia's Czar Peter was a great leader; a little-known fact is that he suffered from epilepsy.

5. After several options had been rejected, I hoped for a quick decision, but the committee delayed action until its next meeting.

POSTTEST Diagraming Sentences

Diagram each sentence.

1. Did you hear?

2. The fans roared and clapped.

3. The orange balloon deflated slowly.

4. There is water at the fountain.

5. Warren offered the girls a ride.

6. Edgar Allan Poe, the famous author, wrote the very scary poem "The Raven."

7. Stacy, remember to stop at the store.

8. The adult lions were resting while the young lions played in the shade of a tree.

9. Checking our e-mail before dinner has become a habit in my family.

10. The plane was due at noon but arrived at three.

11. Puzzled, I looked out the window at the elephant.

12. The car shining, I put the wax away.

13. Why he went to California is not known.

14. There is a protest about what workers should earn.

15. The table still stands although it is very shaky.

16. One mystery is how she got there.

17. Running fast, I caught the bus before it left.

18. Can you help me with this?

19. After she had finished in the library, Stephanie went to her next class, which was in the gym.

20. We know where we are going, but nobody knows how soon we will get there.

Chapter 10

Capitalizing

● ● ● ● ● ● ● ● ● ● ● ● ● ● ● ●

PRETEST **Correcting Errors in Capitalization**

Rewrite any incorrect sentences, correcting errors in capitalization. If a sentence is correct, write C.

1. Several youth clubs invited both democrats and republicans to speak at their events.
2. The season came to an end for the River falls mustangs. (they finished second for the third year in a row.)
3. I need only two things: Dinner and a good night's sleep.
4. "Hey, mom," Leif asked, "Can you come here?"
5. Who was President Garfield's Secretary of State?
6. "Were you in World war II, grandpa?" asked Kathleen.
7. Sarah laughed when someone said that the native language of Latin America is Latin.
8. Dad is norwegian, and my Mom is japanese.
9. Driving North, Harriet saw signs for the great smoky mountains National Park.
10. At night in the Sahara desert, one can see the milky way.
11. The harsh laws of queen Mary I ("bloody Mary") resulted in the deaths of several high-ranking Clergymen.

12. The Vice President's airplane is *air force two.*

13. School usually starts after Labor day.

14. Will the Chicago cubs play in the world series this year?

15. I received a C in Geometry, but I received an A in Calculus II.

16. There is a small quaker church near highway 12 and bent branch road.

17. Tammie, who loves everything about the Movies, holds a party every year during the academy awards.

18. Ms. Burke's favorite movie is *Music Of The Heart.*

19. The industrial revolution began in England.

20. Before Mr. Rogers, captain Kangaroo hosted a television show for children.

21. Hyacinth always signed her letters, "Best Wishes."

22. "Stopping by woods on a snowy Evening" is one of Robert Frost's most famous poems.

23. Cnn stands for Cable News network.

24. The senator and the congressman discussed healthcare on the steps of the Lincoln Memorial.

25. The language of the utes is shoshonean.

10.1 CAPITALIZING SENTENCES AND QUOTATIONS

The use of capitalization across the English-speaking world varies. In business writing particularly, people capitalize terms according to company style, which may vary from the rules in this chapter. However, for your own writing, mastering these rules will enable you to express yourself clearly in any situation.

Rule 1 Capitalize the pronoun *I* and the first word of a sentence.

EXAMPLE   Today I am graduating.

EXAMPLE   What are your plans for the summer?

Rule 2 Capitalize the first word of a sentence in parentheses that stands by itself. Don't capitalize a sentence within parentheses that is contained within another sentence.

EXAMPLE   When spring arrives, I will plant flowers. (There are five flower beds in my yard.)

EXAMPLE   I read that book (it was over four hundred pages long) in a week.

Rule 3 Capitalize the first word of a complete sentence that follows a colon. Lowercase the first word of a sentence fragment that follows a colon.

EXAMPLE   She took her dog to the vet: He needed his yearly vaccinations.

EXAMPLE   The photographer needed supplies: film, a zoom lens, and chemicals for developing photographs.

Rule 4 Capitalize the first word of a direct quotation that is a complete sentence. A **direct quotation** gives the speaker's exact words.

EXAMPLE   Jone asked, "Will you take care of my cat while I am on vacation?"

Unless it begins a sentence, don't capitalize the first word of a direct quotation that cannot stand as a complete sentence.

EXAMPLE   Rottweillers are "commonly used as guard dogs," but more importantly, they make loving companions.

Rule 5 Do not capitalize an indirect quotation. An **indirect quotation** does not repeat a speaker's exact words and should not be enclosed in quotation marks.

EXAMPLE   She says she will be late.

An indirect quotation is often introduced with the word *that*.

EXAMPLE   He said that the party will begin at seven.

Rule 6 In a traditional poem, the first word of each line is capitalized.

EXAMPLE   The rain set early in tonight,
            The sullen wind was soon awake,
            It tore the elm tops down for spite,
            And did its worst to vex the lake;
            —from "Porphyria's Lover" by Robert Browning.

PRACTICE   Capitalizing Sentences and Quotations

Copy the sentences, correcting any errors in capitalization. If a sentence is correctly capitalized, write C.

1. José insisted that The best man won.
2. How can you call this "A minor problem"?
3. We heard the same complaint over and over: it's too hard!
4. "That one," I said, "Is the one I want."
5. One critical quality he's lacking is Self-respect.
6. When do i make my entrance in the play?
7. Pesto (It's a sauce made with basil) is my favorite food.
8. More and more people drink filtered water. (this is a sad commentary on public faith in the water supply.)
9. as soon as he'd tied his shoes, Lou said, "let's get going!"
10. "You can't go on that trail," said the forest ranger. "It's closed."

10.2 CAPITALIZING LETTER PARTS AND OUTLINES

Rule 1 Capitalize the first word in the salutation and the closing of a letter. Capitalize the title and the name of the person addressed.

EXAMPLES   **Dear Miss Jones,**
Dear Sir or Madam:
Dear General Motors:

EXAMPLES   **Best regards,**
Yours truly,
Sincerely yours,

Rule 2 In a topic outline, capitalize the Roman numerals that label main topics and the letters that label subtopics. Don't capitalize letters that label subdivisions of a subtopic. Capitalize the first word in each heading and subheading.

    I. Main topic

        A. Subtopic

            1. Division of a subtopic

                a. Subdivision of a subtopic

                b. Subdivision of a subtopic

    II. Main topic

PRACTICE **Capitalizing Letter Parts**

Write the letter of the correctly capitalized line in each pair.

1. a. Best Wishes,
    b. Best wishes,

2. a. Most sincerely yours,
    b. Most Sincerely yours,

3. a. Dear Commissioner:
    b. dear Commissioner:

4. a. With Many Thanks,
    b. With many thanks,

5. a. To Whom It May Concern:
    b. To whom it may concern:

GRAMMAR/USAGE/MECHANICS

Rewrite the partial outline, correcting any errors in capitalization.

     I. Monday's To-Do
        A. Business Activities
           1. financial
              a. Make Bank deposit
              b. Balance Checkbook
              c. pay bills
           2. filing
        B. Personal Activities
           1. shopping

10.3 CAPITALIZING PROPER NOUNS AND PROPER ADJECTIVES

A **proper noun** names a particular person, place, thing, or idea. **Proper adjectives** are formed from proper nouns.

Rule 1 Capitalize both proper nouns and proper adjectives.

EXAMPLES	PROPER NOUNS	PROPER ADJECTIVES
	Australia	Australian vacation
	Victoria	Victorian England
	Christianity	Christian organization

When proper nouns and adjectives are made up of more than one word, capitalize all words except articles, coordinating conjunctions, and prepositions of fewer than five letters.

EXAMPLES	PROPER NOUNS	Struthers High School
		Parent Teacher Association
		War of 1812
EXAMPLES	PROPER ADJECTIVES	Struthers High School alumni
		Parent Teacher Association member

Note: Many proper nouns do not change form when used as adjectives.

Rule 2 Capitalize the names of people and pets and the initials that stand for their names.

EXAMPLES   Barbara Walters   Rover   W. E. B. Du Bois

Note: Foreign names are often compounded with an article, a preposition, or a word meaning "son of" or "father of." These names often follow different rules of capitalization. The capitalization also depends on whether you are using the full name or just the surname, so be sure to look up the names in a reference source for proper capitalization.

EXAMPLES   **FULL NAME**   **SURNAME ONLY**

Charles de Gaulle   de Gaulle

Vincent van Gogh   van Gogh

Ludwig van Beethoven   Beethoven

Aziz ibn Saud   Ibn Saud

Capitalize nicknames.

EXAMPLES   Catherine the Great   Bogie   the Cos

Enclose nicknames in quotation marks when they are used with a person's full name.

EXAMPLE   Michael "Air" Jordan   Thomas "Stonewall" Jackson

Rule 3 Capitalize adjectives formed from the names of people.

EXAMPLE   Copernicus   Copernican system

EXAMPLE   Jefferson   Jeffersonian writings

EXAMPLE   King George   Georgian architecture

Rule 4 Capitalize a title or an abbreviation of a title used before a person's name.

EXAMPLES   **M**rs. Handel
                 Mr. Peabody
                 Ms. Mason

EXAMPLES   **P**ope Theodore I
                 Dr. Hsai
                 President Carter

EXAMPLES   **R**epresentative Jones
                 King George V
                 Chief Geronimo

Capitalize a title used in direct address.

EXAMPLE   I feel much better, **D**octor.

In general, don't capitalize a title that follows a person's name.

EXAMPLE   Ronald Reagan, **p**resident of the United States, served two terms.

Do not capitalize a title that is simply being used as a common noun.

EXAMPLE   George Bush served as his **v**ice **p**resident.

EXAMPLE   To be **e**mperor of the **u**niverse would be a hard job.

Rule 5 Capitalize the names and abbreviations of academic degrees that follow a person's name. Capitalize *Jr.* and *Sr.*

EXAMPLES   Julie Schenk, **D**octor of **P**hilosophy
                 Eli Washington, **M.B.A.**
                 Jon O'Neill **J**r.

Rule 6 Capitalize a word showing family relationship when it is used either

- **before a proper name** or
- **in place of a proper name**

EXAMPLE When Cousin Tina arrived, the children were delighted.

EXAMPLE I hope Mom made peach cobbler.

Don't capitalize a word showing family relationship if it is preceded by a possessive noun or pronoun.

EXAMPLE Carol's mom is a good baker.

EXAMPLE Your cousin has a swimming pool.

Rule 7 Capitalize the names of ethnic groups, nationalities, and languages.

EXAMPLE	**ETHNIC GROUPS**	Basque, Asian, Indian
EXAMPLE	**NATIONALITIES**	German, Nigerian, Canadian
EXAMPLE	**LANGUAGES**	Greek, Arabic, Hebrew

Rule 8 Capitalize the names of organizations, institutions, political parties and their members, government bodies, business firms, and teams.

EXAMPLES

ORGANIZATIONS	National Geographic Society World Wildlife Fund
INSTITUTIONS	New York University Austin Metropolitan Library Fairfield Union High School
POLITICAL PARTIES AND MEMBERS	Socialist Party/Socialist Democratic Party/Democrat
GOVERNMENT BODIES	Tennessee Valley Authority Peace Corps Bureau of the Census
BUSINESS FIRMS	Bank One, Incorporated Illinois Central Railroad Ameritech
TEAMS	Dallas Cowboys Pittsburgh Pirates

Note: Don't capitalize words such as *court, school,* and *university* unless they are part of a proper noun.

EXAMPLE   I left **s**chool at three o'clock.

EXAMPLE   I attend **L**ancaster **H**igh **S**chool.

Note: When referring to a specific political party or party member, words such as *democrat* and *republican* should be capitalized. However, when used to describe a way of thought or an ideal, such words should be lowercase.

EXAMPLE   Are they members of the **R**epublican or the **D**emocratic **P**arty (or **p**arty)?

EXAMPLE   We discussed **r**epublican theories last night.

EXAMPLE   How does a **d**emocratic government work?

Note: Capitalize brand names of products but not the nouns following them.

EXAMPLES   **L**ay's™ potato chips   **B**ayer™ aspirin

Rule 9 Capitalize the names of roads, parks, towns, cities, counties, townships, provinces, states, regions, countries, continents, other land forms and features, and bodies of water.

EXAMPLES

Third **A**venue	**J**ersey **C**ity	**E**verglades **N**ational **P**ark
Saguaro **C**ounty	**N**ebraska	the **M**idwest
Taiwan	**A**sia	**J**ervis **B**ay
Ozark **P**lateau	**L**ake **S**uperior	**G**alápagos **I**slands

Note: Capitalize words such as *city, island,* and *mountains* only when they are part of a proper name.

Capitalize compass points, such as *north, south, east,* and *west,* when they refer to a specific region or when they are part of a proper name. Don't capitalize them when they indicate direction.

EXAMPLE	REGIONS/PROPER NAMES	DIRECTIONS
	the South	south of the city
	East Haven	driving east

Capitalize *northern, southern, eastern,* and *western* when they refer to hemispheres and cultures.

EXAMPLES   Northern Hemisphere   Eastern culture

Capitalize adjectives that are formed from place names.

EXAMPLES   African art   Tibetan monks

Rule 10 Capitalize the names of planets and other astral bodies.

EXAMPLES	Saturn	Neptune	Uranus
	Beta Crucis	Castor	Orion

Rule 11 Capitalize the names of monuments, buildings, bridges, and other structures.

EXAMPLES	Statue of Liberty	Washington Bridge
EXAMPLES	Chrysler Building	Midtown Tunnel
EXAMPLES	Great Wall of China	Otago Harbor

Rule 12 Capitalize the names of ships, planes, trains, and spacecraft. Note that these names are italicized, but the abbreviations before them are not.

EXAMPLES   *Enola Gay*   *Sputnik 1*   *Santa Maria*
             USS *Constitution*

Rule 13 Capitalize the names of historical events, special events, and holidays and other calendar items.

Historical events require capitalization, as do some historical periods. However, most historical periods are not capitalized. It is best to check a dictionary or other reference source for the proper capitalization of historical periods.

EXAMPLE	HISTORICAL EVENTS	Spanish Civil War, World War I, Louisiana Purchase
EXAMPLE	HISTORICAL PERIODS	Dark Ages, Renaissance, Ice Age, fifteenth century, the sixties, classical period

Note: Historical periods using numerical designations are lowercase unless they are part of a proper name.

The names of special events should be capitalized.

EXAMPLES   Chicago World's Fair   Kentucky Derby   Super Bowl

The names of holidays and other calendar items require capitalization.

EXAMPLES	Inauguration Day	Groundhog Day
EXAMPLES	Tuesday	September

Note: Names of the seasons—*spring, summer, winter, fall*—are not capitalized.

Rule 14 Capitalize the names of deities and words referring to deities, words referring to a revered being, religions and their followers, religious books, and holy days and events.

EXAMPLES

NAMES OF AND WORDS REFERRING TO DEITIES	Holy Spirit	Vishnu	Joseph
WORDS REFERRING TO A REVERED BEING	the Prophet	the Beloved Apostle	
RELIGIONS	Catholicism	Amish	Judaism
FOLLOWERS	Jew	Muslim	Rastafarian
RELIGIOUS BOOKS	Analects	Upanishads	Talmud
RELIGIOUS HOLY DAYS AND EVENTS	Ramadan	Advent	Hanukkah

Note: When referring to ancient Greek or Roman deities, don't capitalize the words *god, gods, goddess,* and *goddesses.*

Rule 15 Capitalize only those school courses that name a language, are followed by a number, or name a specific course. Don't capitalize the name of a general subject.

EXAMPLES **Portuguese**   **foreign language**

EXAMPLES **Women's Studies 152**   **women's studies**

Rule 16 Capitalize the first word and the last word in the titles of books, chapters, plays, short stories, poems, essays, articles, movies, television series and programs, songs, magazines, newspapers, cartoons, and comic strips. Capitalize all other words except articles, coordinating conjunctions, and prepositions of fewer than five letters.

EXAMPLES

To the Lighthouse   the *London Times*
You Can't Take It with You   *Much Ado About Nothing*
Dog Fancy   *"Lady Be Good"*

Note: It is common practice not to capitalize or italicize articles preceding the title of a newspaper or a periodical.

Rule 17 Capitalize the names of documents, awards, and laws.

EXAMPLES **Fifth Amendment**   **India Act**

EXAMPLES **Academy Award**   **Articles of Confederation**

Copy the sentences, correcting errors in capitalization.

1. Loretta, a good friend of mine from High School, told me how her family observes passover.

2. e. b. White wrote *Charlotte's Web* and co-authored the helpful book *the Elements of Style.*

3. Dorothy "dot" Jacobs is the saleswoman who sold aunt Dorothy her red chevrolet.

4. When I visit Washington, d.c., I always go to see the Washington monument and then spend a few hours at the smithsonian.

5. On their Western expedition, Lewis and Clark built fort Clatsop near the coast of the pacific ocean.

6. In Chicago, Southwest airlines flies into midway airport.

7. Many people travel to new England in the Fall to see the foliage.

8. In College, Victor signed up for Chinese and Art classes, but his favorite class was introduction to Psychology.

9. I always get Seafood when I'm near Chesapeake bay.

10. Seamus Heaney, a translator, wrote the book *Beowulf: a new verse Translation.*

11. How far is the big dipper from earth?

12. The navaho and hopi in arizona have disputed territorial land use since 1882.

13. My beagle, bowser, loves Winner's Cup Dog Food.

14. The newbery medal, which is awarded by the Association for library service to children, is an annual literary award.

15. The Emancipation proclamation did not free all the enslaved people, only those in the confederacy.

16. My favorite Cousin, Martha, is the family eccentric.

17. An islamic mosque is located on Elm street.

18. "Oh, dad," said Zeke, "mom said I could take the car tonight to go to Ahrvano's pizza."

19. The articles of Confederation proved to be inadequate for governing the new United States.

20. The guest lecturer, professor Corinne Lyon, lectured on the principles of jeffersonian Democracy.

PRACTICE **Correcting Errors in Capitalization**

Rewrite each item, correcting any errors in capitalization.

1. My Mom likes the song "Dream A Little Dream Of Me."

2. Mom and dad believe in using a Democratic approach to family decision-making; everyone but daisy (She's our dog) gets a vote.

3. Some people believe that all the native Americans migrated to the americas from Asia.

4. To do this, they must have traveled over the Bering strait.

5. Dear señora Ramirez,

Thank you for tutoring me in spanish while I was a student at Langston tech. I have since become a translator for unicef. If it weren't for your help, I would not be doing this wonderful work.

With Best Regards,

Edgard Nau

6. Before he became President, Warren g. Harding was publisher of a newspaper in marion, Ohio.

7. The article is entitled "on the Sea: A memory."

8. My Mom is always saying, "remember to tell grandma that story."

9. Ann did well in physics 101 but better in her music class.

10. I. the 1960s

a. The Fight for Equality

1. Southern christian leadership conference

A. Martin Luther King jr.

B. Fannie lou Hamer

2. National organization for Women

A. Betty Friedan

SUMMARY OF CAPITALIZATION RULES

NAMES AND TITLES OF PEOPLE

CAPITALIZE	DO NOT CAPITALIZE
D. H. Lawrence	an **a**uthor
Miss **J**ones, **Ph. D.**	a **n**eighbor
Pope **J**ohn **P**aul II	a **r**eligious **l**eader
General **S**herman	a **g**eneral
Great-aunt **L**ouise	my **g**reat-aunt

ETHNIC GROUPS, NATIONALITIES, AND LANGUAGES

Latino	an **e**thnic group
South **A**frican	a **n**ationality
Swahili	a **l**anguage

ORGANIZATIONS, INSTITUTIONS, POLITICAL PARTIES AND THEIR MEMBERS, GOVERNMENT BODIES, BUSINESS FIRMS, AND TEAMS

League of **W**omen **V**oters	an **o**rganization
Metropolitan **M**useum of **A**rt	an **a**rt **m**useum
Republican **P**arty / **R**epublican	**r**epublican theories
Supreme **C**ourt	a **c**ourt
Coca-**C**ola **C**ompany	a soft-drink **c**ompany
Nebraska **C**ornhuskers	a football **t**eam

NAMES OF PLACES

Perry **S**treet	a **s**treet
Badlands **N**ational **P**ark	a **p**ark
the **S**outh	**s**outh of the border
Amazon **R**iver	a **r**iver
Mojave **D**esert	a **d**esert

Summary of Capitalization rules, continued

PLANETS AND OTHER HEAVENLY BODIES	
CAPITALIZE	DO NOT CAPITALIZE
Uranus	a planet
North Star	a star
MONUMENTS, BUILDINGS, BRIDGES, AND OTHER STRUCTURES	
Tomb of the Unknowns	a tomb
World Trade Center	a building
Brooklyn Bridge	a bridge
Hadrian's Wall	a wall
SHIPS, PLANES, TRAINS, AND SPACECRAFT	
Santa Maria	a ship
Spirit of Saint Louis	a plane
Columbia	a spacecraft
HISTORICAL EVENTS, SPECIAL EVENTS, AND CALENDAR ITEMS	
World War II	a war
World Series	a baseball game
Labor Day	a holiday
January, June	winter, summer
Wednesday	a day of the week
RELIGIOUS TERMS	
Allah	a deity
the Beloved Apostle	a revered being
Protestantism / Protestant	a religion / a religious follower
Bhagavad Gita	a religious book
Easter Sunday	a religious holiday

Summary of Capitalization rules, continued

SCHOOL COURSES	
CAPITALIZE	DO NOT CAPITALIZE
Russian	a **f**oreign **l**anguage
Statistics 152	**s**tatistics
TITLES OF WORKS	
*Lonesome **D**ove*	a **b**ook
"Everyday **U**se"	a **s**hort **s**tory
*Vanity **F**air*	a **m**agazine
the *Chicago **T**ribune*	a **n**ewspaper
DOCUMENTS, AWARDS, AND LAWS	
Articles of **C**onfederation	a **d**ocument
Nobel **P**rize	an **a**ward
First **A**mendment	a **l**aw

PRACTICE Proofreading

Rewrite the following passage, correcting errors in spelling, capitalization, grammar, and usage. Add any missing punctuation. Write legibly to be sure one letter is not mistaken for another. There are ten mistakes.

Edith Wharton

¹Edith Wharton won the highly prestigious Pulitzer Prize in 1921 for her classic novel of manners *The age of Innocence,* which is still highly regarded.

²Wharton was born into a wealthy and socially prominent New York family. ³She gave up writing when she married (She married in 1885) but took it up again later. ⁴Most of her novels deals with the moral, social and cultural values of middle-class and upper-class society in New England. ⁵When she began writing few women were taken seriously as writers,

especially in the United States. [6]Possibly to gain more personal freedom to pursue her career, she moved to Paris France. [7]It was their that she wrote the majority of her books. [8]It was also in France that she received an important award—the French legion of honor—for her charitable work during World war I.

[9]Although she wrote 22 novels, many collections of short stories, poetry, and nonfiction, Wharton is best remembered for her short novel *Ethan Frome.*

POSTTEST Correcting Errors in Capitalization

Rewrite any incorrect sentences, correcting errors in capitalization. If a sentence is correct, write C.

1. Pedro wondered If the plan could possibly work.
2. The Doctor asked, "are you allergic to any Antibiotics?"
3. Ana bought two books: One by Neruda and one by Dickens.
4. The name slammin' Sammy now refers to Sammy Sosa, not to Golfer Sam Snead.
5. Iran is next to iraq, which is next to kuwait, and all are near the Persian gulf.
6. The Bill of Rights guarantees essential freedoms.
7. Sara said, "in Brazil the language is Portuguese; however," she continued, "in Chile people speak Spanish."
8. Bill's list for the camping trip includes a canteen, Kill'em dead Bug Spray, Sunglow sunscreen, and extra socks.
9. Edwin Booth, brother of John wilkes Booth, was a famous shakespearean actor.
10. [*letter form*] Dear mayor Hughes:
11. "Svetlana Arkaev, m.d.," announced the proud woman, "Is my daughter."
12. The governor met with the secretary of state.
13. Hector went with his Aunt to see his Cousins, Pat and Al.
14. Are the ethics of judaism and christianity based primarily on the ten commandments?

15. The Austins used the book *What's In A Name?* to choose a name for their baby.

16. The Dalai lama is the leader of Tibetan buddhism.

17. The Managers of my Dad's company, counterpoint electronics, met at the Sherwood hotel.

18. Most people forget about Arbor day.

19. The *lusitania,* a british passenger ship, was attacked by a German Submarine in 1915.

20. In the United States, the "supreme law of the land" is the Constitution.

21. The grouping of stars called the little dipper is my favorite; it's the constellation the romans called ursa minor, or little bear.

22. I enjoy Indian and ethiopian food, but my Brother's favorite is food from the middle east.

23. We traveled across the Rio Grande river to Northern Mexico.

24. In India, according to legend, the God Ganesha was created by the Goddess Parvati.

25. [*letter form*] With Many Thanks,

Chapter 11

Punctuation, Abbreviations, and Numbers

● ● ● ● ● ● ● ● ● ● ● ● ● ● ● ●

PRETEST **Correcting Errors in Punctuation**

Rewrite each sentence, correcting any errors in punctuation.

1. The storm brought thunder, and lightning, rain, and winds that toppled a tree onto our car, before we could shelter it.

2. Please remember, to bring in your signed permission slips by Monday not Tuesday.

3. With a gasp that broke her composure Missy asked me if Harry had just run ten miles?

4. How did James' first day on the job go.

5. We saw Act 1 Scene 1 of "A Doll's House."

6. In the area of jazz some all time greats are these, Miles Davis Charlie Parker and Ella Fitzgerald.

7. "If you don't mind" said Sylvia giving a snort of disbelief "I'll just try that for myself"!

8. The sign disturbed Grandma, signs about falling rocks always disturb her to tell the truth.

9. As most of our grandparents know Lassie often saved Timmy on the TV show "Lassie."

10. If you eat a big Thanksgiving dinner you may get sleepy, after all turkey has a chemical that can make one drowsy.

11. For the Halloween dance, Gia, was a cat, Ted, was a king, Lisa was a clown, but Lara didn't wear a costume.

12. My favorite joke, stop me if youve heard this, has to do with someone trying to spell "ludicrous."

13. "Have I mentioned?" asked Charlotte, "That I just love these little beasts to pieces"?

14. The book, that I just read, belongs to my best friend Anya.

15. They dont expect me to stay after class do they!

16. After seeing him perform in *Glory* Rory said "Wow Andre Braugher is a really great actor".

17. Look out There are limbs falling from the trees.

18. Neither Fred nor Lester's shoes will fit me but your's might dont you think?

19. The NFL National Football League, and the AFL American Football League merged in 1970.

20. And then don't interrupt me, Jake said in an awful French accent, "I have to go now, so au revoir."

Rewrite each item, correcting any errors in the use of abbreviations and numbers.

21. $2.00 is way too much to pay for a cup of coffee.

22. The Peasants' Revolt began in England in 1381 ad.

23. I need to take one tsp of the medicine around 8 o'clock in the morning and another 12 hrs. later.

24. Mrs. Garcia weighs 150 lbs, while her sister weighs only one hundred.

25. Even though she's only 22, Leona is paid a salary of thirty-five thousand, five hundred dollars.

26. Mina paid an income tax amounting to 25% of her salary.

27. My best friend lives at five fifteen Elm Street, Troy NY.

28. On December seven, 1941, at about 7:55 am, the first bombs dropped on Pearl Harbor, HI.

29. The earliest Greek civilization began to develop about two thousand bc.

30. 300 people from more than twenty states came to the reunion, some traveling 1,000 mi. or more.

There are three punctuation marks used at the ends of sentences: the period, the exclamation point, and the question mark.

11.1 THE PERIOD

Use a period at the end of a declarative sentence—a statement—and at the end of an imperative sentence—a polite command or a request.

EXAMPLE **DECLARATIVE SENTENCE** The banjo is a folk instrument.

EXAMPLE **IMPERATIVE SENTENCE** Please play me a song on your banjo.

11.2 THE EXCLAMATION POINT

Use an exclamation point to show strong feeling and to indicate a forceful command.

EXAMPLES	**EXCLAMATORY SENTENCE**	What a great movie that was!
		How lovely you look!
		Woe is me!
EXAMPLES	**FORCEFUL COMMAND**	Don't you dare go without me!
		Look out!
		Help!

Use an exclamation point after an interjection that expresses a strong feeling.

EXAMPLES Ow!   Wahoo!   Oh, boy!

11.3 THE QUESTION MARK

Use a question mark at the end of a direct question.

EXAMPLE   Was Aaron Copland an American composer?

EXAMPLE   Did Copland write *Appalachian Spring*?

Don't use a question mark after an indirect question (one that has been reworded so that it is part of a declarative sentence).

EXAMPLE   My friend asked whether Aaron Copland wrote *Appalachian Spring*.

EXAMPLE   She wondered what folk tune is the central melody in *Appalachian Spring*.

Periods, Exclamation Points, and Question Marks

Rewrite each item, adding the correct end punctuation.

1. Yikes I forgot to turn off the stove
2. When was Tibet invaded by China
3. Halt Who goes there
4. Was your grandmother really on the *Titanic*
5. For the last time, stop leaving wet towels on either the bed or the floor
6. Jennie asked me why I wanted a pencil
7. I really like pepperoni, mushroom, and green pepper pizza, don't you
8. What a great idea
9. Find out when the next band practice is scheduled
10. Please tell me what you thought of my story

11.4 THE COLON

COLONS TO INTRODUCE

Use a colon to introduce a list, especially after a statement that uses such words as *these, namely, the following,* or *as follows.*

EXAMPLE The kinds of fiction in which justice prevails include **these:** fairy tales, Westerns, and detective stories.

EXAMPLE Listen to a recording of one of **the following** concert vocalists: Justino Diaz, Martina Arroyo, or Jessye Norman.

Don't use a colon to introduce a list if the list immediately follows a verb or a preposition. In other words, check to be sure that the words preceding the colon make up a complete sentence.

GRAMMAR/USAGE/MECHANICS

EXAMPLE   Three important composers from the United States **are** Aaron Copland, Scott Joplin, and Arthur Cunningham. **[The list follows the verb *are* and acts as the sentence's predicate nominative. Don't use a colon.]**

EXAMPLE   What kinds of music are most popular **in** South America, Asia, Africa, and Oceania? **[The list follows the preposition *in* and acts as the object of the preposition. Don't use a colon.]**

Use a colon to introduce material that illustrates, explains, or restates the preceding material.

Note: A complete sentence following a colon should be capitalized.

EXAMPLE   The cause of the fire was obvious: **C**hildren had been playing with butane lighters.

EXAMPLE   The joyous news was announced to the patiently waiting crowd: **T**he queen had given birth to a healthy daughter.

Use a colon to introduce a long or a formal quotation. A formal quotation is often preceded by such words as *this, these, the following,* or *as follows.*

EXAMPLE   Patrick Henry, speaking before the Virginia Convention, closed his memorable speech with **these** words: "I know not what course others may take; but as for me, give me liberty or give me death!"

Poetry quotations of more than one line and prose quotations of more than four or five lines are generally written below the introductory statement and are indented on the page.

EXAMPLE Walt Whitman responded to critics with **the following** lines:

> Do I contradict myself?
> Very well, then I contradict myself,
> (I am large. I contain multitudes.)

OTHER USES OF COLONS

- Use a colon between the hour and the minute of the precise time.
- Use a colon between the chapter and the verse in biblical references.
- Use a colon after the salutation of a business letter.

EXAMPLES 6:40 A.M.   2:15 P.M.   Exodus 3:4   Matthew 2:5

EXAMPLE Greetings:

EXAMPLE Dear Ford Motor Company:

EXAMPLE Dear Sir or Madam:

EXAMPLE Dear Volunteers:

PRACTICE Colons

Rewrite each sentence below, correcting any errors in the use of colons.

1. The marsupials of Australia include the following koalas, bandicoots, and kangaroos.
2. Some professional baseball players who have hit at least five hundred home runs in their careers are: Ernie Banks, Harmon Killebrew, Mel Ott, and Frank Robinson.
3. The reason for many car accidents is obvious, drunk drivers.
4. The following are favorite Mexican dishes in the United States tacos, burritos, enchiladas, tostadas, and guacamole.

GRAMMAR/USAGE/MECHANICS

5. In the *Analects,* Confucius wrote these words, "The superior man . . . does not set his mind either for anything, or against anything; what is right he will follow."

6. [*Letter form*] To Whom It May Concern,

7. The schedule for Tuesday's showing of *Dreamers* is as follows, 415: P.M., 710 P.M., and midnight.

8. Whether any individual citizen is pleased with the results, every voting day makes one thing clear, the will of the people prevails.

9. My favorite subjects are these, English, history, and art.

10. The biblical reference I used is in Matthew 25, 40, and I quoted it, word for word, as follows, "Inasmuch as ye have done it unto one of the least of these my brethren, ye have done it unto me."

11.5 THE SEMICOLON

SEMICOLONS TO SEPARATE MAIN CLAUSES

Use a semicolon to separate main clauses that are not joined by a comma and a coordinating conjunction (*and, but, or, nor, so, yet,* or *for*).

EXAMPLE   I love jazz**, and** the blues are my favorite kind of jazz.

EXAMPLE   I love jazz**;** the blues are my favorite kind of jazz.

EXAMPLE   George Gershwin wrote music during the Jazz Age**;** his compositions were influenced by jazz.

Use a semicolon to separate main clauses that are joined by a conjunctive adverb (such as *however, therefore, nevertheless, moreover, furthermore,* and *subsequently*) or by an expression such as *for example* or *that is.*

In general, a conjunctive adverb or an expression such as *for example* is followed by a comma.

George Gershwin wrote popular as well as traditional music; **in fact,** he combined the two forms in pieces such as *Rhapsody in Blue.*

EXAMPLE The jazz-opera *Porgy and Bess* is generally considered to be Gershwin's masterpiece; **consequently,** Gershwin enthusiasts call its hit songs "Summertime" and "It Ain't Necessarily So" gems.

SEMICOLONS AND COMMAS

Use a semicolon to separate the items in a series when one or more of the items already contain commas.

EXAMPLE Three important jazz musicians of the twentieth century were Louis Armstrong, a trumpet player; Duke Ellington, a composer; and Sarah Vaughan, a singer.

Use a semicolon to separate two main clauses joined by a coordinating conjunction when one or both of the clauses already contain several commas.

EXAMPLE Arthur Mitchell, as a leading dancer with the New York City Ballet, danced in such works as *A Midsummer Night's Dream, Agon,* and *Western Symphony;* but he is also famous as the founder of the Dance Theater of Harlem, an internationally acclaimed dance company.

GRAMMAR/USAGE/MECHANICS

PRACTICE Semicolons

Rewrite each sentence below, correcting errors in the use of semicolons.

1. My sister keeps her room very clean she's a tidy person.
2. Willie McCovey, a first baseman, Hank Aaron, a right fielder, and Ernie Banks, a shortstop, were all important home run hitters.

3. Cheyenne went to the circus on Tuesday, she went to the movies on Friday.

4. I have lived in Chicago; Illinois for many years, my sister has always lived in Texas.

5. Mark never studied for tests nonetheless; he got good grades.

11.6 THE COMMA

As you study the rules for comma usage, keep in mind that to *separate* elements means to place a comma between two equal elements. To *set off* an element means to put a comma before and after it. Of course, you never place a comma at the beginning or the end of a sentence.

COMMAS IN A SERIES

Use commas to separate three or more words, phrases, or clauses in a series.

EXAMPLE Langston Hughes wrote poetry, drama, screenplays, and popular songs.

EXAMPLE We hung party decorations in the gym, in the halls, and around the courtyard.

EXAMPLE Some movies make audiences laugh, others make them cry, and still others amaze them with state-of-the-art special effects.

Note: The comma before the *and* is called the serial comma. Some authorities do not recommend it. However, many sentences may be confusing without it. We recommend that you always insert the serial comma for clarity.

EXAMPLE UNCLEAR Michelle, Susan and Henry are going to the store. [This sentence might be telling Michelle that Susan and Henry are going to the store.]

CLEAR	Michelle, Susan, and Henry are going to the store. **[This sentence clearly states that three people are going to the store.]**

When all items in a series are connected by conjunctions, no commas are necessary.

EXAMPLE Langston Hughes's poetry is insightful and expressive and powerful.

EXAMPLE You won't want the orange or the green or the red.

Nouns that are used in pairs to express one idea *(pen and ink, spaghetti and meatballs, thunder and lightning)* are usually considered single units and should not be separated by commas. If such pairs appear with other nouns or groups of nouns in a series, however, they must be set off from the other items in the series.

EXAMPLE I like oil and vinegar, salt and pepper, and croutons on my salad.

EXAMPLE Swimming and diving pools, football and baseball fields, and tennis and volleyball courts can be found in the park.

COMMAS AND COORDINATE ADJECTIVES

Place a comma between coordinate adjectives that precede a noun.

Coordinate adjectives modify a noun equally. To determine whether adjectives are coordinate, try to reverse their order or put the word *and* between them. If the sentence still sounds natural, the adjectives are coordinate.

EXAMPLE Hea is a happy, intelligent, graceful child.

Don't use a comma between adjectives preceding a noun if the adjectives sound unnatural with their order reversed or with *and* between them. In general, adjectives that describe size, shape, age, and material do not need to be separated by commas.

EXAMPLE   Julia wore a long blue wool scarf.

Commas may be needed between some of the adjectives before a noun and not between others.

EXAMPLE   It was a cozy, clean, old-fashioned living room.

In the preceding sentence, *and* would sound natural between *cozy* and *clean* and between *clean* and *old-fashioned,* but it would not sound natural between *old-fashioned* and *living.*

COMMAS AND COMPOUND SENTENCES

Use a comma between the main clauses in a compound sentence.

Place a comma before a coordinating conjunction *(and, but, or, nor, for, so,* or *yet)* that joins two main clauses.

EXAMPLE   The Marx Brothers were a comedy team, **but** each brother did work on his own.

EXAMPLE   Groucho Marx made wisecracks, **and** his brother Harpo played music.

PRACTICE **Commas in a Series, with Coordinate Adjectives, and in Compound Sentences**

Rewrite each item below, correcting any errors in the use of commas.

1. My favorite activities are planting flowers going to movies and sailing.
2. You will need to learn, think and study while attending this class.
3. The group of hunters stopped for the night at the small, log, cabin.

4. Marita's first day at the new, high, school dawned sunny crisp and clear.

5. Vladimir struggled to learn English but he found it very difficult.

COMMAS AND NONESSENTIAL ELEMENTS

Use commas to set off participles, infinitives, and their phrases if they are not essential to the meaning of the sentence.

EXAMPLE   The children, **exhilarated,** ripped open their presents.

EXAMPLE   Mari made her way down the street, **happily calling out to her neighbors.**

EXAMPLE   I have no idea, **to tell the truth,** what he meant by that remark.

Don't set off participles, infinitives, and their phrases if they are essential to the meaning of the sentence.

EXAMPLE   The most famous documentary film **directed by Robert J. Flaherty** is *Nanook of the North.* [adjective phrase]

EXAMPLE   Flaherty made the film **to show the realities of Inuit life.** [adverb phrase]

EXAMPLE   **To film *Nanook of the North*** was a difficult undertaking. [infinitive phrase as subject]

Use commas to set off a nonessential adjective clause.

A nonessential clause can be considered an extra clause because it gives optional information about a noun. Because it is an extra clause that is not necessary, it is set off by commas.

EXAMPLE   My cousin Ken, **who lives in California,** works as a film editor. [The adjective clause *who lives in California* is nonessential.]

GRAMMAR/USAGE/MECHANICS

Don't set off an essential adjective clause. Because an essential adjective clause gives necessary information about a noun, it is needed to convey the exact meaning of the sentence.

EXAMPLE   The person **who actually films a movie** is called the camera operator. [The adjective clause *who actually films a movie* is essential. It tells *which* person.]

EXAMPLE   The director first interviewed the actors, **who were very talented.** [This clearly states that all the actors were very talented.]

EXAMPLE   The director first interviewed the actors **who were very talented.** [This clearly states that the director first interviewed those actors who were very talented and then interviewed other actors.]

Use commas to set off an appositive if it is not essential to the meaning of a sentence.

A nonessential appositive can be considered extra information; it calls for commas.

EXAMPLE   James Wong Howe**, a famous camera operator,** was born in China.

EXAMPLE   Howe first worked for Cecil B. DeMille**, a director of many Hollywood films.**

EXAMPLE   *The Ten Commandments***, a classic film from the 1950s,** is one of DeMille's most successful films.

A nonessential appositive is sometimes placed before the noun or pronoun to which it refers.

EXAMPLE   **A camera operator for Cecil B. DeMille,** James Wong Howe was important to the film industry. [The appositive, *A camera operator for Cecil B. DeMille,* precedes the noun it identifies, *James Wong Howe.*]

An essential appositive gives necessary information about a noun and is not set off with commas.

EXAMPLE James Wong Howe operated the camera for Martin Ritt's film *The Molly Maguires.* **[If a comma were placed before the essential appositive, *The Molly Maguires,* the sentence would say that this was Ritt's only film.]**

PRACTICE **Commas and Nonessential Elements**

Rewrite each sentence below, correcting any errors in the use of commas.

1. The girl, who is sitting on the porch, is my niece.
2. The brown horse, which happens to be my favorite already has a rider.
3. The borzoi, a Russian dog is quite large.
4. L. J. walking quietly, through the halls, thought about his homework.
5. I'm concerned, about the test to tell the truth.

COMMAS WITH INTERJECTIONS, PARENTHETICAL EXPRESSIONS, CONJUNCTIVE ADVERBS, AND ANTITHETICAL PHRASES

Use commas to set off the following:

- interjections (such as *oh, well, alas,* and *good grief*)
- parenthetical expressions (such as *in fact, on the other hand, for example, on the contrary, by the way, to be exact,* and *after all*)
- conjunctive adverbs (such as *however, moreover, therefore,* and *consequently*)

EXAMPLE **Indeed,** Francis Ford Coppola is a talented scriptwriter.

EXAMPLE He wrote the screenplay for *Patton,* **for example.**

EXAMPLE He is also a gifted director; **after all,** he won an Academy Award for his direction of *The Godfather.*

Chapter 11 Punctuation, Abbreviations, and Numbers **331**

In fact, Coppola comes from an artistic family.

Talia Shire is Francis Ford Coppola's sister; **moreover,** she is a talented actor.

Use commas to set off an antithetical phrase. An antithetical phrase uses a word such as *not* or *unlike* to qualify what precedes it.

EXAMPLE Augusta**, not Bangor,** is the capital of Maine.

EXAMPLE **Unlike Kansas,** Colorado is very mountainous.

| **PRACTICE** | **Commas with Interjections, Parenthetical Expressions, Conjunctive Adverbs, and Antithetical Phrases** |

Rewrite each sentence below, correcting any errors in the use of commas.

1. Oh I guess you'll be playing first base not Louie.
2. Avocados unlike other fruits are high in fat, however they are rich in several vitamins.
3. It did indeed turn out to be a lovely day after all.
4. By the way Nell has seemed, well a little confused lately.
5. Sharon wanted to live in Prague in fact she was working to accomplish her dream.

COMMAS WITH OTHER ELEMENTS

Set off two or more introductory prepositional phrases or a single long one with a comma.

EXAMPLE **During the winter in New England,** snowstorms are common. **[two prepositional phrases—*During the winter* and *in New England*]**

EXAMPLE **Above one thousand twinkling holiday lights,** the snowy mountains drowsed. **[one long prepositional phrase—*Above one thousand twinkling holiday lights*]**

You need not set off a single short introductory prepositional phrase, but it's not wrong to do so.

EXAMPLE   **In 1862** Victor Hugo published *Les Misérables.*

or

In 1862, Victor Hugo published *Les Misérables.*

Don't use a comma if the introductory prepositional phrase is immediately followed by a verb.

EXAMPLE   On the rug by the fireplace slept a large white dog.

Use commas to set off introductory participles and participial phrases.

EXAMPLE   **Smiling,** I watched Whoopi Goldberg's award-winning performance in *Ghost.* **[introductory participle]**

EXAMPLE   **Beginning as a comic actor,** Sally Field graduated into more serious roles. **[introductory participial phrase]**

Use commas after all introductory adverbs and adverb clauses.

EXAMPLE   **Finally,** the lights dimmed and the movie started. **[introductory adverb]**

EXAMPLE   **Although the usher tried to hush the noisy children,** I could not hear the dialogue. **[introductory adverb clause]**

Also use commas to set off internal adverb clauses that interrupt the flow of a sentence.

EXAMPLE   Denzel Washington, **before he became a movie star,** appeared in the television series *St. Elsewhere.* **[*before he became a movie star* interrupts the flow of the sentence.]**

In general, don't set off an adverb clause at the end of a sentence unless the clause is parenthetical or the sentence would be misread without the comma.

EXAMPLE Denzel Washington appeared in the television series *St. Elsewhere* before he became a movie star. **[no comma needed]**

EXAMPLE We held our car wash**, although it was raining.** [nonessential adverb clause needs comma]

PRACTICE Commas with Other Elements

Rewrite each sentence below, correcting any errors in the use of commas.

1. Fortunately I got all the research material I needed, before the library closed.
2. In the middle of the night the dog began barking and wouldn't stop.
3. Smiling mysteriously Mom merely shook her head.
4. I noticed that the kitten after it began eating well was growing rapidly.
5. Although they were pretty the flowers were dying of a fungal disease.

ADDITIONAL USES OF COMMAS

Use commas to set off a title when it follows a person's name.

EXAMPLE Henry VIII, **king of England,** had six wives.

EXAMPLE Lucia Sanchez, **Ph.D.,** will chair the new committee.

Set off the name of a state or a country when it's used after the name of a city. Set off the name of a city when it's used after a street address. Don't use a comma after the state if it's followed by a ZIP code.

EXAMPLE Paris, France, is the setting of some of Hemingway's novels.

EXAMPLE The company is located at 840 Pierce Street, Friendswood, Texas 77546.

In a date, set off the year when it's used with both the month and the day. Don't use a comma if only the month and the year are given.

EXAMPLE On October 12, 1492, Christopher Columbus landed on the island now called San Salvador.

EXAMPLE It was July 1776 when the Declaration of Independence was signed.

Use commas to set off the parts of a reference that direct the reader to the exact source.

EXAMPLE We performed Act 1, Scene 1, of William Shakespeare's *Julius Caesar.*

Use commas to set off words or names in direct address.

EXAMPLE **Mona,** can you meet me this afternoon?

EXAMPLE You, **my dear,** are leaving at once.

EXAMPLE Thank you for the book, **Mrs. Gomez.**

Use commas to set off tag questions.

A tag question (such as *shouldn't I?* or *have you?*) suggests an answer to the question that precedes it.

EXAMPLE *Bye Bye Birdie* starred Chita Rivera, **didn't it?**

EXAMPLE Chita Rivera was not in the film version of *Bye Bye Birdie,* **was she?**

Place a comma after the salutation of an informal letter. Place a comma after the closing of all letters. In the inside address, place a comma between the city and state and between the day and year.

23 Silver Lake Road
Sharon, Connecticut 06069
February 15, 2000

EXAMPLE Dear Cousin Agnes,

EXAMPLE Best wishes,

PRACTICE **Additional Uses of Commas**

Rewrite each sentence below, correcting any errors in the use of commas.

1. Daphne was born in October, 1989.
2. Martin Van Buren president of the United States is not well remembered is he?
3. My annual exam is scheduled for May 23 2001.
4. I will visit again soon Mrs. Potter.
5. Melvin spent his summer in Dakar Senegal.

MISUSE OF COMMAS

In general, don't use a comma before a conjunction that connects a compound predicate or a compound subject.

EXAMPLE **INCORRECT** Our school never wins the championship, but always has a spectacular loser's party. **[compound predicate]**

CORRECT Our school never wins the championship but always has a spectacular loser's party.

EXAMPLE **INCORRECT** The cheerleaders with their little trampoline, and the band members with their instruments make a lively display. **[compound subject]**

CORRECT The cheerleaders with their little trampoline and the band members with their instruments make a lively display.

Don't use only a comma to join two main clauses unless they are part of a series of clauses. Such a sentence punctuated with a comma alone is called a *run-on sentence* (or a *comma splice* or a *comma fault*). To join two clauses correctly, use a coordinating conjunction with the comma, or use a semicolon.

EXAMPLE	**INCORRECT**	The navigator Juan Rodríguez Cabrillo sighted land in 1542, the history of California entered a new chapter.
	CORRECT	The navigator Juan Rodríguez Cabrillo sighted land in 1542, **and** the history of California entered a new chapter.
	CORRECT	The navigator Juan Rodríguez Cabrillo sighted land in 1542; the history of California entered a new chapter.

Don't use a comma between a subject and its verb or between a verb and its complement.

EXAMPLE	**INCORRECT**	What she considered an easy ballet step to master, was quite difficult for me.
	CORRECT	What she considered an easy ballet step to master was quite difficult for me.
EXAMPLE	**INCORRECT**	Popular tourist attractions in Florida include, Disney World, Palm Beach, and the Everglades.
	CORRECT	Popular tourist attractions in Florida include Disney World, Palm Beach, and the Everglades.
EXAMPLE	**INCORRECT**	Their motto was, "All for one and one for all."
	CORRECT	Their motto was "All for one and one for all."

Rewrite each sentence below, correcting any errors in the use of commas.

1. I listen to reggae, and salsa music a lot, I don't care for what I call "elevator music."

2. Our coach's favorite saying is, "Failure teaches success" and that's one reason he's such a good coach.

3. Some newspapers reported that Dewey had beaten Truman in the 1948 election but Truman's victory was discovered when all the votes were counted.

4. There are many different blues; they include, navy blue, sky blue, and powder blue.

5. Wherever she goes, and whatever she does, will be fine.

"THEN, AS YOU CAN SEE, WE GIVE THEM SOME MULTIPLE CHOICE TESTS."

Sidney Harris

Rewrite each sentence below, correcting any errors in the use of commas.

1. Twenty miles from the nearest town on the map the car's engine died, and wouldn't start again.
2. Well we have pears apples peaches and grapes.
3. Flowers that are fragrant, are a welcome addition to any garden.
4. A frightened wounded animal can be very dangerous; but don't think a courageous healthy bear is safe.
5. Ralph Bunche negotiated the first Arab-Israeli armistice in 1949 moreover he won a Nobel Peace Prize, for his efforts.
6. By the way the blonde woman running to answer the phone, is my aunt.
7. When Laura was ten she moved to Denver Colorado didn't she?
8. I addressed the envelope to the president not the vice president at 1600, Pennsylvania Avenue, Washington D.C., 20016.
9. I was running to catch the bus, and, of course, caught my heel in a grate, and tripped.
10. I'll lock the back door, and check to see if the windows are closed all right?

11.7 THE DASH

On a typewriter, indicate the dash with two hyphens (--). If you're using a computer, you may make a dash with a certain combination of keystrokes. Refer to the manual of your word-processing program for instructions.

Don't place a comma, a semicolon, a colon, or a period before or after a dash.

GRAMMAR/USAGE/MECHANICS

DASHES TO SIGNAL CHANGE

Use a dash to indicate an abrupt break or change in thought within a sentence.

EXAMPLE   "I think the answer is—I've forgotten what I was going to say."

EXAMPLE   All of us—I mean most of us—look forward to vacations.

DASHES TO EMPHASIZE

Use a dash to set off and emphasize extra information or parenthetical comments.

EXAMPLE   Operatic soprano Dame Kiri Te Kanawa—she is the Maori superstar who sang at the wedding of the Prince and Princess of Wales in 1981—published *Land of the Long White Cloud: Maori Myths and Legends* in 1989.

Don't overuse dashes in your writing. Dashes are most often found in informal or personal letters. In formal writing situations, use subordinating conjunctions (such as *after, until, because,* and *unless*) or conjunctive adverbs (such as *however, nonetheless,* and *furthermore*), along with the correct punctuation, to show the relationships between ideas.

PRACTICE   Dashes

Rewrite each sentence, correcting errors in the use of the dash.

1. Quilting a global art form requires a good eye for matching colors and patterns.
2. I really like, no, I love, jazz music.

3. Measure exactly one cup of cornmeal, hey, you need to listen to this, and stir it in.
4. The earliest existing poem by an African American, "Bars Fight," *bars* refers to meadows was written in 1746 by Lucy Terry Prince.
5. Last week the hottest on record, I hear, was terrible.

11.8 PARENTHESES

PARENTHESES TO SET OFF SUPPLEMENTAL MATERIAL

Use parentheses to set off supplemental, or extra, material.

Commas and dashes as well as parentheses can be used to set off supplemental material; the difference between the three marks of punctuation is one of degree. Use commas to set off supplemental material that is closely related to the rest of the sentence. Use parentheses to set off supplemental material that is not important enough to be considered part of the main statement. Use dashes to set off and emphasize any material that interrupts the main statement.

EXAMPLE   Mary Jane Canary (Calamity Jane) knew Wild Bill Hickok.

EXAMPLE   The ASL (Amateur Storytellers League) entertains listeners at their monthly meetings.

A complete sentence within parentheses is not capitalized and needs no period if it is contained within another sentence. If a sentence within parentheses is not contained within another sentence—that is, if it stands by itself—both a capital letter and end punctuation are needed.

EXAMPLE Mary Jane Canary (she was known as Calamity Jane)
was a good friend of Wild Bill Hickok's.

EXAMPLE Paul Bunyan is a famous figure in the folklore of the
United States. (You can learn all about him at the Paul
Bunyan Center in Minnesota.)

PARENTHESES WITH OTHER MARKS OF PUNCTUATION

Place a comma, a semicolon, or a colon *after* the
closing parentheses.

EXAMPLE The writer Bret Harte is associated with the West (his
stories include "The Luck of Roaring Camp" and "The
Outcasts of Poker Flat"), but this celebrated western
author was actually born in Albany, New York.

Place a question mark or an exclamation point
inside the parentheses if it is part of the parenthetical
expression.

EXAMPLE Owatonna is the name of a Native American princess
(a member of the Santee nation?) who lived hundreds
of years ago.

EXAMPLE A novel based on the life of Sacagawea (what a fascinating person she must have been!) was published
recently.

Place a period, a question mark, or an exclamation
point *outside* the parentheses if it is part of the entire
sentence.

EXAMPLE The code of laws that governed Iroquois society was
the Great Binding Law (known as the Iroquois
Constitution).

EXAMPLE   How surprised I was to learn that the British call corn
           maize **(**which comes from the West Indian name for
           corn**)!**

PRACTICE Parentheses

Rewrite each sentence, adding parentheses and any other necessary punctuation for clarity.

1. In one system of grouping nutrients, four major groups, fruits and vegetables, grains, meat and legumes, and dairy are used.
2. The NAACP National Association for the Advancement of Colored People was founded in 1909.
3. Fiona used henna you know, the hair dye, to paint Indian patterns on her hand.
4. In twelve years from 1630 to 1642 sixteen thousand people migrated from England to this area.
5. Henry Jones he's someone I've known for years is a really nice guy.

11.9 BRACKETS AND ELLIPSIS POINTS

BRACKETS

Use brackets to enclose information that you have inserted into a quotation for clarity.

EXAMPLE   We cannot be free until they **[**all Americans**]** are.
                                              —James Baldwin

Use brackets to enclose a parenthetical phrase that already appears within parentheses.

EXAMPLE   The name *Oregon* comes from the French word *oura-gan* (which means "hurricane" **[**referring to the Columbia River**]**).

Chapter 11 Punctuation, Abbreviations, and Numbers   **343**

GRAMMAR/USAGE/MECHANICS

Rewrite the following sentences, adding brackets where they are needed.

1. Adrian exclaimed, "I have always dreamed of visiting the City of Lights Paris, and now I am finally here!"
2. The article reported, "Wherever he went, they the townspeople followed."
3. Martha replied, "I have never read it *The Bluest Eye,* but I've heard it's really good."
4. "It pecan pie is the best I've ever tasted," cried the famous chef.
5. Stephen Biko (who was from South Africa the country that recently abolished its apartheid policies) died in 1977.

ELLIPSIS POINTS

Use a series of three spaced periods, called ellipsis points, to indicate the omission of material from a quotation.

Use three spaced periods if the omission is at the beginning of the sentence. If the omission is at the middle or the end of the sentence, include any punctuation immediately preceding the omitted material (for instance, a comma, a semicolon, or a period) plus the three spaced periods. When it is necessary to use a period, do not leave any space between the last word and the first ellipsis point, which is the period.

EXAMPLE   "Listen, my children, and you shall hear. . . ."
                                  —Henry Wadsworth Longfellow

If the remaining material becomes the end of the sentence, replace the internal punctuation mark with a period, followed by three ellipsis points.

EXAMPLE	ORIGINAL QUOTATION	She spoke sullenly, careful to show no interest or pleasure, and he spoke in a fast bright monotone.
		—Joyce Carol Oates
	QUOTATION WITH OMISSION	She spoke sullenly, careful to show no interest or pleasure. . . .
		—Joyce Carol Oates

PRACTICE   Ellipsis Points

Rewrite the following passage from Patrick Henry's Speech in the Virginia Convention, adding ellipsis points in place of the underlined material.

<u>Mr. President</u>, it is natural <u>to man</u> to indulge in the illusions of hope. We are apt to shut our eyes against a painful truth, <u>and listen to the song of that siren till she transorms us into beasts</u>. Is this the part of wise men, engaged in a great <u>and arduous</u> struggle for liberty? Are we disposed to be of the number of those who, having eyes, see not, and having ears, hear not, the things which <u>so nearly</u> concern their temporal salvation? For my part, <u>whatever anguish of spirit it may cost</u>, I am willing to know the whole truth; to know the worst, and to provide for it.

GRAMMAR/USAGE/MECHANICS

11.10 QUOTATION MARKS

QUOTATION MARKS WITH DIRECT QUOTATIONS

Use quotation marks to enclose a direct quotation.

Place quotation marks around the quotation only, not around purely introductory or explanatory remarks. Generally, separate such remarks from the actual quotation with a comma. (For the use of colons to introduce quotations, see page 322.)

EXAMPLE   "Weave us a garment of brightness," says a Native American song.

EXAMPLE   Phil Rizzuto, in an observation famous for its optimism, said, "They still can't steal first base."

EXAMPLE   The first verse of the national anthem of the United States begins with the words "Oh, say, can you see. . . . " and ends with ". . . and the home of the brave."

Do not use a comma after a quotation that ends with an exclamation point or a question mark.

EXAMPLE   "Look at me! Look at my arm. I have ploughed and planted, and gathered into barns, and no man could head me! And ain't I a woman?" said Sojourner Truth when she addressed the Ohio Women's Rights Convention in 1851.

When a quotation is interrupted by explanatory words such as *he said* or *she wrote,* use two sets of quotation marks.

Separate each part of the quotation from the interrupting phrase with marks of punctuation before and after the phrase. If the second part of the quotation is a complete sentence, begin it with a capital letter and use a period, not a comma, after the interrupting phrase.

EXAMPLE   "Writing free verse," Robert Frost begins a famous poetry definition, "is like playing tennis with the net down."

EXAMPLE   "The Lord prefers common-looking people," Abraham Lincoln once said. "That is why he makes so many of them."

Don't use quotation marks in an indirect quotation.

EXAMPLE   **ORIGINAL QUOTATION**   Toni Morrison said, "I write the kind of books I want to read."

                     INDIRECT QUOTATION   Toni Morrison said she writes the kind of books she wants to read.

Use single quotation marks around a quotation within a quotation.

EXAMPLE   The teacher said to her students, "Benjamin Franklin once wrote, 'Lose no time; be always employed in something useful.'"

In writing dialogue, begin a new paragraph and use a new set of quotation marks every time the speaker changes.

EXAMPLE   "Are you going to pass this collection of abalone shells on to your children?" I said.

"No," he said. "I want my children to collect for themselves. I wouldn't give it to them."

"Why?" I said. "When you die?"

Mr. Abe shook his head. "No. Not even when I die," he said. "I couldn't give the children what I see in these shells. The children must go out for themselves and find their own shells."

—Toshio Mori

QUOTATION MARKS WITH OTHER MARKS OF PUNCTUATION

Always place a comma or a period *inside* closing quotation marks.

EXAMPLE   Nadine Gordimer said in a lecture, "The creative act is not pure."

EXAMPLE   "Literature is a state of culture," Juan Ramón Jiménez said; "poetry is a state of grace."

Always place a semicolon or a colon *outside* closing quotation marks.

EXAMPLE The Greek writer Nikos Kazantzakis said, "My entire soul is a cry"; his meaning escaped me until I read the rest of the quotation, in which he explained, "and all my work is a commentary on that cry."

EXAMPLE According to Rousseau, *"Vivre ce n'est pas respirer, c'est agir"*: "Living is not breathing but doing."

Place the question mark or the exclamation point *inside* the closing quotation marks when it is part of the quotation.

EXAMPLE We read Leonard Bernstein's essay "What Makes Music American?"

EXAMPLE The toddler cried, "No! Cookie *my*!"

Place the question mark or the exclamation point *outside* the closing quotation marks when it is part of the entire sentence.

EXAMPLE When did he say, "We'll be there at nine sharp"?

EXAMPLE How I hate to make a hurried phone call only to hear "Please hold"!

If both the sentence and the quotation at the end of the sentence need a question mark (or an exclamation point), use only one punctuation mark, and place it *inside* the closing quotation marks.

EXAMPLE What was the name of the French poet who asked, "Where are the snows of yesteryear?"

EXAMPLE How astounded we were to hear little Timmy pipe up, "I know! It was François Villon!"

Don't use a comma after a quotation that ends with a question mark or an exclamation point.

EXAMPLE "That's a surprise!" my mother said, smiling.

QUOTATION MARKS WITH TITLES, UNUSUAL EXPRESSIONS, AND DEFINITIONS

Use quotation marks to enclose titles of short works, such as short stories, short poems, essays, newspaper articles, magazine articles, book chapters, songs, and single episodes of a television series.

EXAMPLE   "Abalone, Abalone, Abalone" [short story]

EXAMPLE   "Dream Variations" [short poem]

EXAMPLE   "A Chicano in China" [essay]

EXAMPLE   "Bald Eagle Coming Off Endangered Species List" [newspaper article]

EXAMPLE   "Ahab" [book chapter]

EXAMPLE   "The Star-Spangled Banner" [song]

EXAMPLE   "Lions and Tigers and Bears, Oh, My!" [episode in a television series]

Note: For the use of italics with longer titles, see page 351.

Use quotation marks to enclose unfamiliar slang and other unusual or original expressions.

EXAMPLE   "Groovy" was a word of high praise in the late 1960s.

EXAMPLE   In the late 1990s, "fresh" and "fly" were complimentary adjectives.

Be careful not to overuse quotation marks with unusual expressions. Generally, use quotation marks only the first time you use the unusual expression in a piece of writing.

Use quotation marks to enclose a definition that is stated directly.

EXAMPLE   *Ukulele* comes from the Hawaiian words for "jumping flea."

The word *beige* in French means "of the natural color of undyed wool."

PRACTICE Quotation Marks

Rewrite each item, correcting errors in the use of quotation marks and other punctuation.

1. The English word *petite* comes from French and means small and dainty.
2. "My favorite Shakespearean speech," said Titus, "begins with the line, "What a piece of work is man!"
3. Juana told me that she "loves the feeling and the sound of her bat making solid contact with the ball."
4. "Satire is a sort of glass wrote Jonathan Swift wherein beholders do generally discover everybody's face but their own."
5. Where have you been is a question my mother often asks.
6. Why is she so frustrated when I respond Out?
7. My mother's favorite poem is Dylan Thomas's Fern Hill.
8. Did Jean say When is the movie? or Where is the movie?
9. I used to love to throw my nephew his bay-baw, which was, of course, a baseball.
10. I can't wait for summer crowed Isabella unless I have to go to summer school!

11.11 ITALICS (UNDERLINING)

Italic type is a special slanted type that is used in printing. (*This sentence is printed in italics.*) Indicate italics on a typewriter or with handwriting by underlining. (<u>This sentence is underlined</u>.) When you are using a computer, learn the special keystrokes for italics by referring to your software manual.

ITALICS WITH TITLES

Italicize (underline) the following: titles of books, long poems, plays, films, television series, paintings, sculptures, and long musical compositions. Also italicize (underline) the names of ships, airplanes, spacecraft, newspapers, magazines, and court cases.

A "long poem" or a "long musical composition" is any poem or musical composition published under its own title as a separate work.

EXAMPLES

The Invisible Man [book]

A Raisin in the Sun [play]

Nature [television series]

David [sculpture]

USS *Intrepid** [ship]

Apollo 9 [spacecraft]

Psychology Today [magazine]

Leaves of Grass [long poem]

Casablanca [film]

Christina's World [painting]

Ninth Symphony [long musical composition]

Spruce Goose [airplane]

St. Louis Post-Dispatch [newspaper]

Brown v. Board of Education of Topeka Kansas [court case]

*Don't italicize abbreviations such as USS in the name of a ship.

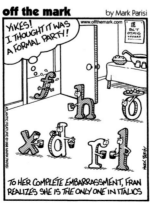

off the mark by Mark Parisi

www.offthemark.com

YIKES! I THOUGHT IT WAS A FORMAL PARTY!

TO HER COMPLETE EMBARRASSMENT, FRAN REALIZES SHE IS THE ONLY ONE IN ITALICS

off the mark © Mark Parisi. Reprinted with permission of Atlantic Feature Syndicate.

Italicize (underline) and capitalize articles (*a*, *an*, *the*) written at the beginning of a title only when they are a part of the title itself. It is common practice not to italicize (underline) the article preceding the title of a newspaper or a magazine. Do not italicize the word *magazine* unless it is a part of the title of a periodical.

EXAMPLE

The Old Man and the Sea   *A Night at the Opera*

but

the *Arabian Nights*   the *New Yorker* magazine

ITALICS WITH FOREIGN WORDS

Italicize (underline) foreign words and expressions that are not used frequently in English.

EXAMPLE   James always ends his letters to me with the words ***hasta la vista.***

Don't italicize (underline) a foreign word or expression that is commonly used in English. Consult a dictionary; if a foreign word or expression is a dictionary entry word, don't italicize (underline) it.

EXAMPLE   The health spa offers courses in **judo** and **karate.**

ITALICS WITH WORDS AND OTHER ITEMS USED TO REPRESENT THEMSELVES

Italicize (underline) words, letters, and numerals used to represent themselves—that is, words used as words, letters used as letters, and numerals used as numerals.

EXAMPLE   To make your essays read more smoothly, connect ideas with conjunctive adverbs such as ***therefore*** and ***however.***

EXAMPLE   The *t* and the *v* sometimes stick on this typewriter.

EXAMPLE   Should I use the dollar sign (*$*) or spell out the word?

PRACTICE   **Italics (Underlining)**

Rewrite each item, correcting errors in the use of italics (underlining).

1. The musical Rent is based on an opera.
2. Thoreau's book Walden has become an American classic.
3. The TV newsmagazine 60 Minutes has been popular for many years.
4. Mom says she is "non compos mentis" whenever she feels mentally incompetent, since that's what the Latin phrase means.
5. The word professional is spelled with only one f .

11.12 THE APOSTROPHE

APOSTROPHES TO SHOW POSSESSION

Use an apostrophe and *-s* for the possessive form of a singular indefinite pronoun.

Do not use an apostrophe with other possessive pronouns.

EXAMPLE   somebody**'s** hat

EXAMPLE   each other**'s** books

EXAMPLE   no one**'s** business

           but

EXAMPLE   **its** engine

EXAMPLE   **whose** mail

EXAMPLE   The responsibility is **theirs.**

EXAMPLE   The rewards are **yours.**

EXAMPLE   The car is **ours.**

Use an apostrophe and -*s* to form the possessive of a singular noun, even one that ends in *s*.

EXAMPLES the child**'s** toys	Ray Charles**'s** music
EXAMPLES the bus**'s** muffler	Wallace Stevens**'s** poetry
EXAMPLES the duchess**'s** plans	Harpo Marx**'s** sweet smile
EXAMPLES the lynx**'s** habitat	Peru**'s** mountains

There are some exceptions to this rule, however. To form the possessive of ancient proper nouns that end in *es* or *is*, the name *Jesus,* and expressions with such words as *conscience* and *appearance,* just add an apostrophe.

EXAMPLES Ulysses**'** journey	Hercules**'** cradle
EXAMPLES Iris**'** apple of discord	Jesus**'** parables
EXAMPLES Xerxes**'** army	her conscience**'** voice

Use an apostrophe alone to form the possessive of a plural noun that ends in *s*.

EXAMPLES the Girl Scouts**'** badges	the teachers**'** cafeteria
EXAMPLES the Hugheses**'** vacation	the tennis rackets**'** grips

Use an apostrophe and -*s* to form the possessive of a plural noun that does not end in *s*.

EXAMPLES the children**'s** surprise	her teeth**'s** crowns
EXAMPLES the women**'s** decision	his feet**'s** arches

Put only the last word of a compound noun in the possessive form.

EXAMPLES	my sister-in-law**'s** computer
	the foster child**'s** happiness
EXAMPLES	my great-grandfather**'s** watch
	my pen pal**'s** photograph

If two or more persons (or partners in a company) possess something jointly, use the possessive form for the last person named.

EXAMPLE   my father and mother**'s** house

EXAMPLE   Lerner and Loewe**'s** musicals

EXAMPLE   Lord and Taylor**'s** department store

EXAMPLE   Procter and Gamble**'s** e-mail address

If two or more persons (or companies) possess an item (or items) individually, put each one's name in the possessive form.

EXAMPLE   Julio**'s** and Emma**'s** test scores

EXAMPLE   the Murphys**'** and the Ramirezes**'** houses

EXAMPLE   the winner**'s** and losers**'** times

Use a possessive form to express amounts of money or time that modify a noun.

The modifier can also be expressed as a hyphenated adjective. In that case, no possessive form is used.

EXAMPLE   two hours' drive   *but*   a two-hour drive

EXAMPLE   eighty cents' worth   an eighty-cent loaf

EXAMPLE   five miles' walk   a five-mile walk

APOSTROPHES IN CONTRACTIONS

Use an apostrophe in place of letters that are omitted in contractions.

A **contraction** is a single word made up of two words that have been combined by omitting letters. Common contractions combine a subject and a verb or a verb and the word *not*.

EXAMPLE	I'd	*is formed from*	I had, I would
EXAMPLE	you're		you are
EXAMPLE	who's		who is, who has
EXAMPLE	it's		it is, it has
EXAMPLE	won't		will not
EXAMPLE	can't		cannot

Use an apostrophe in place of the omitted numerals of a year.

EXAMPLES   the summer of '62   the '92 election results

PRACTICE Apostrophes

Rewrite each sentence, correcting errors in the use of the apostrophe.

1. The lightning struck Beths' car as well as Chris' truck.
2. My sister and brother's-in-law's house is on the Olympic Peninsula, about three hours drive from our's.
3. The boys bikes were at the mall, but theyd gone to Armand's and Barrys' house.
4. The Beatles became one of Englands top groups in 62.
5. James' house is five blocks away, and thats not far at all.
6. Id like to babysit for the Green's new baby because shes such a sweetie, but I cant today.
7. The scissors blades arent very sharp; that makes them good for childrens' use.
8. Much of the storys plot has to do with the problems caused by Zeus's temper.
9. A three blocks walk from here is a nice womens' clothing store.
10. The geeses' habitat was slowly disappearing.

11.13 THE HYPHEN

HYPHENS WITH PREFIXES

A hyphen is not ordinarily used to join a prefix to a word. There are a few exceptions, however. If you are in doubt about using a hyphen, consult a dictionary. Also keep in mind the following guidelines:

Use a hyphen after any prefix joined to a proper noun or a proper adjective. Use a hyphen after the prefixes *all-, ex-* (meaning "former"), and *self-* joined to any noun or adjective.

EXAMPLES	pre-Raphaelite	ex-senator
EXAMPLES	all-purpose	self-sealing

Use a hyphen after the prefix *anti-* when it joins a word beginning with *i*. Also use a hyphen after the prefix *vice-*, except in *vice president*.

EXAMPLES anti-inflammatory

     vice-consul

     but vice president

Use a hyphen to avoid confusion between words beginning with *re-* that look alike but are different in meaning and pronunciation.

EXAMPLE	re-cover the sofa	*but*	recover a loss
EXAMPLE	re-store the supplies		restore confidence
EXAMPLE	re-lease the car		release the captives

HYPHENS WITH COMPOUNDS AND NUMBERS

Use a hyphen in a compound adjective that precedes a noun.

In general, a compound adjective that follows a noun is not hyphenated.

EXAMPLE   a plum-colored shirt
but
The shirt is plum colored.

EXAMPLE   the well-liked performer
but
The performer is well liked.

Compound adjectives beginning with *well, ill,* or *little* are usually not hyphenated when they are modified by an adverb.

EXAMPLE   an ill-tempered man
but
a rather ill tempered man

Do not hyphenate an expression made up of an adverb that ends in -*ly* and an adjective.

EXAMPLE   a badly torn blanket

EXAMPLE   a perfectly balanced mobile

Hyphenate any spelled-out cardinal number (such as *twenty-one*) or ordinal number (such as *twenty-first*) up to *ninety-nine* or *ninety-ninth.*

EXAMPLE   I counted **twenty-seven** birds at the feeder.

EXAMPLE   The **twenty-seventh** bird was a goldfinch.

EXAMPLE   Most people have **thirty-two** teeth.

EXAMPLE   The **thirty-second** day of the year is February first.

Hyphenate a fraction that is expressed in words.

EXAMPLES   one-half teaspoon   one-quarter of the pie
a two-thirds majority

Hyphenate two numerals to indicate a span.

EXAMPLES   1899–1999   pages 152–218

When you use the word *from* before a span, use *to* rather than a hyphen. When you use *between* before a span, use *and* rather than a hyphen.

EXAMPLES   **from** 1899 **to** 1999   **between** 2:45 **and** 3:15 P.M.

HYPHENS TO DIVIDE WORDS AT THE END OF A LINE

Words are generally divided between syllables or pronounceable parts. Because it is often difficult to decide where a word should be divided, consult a dictionary.

In general, if a word contains two consonants occurring between two vowels or if it contains double consonants, divide the word between the two consonants.

EXAMPLES   con-sonant   per-sistent   pul-ley   scis-sors

If a suffix has been added to a complete word that ends in two consonants, divide the word after the two consonants. Remember, the object is to make the hyphenated word easy to read and understand.

EXAMPLES   dull-est   reck-less   steward-ship   fill-ing

Rewrite each sentence, correcting errors in the use of hyphens. Then make a list of all the italicized words, showing where each would be divided if it had to be broken at the end of a line. Don't consult a dictionary; divide each word as you have been taught in this lesson.

1. I spent three quarters of an hour at the ironing board because I had to repress my peach colored blouse.
2. Is the *babysitter* prepared to deal with bad mannered and foul mouthed children?
3. On the twenty first of *December,* Clarissa's party lasted from 11:00 A.M.-8:00 P.M.
4. The second *millennium* (A.D.1000-2000) saw *enormous* growth in self government.
5. The chair of the *committee* is a sharp tongued woman who believes she is all knowing.

11.14 ABBREVIATIONS

Abbreviations are shortened forms of words.

Abbreviations save space and time and prevent unnecessary wordiness. Most abbreviations require periods. If you are unsure of how to write an abbreviation, consult a dictionary.

Use only one period, not two, if an abbreviation that has a period occurs at the end of a sentence that would ordinarily take a period of its own.

If an abbreviation that has a period occurs at the end of a sentence that ends with a question mark or an exclamation point, use the abbreviation's period *and* the question mark or the exclamation point.

EXAMPLE   He awoke at 5:00 A.M.

EXAMPLE   Did he really awake at 5:00 A.M.?

CAPITALIZING ABBREVIATIONS

Capitalize abbreviations of proper nouns.

EXAMPLES   **Thurs.**   **U.S.A.**   **U.S. Army**   **Sept.**

Abbreviations of organizations and government agencies are often formed from the initial letters of the complete name. Such abbreviations, whether pronounced letter by letter or as words, do not use periods and are written with capital letters.

EXAMPLES   UN   NASA   ABC   IRS   NBA

When abbreviating a person's first and middle names, leave a space after each initial.

EXAMPLES   Robert **E.** Lee   **W. H.** Auden   **J. S.** Bach

Capitalize the following abbreviations related to dates and times.

A.D. (*anno Domini*, "in the year of the Lord" [since the birth of Christ]); place before the date: A.D. 5

B.C (before Christ); place after the date: 1000 B.C.

B.C.E. (before the common era, equivalent to *B.C.*); place after the date: 164 B.C.E.

C.E. (common era; equivalent to *A.D.*); place after the date: 66 C.E.

A.M. (*ante meridiem*, "before noon"); place after exact times: 7:45 A.M.

P.M. (*post meridiem*, "after noon"); place after exact times: 2:30 P.M.

POSTAL ABBREVIATIONS

In ordinary prose, spell out state names. On envelopes, however, abbreviate state names using the two-letter abbreviations approved by the United States Postal Service.

A complete list of these abbreviations can be found in the Ready Reference section on pages 90–91.

Alabama	**AL**
Florida	**FL**
Louisiana	**LA**
Nebraska	**NE**
Rhode Island	**RI**

The two-letter form for the District of Columbia, for use on envelopes only, is **DC.** In ordinary prose, however, use periods to write **Washington, D.C.**

EXAMPLE   We visited **Washington, D.C.,** on our vacation.

ABBREVIATIONS OF TITLES AND UNITS OF MEASURE

Use abbreviations for some personal titles.

Titles such as *Mrs., Mr., Ms., Sr.,* and *Jr.* and those indicating professions and academic degrees *(Dr., Ph.D., M.A., B.S.)* are almost always abbreviated. Titles of government and military officials and members of the clergy are frequently abbreviated when used before a full name.

EXAMPLES   Maria García, **M.F.A.**   **Mr.** Christopher Reeve

EXAMPLES   Victoria Proudfoot, **M.D.**   Lydia Stryk, **Ph.D.**

EXAMPLES   **Mrs.** Hillary Clinton   **Dr.** Jonas Salk

EXAMPLES   Douglas Fairbanks **Jr.**   Paul Chin, **D.V.M.**

Abbreviate units of measure used with numerals in technical or scientific writing. Do not abbreviate them in ordinary prose.

The abbreviations that follow stand for both singular and plural units.

U.S. SYSTEM		METRIC SYSTEM	
ft.	foot	cg	centigram
gal.	gallon	cl	centiliter
in.	inch	cm	centimeter
lb.	pound	g	gram
mi.	mile	kg	kilogram
oz.	ounce	km	kilometer
pt.	pint	l	liter
qt.	quart	m	meter
tbsp.	tablespoon	mg	milligram
tsp.	teaspoon	ml	milliliter
yd.	yard	mm	millimeter

For more information on abbreviations, see pages 85–92 in the Ready Reference.

For more information on abbreviations, see pages 85–92 in the Ready Reference.

PRACTICE Abbreviations

Rewrite each sentence, correcting errors in the use of abbreviations.

1. Henry VII was crowned Holy Roman emperor in 1312 AD.
2. The train went to Philadelphia, PA, and Washington DC.
3. What advice do you think the patients of John H Salt, MD, get from him?
4. Two N.F.L. teams play in the Super Bowl every year.
5. Jeffrey earned a BA, an MFA, and a PhD, and then he went to work for the US Army.
6. Augustus became the first emperor of Rome in 27 bc. *(acc to EB—my comment))*
7. I'm writing a paper on TS Eliot for my 8:00 am class.
8. Are there two qts or four in a gal?
9. My father is Paul Connor jr, and folks call him Junior.
10. My sister is five ft., three in. tall.

Chapter 11 Punctuation, Abbreviations, and Numbers **363**

GRAMMAR/USAGE/MECHANICS

11.15 NUMBERS AND NUMERALS

In nontechnical writing, some numbers are spelled out, and some are expressed in figures. Numbers expressed in figures are called numerals.

NUMBERS SPELLED OUT

In general, spell out cardinal numbers (such as *twenty*) and ordinal numbers (such as *twentieth*) that can be written in one or two words.

EXAMPLE   We needed **twenty-two** tickets for the whole family.

EXAMPLE   There were **fifteen hundred** people in line.

Spell out any number that occurs at the beginning of a sentence. (Sometimes, it is better to revise the sentence to move the spelled-out number.)

EXAMPLES

Two hundred twenty-five singers performed.

BETTER   There were 225 singers in the performance.

Nineteen ninety-eight was the year my dog was born.

BETTER   My dog was born in 1998.

NUMERALS

In general, use numerals to express numbers that would be written in more than two words.

EXAMPLE   There were **220** marching in the band.

EXAMPLE   We worked **150** hours of community service.

Very large numbers are often written as a numeral followed by the word *million* or *billion.*

EXAMPLE   The area of Canada is roughly **3.85 million** square miles.

If related numbers appear in the same sentence and some can be written out while others should appear as numerals, use all numerals.

EXAMPLE This year the number of women marathon runners increased from **78** to **432.**

Use numerals to express amounts of money, decimals, and percentages. Spell out the word *percent,* however.

EXAMPLE She owed me **$2.75.**

EXAMPLE The bottle holds **1.5** quarts of shampoo.

EXAMPLE The bank paid **6** percent interest.

Amounts of money that can be expressed in one or two words, however, should be spelled out.

EXAMPLES **forty-six** cents   **twenty-two thousand** dollars

Use numerals to express the year and day in a date and to express the precise time with the abbreviations A.M. and P.M.

EXAMPLE Newfoundland became Canada's tenth province on March **31, 1949.**

EXAMPLE The movie was scheduled to begin at **7:05 P.M.**

Spell out expressions of time that do not use A.M. or P.M.

EXAMPLE The movie starts at **seven** o'clock.

To express a century when the word *century* is used, spell out the number. Likewise, to express a decade when the century is clear from the context, spell out the number.

The **twentieth** century saw the beginnings of rock-and-roll music in the **fifties.**

When a decade is identified by its century, use numerals followed by an -*s*.

EXAMPLE The baby boom reached its peak in the **1950s.**

Use numerals for numbered streets and avenues above ninety-nine and for all house, apartment, and room numbers. Spell out numbered streets and avenues of ninety-nine and below.

EXAMPLE The office is near **Fifth** Avenue, at **4** West **347th** Street, Suite **220.**

PRACTICE Numbers and Numerals

Rewrite each item, correcting errors in the use of numbers and numerals.

1. At around 5 o'clock, many people leave work.
2. 1492 is a famous date in American history.
3. During the nineteen eighties, my uncle lived in Algiers, but he returned to the States in nineteen ninety-two.
4. I bought a pen for four dollars and seventy-five cents.
5. During the late 60s, extremely short skirts became popular, and my mom and her 3 sisters all wore them.
6. 5th Avenue in New York is one of the world's most famous streets.
7. There were at least two hundred and fifty people at the first performance, but only about eighty at the second.
8. I have a twenty-five percent share in the family business.
9. 1,000,000 dollars is a lot of money.
10. I wanted to go to One hundred and eighteenth Street, but I ended up on 1st Avenue.

Rewrite the following passage, correcting errors in spelling, capitalization, grammar, and usage. Add any missing punctuation. Write legibly to be sure one letter is not mistaken for another. There are ten errors.

The Phoenicians

[1]The Phoenicians, who lived near the coast in what is now Syria, Israel, and Lebanon, were among the earliest seafaring explorers and all purpose shipbuilders. [2]At the peak of their power and influence the entire Mediterranean region became an area of commerce for them. [3]They established colonies on the coasts of Spain, Sicily, and Africa and exported both products (The famed "cedars of Lebanon" came from Phoenicia) and ideas. [4]The biblical reference in 1 Kings 9,27 to "shipmen that had knowledge of the sea" is referring to Phoenicians.

[5]The Greek historian Herodotus tells of the Phoenicians' voyage in the late 7th or early 6th century B.C. around the entire continent of Africa (the Portuguese did not repeat this feet until 1498 ad), and they may have sailed as far as Britain. [6]Many scholars believe that they colonized areas on the Greek mainland; however, this is not a proven fact. [7]During the Persian Wars (from 492-449 B.C.), the Phoenician naval forces were strong enemies of Greece, but the Phoenician fleet was almost completely destroyed by Greece, before the wars were over.

[8]More information about the Phoenicians as well as other explorers can be found in Paolo Novaresio's book "The Explorers."

Rewrite each sentence, correcting any errors in punctuation.

1. "Grab Bill's hand He can't swim"! shouted Elaine.
2. About three quarters of the time, I can't keep up with my grandmother who jogs regularly.

3. Hilton wondered if he'd ever graduate?

4. Is that an antique civil war uniform.

5. In "Romeo and Juliet," Juliet asks the following question, "What's in a name?"

6. There were twenty six serious fires in our town between 1998-2001.

7. The students on the debate team are as follows, Alec Lena Leon Lydia and Chuck.

8. The warning stated the obvious: smoking is bad for your health.

9. Self confidence is an attractive trait but arrogance is not don't you agree?

10. Oslo is a beautiful city, in fact it is my fathers favorite place in the world.

11. When she got to Buckingham Palace all Billy Jean could think of to say was, "why are the guards wearing those silly hats"?

12. Leanne had to decide where to go to college, Stanford which promised top notch science courses, UCLA which excelled in film, or Williams which offered fabulous art history courses.

13. Lysette uses rayon nylon silk and cotton in her textile art, however she refuses to use polyester.

14. The little red wagon the childrens' favorite toy went plummeting down the hill and ran into the impressive shiny black van parked at the corner.

15. Marion Jones ran around the track holding an American flag, and waving to the crowd.

16. "Well there you are!" said Mrs. Miniver "Now how did you get up in that tree you naughty cat?"

17. We're supposed to have the entire "Iliad" read by tomorrow, yes, we really are, and I dont think I'm the only one who wont have finished.

18. I like Indian food, especially dal and chapatis.

19. "Those years were harder ones for my family than for your's" said Lucy sighing.

20. If everyones breakfast is eaten we can leave.

POSTTEST Correcting Errors in the Use of Abbreviations and Numbers

Rewrite each item, correcting any errors in the use of abbreviations and numbers.

21. Linda's assignment was to read from page one hundred to page 126 in her history textbook.

22. At 7:00 o'clock, I called my brother in Washington, DC.

23. I bought this book about synonyms, by SI Hayakawa, for only $2.00 at a thrift shop.

24. Mia got her b a and went to work for the I.R.S.

25. About 8 km farther south, archaeologists uncovered the remains of a town that they estimated had been abandoned around two thousand b.c.

26. The sign said that the auditions would begin at 200 p.m.

27. My dad graduated from Brown University in Providence, RI, in nineteen eighty.

28. Although 95 % of the crowd was peaceful, the remaining five % caused some trouble.

29. I have 30 lbs. of sugar in my pantry!

30. To call Dr Barnett, should I use the number listed for Rita Barnett, DVM, or Rita Barnett, M.D?

GRAMMAR/USAGE/MECHANICS

Chapter 12

Sentence Combining

● ● ● ● ● ● ● ● ● ● ● ● ● ● ● ●

PRETEST **Combining Sentences**

Read each group of sentences below. Combine the sentences in the way that seems best to you.

1. Gayla needs to practice the piano. She also needs to study.
2. Carbon has a high melting point. It is a basic element.
3. The football fans yelled. They were filled with glee.
4. Dolphins are intelligent animals. They are mammals.
5. The day was rainy. The day was foggy. It was winter.
6. Children were on the playground. They were the youngest children. The playground was new.

7. The scientist discovered an element. The element was radioactive. The scientist was brilliant.

8. The room was filled with the smell of hot cider. The smell made everyone feel comfortable.

9. The U. S. Post Office printed a stamp showing George Washington. It printed a stamp showing Benjamin Franklin. It did this when it first printed stamps.

10. I collect buttons and beads. The beads are from all over the world. The buttons are vintage.

11. I will take French next semester. If I don't take French, I will take Spanish.

12. The most remembered song from *The Wizard of Oz* is "Somewhere over the Rainbow." The song was almost cut from the movie.

13. Kathy slurped her chicken noodle soup. She ate it from a large spoon.

14. Erato is the daughter of the goddess of memory. Erato is also one of the muses.

15. The octopus has eight arms. The squid has ten.

16. Henri Rousseau was self-taught. He was a famous French painter.

17. The glasses were broken. They were fixed with masking tape.

18. Spencer Tracy won the Oscar for best actor two years in a row. So did Tom Hanks.

19. Aaron Burr was indicted for murder. At the same time, he was vice president of the United States.

20. Insects pollinate crops. They disperse seeds. They control harmful organisms.

12.1 TIPS FOR SENTENCE COMBINING

A distinctive writing style is one way of communicating your personality. Developing a clear, expressive writing style requires practice, of course. By writing regularly in your journal and by trying out different kinds of writing—poems, essays, stories, letters to the editor—you practice a range of skills. Another excellent approach for developing style is sentence combining.

The process of combining short sentences into more complex ones is the focus of this chapter. Your goal, though, is not to make long sentences, but to make good ones. Sometimes you'll find that longer, complex sentences let you express your ideas clearly and precisely. At other times, shorter is better.

Sentence combining is easy and fun. Here are some suggestions that have worked for other high school students—suggestions you might try as you explore your style.

1. **Whisper sentences to yourself.** This is faster than writing, and it helps you decide on the best sentence to write down.

2. **Work with a partner.** By trying out sentences on a partner and hearing your partner's ideas, you will often discover new, interesting ways to solve specific challenges. Feel free to borrow ideas.

3. **Use context when choosing sentences for a paragraph.** Each paragraph has an emerging context: the sentences you have already combined. Reading this context aloud helps you decide on the best next sentence.

4. **Compare your sentences with those of other students.** Seeing how others have solved combining tasks broadens your awareness of sentence options. Keep asking yourself, "Which do I prefer?"

5. **Look for stylistic patterns in your writing.** Calculate the average number of words per sentence; study your sentence openers; listen to rhythms in your style. Try new patterns to stretch yourself.

6. **Take risks.** It makes good sense to take risks and make mistakes as you combine sentences. Mistakes provide feedback. As you learn from them, you develop a personal style, a voice. You come to know yourself as a writer.

The point of sentence combining is to improve your revising and editing skills. Practice in combining sentences helps you see that sentences are flexible tools for thought, not rigid structures cast in concrete. The simple fact that you feel confident in moving sentence parts around increases your control of revising and editing. To acquire this sense of self-confidence—based on your real competence in combining and revising sentences—try strategies like these:

1. **Vary the length of your sentences.** Work for a rhythmic, interesting balance of long and short sentences, remembering that short sentences can be dramatic.

2. **Vary the structure of your sentences.** By using sentence openers occasionally and by sometimes tucking information into the middle of a sentence, you can create stylistic interest.

3. **Use parallelism for emphasis.** Experiment with repeated items in a series—words, phrases, clauses.

4. **Use interruption for emphasis.** Commas, colons, semicolons, dashes, parentheses—all of these are useful in your stylistic toolkit.

5. **Use unusual patterns for emphasis.** That you might sometimes reverse normal sentence patterns may never have occurred to you, but it can strengthen your writing.

You'll use these four main strategies when you combine sentences:

- deleting repeated words
- adding connecting words
- rearranging words
- changing the form of words

12.2 COMBINING SENTENCES BY INSERTING WORDS

When two sentences talk about the same idea, sometimes you can effectively combine them simply by taking a word or words from one sentence and inserting them into the other sentence. Occasionally the word or words you are inserting must change their form.

ORIGINAL VERSION	COMBINED VERSION
Sharks detect electrical fields The electrical fields are faint.	Sharks detect **faint** electrical fields. **[no change]**
A homing pigeon can hear wind sounds. The wind sounds have low frequencies. The sounds are thousands of miles away.	A homing pigeon can hear **low-frequency** wind sounds **thousands of miles away.** **[The noun phrase *low frequencies* has changed to the compound adjective *low-frequency*.]**

Read each group of sentences below. Combine the sentences in each group by inserting a word or words from the later sentences into the first sentence.

1. Sara ate the grapes straight from the vine. They were sweet. They were juicy.
2. The dog barked. It did this loudly. It did this angrily.
3. The train surged through the night. The night was still. It was cloudless.
4. Maria hung curtains at the bedroom window. The curtains were lacy.
5. Do you need this pencil to finish that test? It is sharpened. It is yellow.
6. The limb of the tree tapped on the window. It tapped gently.
7. Camels run across the desert. They run quickly. The desert is vast.
8. Do you have butterfly barrettes in your hair? Are they little? Are they purple? Are they silk?
9. Most flowers grow well in good soil. They grow well in rich soil.
10. Do you like that book about the history of the Roman Empire? Why?

12.3 COMBINING SENTENCES BY INSERTING PHRASES

Another way to combine sentences is to insert a phrase from one sentence into another sentence. Sometimes you can use the phrase unchanged; at other times, you must make the words into a phrase. The most useful phrases for this purpose are prepositional phrases, appositive phrases, and participial phrases.

PREPOSITIONAL PHRASES

ORIGINAL VERSION	COMBINED VERSION
Bobolinks sense subtle distortions. The distortions are in the earth's magnetic field.	Bobolinks sense subtle distortions **in the earth's magnetic field.** [no change]
They use this information to navigate. The information helps them map their location.	They use this information **like a map** to navigate. [**The second sentence is changed into a prepositional phrase.**]

Note: For more information on prepositional phrases, see pages 146–148.

PRACTICE Combining Sentences by Inserting Prepositional Phrases

Read each group of sentences below. Combine the sentences by inserting prepositional phrases in the way that seems best to you.

1. The book I am reading is *The World My Wilderness*. It is by Rose Macauley.
2. Ellen ran across the meadow. She was without shoes.
3. Helga has a beautiful violin. It has a deep golden finish.
4. I am growing tomatoes. They are in the garden. They are near the back wall.
5. Our yard has a pond. It is beneath the willow tree.
6. The sun rises every day. The time that it rises is early morning.
7. Jeffrey expected to meet William. Jeffrey thought they would meet at the corner.
8. My mother bakes. She uses real butter.

9. My old teachers greeted me. They had smiles on their faces.

10. George Washington sat. He sat with an ax. He sat beneath the cherry tree.

APPOSITIVE PHRASES

ORIGINAL VERSION	COMBINED VERSION
Charles Dickens was born in 1812. He was a British novelist.	Charles Dickens, **a British novelist,** was born in 1812.

or

British novelist Charles Dickens was born in 1812. |

Note: For more information on appositive phrases, see pages 148–149.

PRACTICE | **Combining Sentences by Inserting Appositive Phrases**

Read each group of sentences below. Combine the sentences by inserting appositive phrases in the way that seems best to you.

1. Experts consider Ben Jonson nearly as important as William Shakespeare. Jonson was an English playwright.

2. Lake Quinault is on the Olympic Peninsula. It is fed by glaciers.

3. The scissor-tailed flycatcher is an odd-looking creature. It is the state bird of Oklahoma.

4. Sir Francis Galton determined that everyone's fingerprints are unique. He was a British anthropologist.

5. During digestion, the human stomach secretes a fluid to break down food. The fluid is dilute hydrochloric acid.

GRAMMAR/USAGE/MECHANICS

6. My little dog accidentally bit the nose off Earl. Earl is my teddy bear.
7. My aunt Wilma ate her regular breakfast. It was a bagel with cream cheese.
8. The wrapping on my present was beautiful. It was a floral design.
9. James Garfield is an ancestor of mine. He was the twentieth president of the United States.
10. The salsa was too spicy for me. It is our grandmother's secret recipe.

PARTICIPIAL PHRASES

ORIGINAL VERSION	COMBINED VERSION
Dickens's novels were immensely popular in the nineteenth century. They contained a hidden agenda.	**Containing a hidden agenda,** Dickens's novels were immensely popular in the nineteenth century.
	or
	Dickens's novels, **containing a hidden agenda,** were immensely popular in the nineteenth century.
Dickens's novels opposed many human rights violations of the time. They were crowded with memorable characters.	Dickens's novels, **crowded with memorable characters,** opposed many human rights violations of the time.
	or
	Crowded with memorable characters, Dickens's novels opposed many human rights violations of the time.

Note: For more information on participial phrases, see pages 150–151.

Combining Sentences by Inserting Participles and Participial Phrases

Read each group of sentences below. Combine the sentences by inserting participles or participial phrases in the way that seems best to you.

1. The doctor was tired. She gave me a smile.
2. Ed tripped on a branch. He was running through a forest.
3. The rock was smooth. It had been worn by tides.
4. John bit his lip. He tried to look serious.
5. I noticed the rabbit. It was peeking through the bushes.
6. That runner won the race. He sprinted to the finish line.
7. Cooper ordered an ice cream sundae. It was made with two scoops of ice cream.
8. Workers near Naples, Italy, were digging in 1748. They began to uncover the ruins of Pompeii.
9. Pompeii had been covered by a volcanic eruption. In A.D. 79. The city had been frozen in time for seventeen hundred years.
10. Experts paid little attention. They did not recognize the importance of the discovery.

12.4 COMBINING SENTENCES USING COORDINATING CONJUNCTIONS

To combine sentences that have equally important ideas, you can form a compound sentence by using a coordinating conjunction *(and, but, or, so, nor, for, yet)* or a pair of correlative conjunctions *(both . . . and, just as . . . so, not only . . . but (also), either . . . or, neither . . . nor, whether . . . or).* As an alternative to using conjunctions to join the independent clauses, you could use a semicolon with or without a conjunctive adverb, such as *however, consequently,* and *furthermore.*

ORIGINAL VERSION	COMBINED VERSION
Jan stood up in the front of the room. She asked for silence.	Jan stood up in the front of the room **and** asked for silence.
My car's engine is good. Its brakes need to be replaced.	My car's engine is good, **but** its brakes need to be replaced.
Let's repair that wobbly table. Alternatively, we could replace it.	Let's **either** repair that wobbly table **or** replace it.
The waiter was slow and rude. For those reasons, I left no tip.	The waiter was slow and rude; **accordingly**, I left no tip.

PARALLELISM

The sentence parts joined by conjunctions must be *parallel;* that is, they must use the same grammatical constructions. For example, a noun should be matched with a noun, an adjective with an adjective, and a phrase with a phrase. A conjunction should not be used to link an adjective with a noun, a noun with a verb, or a phrase with a clause.

EXAMPLE   **INCORRECT**   The man was tall and a hero.

CORRECT   The man was tall and heroic.

PRACTICE   **Combining Sentences Using Conjunctions and Conjunctive Adverbs**

Read each group of sentences below. Combine the sentences, using conjunctions or conjunctive adverbs. Be sure your constructions are parallel.

1. Riva has beautiful hair. She has lovely eyes.
2. The lamp broke. I had to use a flashlight.
3. Koalas are cute. They are not bears.

4. The music that was playing on Beverly's radio was loud. It was an opera.

5. My family believes in eating dinner together. For this reason, no one makes other plans for dinner time.

6. The man who moved in next door seems to be a traditionalist. He seems conservative.

7. I enjoy spending time with Harriet because she is cheerful. She is an optimist.

8. We are going to Wyoming for vacation. If we don't go there, we are going to Arizona.

9. A person's friends are important. A person's family is important too.

10. Sherry did not want to go to the party. Even though she felt this way, she went.

12.5 COMBINING SENTENCES USING SUBORDINATION IN ADVERB CLAUSES, ADJECTIVE CLAUSES, AND NOUN CLAUSES

Sometimes the ideas in two sentences are not equally important. Instead, one idea is more important than the other. You can combine these kinds of sentences by making the less important idea into a subordinate clause.

ADVERB CLAUSES

One kind of subordinate clause is an adverb clause. An adverb clause is introduced by a subordinating conjunction and modifies a verb, an adjective, or another adverb in the main clause. Following are some subordinating conjunctions you might use to show the relationship between the two clauses.

SUBORDINATING CONJUNCTIONS

FOR EXPRESSING TIME RELATIONSHIPS	after, as, as soon as, before, since, so long as, until, when, whenever, while
FOR EXPRESSING PLACE RELATIONSHIPS	as far as, where, wherever
FOR EXPRESSING CAUSE-AND-EFFECT RELATIONSHIPS	as, because, since, so (that)
FOR EXPRESSING CONDITIONAL RELATIONSHIPS	although, as if, as long as, as though, considering (that), if, inasmuch as, in order that, provided (that), since, than, so (that), though, unless, whereas

In the following examples, some of the techniques you have already seen are used along with subordinating conjunctions to combine several sentences into one. Study the examples to see how the techniques can be used together.

ORIGINAL VERSION	COMBINED VERSION
His destination was a truck stop. The truck stop was familiar. He would have breakfast there.	His destination was a familiar truck stop **where** he would have breakfast.
The cook poured water into the skillet of venison sausage patties. The patties were sputtering. Venison should cook slowly.	The cook poured water into the skillet of sputtering venison sausage patties **because** venison should cook slowly.
Her stylish shoes pinched her feet cruelly. The shoes were tight. In spite of the pain, she danced every dance with a smile. The smile was blissful.	**Although** her stylish but tight shoes pinched her feet cruelly, she danced every dance with a blissful smile.

Note: For more information on using subordinating conjunctions in adverb clauses, see page 168.

GRAMMAR/USAGE/MECHANICS

Combining Sentences Using Subordination: Adverb Clauses

Read each pair of sentences below. Using adverb clauses, combine the sentences in the way that seems best to you.

1. The Pony Express was not misnamed. Many of the horses on the trail were native ponies.
2. We looked at the museum exhibits. Later each person voted for his or her favorite exhibit.
3. The company decided to close down the plant near our high school. Business there had fallen off drastically in recent months.
4. The lights flashed. The music blared. Right then Dion began to dance.
5. We will arrange the furniture. First we will sand and varnish the floors.
6. Jake likes the sauce on pizza. He doesn't like tomatoes in any other form.
7. Jeff couldn't find a table he liked. He had looked a long time. He made one himself.
8. No one had volunteered for the decoration committee. The party was a great success.
9. Tara worked hard to memorize her music for the recital. She had many other things to do.
10. Em believes she will be the president. She will be grown up at that time.

ADJECTIVE CLAUSES

An adjective clause is a subordinate clause that modifies a noun or a pronoun in the main clause. To combine ideas using an adjective clause, replace the subject of one sentence with the word *who, whose, which,* or *that.*

ORIGINAL VERSION	COMBINED VERSION
My father taught me about the Australian Aborigines. My father was born in Australia.	My father, **who was born in Australia,** taught me about the Australian Aborigines.
	or
	My father, **who taught me about the Australian Aborigines,** was born in Australia.
Oodgeroo Noonuccal was a poet and an Aboriginal rights activist. Her name is pronounced OO-juh-roo nuh-NUCK-ul	Oodgeroo Noonuccal, **whose name is pronounced OO-juh-roo nuh-NUCK-ul,** was a poet and an Aboriginal rights activist.
Her 1964 collection of poems was called *We Are Going.* It made her the first Aboriginal writer to be published in English.	Her 1964 collection of poems, **which made her the first Aboriginal writer to be published in English,** was called *We Are Going.*
	or
	Her 1964 collection of poems, **which was called *We Are Going,*** made her the first Aboriginal writer to be published in English.

PRACTICE Combining Sentences Using Subordination: Adjective Clauses

Read each group of sentences below. Using adjective clauses, combine the sentences in the way that seems best to you.

1. The most crowded state in the United States is New Jersey. It has the most people per square mile.
2. *Vermont* is a good name for that beautiful state. The name means "green mountain."

3. Most Eskimos would not think of living in igloos. They are sometimes used as temporary dwellings for travelers.

4. The Danube River begins in the Black Forest of Germany and empties into the Black Sea. It is called the "beautiful blue Danube."

5. Daylight Savings Time wasn't adopted in the United States until 1918. It was originally proposed by Benjamin Franklin in 1784.

6. Lillian Gish made her first film in her teens. She made her last film at the age of ninety-one.

7. King George I of England was born and raised in Germany. He never learned to speak English.

8. Evelyn is not a member of the club. She wants to join it next year.

9. The American one-cent piece does not have the word *penny* anywhere on it. Most people call it a penny.

10. Commemorative postage stamps do not picture living people. They feature many great Americans.

NOUN CLAUSES

A noun clause is a subordinate clause used as a noun. To combine ideas using a noun clause, begin one sentence with one of the words in the following chart. (It will probably be necessary to change some other words in the sentence.) Then put the noun clause you have made into another sentence.

WORDS THAT CAN INTRODUCE NOUN CLAUSES			
how	whatever	which	whoever, whomever
that	when	whichever	whose
what	where	who, whom	why

ORIGINAL VERSION	COMBINED VERSION
I wish I knew something. My notebook is somewhere.	I wish I knew **where my notebook is.** [noun clause acting as direct object]
Give someone the prize. The runner who finishes first is the winner.	Give **whoever is first** the prize. [noun clause acting as indirect object]
A news story should begin with something. It should get the reader's attention.	A news story should begin with **whatever will get the reader's attention.** [noun clause as object of the preposition *with*]
You want to wear clothes that are too big for you. This desire makes no sense to me.	**Why you want to wear clothes that are too big for you** makes no sense to me. [noun clause acting as subject]

PRACTICE Combining Sentences Using Subordination: Noun Clauses

Read each group of sentences below. Using noun clauses, combine the sentences in the way that seems best to you.

1. Did you know this fact? President Gerald Ford was named Leslie King.
2. Jake didn't finish the job until yesterday. I am really disappointed.
3. Why did Dee play that song? I wonder.
4. Parallel lines never meet. I just learned that.
5. Mary Shelley was only twenty when she wrote *Frankenstein?* Are you sure?
6. People throw away perfectly good clothes and buy new ones. I don't understand why.

7. The door was closed when I left the house. I'm sure of that.
8. Why does bread always fall jelly-side down? I wish I knew.
9. Can you help me find something? My ring is somewhere.
10. Allison manages to look good in everything she wears. I don't know how she does it.

PRACTICE **Combining Sentences Using Subordination**

Read each group of sentences below. Using subordination, combine the sentences in the way that seems best to you.

1. The play was over. Then the audience applauded loudly.
2. There was little food on the buffet. Still, we went back.
3. Kayla is a sprinter. She is one of the best athletes and students in our school.
4. What is that red flowering bush over by the back fence? Tell me.
5. I offered to lend you this book. Here it is.
6. Honesty is an important quality in a friend. Many people think this.
7. At times I get tired of rock and roll. Then I listen to classical music or jazz.
8. That house has been for sale for six months. The owner is reducing the price.
9. I can't find my black jacket. I wore it to your party last Friday night.
10. Olives are grown in Spain, Greece, and California. They are the source of olive oil. In these places, they are important to the economy.

The following is a passage about John Boyle O'Reilly. Rewrite the passage, combining sentences that are closely related in meaning. Not all sentences have to be combined.

John Boyle O'Reilly

Many Irish immigrants came to the United States. They came to escape poverty. John Boyle O'Reilly came to escape prison. He was born in Ireland. He was born in 1844. He was a soldier. He was also a member of the Fenian movement. The Fenian movement was an Irish resistance group.

O'Reilly's work for the resistance was discovered. He was court-martialed. He was put in prison. He was deported to Australia. He escaped from the Western Australian Settlement. He was helped by fellow convicts. He was helped by a priest.

Finally O'Reilly ended up in Philadelphia. He arrived there in November of 1869. The Irish-American community welcomed him. He was treated as a hero. He worked for a newspaper. The paper was in Boston. It was an Irish-American newspaper. He began to fight for his people in America. Some were being treated badly. They were poor. They were downtrodden. His writing became more important than his resistance work had ever been. His writing became more powerful.

Read each group of sentences below. Combine the sentences in the way that seems best to you.

1. Jeremy sent me a letter of apology. He wanted my forgiveness.
2. I will put these chairs somewhere. The kitchen is the place where I will put them.

3. Deirdre is the tallest girl in the school. She plays volleyball. She plays it well.
4. Mai likes classical music. She likes music by German composers.
5. That is my favorite mug. It is bright blue.
6. The white-throated capuchin is nimble and slender. It is a small monkey.
7. The doctor was angry. She spoke quietly. She tried to be calm.
8. Verna broke her wrist. For that reason, she had to wear a cast.
9. I left my cap somewhere. I left my muffler there too.
10. The tree fell last night. It is an oak.
11. Someone painted this beautiful picture. I want to meet that person.
12. I don't like to walk over the bridge. My mother reassures me all the time.
13. Anna Jarvis never had a child. She created Mother's Day.
14. How many kinds of apples are there currently? I wonder.
15. The result of the football game seemed sure. The losing team was determined not to give up.
16. Nettie has a great deal of talent. Her talent involves photography.
17. Vera tutors at the library. She was sixteen years old when she started tutoring.
18. Go pick up the tempera paints. During the time you're gone, I'll start sketching in the mural.
19. Someone will present the awards tonight. The person will be a teacher. It will be the teacher who has taught here the longest.
20. Dogs are loyal, loving, appealing, and protective. For these reasons, many people own them as pets.

Chapter 13

Spelling and Vocabulary

• • • • • • • • • • • • • •

13.1 SPELLING RULES

The following rules, examples, and exceptions will help you master the spelling of many words. However, not all words follow the rules. When you're not sure how to spell a word, the best thing to do is check a dictionary.

Spelling *ie* and *ei*

An easy way to learn when to use *ie* and when to use *ei* is to memorize a simple rhyming rule. Then learn the common exceptions to the rule.

RULE	EXAMPLES
"WRITE *I* BEFORE *E*	achieve, believe, brief, chief, die, field, friend, grief, lie, niece, piece, pier, quiet, retrieve, sieve, tie, tier, yield
EXCEPT AFTER *C*	ceiling, conceit, conceive, deceit, deceive, receipt, receive
OR WHEN SOUNDED LIKE *A*, AS IN *NEIGHBOR* AND *WEIGH*."	eight, eighth, eighty, freight, neigh, reign, sleigh, veil, vein, weigh, weight

Some exceptions: *either, caffeine, foreign, forfeit, height, heir, leisure, neither, protein, seize, species, their, weird;* words ending in *cient (ancient)* and *cience (conscience);* plurals of nouns ending in *cy (democracies);* the third-person singular form of verbs ending in *cy (fancies);* words in which *i* and *e* follow *c* but represent separate sounds *(science, society)*

GRAMMAR/USAGE/MECHANICS

Words Ending in *cede, ceed,* and *sede*

The only English word ending in *sede* is *supersede.* Three words end in *ceed: proceed, exceed,* and *succeed.* You can remember these three words by thinking of the following sentence:

If you **proceed** to **exceed** the speed limit, you will **succeed** in getting a ticket.

All other words ending with the "seed" sound are spelled with cede: *concede, intercede, precede, recede, secede.*

Spelling Unstressed Vowels

Listen to the vowel sound in the second syllable of the word *or-i-gin.* This is an unstressed vowel sound, and it can be spelled in many ways. Dictionary respellings use the schwa (ə) to indicate an unstressed vowel sound.

To spell a word that has an unstressed vowel sound, think of a related word in which the syllable containing the vowel sound is stressed.

The word *original,* for example, should help you spell the word *origin.* The chart shows some other examples.

SPELLING UNSTRESSED VOWELS

UNKNOWN SPELLING	RELATED WORD	WORD SPELLED CORRECTLY
leg_l	leg**a**lity	legal
fant_sy	fan**tas**tic	fantasy
host_le	hos**til**ity	hostile
opp_site	op**pose**	opposite
def_nite	de**fine**	definite

Adding Prefixes

Adding prefixes is easy. Keep the spelling of the root word and add the prefix. If the last letter of the prefix is the same as the first letter of the word, keep both letters.

un- + happy = unhappy

dis- + appear = disappear

re- + enlist = reenlist

mis- + spell = misspell

co- + operate = cooperate

il- + legal = illegal

un- + natural = unnatural

im- + migrate = immigrate

Adding Suffixes

When you add a suffix beginning with a vowel, double the final consonant if the word ends in a **single consonant preceded by a single vowel** *and*

- the word has one syllable

mud + -y = muddy   sad + -er = sadder

put + -ing = putting   stop + -ed = stopped

- the word is stressed on the last syllable and the stress remains on the same syllable after the suffix is added

occur + -ence = occurrence

regret + -able = regrettable

begin + -ing = beginning

repel + -ent = repellent

commit + -ed = committed

refer + -al = referral

Don't double the final consonant if the word is not stressed on the last syllable or if the stress shifts when the suffix is added.

murmur + -ed = murmured

refer + -ence = reference

Don't double the final letter if the word ends in *s, w, x,* or *y: buses, rowing, waxy, employer.*

Don't double the final consonant before the suffix -*ist* if the word has more than one syllable: *druggist* but *violinist, guitarist.*

Adding suffixes to words that end in *y* can cause spelling problems. Study the following rules and note the exceptions.

When a word ends in **a vowel and y,** keep the y.

play + -s = plays
obey + -ed = obeyed
buy + -ing = buying
employ + -er = employer
joy + -ful = joyful
joy + -less = joyless

joy + -ous = joyous
annoy + -ance = annoyance
enjoy + -ment = enjoyment
enjoy + -able = enjoyable
boy + -ish = boyish
coy + -ly = coyly

SOME EXCEPTIONS: gay + -ly = gaily, day + -ly = daily, pay + -d = paid, lay + -d = laid, say + -d = said

When a word ends in **a consonant and y,** change the y to i before any suffix that doesn't begin with i. Keep the y before suffixes that begin with i.

carry + -es = carries
dry + -ed = dried
easy + -er = easier
merry + -ly = merrily
happy + -ness = happiness
beauty + -ful = beautiful
fury + -ous = furious
defy + -ant = defiant
vary + -ation = variation

deny + -al = denial
rely + -able = reliable
mercy + -less = merciless
likely + -hood = likelihood
accompany + -ment = accompaniment
carry + -ing = carrying
baby + -ish = babyish
lobby + -ist = lobbyist

SOME EXCEPTIONS: shy + -ly = shyly, dry + -ly = dryly, shy + -ness = shyness, dry + -ness = dryness, biology + -ist = biologist, economy + -ist = economist, baby + -hood = babyhood

Usually a **final silent e** is dropped before a suffix, but sometimes it's kept. The following chart shows the basic rules for adding suffixes to words that end in silent e.

ADDING SUFFIXES TO WORDS THAT END IN SILENT *E*

RULE	EXAMPLES
Drop the *e* before suffixes that begin with a vowel.	care + -ed = cared dine + -ing = dining move + -er = mover type + -ist = typist blue + -ish = bluish arrive + -al = arrival desire + -able = desirable accuse + -ation = accusation noise + -y = noisy
Some exceptions	mile + -age = mileage dye + -ing = dyeing
Drop the *e* and change *i* to *y* before the suffix *-ing* if the word ends in *ie*.	die + -ing = dying lie + -ing = lying tie + -ing = tying
Keep the *e* before suffixes that begin with *a* and *o* if the word ends in *ce* or *ge*.	dance + -able = danceable change + -able = changeable
Keep the *e* before suffixes that begin with a vowel if the word ends in *ee* or *oe*.	see + -ing = seeing agree + -able = agreeable canoe + -ing = canoeing hoe + -ing = hoeing
Some exceptions (There can never be three of the same letter in a row.)	free + -er = freer free + -est = freest
Keep the *e* before suffixes that begin with a consonant.	grace + -ful = graceful state + -hood = statehood like + -ness = likeness care + -less = careless sincere + -ly = sincerely

See next page for some exceptions.

Adding Suffixes to Words That End in Silent E, *continued*

RULE	EXAMPLES
Some exceptions	awe + -ful = awful
	argue + -ment = argument
	true + -ly = truly
	due + -ly = duly
	whole + -ly = wholly
Drop *le* before the suffix *-ly* when the word ends with a consonant and *le*.	possible + -ly = possibly
	sparkle + -ly = sparkly
	gentle + -ly = gently

Don't drop any letters when you add *-ly* to a word that ends in a single *l*. When a word ends in *ll,* drop one *l* when you add the suffix *-ly.*

real + -ly = really   chill + -ly = chilly
cool + -ly = coolly   full + -ly = fully

Don't drop any letters when you add the suffix *-ness* to a word that ends in *n.*

stubborn + -ness = stubbornness   mean + -ness = meanness

Compound Words

Keep the original spelling of both parts of a compound word.

Remember that some compounds are one word, some are two words, and some are hyphenated. Check a dictionary when in doubt.

foot + lights = footlights   fish + hook = fishhook
busy + body = busybody   with + hold = withhold
book + case = bookcase   book + keeper = bookkeeper
light + house = lighthouse   heart + throb = heartthrob

Spelling Plurals

To form the plural of **most nouns,** you simply add -*s.* Remember that simple plural nouns never use apostrophes.

The following chart shows other basic rules.

GENERAL RULES FOR PLURALS

NOUNS ENDING IN	TO FORM PLURAL	EXAMPLES
ch, s, sh, x, z	Add -*es.*	lunch → lunches loss → losses dish → dishes box → boxes buzz → buzzes
a vowel and *y*	Add -*s.*	boy → boys turkey → turkeys
a consonant and *y*	Change *y* to *i* and add -*es.*	baby → babies penny → pennies
a vowel and *o*	Add -*s.*	radio → radios rodeo → rodeos
a consonant and *o*	Usually add -*es.*	potato → potatoes tomato → tomatoes hero → heroes echo → echoes
	Sometimes add -*s.*	zero → zeros photo → photos piano → pianos

NOUNS ENDING IN	TO FORM PLURAL	EXAMPLES
f or *fe*	Usually change *f* to *v* and add -*s* or -*es*.	wife → wives knife → knives life → lives leaf → leaves half → halves shelf → shelves wolf → wolves thief → thieves
	Sometimes add -*s*.	roof → roofs chief → chiefs cliff → cliffs giraffe → giraffes

The plurals of **proper names** are formed by adding -*es* to names that end in *ch, s, sh, x,* or *z.*

EXAMPLE   The **Woodriches** live on Elm Street.

EXAMPLE   There are two **Jonases** in our class.

Just add -*s* to form the plural of all other proper names, including those that end in *y.* Remember that the rule of changing *y* to *i* and adding -*es* doesn't apply to proper names.

EXAMPLE   The **Kennedys** are a famous American family.

EXAMPLE   I know three **Marys.**

EXAMPLE   The last two **Januarys** have been especially cold.

To form the plural of a **compound noun written as one word,** follow the general rules for plurals. To form the plural of **hyphenated compound nouns** or **compound nouns of more than one word,** usually make the most important word plural.

EXAMPLE   The two women's **fathers-in-law** have never met.

EXAMPLE   The three **post offices** are made of brick.

EXAMPLE   There have been three **surgeons general** in this decade.

EXAMPLE   The list of **poets laureate** in Great Britain is a short list.

EXAMPLE   The general presided over two **courts martial** today.

Some nouns have **irregular plural forms** that don't follow any rules.

---

man → men   tooth → teeth
woman → women   mouse → mice
child → children   goose → geese
foot → feet   ox → oxen

Some nouns have the same singular and plural forms. Most of these are the names of animals, and some of the plural forms may be spelled in more than one way.

---

deer → deer   species → species
sheep → sheep   fish → fish *or* fishes
head (of cattle) → head   antelope → antelope *or* antelopes
Sioux → Sioux   buffalo → buffalo *or* buffaloes
series → series   *or* buffalos

Learning to Spell New Words

You can improve your spelling by improving your study method. Try the following method to learn to spell new words. You can also improve your spelling by thoroughly learning certain common but frequently misspelled words.

1. Say It
Look at the printed word and say it aloud. Then say it again, pronouncing each syllable correctly.

2. Visualize It
Picture the word in your mind. Avoid looking at the printed word on the page. Try to visualize the word letter by letter.

3. Write It
Look at the printed word again, and write it two or three times. Then write the word without looking at the printed spelling.

4. Check It
Check your spelling. Did you spell the word correctly? If not, repeat each step until you can spell the word easily.

Get into the habit of using a dictionary to find the correct spelling of a word.

Using a Computer to Check Spelling

A spelling checker is a useful computer tool. If you have misspelled any words, a spelling checker can find them for you. Not only will it save you time, but it will also show you words you need to learn to spell.

Although spelling checkers are handy, they can't do the whole job. When a spelling checker finds a misspelled word, it searches the computer's dictionary for words spelled in a similar way. *You* must choose the correct word from the options the computer gives you.

Furthermore, a spelling checker can't check for sense. If you type *right* instead of *write*, the spelling checker won't highlight the error because both right and write are correctly spelled words. You still need to know correct spellings.

PRACTICE **Spelling Rules**

Find the misspelled word in each group and write it correctly.

1. recieve, field, sleigh
2. cliffs, briefs, halfs
3. relaxed, linning, offered
4. immature, ilogical, unforgettable
5. catchs, pennies, monkeys
6. sunflowers, sisters-in-law, busybodys
7. abley, merely, hopefully
8. impede, interceed, recede
9. alleys, alloys, allys
10. bargeing, fanciful, likeable

13.2 SPELLING DIFFICULT WORDS

Some words are more difficult to spell than others, and not all words follow basic spelling rules. Each person has an individual list of "problem" words. One useful strategy for learning difficult words is to develop a list of words that you frequently misspell and study them often.

A list of frequently misspelled words follows. Use it for quick reference.

FREQUENTLY MISSPELLED WORDS

abdomen
absence
abundant
academically
accelerator
accept
accessible
accidentally
acclimated
accommodate
accompaniment
accomplishment
acknowledge
acknowledgment
acquaintance
adequately
admission
admittance
adolescent
advantageous
advertisement
adviser
aerate
aerial
against
alcohol
allegiance
alliance
allot
allotting
all right
a lot
anonymous
answer

apologetically
apparatus
apparent
arctic
arousing
arrangement
atheistic
attendant
ballet
bankruptcy
beautiful
beginning
behavior
bibliography
biscuit
blasphemy
boulevard
buffet
bureau
bureaucrat
burial
business
cafeteria
calendar
camouflage
canceled
canoe
capitalism
carburetor
caricature
cataclysm
catastrophe
cemetery
changeable

chassis
choir
circumstantial
coliseum
colleague
colonel
coming
commercial
competition
complexion
concede
conceivable
connoisseur
conscience
conscientious
conscious
consciousness
consistency
controlling
controversy
convenient
cruelty
curriculum
decadent
decathlon
deceitful
deference
definite
deodorant
descend
descendant
descent
desirable
detrimental

devastation	exuberant	idiomatic
develop	familiarize	immediate
devise	fascinating	incidentally
dilemma	fascism	independent
diligence	February	inevitable
diphtheria	feminine	influential
disastrous	financier	ingenious
disciple	fission	innocent
discipline	foreign	inoculate
discrimination	forfeit	institution
disease	forty	intellectual
diseased	fulfill	interference
dissatisfied	fundamentally	irresistible
division	funeral	jewelry
efficiency	gaiety	knowledge
eighth	galaxy	knowledgeable
elementary	gauge	laboratory
eligible	genius	larynx
embarrass	government	legitimate
embarrassed	grammatically	leisure
emperor	guarantee	leisurely
emphasize	guidance	library
endeavor	harassment	license
enormous	height	livelihood
entertainment	hereditary	luxurious
entrance	hindrance	magistrate
environment	hippopotamus	magnificence
espionage	horizontal	maintenance
essential	hospital	malicious
exceed	humorous	manageable
except	hygiene	maneuver
exhibition	hypocrisy	marital
exhilaration	hypocrite	marriageable
expensive	ideally	martyrdom

GRAMMAR/USAGE/MECHANICS

mathematics
mediocre
melancholy
melodious
metaphor
miniature
mischievous
misspell
molasses
mortgage
mosquito
municipal
muscle
naive
necessary
necessity
negligence
negotiable
neighborhood
neurotic
newsstand
niece
nucleus
nuisance
nutritious
occasion
occasionally
occur
occurrence
occurring
omission
omitting
opportunity
orchestra

original
outrageous
pageant
pamphlet
parallel
paralysis
parliament
pastime
peasant
pedestal
perceive
permanent
permissible
personnel
perspiration
persuade
pharmacy
physical
physician
picnic
picnicking
pilot
playwright
pneumonia
politician
possessed
precede
preferable
presence
prestige
presumption
prevalent
privilege
procedure

proceed
propaganda
propagate
prophecy
prophesy
psychoanalysis
questionnaire
realtor
rebellion
receipt
receive
recognize
recommend
recommendation
reference
referred
rehearsal
reminiscent
remittance
repetitive
representative
responsibility
restaurant
reveal
rhythm
rhythmical
ridiculous
salable
schedule
seize
separate
separation
sergeant
significance

sincerely
souvenir
specimen
sponsor
statistics
strategic
stubbornness
succeed
succession
sufficient
superintendent
supersede
suppress
surprise
susceptible

symmetrical
synonymous
technique
technology
temperament
tendency
theory
tolerance
tortoise
traffic
tragedy
transparent
truly
twelfth
unanimous

undoubtedly
unmistakable
unnecessary
unscrupulous
usually
vaccine
vacuum
valedictory
variety
vaudeville
vehicle
vengeance
versatile
villain
Wednesday

GRAMMAR/USAGE/MECHANICS

Frank and Ernest

THOSE TWO ARE INSEPARABLE.

THAVES

© 2000 Thaves. Reprinted with permission. Newspaper dist. by NEA, Inc.

Find each misspelled word and write it correctly.

1. James took a liesurely walk through the neighborhood, past the cemetery, libary, and hospital.
2. Stopping briefly in the zoo, he saw a hippopotomos repetatively bellowing at the nearby rhinoceros.
3. Acknowledging the rhino's aparrent tolerance with a nod, James continued down the bullevard.
4. In the park, he saw a couple picnicing merrily with three cute but mischevous children.
5. Supressing the urge to join in the fun, James proceded across the street through the heavy traffick.
6. In the window of an antique shop, James spied an old calender advertising Miller's Marvelous Vacume Cleaners.
7. The eigth of Febuary was circled in red, and an anonymus artist had drawn in a ridiculous minature poodle.
8. "Anna's birthday is tomorrow!" James cried. "How embarassing it would be to forgot my favorite neice!"
9. Relieved at avoiding such a catastrophy, James headed for the jewelcry store.
10. There he bought an inexpencive but iresistable charm— a tiny silver poodle—for Anna's bracelet.

13.3 EXPANDING YOUR VOCABULARY

Increasing your vocabulary improves your reading and writing skills and your chances of scoring well on standardized tests. The following tips suggest ways to expand your vocabulary and remember new words you encounter.

1. **Notice** new words when you're reading or listening. Write the words and their meanings in a notebook.

2. **Check** the meaning and pronunciation of a new word in a dictionary. Use the original context—surrounding words that are familiar—to understand the word's meaning and use.
3. **Relate** the new word to words you already know. Associate its spelling or meaning with a familiar word that will make the new word easier to remember.
4. **Verify** your understanding of the new word with someone else. A teacher, a parent, or a friend may be able to tell you if you correctly understand the meaning of the word.
5. **Practice** using the new word in your writing and conversation. Try to use the new word at least once a day for a week. Using a word repeatedly is the best way to remember it.

LEARNING FROM CONTEXT

You can often figure out the meaning of an unfamiliar word by looking for clues in the words and sentences around it. These surrounding words and sentences are called the context.

USING SPECIFIC CONTEXT CLUES

Writers often give clues to the meaning of unfamiliar words. Sometimes they even tell you exactly what a word means. The following chart shows five types of specific context clues. It also lists clue words to look for. Finally, the chart gives examples of sentences with unfamiliar words whose meanings you should be able to figure out from the context. In the examples, the clue words are in bold type. The unfamiliar words and the helpful context are in italic type.

TYPE OF CONTEXT CLUE	CLUE WORDS	EXAMPLES
Definition The meaning of the unfamiliar word is stated in the sentence.	also known as in other words or that is which is which means	The course emphasized *demography,* **which is** *the study of human populations.* The lecturer was *verbose;* **that is,** he was *wordy.*
Example The meaning of the unfamiliar word is explained through familiar examples.	for example for instance including like such as	Osbert served as the old duke's *amanuensis;* **for example,** *he took dictation and copied manuscripts.* *Miscreants* of all kinds, **including** *pickpockets, thieves, and vandals,* roamed the streets of Victorian England.
Comparison The unfamiliar word is similar to a familiar word or phrase.	also identical like likewise resembling same similarly too	Joan's friend testified to her *veracity.* Her teacher, **too,** said Joan's *truthfulness* was evident to all who knew her. Consuela suffered from *acrophobia;* her father **also** had a *fear of heights.*
Contrast The unfamiliar word is the opposite of a familiar word or phrase.	although unlike however on the contrary	**Unlike** his *despondent* opponent, Kwami appeared *hopeful, happy,* and *sure* he would win.

TYPE OF CONTEXT CLUE	CLUE WORDS	EXAMPLES
Contrast, *continued*	on the other hand though but	Martin always *grouses* about doing his chores, **but** his sister does her work *without complaining.*
Cause and Effect The unfamiliar word is explained as part of a cause-and-effect relationship.	as a result because consequently therefore thus	Maria felt the stranger was being *intrusive* **because** he *asked too many* personal questions. Otis has a *loquacious* nature; **consequently,** the teacher is constantly telling him to stop talking.

GRAMMAR/USAGE/MECHANICS

USING GENERAL CONTEXT

Sometimes there are no special clue words to help you understand an unfamiliar word. However, you can still use the general context. That is, you can use the details in the words or sentences around the unfamiliar word. Read the following sentence:

EXAMPLE Ramon was in a *jocund* mood, laughing and joking with his friends.

Even if you don't know the meaning of *jocund*, you do know that it must be an adjective describing *mood*. From other details in the sentence (*laughing and joking*), you may guess correctly that *jocund* means "merry, cheerful, carefree."

Use context clues to figure out the meaning of the italicized word. Write the meaning. Then write definition, example, comparison, contrast, cause and effect, *or* general *to tell what type of context clue you used to define the word.*

1. I had a *premonition* of defeat, a kind of foreknowledge that we would lose.
2. We didn't need his insults to *exacerbate* the situation; it was bad enough already.
3. Because I didn't want to miss any details, I made *copious* notes on everything that was said.
4. We had great hopes for a warm, sunny afternoon but had to cancel the picnic because of *inclement* weather.
5. Always eager for approval, Brian beamed at his teacher's obvious *approbation* of his story.
6. The three army generals planned to become the ruling *triumvirate* after they had overthrown the prime minister and parliament.
7. The flaw in the fabric was so small as to be almost invisible; it was *infinitesimal.*
8. We weren't being paid fairly, so our union went on strike, demanding pay *commensurate* with our work.
9. In the same way that the man lied in daily life, he also *perjured* himself on the witness stand.
10. The gardener obviously prefers *variegated* leaves to ones that are a solid color.

13.4 ROOTS, PREFIXES, AND SUFFIXES

You can often figure out the meaning of an unfamiliar word by analyzing its parts. The main part of a word is its root. When the root is a complete word, it's sometimes called a base word. A root or base word can be thought of as the "spine" of a word. It gives the word its backbone of meaning.

A root is often combined with a prefix (a word part added to the beginning of a word), a suffix (a word part added to the end of a word), or another root. Prefixes and suffixes change a word's meaning or its part of speech.

Although the English language borrows words from many other languages, a large number of words we use have their origins in Latin and Greek roots. Knowing some of these Latin and Greek roots will help you analyze many unfamiliar words and determine their meanings.

EXAMPLE

encryption

Prefix	The prefix *en-* means "to put into."

Root	The root *crypt* means "hidden" or "secret." The word *encrypt,* therefore, means "to put into a hidden or secret form."

Suffix	The suffix *–ion* changes *encrypt* from a verb to a noun meaning "the state of being encrypted."

The word *encryption,* then, means "something that has been put into a secret code," in other words, "a coded message." Although this word's parts add up to its meaning in a fairly clear way, sometimes an analysis of a word's parts doesn't yield the word's meaning so readily. Use a dictionary to check your analysis.

ROOTS

When you're trying to determine the meaning of an unfamiliar word, think of words that might share a root with it. The meanings of these other words might give you clues to the meaning of the unfamiliar word. The following chart lists some common roots and some words that share them. Keep in mind that one or more letters in a root may change when the root is combined with other word parts.

ROOTS		
ROOTS	**WORDS**	**MEANINGS**
ac or *ag* means "do"	action	act or process of doing
	agenda	list of things to do
agri or *agro* means "field"	agriculture	science of cultivating the soil
	agronomy	study of crop production and soil management
am means "love" or "friend"	amicable	friendly
	amorous	relating to love
anima means "life" or "mind"	animate	having life
	unanimous	being of one mind
anthrop means "human beings"	anthropology	study of human beings
	misanthrope	one who hates or distrusts human beings
aqua means "water"	aquarium	tank of water in which living animals are kept
	aqueduct	structure for moving water
arch means "rule" or "government"	anarchy	absence of government
	archives	government records

ROOTS	WORDS	MEANINGS
astr or *astro* means "star"	astronaut astronomy	traveler among the stars study of stars
audio means "hear"	audience audiometer	group that hears a performance device for measuring hearing
aut or *auto* means "self"	autistic autobiography	absorbed in the self story of a person's life written by that person
bene means "good"	beneficial benevolent	good, helpful inclined to do good
bibli or *biblio* means "book"	bibliography bibliophile	list of books related to a particular subject lover of books
bio means "life"	autobiography biology	story of a person's life written by that person study of living things
brev means "short" or "brief"	abbreviate brevity	shorten a word or phrase shortness of expression
cand means "shine" or "glow"	candle incandescent	molded mass of wax that may be burned to give light bright, glowing
capit means "head"	capital decapitate	place where the head of government sits remove the head
ced means "go"	proceed recede	go forward go back
cent means "hundred"	centimeter century	one hundredth of a meter one hundred years

GRAMMAR/USAGE/MECHANICS

ROOTS	WORDS	MEANINGS
chron or *chrono* means "time"	chronological synchronize	arranged in time order cause to happen at the same time
cid or *cide* means "kill"	germicide homicide	agent that destroys germs killing of one human being by another
circ means "circle"	circumference circus	distance around a circle entertainment usually held in a circular area
cis means "cut"	incision incisor	surgical cut tooth adapted for cutting
cline means "bend," "lean," or "slope"	decline incline	slope downward lean forward
cogn means "know"	cognition recognize	knowledge; awareness know someone or something
corp means "body"	corps corpse	body of military troops dead body
cracy means "government"	democracy technocracy	government by the people government by technical experts
cred means "believe" or "trust"	credible incredible	believable unbelievable
crypt or *crypto* means "hidden" or "secret"	cryptic cryptogram	having a hidden meaning communication in secret code
culp means "blame" or "guilt"	culpable culprit	guilty one who is guilty
cur or *curs* means "run"	current	water running in a stream or electricty running through a wire

Roots, continued

ROOTS	WORDS	MEANINGS
cur or *curs*, continued	cursory	rapidly performed or produced
cycl means "circle" or "wheel"	bicycle cyclone	two-wheeled vehicle storm that rotates in a circle
dec or *deca* means "ten"	decade decathlon	ten years athletic contest consisting of ten events
dem or *demo* means "people"	democracy epidemic	rule by the people affecting many people
di means "two"	dichotomy dichromatic	division into two groups having two colors
dict means "say"	contradict dictate	say the opposite of speak for another to record
duc or *duct* means "lead" or "draw"	conductor deduct	one who leads take away from a total
ectomy means "surgical removal"	appendectomy mastoidectomy	surgical removal of the appendix surgical removal of part of the mastoid bone or process
equi means "equal"	equilateral equitable	having sides of equal length dealing equally with all
err means "wander" or "err"	aberration erratic	result of straying from the normal way inconsistent, irregular
eu means "good" or "well"	eulogize euphoria	praise feeling of well-being

ROOTS	WORDS	MEANINGS
exo means "outside" or "outer"	exoskeleton	outer supportive covering of an animal, as an insect or mollusk
	exotic	outside the ordinary
fac or *fec* means "make" or "do"	effective	done well
	factory	place where things are made
ferous means "bearing" or "producing"	coniferous	bearing cones, as a pine tree
	somniferous	producing sleep
fid means "faith" or "trust"	confidant	person one trusts
	fidelity	faithfulness
fin means "end" or "limit"	define	limit the meaning of
	infinite	having no end
fix means "fasten"	fixate	fasten one's attention intently
	fixative	substance that fastens or sets
frac or *frag* means "break"	fracture	break
	fragile	easily broken
fus means "pour" or "melt"	effusive	demonstrating an excessive pouring out of talk or affection
	fusion	joining by melting
gen means "class," "kind," "descent," or "birth"	general	affecting a whole class
	generate	start or originate
geo means "earth," "ground," or "soil"	geocentric	measured from the center of the earth
	geology	study of the earth

GRAMMAR/USAGE/MECHANICS

ROOTS	WORDS	MEANINGS
grad or *gress* means "step" or "go"	egress gradual	way to go out proceeding by steps or degrees
gram or *graph* means "writing"	autograph telegram	written signature written message sent over a distance
grat means "pleasing" or "thanks"	congratulate gratuity	express sympathetic pleasure something given voluntarily to show thanks for service
hetero means "different"	heterogeneous heteronym	made up of different kinds of things or people word spelled like another word but different in meaning and pronunciation, for example, *bow*
homo means "same"	homogeneous homophone	made up of the same kinds of things or people word pronounced like another word but different in meaning and spelling, for example, *to, too,* or *two*
hydr or *hydro* means "water"	dehydrate hydrant	remove water large pipe used to draw water
ject means "throw"	eject trajectory	throw out path of something thrown

GRAMMAR/USAGE/MECHANICS

ROOTS	WORDS	MEANINGS
jud means "judge"	judicious	using good judgment
	prejudice	judgment formed without sufficient knowledge
junct means "join"	conjunction	word that joins other words
	junction	place where two things join
jur or *jus* means "law"	jurisprudence	system of law
	justice	determination of rights according to the law
lect or *leg* means "read"	lectern	stand used to support a book or paper for reading
	legible	capable of being read
like means "resembling"	businesslike	resembling the conduct of a business
	childlike	resembling the behavior of a child
loc means "place"	local	relating to a place
	location	position, site, or place
locut or *loqu* means "speak" or "speech"	locution	style of speaking
	loquacious	talkative
log or *logo* means "word," "thought," or "speech"	dialogue	speech between two people
	monologue	speech by a single person
logy means "science" or "study"	biology	science of living things
	genealogy	study of ancestors
luc means "light"	lucid	suffused with light; clear
	translucent	permitting the passage of light

GRAMMAR/USAGE/MECHANICS

ROOTS	WORDS	MEANINGS
macro means "large"	macrocosm	world; universe
	macroscopic	large enough to be observed with the naked eye
magn means "large" or "great"	magnificent	large and grand
	magnify	make larger
mal means "bad" or "badly"	maladjusted	badly adjusted
	malice	desire to see another suffer
man means "hand"	manual	done by hand
	manuscript	document written by hand or typed
meter or *metr* means "measure"	metric	relating to meter
	thermometer	instrument for measuring heat
micr or *micro* means "small"	micrometer	device for measuring very small distances
	microwave	a short electromagnetic wave
milli means "thousand"	millimeter	one thousandth of a meter
	million	one thousand times one thousand
mis or *mit* means "send"	remiss	failing to respond
	transmit	send across a distance
mon means "warn"	admonish	express warning or disapproval in a gentle way
	premonition	forewarning
mon or *mono* means "one"	monarchy	rule by one person
	monochromatic	having one color

ROOTS	WORDS	MEANINGS
morph or *morpho* means "form"	metamorphosis morphology	change in physical form study of the form and structure of animals and plants
mort means "death"	mortal mortician	subject to death one who prepares the dead for burial
neo means "new"	neologism neonatal	new word, usage, or expression affecting the newborn
nym means "name"	anonymous pseudonym	not named or identified fictitious or pen name
octa or *octo* means "eight"	octagon octopus	figure with eight sides creature with eight limbs
omni means "all"	omniscient omnivorous	knowing all eating both animal and vegetable matter
oper means "work"	opera operative	musical and dramatic work working
pan means "all" or "whole"	panacea Pan-American	remedy for all problems relating to the whole of North and South America
path or *pathy* means "feeling" or "suffering"	pathology sympathy	study of disease inclination to feel like another
ped means "child" or "foot"	pediatrician quadruped	physician who cares for children animal having four feet
pend or *pens* means "hang" or "weigh"	pendant	something hanging or suspended

ROOTS	WORDS	MEANINGS
pend or *pens,* continued	suspense	feeling that leaves one hanging or unsure of an outcome
phil or *phile* means "loving" or "fondness"	bibliophile philanthropist	lover of books one who loves human beings
phobia means "fear"	acrophobia hydrophobia	fear of heights fear of water
phon or *phono* means "sound," "voice," or "speech"	phonics phonograph	method of teaching relationships between sounds and letters instrument for playing recorded sound
physi or *physio* means "nature" or "physical"	physiognomy physiotherapy	natural features of the face believed to show temperament and character physical therapy
poly means "many"	polyglot polygon	composed of numerous language groups a many-sided figure
pon or *pos* means "place" or "put"	exponent position	symbol placed above and to the right of a mathematical expression place where something is situated
port means "carry"	portable porter	capable of being carried one who carries
prehend means "seize" or "grasp"	apprehend comprehend	arrest by seizing grasp the meaning of
prim means "first"	primary	first in order of time or development

GRAMMAR/USAGE/MECHANICS

ROOTS	WORDS	MEANINGS
prim, continued	primitive	characteristic of an early stage of development
prot or *proto* means "first" or "beginning"	proton prototype	elementary particle original model
pseudo means "false"	pseudoclassic pseudonym	pretending to be classic fictitious or pen name
psych or *psycho* means "mind"	psychology psychotherapy	study of the mind therapy for the mind
punctus means "point"	punctual puncture	on time hole or wound made by a pointed instrument
quadr or *quadri* means "four"	quadrangle quadrilateral	four-sided enclosure having four sides
rect means "right" or "straight"	rectangle rectitude	figure with four right angles quality of being correct in judgment or procedure
reg means "rule" or "direct"	regular regulate	according to rule direct according to rule
rupt means "break"	interrupt rupture	stop or hinder by breaking in break
sang means "blood"	consanguinity sanguine	blood relationship marked by high color and cheerfulness; confident; optimistic
sci means "know"	omniscient science	knowing all things knowledge about the natural world
scope means "a means for viewing"	microscope	a means for viewing small things

ROOTS	WORDS	MEANINGS
scope, continued	telescope	a means for viewing things at a distance
scrib or *script* means "write"	prescribe	write an order for medicine
	prescription	written order for medicine
secu or *sequ* means "follow"	sequel	installment that follows a previous one
	sequence	series in which one item follows another
sens or *sent* means "feel" or "sense"	sensation	feeling
	sentence	group of words that makes sense
sol or *solv* means "dissolve" or "solve"	solution	that which solves a problem
	solvent	that which dissolves
son means "sound"	resonant	continuing to sound
	sonorous	full of sound
soph means "wise" or "clever"	sophisticated	having wise and clever knowledge of the ways of the world
	sophomore	student in the second year of high school or college (a combination of wise and foolish)
spec or *spect* means "look" or "watch"	perspective	way of looking at something
	spectator	one who watches an event
spir means "breath" or "breathe"	inspire	exert an influence on
	respiration	breathing
strict or *string* means "bind"	constrict	draw together
	stringent	strict; severe

GRAMMAR/USAGE/MECHANICS

ROOTS	WORDS	MEANINGS
tact or *tang* means "touch"	contact	touching of two things or people
	tangible	capable of being touched
tele means "far off" or "distant"	telephone	instrument for hearing sound at a distance
	television	instrument for viewing pictures at a distance
terr means "earth"	extraterrestrial	being from beyond earth
	terrain	physical features of a tract of land
therm or *thermo* means "heat"	thermal	relating to heat
	thermometer	instrument for measuring heat
trac means "draw" or "pull"	extract	pull out
	traction	friction caused by pulling across a surface; pulling force
tri means "three"	triangle	figure with three angles
	triathlon	athletic contest consisting of three events
vac means "empty"	evacuation	process of emptying out
	vacant	empty
ven or *vent* means "come"	intervene	come between
	venue	place related to a particular event
verb means "word"	verbal	having to do with words
	verbose	wordy
vers or *vert* means "turn"	avert	turn away
	reverse	turn back
vid or *vis* means "see"	evident	plain to see
	visible	capable of being seen

ROOTS	WORDS	MEANINGS
viv means "live" or "alive"	revive	bring back to life
	vivacious	full of life; lively
vit means "life"	vital	necessary to the maintenance of life
	vitamin	substance necessary for the regulation of life processes
voc or *vok* means "call" or "call forth"	evoke	call forth
	vocation	job a person feels called to do
vol or *volv* means "roll"	evolve	develop
	revolution	rotation

PREFIXES

Prefixes are word parts added to the beginning of a root or a base word to change its meaning. They are important tools for understanding and learning new words. The following chart shows common prefixes and their meanings. Notice that some prefixes have more than one meaning and that some prefixes convey the same meaning as others.

PREFIXES		
PREFIXES	**WORDS**	**MEANINGS**
a- means "without" or "not"; it can also mean "on," "in," or "at"	abloom	in bloom
	aboard	on board
	amoral	without morals
	atypical	not typical

GRAMMAR/USAGE/MECHANICS

PREFIXES	WORDS	MEANINGS
ant- or *anti-* means "against" or "opposing"	antacid	agent that works against acidity
	antiwar	opposing war
ante- means "before"	antecedent	going before
	antediluvian	before the biblical flood
be- means "cause to be"	befriend	act as a friend to
	belittle	cause to seem little or less
bi- means "two"	bimonthly	once every two months or twice a month
	bisect	divide into two equal parts
cat- or *cata-* means "down"	catacomb	subterranean cemetery
	catastrophe	final stage of a tragedy
circum- means "around" or "about"	circumference	distance around a circle
	circumstance	surrounding condition
	circumvent	avoid by going around
co- means "with" or "together"	coworker	person one works with
	cowrite	write together
col-, com-, con-, or *cor-* means "together" or "with"	collaborate	work with others
	companion	one who accompanies another
	confer	consult with others
	correspond	exchange letters with another
contra- means "against"	contradict	speak against
	contrary	opposite
counter- means "opposite" or "opposing"	counterbalance	oppose with an equal weight or force
	counterclockwise	opposite of clockwise

PREFIXES	WORDS	MEANINGS
de- means "do the opposite of," "remove," or "reduce"	de-emphasize	do the opposite of emphasize
	defrost	remove frost
	devalue	reduce the value of
dia- means "through" or "across"	diameter	length through the center of a circle
	diaphragm	a membrane stretching across an area
dis- means "not" or "absence of"	dishonest	not honest
	distrust	absence of trust
e- or *ex-* means "out"; *ex-* also means "former"	eject	throw out
	exceed	go beyond
	ex-president	former president
en- means "cause to be" or "put into"	enlarge	cause to be made large
	enthrall	put into thrall
extra- means "outside" or "beyond"	extralegal	outside of legal means
	extraordinary	beyond the ordinary
for- means "so as to involve prohibition or exclusion"	forgive	give up feelings of resentment
	forgo	give up pleasure or advantage
hemi- means "half"	hemicycle	structure consisting of half a circle
	hemisphere	half a sphere
hyper- means "excessive" or "excessively"	hyperbole	excessive exaggeration
	hypersensitive	excessively sensitive
il-, im-, in-, or *ir-* means "not" or "into"	illegal	not legal
	illuminate	bring light into
	immature	not mature
	immigrant	one who moves into a country

GRAMMAR/USAGE/MECHANICS

Chapter 13 Spelling and Vocabulary **427**

PREFIXES	WORDS	MEANINGS
il-, im-, in-, or *ir-,* continued	inconvenient insight	not convenient power of seeing into a situation
	irregular irrigate	not regular bring water into
inter- means "among" or "between"	international interscholastic	among nations between schools
intra- means "within"	intramural	within the walls (of a school)
	intrastate	within a state
intro- means "in" or "into"	introspection introvert	looking within oneself one who is turned inward
mis- means "bad," "badly," "wrong," or "wrongly"	misspell mistreat	spell wrong treat badly
non- means "not"	nonallergenic nonconformist	not causing allergies one who does not conform
over- means "exceed," "surpass," or "excessive"	overeat overqualified	eat to excess qualified beyond the normal requirements
para- means "beside" or "beyond"	paramedic	one who works beside a physician
	paranormal	beyond the normal
peri- means "around"	perimeter	distance around a plane figure
	periscope	instrument for looking around
post- means "after"	postgame postwar	after the game after the war
pre- means "before"	precede premonition	go before advance warning

PREFIXES	WORDS	MEANINGS
pro- means "in favor of," "forward," "before," or "in place of"	pro-American proceed prologue pronoun	in favor of America go forward introduction before the main text word that takes the place of a noun
re- means "again" or "back"	recall replay	call back play again
retro- means "back," "backward," or "behind"	retroactive retrogress	effective as of a prior date move backward
semi- means "half" or "partly"	semicircle semisweet	half a circle partly sweet
sub- means "under" or "less than"	subhuman submarine	less than human underwater
super- means "over and above"	superabundant superhuman	having more than an abundance over and above what is normal for a human being
sym- or *syn-* means "with" or "together"	symbiosis synchronize	living together of two dissimilar organisms make happen at the same time
trans- means "across"	transmit transport	send across carry across
un- means "not" or "do the opposite of"	unhappy untie	not happy do the opposite of tie
uni- means "one"	unicycle unified	one-wheeled vehicle joined into one

GRAMMAR/USAGE/MECHANICS

SUFFIXES

Suffixes are word parts added to the end of a root or a base word to change its meaning and sometimes its part of speech. The following chart shows common suffixes and their meanings. Notice that some suffixes have more than one meaning and that some suffixes convey the same meaning as others. Notice also that the spelling of a root often changes when a suffix is added. Furthermore, more than one suffix may be added to many words.

SUFFIXES

SUFFIXES	WORDS	MEANINGS
-able or *-ible* means "capable of," "fit for," or "tending to"	agreeable	tending to agree or able to be agreed with
	breakable	capable of being broken
	collectible	fit for collecting
-age means "action," "process," or "result"	breakage	action or process of breaking
	marriage	action, process, or result of marrying
	wreckage	result of wrecking
-al means "relating to" or "characterized by"; it can also mean "action," "process," or "result"	fictional	relating to fiction
	rehearsal	action or process of rehearsing
-an or *-ian* means "one who is of or from"; it can also mean "relating to"	Bostonian	one who lives in Boston
	Elizabethan	relating to the reign of Queen Elizabeth I

SUFFIXES	WORDS	MEANINGS
-ance, -ancy, -ence, or *-ency* means "action," "process," "quality," or "state"	dependency performance persistence vacancy	state of being dependent action or process of performing quality of persisting state of being vacant
-ant means "one who or that which"; it can also mean "being"	contestant observant	one who participates in a contest being observing
-ar means "relating to" or "resembling"; it can also mean "one who"	liar molecular spectacular	one who lies relating to molecules resembling a spectacle
-ard or *-art* means "one who"	braggart dullard	one who brags one who is dull
-ary means "person or thing belonging to or connected with"; it can also mean "relating to or connected with"	complimentary functionary	relating to a compliment person who serves a particular function
-ate means "of," "relating to," or "having"; it can also mean "cause to be"	activate collegiate	cause to be active relating to college
-cy means "state," "quality," "condition," or "fact of being"	accuracy bankruptcy infancy	quality of being accurate condition of being bankrupt state of being an infant
-dom means "state of being"	boredom freedom	state of being bored state of being free

SUFFIXES	WORDS	MEANINGS
-ee means "receiver of action" or "one who"	escapee trainee	one who escapes receiver of training
-eer means "one who"	auctioneer engineer	one who runs an auction one who is concerned with engines
-en means "made of or resembling"; it can also mean "cause to be or become"	golden strengthen	made of or resembling gold cause to be strong
-ent means "one who"	resident superintendent	one who resides in a place one who superintends
-er means "one who" or "native or resident of"; it can also mean "more"	New Yorker reporter sooner stronger	resident of New York one who reports more soon more strong
-ery or *-ry* means "character," "art or practice," "place," or "collection"	bakery cookery jewelry snobbery	place for baking art or practice of cooking collection of jewels character of being a snob
-ese means "originating in a certain place or country"; it can also mean "resident of" or "language of"	Japanese	originating in Japan; resident of Japan; language of Japan
-esque means "in the manner or style of" or "like"	picturesque statuesque	in the manner or style of a picture like a statue

SUFFIXES	WORDS	MEANINGS
-et or *-ette* means "small" or "group"	islet kitchenette quartet	small island small kitchen group of four
-fold means "multiplied by"	fourfold	multiplied by four
-ful means "full of" or "tending to"; it can also mean "amount that fills"	fearful forgetful spoonful	full of fear tending to forget amount that fills a spoon
-fy or *-ify* means "make or form into," "make similar to," or "become"	fortify glorify solidify	make similar to a fort make glorious become solid
-hood means "state," "condition," "quality," or "character"	childhood likelihood statehood	state of being a child quality of being likely condition of being a state
-ic or *-ical* means "having the qualities of," "being," "like," "consisting of," or "relating to"	angelic athletic atomic historical	like an angel having the qualities of an athlete consisting of atoms relating to history
-ile means "tending to" or "capable of"	contractile infantile	capable of contracting tending to be like an infant
-ine means "of," "like," or "relating to"	Alpine crystalline marine	relating to the Alps like crystal of the sea
-ion or *-ation* means "act or process," "result," or "state or condition"	pollution selection sensation	result of polluting process of selecting state or condition of feeling something

GRAMMAR/USAGE/MECHANICS

Suffixes, continued

SUFFIXES	WORDS	MEANINGS
-*ish* means "like," "inclined to," "somewhat," or "having the approximate age of"	bookish	inclined to be interested in books
	foolish	like a fool
	reddish	somewhat red
	thirtyish	about thirty
-*ism* means "act, practice, or process," "prejudice," "state or condition," "doctrine or belief," or "conduct or behavior"	criticism	act of criticizing
	heroism	conduct or behavior of a hero
	Mormonism	belief in the doctrines of the Mormon faith
	parallelism	state of being parallel
	racism	prejudice against a race of people
-*ist* means "one who"	violinist	one who plays a violin
-*ite* means "native or resident of"	Brooklynite	native or resident of Brooklyn
-*ity* means "quality," "state," or "condition"	humanity	condition of being human
	purity	quality of being pure
	sanity	state of being sane
-*ive* means "performing or tending toward"	active	tending toward action
	excessive	tending toward excess
-*ize* means "cause to be," "become," or "make"	Americanize	become American
	modernize	make modern
	sterilize	cause to be sterile
-*less* means "without"	hopeless	without hope
-*ly* means "like"; it can also mean "in a manner" or "to a degree"	easily	in an easy manner
	friendly	like a friend
	partly	to a partial degree

SUFFIXES	WORDS	MEANINGS
-ment means "result," "action," or "condition"	amazement	condition of being amazed
	astonishment	result of being astonished
	development	act of developing
-ness means "state," "condition," or "quality"	darkness	condition of being dark
	goodness	state of being good
	heaviness	quality of being heavy
-or means "one who or that which"	elevator	that which raises people or goods to a higher level
	inventor	one who invents
-ory means "place of or for"; it can also mean "relating to" or "characterized by"	contradictory	characterized by contradiction
	observatory	place for observing
	sensory	relating to the senses
-ose means "full of" or "having"	grandiose	having grand ideas
	verbose	full of words; wordy
-ous means "full of," "having," or "characterized by"	courageous	characterized by courage
	gracious	having grace
	joyous	full of joy
-ship means "state, condition, or quality," "office, dignity, or profession," or "art or skill"	ambassadorship	office of an ambassador
	friendship	state of being a friend
	horsemanship	art or skill of horseback riding
-some means "characterized by"; it can also mean "group of"	foursome	group of four
	troublesome	characterized by trouble
-th or *-eth* is used to form ordinal numbers	seventh	ordinal for *seven*
	twentieth	ordinal for *twenty*

GRAMMAR/USAGE/MECHANICS

SUFFIXES	WORDS	MEANINGS
-ty means "quality," "condition," or "state"	novelty	quality or condition of being novel
	safety	state of being safe
-ure means "act," "process," "state," or "result"	composure	state of being composed
	erasure	result of erasing
	exposure	act of exposing
-ward means "toward" or "in a certain direction"	afterward	at a later time
	homeward	toward home
-y means "characterized by or full of," "like," or "tending or inclined to"; it can also mean "state, condition, or quality" or "instance of an action"	chatty	tending or inclined to chat
	homey	like home
	inquiry	instance of inquiring
	jealousy	state, condition, or quality of being jealous
	juicy	full of juice
	waxy	characterized by wax

GRAMMAR/USAGE/MECHANICS

Frank and Ernest

© 1996 Thaves / Reprinted with permission. Newspaper dist. by NEA, Inc.

Use the following roots, prefixes, and suffixes to make a list of ten words you know or combinations you think might be words. Use at least one root, prefix, or suffix from the chart in each word you write. Check your words in a dictionary.

PREFIXES	ROOTS	SUFFIXES
col-, com-, con-	ced	-able, -ible
de-	cogn	-al
e-, ex-	duc	-ate
il-, im-, in-, ir-	frac, frag	-ion, -ation
intro-	grad, gress	-ize
mis-	junct	-ment
pro-	gram	-ous
re-	mis, mit	-ty
trans-	port	-ship
un-	reg	-ure
	scope	
	sens, sent	
	son	
	trac	

GRAMMAR/USAGE/MECHANICS

Part Three

● ● ● ● ● ● ● ● ● ● ● ● ●

Composition

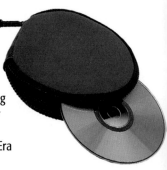

The Writing Process

• • • • • • • • • • • • • • •

Writing is a process done in different stages: prewriting, drafting, revising/editing, and publishing/presenting. These stages are recursive; that is, they do not necessarily follow one another in order; you can go back and forth among steps, repeating those that you need to until you end up with the result you want.

PEANUTS reprinted by permission of United
Feature Syndicate, Inc.

The Writing Process

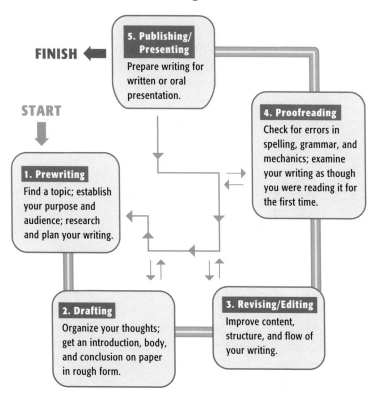

5. Publishing/Presenting
Prepare writing for written or oral presentation.

FINISH

START

1. Prewriting
Find a topic; establish your purpose and audience; research and plan your writing.

4. Proofreading
Check for errors in spelling, grammar, and mechanics; examine your writing as though you were reading it for the first time.

2. Drafting
Organize your thoughts; get an introduction, body, and conclusion on paper in rough form.

3. Revising/Editing
Improve content, structure, and flow of your writing.

STAGE 1: PREWRITING

During Prewriting, you decide what you want to write about by exploring ideas, feelings, and memories. Prewriting is the stage in which you not only decide what your topic is, but

- you refine, focus, and explore your topic
- you gather information about your topic
- you make notes about what you want to say about it
- you also think about your audience and your purpose

COMPOSITION

Your audience is whoever will read your work. Your purpose is what you hope to accomplish through your writing.

After you've decided on a topic and explored it, making notes about what you will include, you will need to arrange and organize your ideas. This is also done during the Prewriting stage, before you actually draft your paper.

There are many techniques you can use to generate ideas and define and explore your topic.

CHOOSING AND EXPLORING YOUR TOPIC

Keeping a Journal

Many writing ideas come to us as we go about our daily lives. A journal, or log, can help you record your thoughts from day to day. You can then refer to this record when you're searching for a writing topic. Every day you can write in your journal your experiences, observations, thoughts, feelings, and opinions. Keep newspaper and magazine clippings, photos, songs, poems, and anything else that catches your interest. They might later suggest questions that lead to writing topics. Try to add to your journal every day. Use your imagination. Be creative and don't worry about grammar, spelling, or punctuation. This is your own personal record. It is for your benefit only, and no one else will read it.

Freewriting

Freewriting means just what it says: writing freely without worrying about grammar, punctuation, spelling, logic, or anything. You just write what comes to your mind. Choose a topic and a time limit and then just start writing ideas as they come to you. If you run out of ideas, repeat the same word over and over until a new idea occurs to you. When the time is up, review what you've written. The ideas that most interest you are likely to be the ones that will be most worth writing about. You can use your journal as a place for freewriting, or you can just take a piece of paper and start the process. The important thing is to allow your mind to follow its own path as you explore a topic. You'll be surprised where it might lead you.

1. Let your thoughts flow. Write ideas, memories, anything that comes to mind.
2. Don't edit or judge your thoughts; just write them down. You can evaluate them later. In fact, evaluating your ideas at this point would probably dry up the flow. Accepting any idea that comes is the way to encourage more ideas.
3. Don't worry about spelling, punctuation, grammar, or even sense; just keep writing.

Brainstorming

Brainstorming is another free-association technique that you can use to generate ideas. It is often most effective to brainstorm with others because ideas can spark new ideas. Start with a key word or idea and list other ideas as they occur to you. Don't worry about the order; just let your ideas flow freely from one to the next.

COMPOSITION

Clustering

Write your topic in the middle of a piece of paper. As you think about the topic, briefly write down everything that comes to mind. Each time you write something, draw a circle around it and draw lines to connect those circles to the main idea in the center. Continue to think about the secondary ideas and add offshoots to them. Draw circles around those related ideas and connect them to the secondary ideas.

COMPOSITION

Clustering

Collecting Information

Whether you're deciding on your topic or exploring a topic you've already chosen, you need to discover as many facts as possible about your topic or possible topic.

Asking Questions To discover the facts you need, begin by writing down a list of questions about your topic. Different questions serve different purposes, and knowing what kind of question to ask can be as important as knowing how to ask it clearly. The chart that follows will help you categorize your list of questions.

KINDS OF QUESTIONS	
PERSONAL QUESTIONS	ask about your responses to a topic. They help you explore your experiences and tastes.
CREATIVE QUESTIONS	ask you to compare your subject to something else or to imagine observing your subject as someone else might. Such questions can expand your perspective on a subject.
ANALYTICAL QUESTIONS	ask about structure and function: How is this topic constructed? What is its purpose? Analytical questions help you evaluate and draw conclusions.
INFORMATIONAL QUESTIONS	ask for facts, statistics, or details.

For Better or For Worse®　　　　　　　　　　**by Lynn Johnston**

Library Research If your topic requires information you do not already have, your school or public library is the best place to find it.

Library Research TIP

1. Search for books by title, author, and subject, using either the card catalog or the online computer system.
2. Use the subject heading for each listing as a cross-reference to related material.
3. Browse among other books in the section where you locate a useful book.
4. Jot down the author, title, and call number of each book you think you will use.
5. Record the titles of books that don't provide help (so you won't search for them again).
6. Examine each book's bibliography for related titles.
7. Try to be an independent researcher but ask a librarian for help if you cannot locate much information on your topic.

If you do your research on the Internet, evaluate your sources carefully and always find at least one more source to verify each point. The reliability of Internet information varies a great deal. It's probably a good idea to use print sources to verify information you find on the Internet, if that is possible.

Observing One good starting point for exploring a topic is simply to observe closely and list the details you see. After you've listed the details, arrange them into categories. The categories you choose depend on the details you observe and your writing goal. For example, you might want to organize your details using spatial order, chronological order, or order of importance.

Interviewing   Get your information directly from the source; interview someone. By asking questions, you can get the specific information you need or want. Follow these steps:

BEFORE THE INTERVIEW	Make the appointment.
	Research your topic and find out about your source.
	Prepare four or five basic questions.
DURING THE INTERVIEW	Ask informational questions (who, what, where, when, why, and how).
	Listen carefully.
	Ask follow-up questions.
	Take accurate notes (or tape-record with permission).
AFTER THE INTERVIEW	Write a more detailed account of the interview.
	Contact your source to clarify points or to double-check facts.

IDENTIFYING PURPOSE AND AUDIENCE

Purpose

Before you start to write, you must determine the primary purpose for your writing: to inform or explain, to persuade, to amuse or entertain, to narrate, or to describe. Sometimes you might want to accomplish more than one purpose, so you will have a primary purpose and a secondary purpose. To determine the primary purpose, answer these questions:

1. Do I want to tell a story?
2. Do I want to describe someone or something?
3. Do I want to inform my readers about the topic or to explain something about it?

4. Do I want to persuade my readers to change their minds about something or take some action?

5. Do I want to amuse or entertain?

Audience

Your audience is anyone who will be reading your writing. Sometimes you write just for yourself. Most often, however, you write to share information with others. Your audience might include a few friends or family members, your classmates, the population at large, or just your teacher. As you write, consider these questions:

1. Who will my audience be? What do I want to say to them?

2. What do my readers already know about my topic?

3. What types of information will interest my audience?

ARRANGING AND ORGANIZING IDEAS

Once you have gathered your information and ideas, you can choose from many kinds of details—examples, facts, statistics, reasons, and concrete and sensory details—to support your main idea. As a writer, you need to organize these details and put them in order. Your purpose and main idea will determine which kinds of supporting details you include as well as the order in which you arrange them. Some possible patterns of organization include

- chronological order (by time)
- spatial order (relationships based on space, place, or setting)
- order of importance
- cause and effect (events described as reason and result, motive and reaction, stimulus and response)
- comparison and contrast (measuring items against one another to show similarities and differences)

The technique you choose to organize details might be as simple as making a list or an outline that shows how the details will be grouped under larger subtopics or headings. You can also organize details visually by making a chart or a diagram similar to the Clustering diagram on page 445. You might better be able to see a plan for organizing your paper when you see the relationships among the parts of your topic.

LET'S SEE, WHERE DID I FILE THOSE NOTES I WAS WORKING ON... UNDER 'H' FOR HOT STORY? NO...

UNDER 'D' FOR DON'T LOSE? NO... UNDER 'G' FOR GOT TO DO IT NOW?

UH-OH... NOW I REMEMBER... UNDER 'L' FOR LEFT IT HOME...

STAGE 2: DRAFTING

When you write your draft, your goal is to organize the facts and details you have accumulated into unified paragraphs. Make sure each paragraph has a main idea and does not bring in unrelated information. The main idea must be stated in a topic sentence, and it must be supported by details that explain and clarify it. Details can be facts and statistics, examples or incidents, or sensory details.

Writing a draft, or turning your ideas into paragraphs, is a stage in the Writing Process and a tool in itself. During Prewriting, you started to organize your details. You will continue to do this as you write your draft because you might find links between ideas that give new meanings to your words and phrases. Continue to organize your details using one of the methods discussed in Prewriting.

To make your sentences interesting, be sure to vary the length of sentences. Don't use too many short, choppy sentences when you can incorporate some of your ideas in subordinate clauses or compound or complex sentences.

Writing Tip

Your composition should consist of three parts: the introduction, the body, and the conclusion (see the outline on page 486). Begin your paper with an **introduction** that grabs the reader's interest and sets the tone. The introduction usually gives the reader a brief explanation of what your paper is about and often includes the **thesis.** The thesis states your paper's main idea or what you're trying to prove or support.

Each paragraph in the **body,** or main part, of your paper should have a topic sentence that states what the paragraph is about. The rest of the paragraph should include details that support the topic sentence. Similarly, each topic sentence should support the thesis, or main idea of the paper.

End your paper with a good **conclusion** that gives a feeling of "completeness." You might conclude your paper in any of the following ways:

- Summarize what you've said in the body of your paper.
- Restate the main idea (using different words).
- Give a final example or idea.
- Make a comment on or give a personal reaction to the topic.
- End with a quotation that sums up or comments on the topic.
- Call for some action (especially in persuasive papers).

STAGE 3: REVISING/EDITING

The purposes of Revising are to make sure that your writing is clear and well organized, that it accomplishes your goals, and that it reaches your audience. The word *revision* means "seeing again." You need to look at your writing again, seeing it as another person might. You might read your paper very carefully, you might tape-record yourself reading your paper aloud, or you might share your writing with another student, a small group of students, or your teacher. After evaluating your work, you might want to move things around or change them completely. You might want to add or cut information. Mark these changes right on your draft and then incorporate them.

The revision stage is the point at which you can

- improve paragraphs
- implement self-evaluation and peer evaluation
- check content and structure
- make sure the language is specific, descriptive, and nonsexist
- check unity and coherence
- check style and tone

Writing Tip

When you are writing about people in general, people who may be either male or female, use nonsexist language. That is, use words that apply to all people, not specifically to males or females. For example, instead of *mailman,* which is gender-specific, you could use the term *mail carrier.*

Traditional nouns for males and females in the same occupation (for instance, *poet* and *poetess*) are no longer encouraged. The noun *poet* now refers to both males and females. Refer to the following list for other gender-neutral terms to use in your writing.

Use	Instead of
actor	actress
Briton	Englishman
businesspeople	businessman/woman
chairperson, chair, moderator	chairman/woman
a member of the clergy	clergyman
craftspeople	craftsmen
crewed space flight	manned space flight
fisher	fisherman
flight attendant	stewardess
Framers, Founders	Founding Fathers

Writing Tip (continued)

Use	Instead of
handmade, synthetic, manufactured	manmade
homemaker	housewife
humanity, human beings, people	mankind
it/its (in reference to ships, countries)	she/her/hers, he/his
land of origin, homeland	mother country
letter carrier/mail carrier	mailman
police officer	policeman
representative	congressman/woman
server	waiter or waitress
supervisor	foreman
watch, guard	watchman
worker	workman
workforce	manpower

Masculine pronouns (such as *he, him, his*) were once used to refer to mixed groups of people. Females were understood to be included. That is, a sentence like *A reporter must check his facts* was understood to apply to both male and female reporters. Now everyone is encouraged to use gender-neutral wording. Some gender-neutral possibilities for that sentence are *Reporters must check their facts, A reporter must check the facts,* and *A reporter must check his or her facts.* (See page 245.)

STAGE 4: PROOFREADING

The purposes of Proofreading are to make sure that you've spelled all words correctly and that your sentences are grammatically correct. Proofread your writing and correct mistakes in capitalization, punctuation, and spelling. Refer to the following chart for Proofreading symbols to help you during this stage of the Writing Process.

Proofreading Marks

Mark	Meaning	Example
∧	Insert	My gra*d*nmother is eighty-six years old.
℘	Delete	She grew up on a dair*y*y farm.
# ∧	Insert space	She milked#cows every morning.
‿	Close up space	She fed the chickens in the barn‿yard.
≡	Capitalize	times have changed.
/	Make lowercase	Machines now do the /Milking.
◯ Sp	Check spelling	Chickens are fed ⟨autommatically.⟩ Sp
‿	Switch order	Modern farms are⁀like⁀more⁀factories.
⁋	New paragraph	⁋Last year I returned to the farm.

STAGE 5: PUBLISHING/PRESENTING

This is the stage at which you share your work with others. You might read your work aloud in class, submit it to the school newspaper, or give it to a friend to read. There are many avenues for Presenting your work.

Chapter 15

Modes of
Writing

● ● ● ● ● ● ● ● ● ● ● ● ● ● ● ●

15.1 DESCRIPTIVE WRITING

Descriptive writing helps the reader experience the subject described. This type of writing requires

- strong observation skills
- precise, informative word choice
- effective organization of details

BEFORE YOU WRITE

Choose a Subject Your descriptive writing may take the form of a character sketch, which is a quick profile that reveals a person's personality and physical appearance. Instead, you may wish to describe an object, an event, or a setting. As you look for people, objects, settings, or incidents to describe in your writing, ask yourself the following questions:

- What is most striking about this subject?
- What memories does this person, object, event, or setting evoke?

- How can I express my impressions of this subject in my writing?
- What aspects of my subject do I want my reader to experience?

Choose a Vantage Point The vantage point is the angle from which the actions are witnessed. You may either write from a stationary vantage point, a fixed position from which to view a scene, or from a moving vantage point. Choosing a vantage point selects and limits the details available to you. You should, therefore, determine your purpose before you choose your vantage point. Note how the purpose of describing a baseball game changes the choice of a vantage point in the chart below.

PURPOSE	VANTAGE POINT
To describe for the reader how it feels to be a baseball player	Dugout; locker room
To show the reader the thrill of watching a baseball game	Stands

Keep these questions in mind as you describe an event:
- Is my vantage point clearly defined and consistent?
- Can I see, hear, smell, taste, or touch the things I am describing from my vantage point?
- Is the passage of time logical and believable?

Writing Tip

When you begin writing, be sure to alert the reader if you shift vantage points. Begin a new paragraph or say something like "Meanwhile, at Sue's house . . ."

Observe and Take Notes Once you decide what you will describe and from which vantage point you will describe it, you will need to capture striking, image-creating details through direct observation and note taking. Videotape, sketch, or jot down notes on your subject to refer to as you write. If you are describing an event that has already occurred, you may "observe" the scene using your memory or photographs.

WRITE A UNIFIED, COHERENT, AND VIVID DESCRIPTION

Create a Topic Sentence The topic sentence states the main idea of your writing. It may entice or tantalize readers, set the stage for the description that follows, or focus the reader's attention in a particular direction. Each paragraph in your writing should have a topic sentence.

Include Details That Support the Topic Sentence A unified paragraph uses only those supporting details that reinforce the main idea of the topic sentence.

Main Idea: Except for an occasional gust of fretful wind that flattened the high, corn-like grass, nothing uttered— nothing in the valley stirred.

Supporting Details: • *drone of grasshoppers was dead*
• *birds left sky unmarked*

Use Sensory Details Well-chosen words based on the five senses—sight, smell, hearing, touch, and taste—can draw your reader into a description. Be aware, however, that too many strong sensory details can numb your reader. Pick a few good details and let these carry the description.

Organize Details Noting details is only one part of your job as a writer. Equally important is the task of selecting and

COMPOSITION

arranging details to achieve the effects you want. You may organize your details in four ways: by order of impression, by order of importance, by spatial order, or by chronological order.

- **Order of Impression** organizes details in the order in which you notice or experience them. If you want to create a "you are there" impression in your writing, use order of impression.
- **Order of Importance** organizes details by their significance or importance. If you want to show that some details are more significant than others, use order of importance.
- **Spatial Order** presents details by their location. If you want readers to visualize details as they truly exist in relationship to one another, use spatial order.
- **Chronological Order** gives details in the order in which they occurred. Use chronological order to describe an event or a process.

Use Transitions to Achieve Coherence Use transitional words and phrases to achieve coherence and to show

- movement in time (*when, before, soon, first, second*)
- movement in space (*beyond, farther, in front of*)
- movement in importance (*in fact, especially, above all*)

Use Descriptive Language You can bring energy to your writing by using specific, action-packed words. Stay away from overused modifiers, such as *good, bad, really,* and *very.* Use exact verbs to evoke a mood and strong mental images. To choose just the right verb, use a thesaurus, which is a collection of synonyms. Keep in mind, however, that synonyms are not always interchangeable. For example, you

COMPOSITION

wouldn't write "The horse *jogs*" when you mean "The horse *gallops*." Use a dictionary to find the exact meanings of words.

Her love affair had ended. She didn't want to live.

She threw herself in front of a Zamboni.

THAT'S THE DUMBEST THING I'VE EVER READ!

She threw herself in front of a skateboard.

PEANUTS reprinted by permission of United
Feature Syndicate, Inc.

Use Analogies An analogy is an extended comparison between two things that are usually considered dissimilar but share common features. An analogy makes an extended comparison, supported point by point with examples and details. It can last through several paragraphs or an entire essay.

CREATING SUCCESSFUL ANALOGIES
1. Find a minimum of three similarities between the ideas you are comparing.
2. Use specific details and examples to support your comparisons.
3. Write a topic sentence that establishes the basis of the comparison.
4. Decide on a logical order for the points of the analogy and use transitions, such as *similarly* and *also,* to link them clearly.

Produce a Mood The overall feeling, or mood, of a piece of writing is constructed through the details chosen and the language used to describe these details. The mood of a piece will depend on your purpose. Do you want your reader to get a sense of excitement? Calm? Sadness? Changing the mood of a description can alert the reader to a change in feeling toward the subject or to a shift in the action.

GUIDELINES FOR DESCRIPTIVE WRITING
1. Gather vivid details that will help you describe a person or re-create a scene or an experience for your readers.
2. Decide which kind of organization will be more appropriate for your subject— spatial order, chronological order, order of importance, or order of impression.
3. Write a topic sentence for each paragraph.
4. Use appropriate transitions to make the organization and relationships among ideas clear.
5. Use descriptive language and analogies to make your writing vivid and interesting.

15.2 NARRATIVE WRITING

When you write a narrative, you tell a story of an event.

- A **fictional narrative** is a story from a writer's imagination.
- A **nonfiction narrative,** such as a biography or a history, is about events that really happened.

Fictional and nonfiction narratives have the same basic elements: character, plot, point of view, theme, and setting.

DEVELOP YOUR NARRATIVE

Set the Scene Use the details of setting to create mood and develop readers' expectations about character and action. The elements of setting are **time, place, weather, culture,** and **historical period.** As you write, consider how each element of setting can contribute to your narrative.

Reveal Character Use interesting dialogue and vivid description to make your characters as lifelike as possible.

- **Use Interesting Dialogue** Dialogue gives the reader important information about the characters. What characters say and how they say it reveal personality and show relationships among characters. Use language that reflects the age, background, and personality of each character.

- **Use Vivid Description** A description that reveals character has more impact than one that merely tells what you think. Notice how the specific observation that follows is more interesting and descriptive than the general statement:

  General statement: "Bob is soft-hearted and impractical."

  Specific observation: "Bob can't pass a musician on the street without giving away all his change, so he never has a quarter for the telephone."

Writing Tip

Answer these questions as you describe the characters in your narrative:

- How do the characters look, move, and speak?
- How do the characters behave toward others?
- How do others react to the characters?
- What personality traits do the characters have?
- What overall impression should my descriptions convey?

Convey a Mood Writers use word choice and description to create moods in their stories. Notice how two different moods can be created for the same desert setting:

TWO MOODS OF THE DESERT	
UPBEAT: LOCATION IS INVITING	rich golds of the sunset, aroma of mesquite on the fire, clear music of mission bells
NEGATIVE: LOCATION IS HOSTILE	sharp needles of cacti, parched streambed, threatening hiss of a snake

COMPOSITION

Communicate a Theme The theme of a story is the insight into human life that the writer conveys through the narrative. One way to express the theme of your narrative is through your description of the setting. Ask yourself how you can create mood and hint at theme through scenery, props, color, and sound. Then use concrete, evocative words to describe these details.

Choose a Point of View Once you have decided on the characters, plot, and setting, you must choose the point of view from which you will tell the story.

- **First-person point of view:** The narrator is a character in the story; he or she uses the pronoun *I*.
- **Third-person point of view:** The narrator is not a character in the story but an observer of it. Using this point of view, you may choose a **third-person limited narrator,** who sees the world through the eyes of one character and knows and relays the thoughts and actions of only this character. Alternatively, you may choose a **third-person omniscient narrator,** who knows and relays the thoughts and actions of all of the characters.

Remember that the point of view you choose significantly affects the story. It can give the story a bias, or it can limit what the audience knows until the very end. Think carefully about the point of view and how it will affect the development of the plot.

ORGANIZE YOUR NARRATIVE

Construct a Plot A narrative is comprised of a series of events. Plot is the writer's arrangement of events to dramatize a particular conflict or theme. When you begin to organize the information you have decided to include in your story, review the basic plot structure diagram that follows.

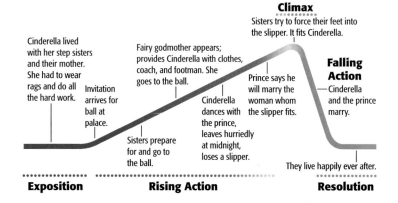

Climax
Sisters try to force their feet into the slipper. It fits Cinderella.

Cinderella lived with her step sisters and their mother. She had to wear rags and do all the hard work.

Invitation arrives for ball at palace.

Fairy godmother appears; provides Cinderella with clothes, coach, and footman. She goes to the ball.

Prince says he will marry the woman whom the slipper fits.

Falling Action
—Cinderella and the prince marry.

Cinderella dances with the prince, leaves hurriedly at midnight, loses a slipper.

Sisters prepare for and go to the ball.

They live happily ever after.

Exposition   **Rising Action**   **Resolution**

Most plots develop in five stages.

- **Exposition** is background information about the characters and setting. This sets the scene for the conflict that follows.
- **Rising action** develops the conflict.
- **Climax** is the point of highest interest, conflict, or suspense in the story.
- **Falling action** shows what happens to the characters after the climax.
- **Resolution** shows how the conflict is resolved or the problem solved.

Establish Conflict Conflict is the heart of narrative writing. It sets the plot in motion and causes changes in the characters.

- In an **external conflict,** a character struggles with another character or an element of nature.
- In an **internal conflict,** a character struggles to make a decision or to act in a certain way.

Order Time in Your Narrative Writers don't always begin a narrative with the event that happened first, because this event is not always the one that best sets the mood or introduces the conflict. You can manipulate your readers' perceptions of time. You can use flashbacks to show the complicated relationship between past and present; you can use fantasies, dreams, and flash-forwards to offer glimpses of events to come.

- **Chronological narratives** describe events in the order in which they occur.
- **Flashbacks** interrupt chronological narratives to relate events that occurred in the past.

Writing Tip

Some writers use a character's musings and memories to introduce a flashback; others have characters relate past events to a first-person narrator.

Few, if any, narratives take place in real time. A ten-day train ride may be described in only one sentence, while a ten-minute conversation may take several pages to describe.

Build Narrative Suspense Suspense is the uncertainty about the outcome of a story—what makes a reader's pulse quicken. Add suspense to a narrative to give readers a pressing desire to read on to the end.

Use any of the following techniques to create suspense in your narrative:

- Construct an eerie setting.
- Use delaying tactics. Slow down time at a crucial moment with precise descriptions, flashbacks, or scene changes.
- Use foreshadowing—a hint of what is to come.

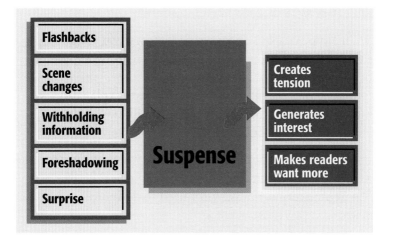

Flashbacks

Scene changes

Withholding information

Foreshadowing

Surprise

Suspense

Creates tension

Generates interest

Makes readers want more

15.3 EXPOSITORY WRITING

Giving directions, explaining an idea or a term, comparing one thing to another, and explaining how to do something are all forms of expository writing. The purpose of expository writing is to inform your readers or to explain something to them. Effective expository writing

- gives the reader a logical step-by-step path through new information
- allows writers to share information and explanations directly with the reader

USE EXPOSITORY WRITING TO
• explain a process
• show a cause-and-effect relationship
• compare and contrast
• identify problems and propose solutions
• build and support a hypothesis

EXPLAIN A PROCESS

This type of expository writing allows you to explain either how to do something or how something happens.

Consider Your Audience As you write your explanation, you should keep your audience's background knowledge in mind. Answer the following questions:

- How much does my audience know about the process?
- How much detail are they likely to need?
- Which terms, if any, will I need to define?

Understand the Process To explain a process, the writer must first understand the steps involved in the process and then present these steps in order.

Writing Tip

Effective instructions are straightforward, precise, and clearly organized. Obscure language or garbled logic can confuse your reader.

Write the Essay Follow the three steps below to write an essay that explains a process.

- **Prewriting:** Research by reading, watching others, or performing the process.
- **Drafting:** Arrange the steps of the process in chronological order. Break one step into two if more detail is needed. Omit unnecessary steps.
- **Revising:** Reread the explanation. Make sure you've included all necessary details and signaled separate steps with transition words. Reorder steps as necessary.

CAUSE AND EFFECT

In cause-and-effect writing, you give reasons and explanations for events, conditions, or behavior. Whenever you explain "why" in writing, you will use some form of cause-and-effect exposition. Cause-and-effect relationships can

- start with one cause and lead to one effect
- start with one cause and lead to several effects
- start with several causes and lead to one effect
- start with several causes and lead to several effects
- start with one cause that leads to an effect, which in turn leads to another effect, resulting in a chain of events

Plan Your Essay When planning a cause-and-effect essay,

1. identify the event or condition you want to explain
2. ask yourself the following questions:
   - Who or what was responsible?
   - Who or what was affected?
3. list and explain the causes and the effects
4. answer the questions in the following chart to be sure you have not drawn any faulty conclusions

FAULTY CAUSE-AND-EFFECT RELATIONSHIPS	
• HAVE YOU ASSUMED A CAUSE-AND-EFFECT RELATIONSHIP WHEN THERE IS NONE?	*My mother knows everyone; therefore, I can get into any college in the country.*
• HAVE YOU ASSUMED ONLY ONE CAUSE WHEN MANY CAUSES MAY BE APPROPRIATE?	*The team lost the pennant because of the umpire's bad call.*
• HAVE YOU INCORRECTLY ASSUMED A CAUSAL RELATIONSHIP BETWEEN TWO EVENTS THAT FOLLOWED EACH OTHER?	*Unemployment skyrocketed once he began his term as governor. He should claim responsibility for the horrible state of the economy.*

Write Your Essay Follow these steps to write a cause-and-effect essay.

1. Compose a thesis statement that clearly states your topic. Include this thesis statement in your introduction.
2. Organize and write your essay. Cause-and-effect essays need a logical structure, so you might begin with a cause and then present its effect. You can also reverse this order—you might begin with an effect and trace it back to its original cause.
3. Summarize your arguments in your conclusion.

COMPARE AND CONTRAST

A compare-and-contrast essay expresses the essential differences and similarities between two subjects. Compare-and-contrast essays should be carefully constructed around thesis statements to explain the similarities and differences between items or events. The thesis gives the essay a shape—it determines what information belongs in the essay.

Choose a Method of Organization Some writers choose to organize their compare-and-contrast essays according to subject. Using this method, writers will discuss all the details about one subject first and then all the details about the next subject. Then they will compare and contrast the subjects. Other writers prefer to organize details by feature. They will select one feature of the subjects at a time and list all the similarities and differences for both subjects.

IDENTIFY PROBLEMS AND PROPOSE SOLUTIONS

When writing about a problem and its solutions, define the problem carefully and try to present a range of possible solutions.

1. Begin your essay by gathering information at the library, on the Internet, or from interviews or observation.
2. Ask yourself such questions as the following:
   - What is the nature and extent of the problem?
   - What are its causes?
   - How does it affect people?
3. Draw on different types of information to explain the dimensions of a problem.
   - Use personal anecdotes to help your readers relate a problem to their own lives.
   - Use statistics to help you present an overview of a problem.
4. Present solutions. Most problems have more than one possible solution. Examine the advantages and disadvantages of proposed solutions carefully and systematically. Be realistic when you explain solutions—it may be that no solution will completely solve a problem.

BUILD A HYPOTHESIS

A **hypothesis** is a statement of a belief that you assume to be true.

	THE STEPS TO BUILDING A HYPOTHESIS
STEP 1	Decide on the issue or question you want to explore. For example, you might build a hypothesis to explain a foreign policy decision or a chemical reaction.
STEP 2	Identify what you are trying to explain.
STEP 3	Collect data and consult experts.
STEP 4	Compare and contrast data to identify patterns or trends.
STEP 5	Decide on the most reasonable hypothesis based on the data.
STEP 6	Test the conclusion for acceptance, modification, or rejection.

COMPOSITION

Present Your Data After you have tested your hypothesis, you can begin writing. Follow these steps when you begin your essay.

1. Present your hypothesis in a thesis statement. This statement should be part of an introductory paragraph that tells how and why your topic and thesis are important.
2. Develop your explanation in the body of your essay by supporting each point with specific examples, facts, or expert testimony.
3. Summarize your main points in your concluding paragraph. Draw a conclusion by evaluating the evidence you've assembled or by expressing a judgment or a realization.

15.4 PERSUASIVE WRITING

Persuasive writing is used to motivate readers—to change their minds about a topic, to convince them to buy a product, or to get them to vote for a certain candidate or issue. The main reason for persuasive writing is to convince readers to take action, in whatever form that might be. To make a persuasive argument, you must

- state your opinion clearly as early in the essay as possible
- support your position with facts, reasons, and examples
- choose a presentation that is designed to appeal to your audience

CHOOSE A TOPIC

You are writing to convince your reader to agree with your opinion. Choose an argument about which you and others feel strongly.

KNOW YOUR AUDIENCE

A particular topic or issue may be insignificant to one group of people and yet be of great interest to another group. Make a list of information about your audience, including their likes and dislikes, their biases, and what they probably know about the subject. Keep this list in mind when constructing your argument.

CONSTRUCT AN ARGUMENT

Begin by clearly expressing your opinion in a thesis statement. Compare the thesis statements in the following chart.

SAMPLE THESIS STATEMENT		
Not So Good	**Better**	**Best**
In a democracy, all citizens are allowed to participate.	*Democratic rule requires participation; therefore, everyone should vote.*	*Low voter turnout is undermining our democracy; we must encourage greater participation through voter information.*
(Not an opinion, just a statement of fact)	(Vague)	(Well-defined position, specific solution)

To test your thesis, summarize the opposing view. If you cannot state an opposing view, you probably do not have a strong point to make.

Next gather evidence to support your thesis and develop a strategy for presenting it. You may choose to begin your essay by analyzing and refuting the arguments of the opposing side. You might choose to present information in one of the following ways:

- **decreasing order of importance,** placing the most important evidence first
- **increasing order of importance,** placing the most important evidence last

Increasing order of importance can fail if you don't hold the audience's attention until the end. An attention-getting introduction and a strong middle are essential to this strategy.

EVALUATE THE EVIDENCE

To support your argument, you must choose and evaluate a variety of evidence. Each type of evidence you use adds a different kind of support to your position.

- **Factual information and concrete details,** such as statistics, observations, scientific reports, and historical perspectives, are convincing because they are verifiable.
- **Opinions** are effective if they are from a respected authority or are deduced from factual evidence.
- **Examples, anecdotes, and analogies** can bring your subject to life or illuminate a point.
- **Reasons** guide your audience through the logic of your position.

The wider your range of supporting evidence, the stronger your arguments. However, collecting mountains of evidence does not guarantee that you'll have a strong argument. You need to judge the quality of the evidence. The following questions can help you analyze your research:

- Does the evidence come from a reliable, unbiased, up-to-date source?
- Is the evidence consistent with what you or authorities on the subject believe to be true?
- Does the evidence address all sides of the issue, taking all objections into account?

Sift Fact from Opinion A strong persuasive argument supports opinions with relevant facts. Recognizing the difference between fact and opinion can help you more clearly define your position. It can also guide you in presenting facts and opinions appropriately in your writing.

Follow these guidelines to help you determine whether the "facts" you read and hear are actually opinions in disguise.

RECOGNIZING FACTS AND OPINIONS	
RECOGNIZING FACTS	RECOGNIZING OPINIONS
Can the statement be verified?	**Is the statement based on personal preference or belief?**
Facts can be proven or measured; you can check them in reference works. Sometimes you can observe or test them yourself.	Often, although not always, opinions are open to interpretation and contain phrases such as "I believe" or "in my view."

COMPOSITION

Evaluate Facts and Opinions To evaluate the strength of an argument, you need to do more than distinguish between fact and opinion. You also need to determine whether facts are relevant and whether they tell the whole story.

Opinion, as well as fact, should be evaluated carefully. Informed opinions, based on facts and on the experiences of eyewitnesses or experts, carry the most weight.

Use Inductive and Deductive Reasoning Both inductive and deductive reasoning involve using facts to arrive at conclusions, but they work in different ways. When you use inductive reasoning, you

1. begin with a series of facts
2. study the facts, looking for a connection among them
3. draw a conclusion or a generalization

We rely on this kind of reasoning for much of our knowledge.

Inductive reasoning proceeds logically from limited facts or observations to a general conclusion. An inductive argument will hold up only if the evidence is accurate and the conclusion follows reasonably from the evidence. Check your reasoning by asking whether you can draw another conclusion from the evidence.

EVALUATE INDUCTIVE REASONING
1. What are the specific facts or evidence from which the conclusion is drawn?
2. Is each fact or piece of evidence accurate?
3. Do the facts form a representative and sufficiently large sample?
4. Do all of the facts or the evidence lead to the conclusion?
5. Does the argument contain any logical fallacies?

COMPOSITION

Sidney Harris

When you use deductive reasoning, you

1. begin with a generalization
2. apply that generalization to a specific example
3. arrive at a conclusion

Deductive reasoning may involve a **syllogism,** which consists of a major premise, or a general statement; a minor premise, or a related fact; and a conclusion based on the two.

SYLLOGISM	
START WITH A GENERALIZATION OR MAJOR PREMISE.	A diet high in fat is unhealthful.
STATE A RELATED FACT OR MINOR PREMISE.	A typical teenager's diet is high in fat.
DRAW A CONCLUSION BASED ON THE TWO.	A typical teenager's diet is unhealthful.

Note: A syllogism is valid if it follows the rules of deductive reasoning. It is true if the statements are factually accurate. A syllogism, then, can be valid but untrue. For example:

Major premise: Basketball players are the best athletes. [This can't be proved true.]

Minor premise: Michael Jordan is the best basketball player. [This, too, can be debated.]

Conclusion: Therefore, Michael Jordan is the best athlete. [This conclusion is valid according to the premises, but it isn't necessarily true.]

EVALUATE DEDUCTIVE REASONING
1. What are the major premise, the minor premise, and the conclusion?
2. Is the major premise a universal statement?
3. Are both premises true?
4. Does the conclusion follow logically from the major and the minor premises?
5. Does the argument contain any logical fallacies?

Recognize Logical Fallacies Faulty reasoning involves errors called logical fallacies. Learning to recognize your own and others' logical fallacies will strengthen your skills in persuasive writing. Listed are some of the most common types of flaws.

- A **red herring** statement diverts attention from the issue at hand. A senator who is attacked for irregular attendance might describe her charitable work to prove she is productive. However, she has not addressed the criticism about the missed meetings.

- **Circular reasoning** is an argument that apparently leads to a logical conclusion but actually takes you back to where you started. The statement "Shaquille O'Neal is a great basketball player because he has so much talent" sounds true, but the statement doesn't prove anything; it merely repeats the point in different words. To say that talent makes O'Neal great is just another way of saying he's a great basketball player.

- **Bandwagon Reasoning** The term "jumping on the bandwagon" means doing or thinking something because everyone else is doing or thinking it. This type of reasoning provides no evidence to support a decision or a viewpoint.

Anticipate Objections When you present an argument, anticipate objections to your view and then try to answer those objections. A good strategy for handling opposition is to make concessions—to admit that some point in your argument is weak or to agree with some part of your opponent's argument.

Chapter 16

Research Paper Writing

●●●●●●●●●●●●●●●●

When you write a research paper, you collect factual information from a variety of sources, analyze and organize this information, and present it to your readers in a clear and interesting way.

Follow these steps to write a research paper:

- Choose a topic that interests you.
- Narrow the topic to fit your paper's length.
- Perform extensive research to gather information about the topic.
- Organize your research and write an outline.
- Form a thesis statement and support the thesis with the information you gathered in your research.
- Compile a list of works cited.

16.1 PREWRITING

CHOOSE A TOPIC

Researching and writing will be easier if you are curious about the topic you choose, so try to find a topic that interests you. Keep in mind how much information will be manageable given the length of your research paper. If the topic is too broad, you'll have too much information. Narrow your topic until you feel you can cover it adequately in your paper.

TOO BROAD	NARROW	NARROWER
Sports	Tennis	The History of Wimbledon
Dance	Ballet	Romantic Ballet
History	History of Art	Art in the Romantic Era

Research TIP

If your teacher assigns a topic, do some preliminary research at the library or on the Internet to find an aspect of this topic that appeals to you.

Decide on a Central Idea

After choosing a topic, you need to decide on your paper's central idea, which will guide your selection of research questions. Identify three to seven research questions, each question focusing on one aspect of the topic. Ask the *whats, whys,* and *hows* about your topic. As you begin to find answers, you'll come up with more sharply focused questions. Feel free to modify your central idea as you learn more about the topic.

QUESTIONS FOR A RESEARCH PAPER ABOUT THE ROMANTIC ERA
• What were the beliefs of the Romantics?
• Why did Romantics believe in these things?
• How did artists, musicians, and poets of the Romantic Era express these beliefs in their works?
• Which artists are considered Romantics?
• What did these artists have in common? How were they different?

FIND INFORMATION ON YOUR TOPIC

Use two types of sources—primary and secondary.

- A **primary source** is first-hand information that has not been evaluated or analyzed by someone else. A witness to an event, letters and original documents from the historical era you are studying, and interviews with experts on your topic are considered primary sources.
- A **secondary source** is information that has been organized, evaluated, and analyzed by someone else. An article analyzing a witness's comments would be a secondary source. Most books and magazine articles are considered secondary sources.

Technology Tip

The Internet can be a valuable tool for finding both primary and secondary sources. Evaluate Internet sources carefully; not all Internet sites contain accurate information. To make certain that the sources are valid, find another source that contains the same information.

Take Notes

Once you have found some sources, you can begin taking notes and collecting information. Taking notes efficiently and accurately is one of the most important steps in writing a good research paper. You will probably take many more notes than you will use, but at this point, it is better to have too much information than too little.

Prepare Note Cards Read your sources thoroughly for information, ideas, statements, and statistics that relate to your research topic and to your main idea. When you find something you can use, write it on a three-by-five note card, with one piece of information per card, and record the number of that source's bibliography card. There are three ways to record the information you find.

- **Paraphrase:** Write the information in your own words.
- **Quote Directly:** Copy the information exactly as it appears in the text. Use quotation marks to indicate when you quote directly.
- **Summarize:** Write a brief summary of the information, focusing on key points and concepts.

Develop a Working Bibliography Assemble a record of the books, articles, Internet sites, and other sources you consult. This record is your working bibliography. When you find a useful source, record the publishing data on a three-by-five index card. This way you can easily find and use the information later. Complete bibliography cards will also help you write your list of works cited.

Different types of sources need different data on their bibliography cards, as the following samples illustrate. Examples of other kinds of sources can be found in the List of Works Cited on pages 494–495.

Number Your Sources Number each card. This number will later serve as an easy way to identify the source. You can also write brief notes indicating the type of information in the source.

Types of Bibliography Cards

EXAMPLE **Book**

> 1
>
> Kerner, Mary. *Barefoot to Balanchine: How to Watch Dance*. New York: Doubleday, 1990.

EXAMPLE Internet Source

> 3
>
> Wordsworth, William. *Literary Ballads*. Comp. Thomas Gannon. London: Routledge, 1991. *Favorite Quotations from William Wordsworth*. 25 May 1995. Preface. University of South Dakota. 15 July 1998
>
> <http://www.usd.edu/~tgannon/txts/wordquot.txt>.

Avoid Plagiarism Presenting the ideas or statements of another writer without crediting the original source is plagiarism. Plagiarism occurs when

- a writer directly quotes a source without using quotation marks or paraphrases a source too closely, substituting only a few words of his or her own. Even if credit is given to the source, this use of information is still considered plagiarism.
- a writer summarizes a source's ideas or observations without giving credit

Frank and Ernest

© 1989 Thaves / Reprinted with permission. Newspaper dist. by NEA, Inc.

Research TIP

To avoid paraphrasing a source too closely, look away from the source while you take notes. After you have finished paraphrasing, reread the source to make sure that you have used your own words.

Read Sources Critically As you do research, evaluate each source for bias. If a source's bias detracts from the objectivity of your paper, you may not want to use it unless you present one or more opposing views. To detect bias, ask yourself whether you think the source is treating the topic fairly or not. Does the author make unqualified assertions?

COMPOSITION

Are the views of the author often disputed? Answering these questions will help you choose the best sources.

PEANUTS reprinted by permission of United
Feature Syndicate, Inc.

CHOOSE A METHOD OF ORGANIZATION

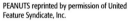

How can you decide on the best way to arrange the ideas in your notes? You have a number of options, depending on the nature of your information.

- **Chronological:** Arrange the information according to when it happened. This organization is often used in papers describing historical changes.
- **Cause and Effect:** Arrange items in causal order to show how one idea or event directly determines another. This organization is often used in papers exploring why something happened.
- **Cumulative:** Arrange items according to how important or how familiar to the reader each one is. This organization is often used in papers evaluating results.

Develop an Outline

An outline is a summary of the main points and the ideas that support them. As you take notes, look for ways to classify the facts and the ideas you find. Begin to group the note cards as you classify them. As you make decisions about how to organize your cards, you are developing the information you need to write a working outline. You will continue to write and revise this outline as you conduct research. The following tip will help you write your working outline, which will eventually become the formal outline you will use when you write your first draft.

1. Look for similarities among notes; group note cards on similar topics together. Use each group as a main topic in your outline.
2. Within groups, cluster similar note cards into subgroups that elaborate on the main topic. Use these subgroups as the subheadings in your outline.
3. Arrange main topics to build on your central idea. Under each topic, arrange subheadings so they elaborate on the heading, or main topic, in a logical way.
4. As you continue your research and learn more, revise your outline. Subdivide information in subheadings into outline entries as well.
5. Set aside note cards that don't fit under any of your headings, but don't throw them away.
6. Before you begin your first draft, prepare a formal outline.

Title of Paper

I. Introduction
   Central idea (thesis statement)

II. Heading (main topic)
   A. Subheading (supporting detail)
      1. sub/subheading
      2.
   B. Subheading (supporting detail)
      1.
      2.

Body—

III. Heading (main topic)

IV. Heading (main topic)

V. Conclusion

Outlining TIP

Make Smooth Transitions: Note how the writer of the following outline organizes the information to provide smooth transitions between the headings. For example, the writer places "natural settings" at the end of heading III and at the beginning of heading IV; doing so gives the writer an effective way to connect the two paragraphs.

COMPOSITION

Art in the Romantic Era: How Writers, Dancers, Musicians, and Artists Were Influenced by Romantic Philosophy

I. Introduction

Artists, poets, musicians, and dancers all shared common elements of Romantic thought.

II. Definition and history of Romantic Era
   A. History of the term
   B. Shared beliefs
      1. Emotional over intellectual
      2. New forms
      3. Love of nature

III. Romanticism in Literature
   A. William Wordsworth; Samuel Taylor Coleridge
      1. Emotions
      2. Reaction against Classicists
   B. New forms
      1. Wordsworth
      2. William Blake
   C. Natural settings

IV. Romanticism in the visual arts
   A. Natural settings
   B. Personal feelings
      1. Comparison to poets
      2. New techniques

V. Romanticism in music
   A. Personal feelings
   B. Shared goals of Romantic composers

VII. Conclusion

16.2 DRAFTING

DEVELOP A THESIS STATEMENT

Until now, you have guided your research and outline according to a central idea about your topic. Now you should turn your central idea into a **thesis statement**—that is, a concise idea you will try to prove, expand on, or illustrate in your writing. Your thesis statement gives your writing a focus from start to finish.

THREE STEPS TO CONSTRUCTING A THESIS STATEMENT
1. Examine your central idea and refine it to reflect the information that you gathered in your research. The information you find may be very different from what you expected to find.
2. Consider your approach to the topic. What is the purpose of your research? Are you proving or disproving something? Illustrating a cause-and-effect relationship? Offering a solution to a problem? Examining one aspect of your topic thoroughly?
3. Revise your central idea to reflect your approach and polish your wording to form a concise thesis statement.

USE YOUR OUTLINE AND NOTES

Using the structure of your formal outline, you will be able to transform your piles of note cards into the basis for a first draft. Look at your outline again to be sure you're satisfied with the way each idea leads to the next. Then begin drafting.

DRAFTING TIP

1. Try to draft as smoothly and logically as possible without getting stalled on details. Don't worry about finding the perfect word or phrase; you can revise later.
2. Use your outline as a map to help guide you in your writing. The outline should remind you of what comes before or after a particular idea.
3. Write at least one paragraph for each heading, or main topic, in your outline. Each paragraph should have a topic sentence and supporting details.
4. When you use data from a note card, write the number of that card near the data in the text to help you document the idea later.

Write the Introduction and Conclusion

Your paper's introduction and conclusion work together to frame your research paper. A good introduction should grab your reader's attention and make him or her want to read on. The introduction can be a good place to use a special bit of information you have found in your research, perhaps a little-known fact, a vivid description, or a funny anecdote that you want to highlight. Your conclusion should alert the reader that you are wrapping up. You might summarize your main points or mention any new questions your paper raises.

TRAITS OF EFFECTIVE INTRODUCTIONS AND CONCLUSIONS	
Introduction	**Conclusion**
Contains a clear, concise thesis statement	Restates the thesis statement
Grabs and keeps the reader's interest	Reviews the main points of the paper
Identifies your approach to the topic	Notes the significance of the research
Presents a bit of enticing background information on unfamiliar subjects	Identifies possible implications for the future (if appropriate)

RESEARCH PAPER FORMAT

Use the following format for your research paper:

- At the top, bottom, and both sides of each page, leave margins of one inch.
- Double-space every line, including the title if it is more than one line long.
- Unless you are told to include a cover page, put your name, your teacher's name, the name of the course, and the date on four lines at the start of page one, even with the left margin.
- Center the title on the next line.
- For all but the first page, put the first line of text one inch from the top edge of the paper.
- Put your last name and the page number at the upper right corner of each page, one-half inch from the top and even with the right margin. Number all pages, even the first, consecutively.
- Indent each paragraph's first line one-half inch from the left margin.
- If you use a set-off quotation, indent each line of it one inch from the left margin.

- At the end of your research paper, on a new page, begin your list of works cited. Center the title, *Works Cited,* an inch from the top of the page. Begin each entry even with the left margin. If an entry is more than one line long, indent the next line or lines one-half inch from the left margin.

16.3 CITING SOURCES

Document Information You need to name the sources of words, ideas, and facts that you borrow. Readers should be able to distinguish your ideas from those of your sources. Documenting your sources enables your reader to check the source personally and to judge how believable or important a piece of information is. Documentation also decreases the chance of plagiarism.

What to Document You should document your information

- whenever you use someone's exact words
- whenever you paraphrase a particular idea or series of ideas
- whenever you use information that is not generally known or found in most books on the subject

You do not need to document the following information:

- widely known proverbs, famous quotations, and simple definitions
- information that is common knowledge or is found in most sources about the topic

Use Parenthetical Documentation Cite sources in the text of your report by inserting the author's last name and a page reference in parentheses after the information that requires citation.

- **Name in text:** If you mention the author in the text (for example, if the text reads "As Ferguson points out, . . ."), then you can merely insert the page number in parentheses.
- **Two or more authors:** For two authors, insert both authors and the page numbers in parentheses (Smith and Brown 42). If the source has more than two authors, just give the last name of the first author listed, followed by *et al.* ("and others") and the page number (Wold et al. 42).
- **More than one work by the same author:** Use the author's name, a shortened version of the title, and give the page number (Longyear, <u>Romanticism in Music</u> 12).
- **No author or editor:** Use a shortened version of the title and give the page number (<u>Britannica</u> 160).
- **No page numbers:** Use *n. pag.* in place of a page reference (Clark n. pag.).
- **More than one source at the same time:** Include both sources, and separate them with a semicolon (Wold et al. 42; <u>Britannica</u> 160).
- **Author quoted in another source:** Use the abbreviation *qtd. in* for "quoted in" and the author and page number of the source (qtd. in Longyear 33).

Use Quotations

You may quote from a source in the following ways:

1. You may quote one word or part of a sentence, including it in a sentence of your own.

   This ideal differed greatly from the thoughts of eighteenth-century poets, who felt that poetry was "primarily an imitation of human life" (Abrams 5).

2. You may quote a complete sentence, which you should introduce in your own words.

The Romantics favored natural settings over newly industrial cities such as London. In his poem "The Tables Turned," Wordsworth wrote, "Come forth into the light of things, Let Nature be your teacher" (Bartlett 372).

3. You may omit words or sentences from a quotation by using ellipses in place of the omitted words or sentences. Place brackets around words you have inserted in place of the omitted words or sentences. Be careful not to change the meaning of the original sentences.

Composers wrote works that they felt would appeal to the public or "satisfy . . . [their] intense feeling for expression" (Wold et al. 253).

4. You may use a quotation of more than four lines by starting a new line and indenting the quote. In this case, you do not need to use quotation marks.

Which Page Numbers Should I Include? Page numbers in parenthetical documentation indicate the pages from which the information is taken. Page numbers in works cited entries are for the page span of the entire newspaper or magazine article or anthologized work.

Compile a List of Works Cited

From your bibliography cards, record the publishing information about the source in the form of a list of works cited. This list should appear on a new page at the end of your report. Write the information about the sources in the order in which you wrote it on your bibliography card. List the sources in alphabetical order by authors' last names, or if no author is given, by title.

The following chart shows the proper bibliographic style for various sources. The style is based on the recommendations of the Modern Language Association. If your teacher asks you to use a different style to document your sources, you can still refer to this chart to be sure you have included everything necessary.

A LIST OF WORKS CITED

TYPE OF CITATION	EXAMPLE
Book with Single Author	Kerner, Mary. <u>Barefoot to Balanchine: How to Watch Dance</u>. New York: Doubleday, 1990.
Book with Two Authors	Collier, Peter and Robert Lethbridge. <u>Artistic Relations: Literature and the Visual Arts in Nineteenth-Century France</u>. New Haven: Yale University Press, 1994.
Book with Three or More Authors	Wold, Milo, et al. <u>An Introduction to Music and Art in the Western World</u>. Dubuque: Brown and Benchmark, 1996.
Articles in a Periodical	Furst, Lilian. "Poetic Madness and the Romantic Imagination." <u>Nineteenth-Century Literature</u> Vol. 52 June 1997: 110–112.
Encyclopedia Article	"Romanticism." <u>The New Encyclopaedia Britannica: Micropaedia</u>. 15th ed. 1998.

TYPE OF CITATION	EXAMPLE
Internet Site with a Print Version	Wordsworth, William. <u>Literary Ballads</u>. London: Routledge, 1991. <u>Favorite Quotations from William Wordsworth</u>. Comp. Thomas Gannon. 25 May 1995. Preface. University of South Dakota. 15 July 1998 <http://www.usd.edu/~tgannon/txts/word quot.txt>.

Not all sources fit the categories listed in the preceding chart. To cite such sources, refer to the *MLA Handbook for Writers of Research Papers* and adapt one of the above entries, arranging the information in the following order:

Author information should appear at the beginning of the entry, with the author's last name first.

- If the source has two or more authors, reverse only the first author's name.
- If no author is listed, list the editor. If no editor is listed, begin with the title.
- If you use more than one work by the same author, you do not need to repeat the author's name for each entry. Instead, use three hyphens followed by a period to begin the entry.

Title information follows any author information and lists the title of the article, essay, or other part of the book first if applicable, then the title of the book.

COMPOSITION

Publication information follows the author and title and, as needed, lists the editor's name, edition number, volume number, and series name. List the city of publication, publisher's name, and the publication date. (Note: This information may not be available on Internet sources. Just include the information given at the site.) If appropriate, list page numbers. If a newspaper or magazine article does not appear on consecutive pages, include the first page number and a plus sign (10+).

Citing Online Sources

You will not need to include everything from the following list in a single citation; most sources don't offer all this information. If you cannot find all the information needed for a particular source, provide as much information as is available.

1. Author, editor, or compiler of the source
2. Title of an article, poem, or short work (in quotation marks); or title of a posting to a discussion line or forum followed by the phrase *Online posting*
3. Title of a book (underlined)
4. Editor, compiler, or translator of the text (if not mentioned earlier)
5. Publication information for any print version of the text
6. Title of the scholarly project, database, periodical, or professional or personal site (underlined). If the professional or personal site has no title, use a description such as *Home page.*
7. Editor or director of the scholarly project or database
8. Version number of the source, or for a journal, the volume number, issue number, or other identifying number
9. Date of electronic publication, of the last update, or of the posting

10. Total number of pages (if they are numbered)
11. Name of the institution or organization sponsoring or associated with the Internet site
12. Date when you accessed the source
13. Electronic address of the source (in angle brackets)

16.4 REVISING/EDITING

When you revise your first draft, you can improve your choice of words, your transitions, and—most important—the way you present your ideas. Use the following chart to help you revise your draft.

SOLVING REVISION PROBLEMS	
Problem	**Solution**
My first draft needs a clearer focus.	Review your thesis statement; delete or rewrite anything in the paper that doesn't support it.
My argument should be easier to follow.	Add transitions and rearrange and add ideas to make the paper more coherent; delete irrelevant information.
My paragraphs do not flow smoothly from one to another.	Add or change transitions between paragraphs; rearrange paragraphs in a more logical order.
My introduction doesn't connect well with the rest of my paper.	Add transitions or rewrite the introduction to conform with the purpose and the main idea.
My sentences sound repetitive.	Vary sentence structure. Use precise, lively language. Find synonyms for repeated words.

16.5 PROOFREADING

After you have revised your paper, proofread it several times, looking for a different kind of flaw each time. Read your paper once for sense, looking for mistakes in usage, omitted words, and transposed elements. Read again for typing, spelling, and punctuation errors. Finally, proofread your citations, cross-checking your bibliography cards, note cards, and first draft as necessary. Use the following checklist to help you catch any remaining problems.

FINAL PROOFREADING CHECKLIST
❏ Are words omitted?
❏ Do typing errors exist?
❏ Are grammar and usage correct?
❏ Is punctuation correct?
❏ Are all words spelled correctly and consistently?
❏ Are proper names capitalized?
❏ Are unfamiliar words defined or explained?
❏ Is each source properly documented?

16.6 PUBLISHING/PRESENTING YOUR RESEARCH PAPER

Your teacher will probably ask you to make a cover sheet for your research paper, containing the title of the paper as well as your name and other identifying information. Center your name and the date under the title. Your teacher may also ask you for other materials to check the extent of your research and the construction of your paper. You may be asked to include a clean copy of your formal outline.

Your teacher may ask you to include a summary statement. This is a brief restatement of your thesis statement, no more than two sentences long and inserted before your report.

SAMPLE RESEARCH PAPER

Dorothea Brooke

Mr. Garcia

English III

March 15, 2001

Art in the Romantic Era: How Writers,

Dancers, Musicians, and Artists Were Influenced

by Romantic Philosophy

"Every intellectual product must be judged
from the point of view of the age and the people in
which it was produced."

—Walter Pater (qtd. in <u>Familiar Quotations</u>)

Until the nineteenth century, painters, sculptors, writers, and musicians in England received
most of their income from wealthy patrons (lords,
ladies, and sometimes kings and queens) or from
the church. This system of patronage began to
change in the early nineteenth century. Artists no
longer received an income from the church and the

aristocracy; instead composers gave performances, poets and novelists sold copies of their works, and painters and sculptors sold their artworks (Wold et al. 244–245). These artists had to cater to the tastes of an entirely new audience—the general public—who now had the income and the education to enjoy artistic pursuits. This new audience gave artists a new freedom; with a wider audience to which to appeal, they could experiment with new forms and express emotions that had once been considered off-limits. The time was right for the birth of a new movement—and this new movement was Romanticism. Romantic artists believed in the individual, and each looked for individual ways to express his or her ideals. However, the writers, visual artists, and composers of this time shared common elements of Romantic thought, such as a love of nature, an interest in new forms, and an emphasis on expressing spontaneity and emotion.

> The thesis statement clearly states the main idea of the paper.

The Romantic Era was named after the medieval romances that had become popular at the end of the eighteenth century. These romances were tall tales of heroic individuals who battled evil creatures and returned home victorious. The Romantics of literature did not tell these tall tales, but they did place an emphasis on the individual. Unlike their predecessors, the Classicists, who had favored intellectual pursuits and material goods, the Romantics favored emotions, spontaneous thought, and nature. If Classicism was the Age of Reason, then this was the Age of Emotion.

The Romantic Era began in the 1790s, when William Wordsworth published a book of poems called *Lyrical Ballads*. In the preface to the second edition, he summed up the ideals of the Romantics when he described poetry as "the spontaneous overflow of powerful feelings" (qtd. in <u>Favorite Quotations</u>). This ideal differed greatly from the thoughts of eighteenth-century poets, who had felt

COMPOSITION

that poetry was "primarily an imitation of human life" (Abrams 5). To the Romantics, feelings were more important than intellectual thoughts; in fact, Romantics felt it was impossible to think deeply without emotion. Wordsworth's friend Samuel Taylor Coleridge expressed this idea when he wrote, "Deep thinking is attainable only by a man of deep feeling" (Abrams 7).

Romantic poets chose new, freer forms and natural settings to express their emotions and ideas. Wordsworth felt that the Classicists had imposed artificial limits on poetry. He rejected the highly stylized language and heroic topics of the seventeenth century. Instead, he wrote in the *Lyrical Ballads* that he had decided to "choose incidents and situations from common life, and to relate or describe them . . . in a selection of the language really used by men" (qtd. in <u>Favorite Quotations</u>). William Blake, another Romantic poet, wrote from "Inspiration and Vision" (Abrams 5).

> The topic sentence of each paragraph supports or explains the thesis statement; the rest of the paragraph supports or explains the topic sentence.

COMPOSITION

Romantic poets often wrote about their emotions, which they felt most acutely in nature. They favored natural settings over newly industrialized cities such as London. In his poem "The Tables Turned," Wordsworth wrote, "Come forth into the light of things, Let Nature be your teacher" (Bartlett 372). Wordsworth's poems tell of the great joy and serenity people can find in natural settings.

Many of the visual artists of the nineteenth century shared the Romantic poets' love of nature. Instead of finding inspiration in history or in classical literature as artists before them had often done, many Romantic artists were inspired by nature. Painters such as J. M. W. Turner and John Constable became famous for their sweeping landscapes and seascapes; they used shading, lighting, and bold colors to express the magnificence of natural settings (<u>Britannica</u> 161).

The artists of this era also expressed their personal feelings in their art—and their personal feelings could take the form of joy, rage, or violence. William Blake (who was both a poet and a painter) expressed the ideals of the Romantics with bold, sometimes violent paintings. Probably because they no longer had to cater to aristocratic tastes, Romantic artists were less concerned with depicting things as they really were and more with expressing their feelings toward their subjects. Turner "used rapid brush techniques to create the spirit of the object rather than a mere photographic likeness" (Wold et al. 248). Just as the poets used new, freer forms to express their emotions, Romantic artists expressed their feelings using light and shadow in new ways.

The music of this time also reflected changes in form and function. Romantic music is intense and passionate because composers began to express their feelings in their works. They shared a belief that "musical tension is necessary to achieve . . . [an] emotional response" (Wold et al. 253). Released from aristocratic patronage, composers such as Ludwig van Beethoven and Franz Schubert wrote works that they felt would appeal to the public or "satisfy . . . [their] intense feeling for expression" (Wold et al. 253). Like the Romantic poets, many composers of this era shared a love of nature; Beethoven, for example, wrote a "Pastoral" symphony that celebrated nature. The work was not meant to depict nature, however; he described it as having "more of an expression of feeling than painting" (qtd. in Longyear 12).

Each Romantic composer, artist, poet, and dancer was an individual, but together they produced a body of work that shares elements of the Romantic philosophy—a love of nature, a spontaneous response to life, and a reaction against the ideals of the Classicists. Romantic works—such as Wordsworth's poems, Blake's paintings, and Beethoven's music—can be distinguished by their passion, their emotion, and their intensity of feeling.

The conclusion might restate the thesis statement, summarize the main points, or mention new questions the paper raises.

COMPOSITION

Works Cited

Abrams, M. H., ed. <u>The Norton Anthology of English Literature</u>. New York: W. W. Norton and Company, 1993.

Bartlett, John. "Walter Pater." <u>Familiar Quotations: A Collection of Passages, Phrases, and Proverbs Traced to Their Sources in Ancient and Modern Literature</u>. Boston: Little, Brown, and Company: 16th ed. 1992.

---. "William Wordsworth." <u>Familiar Quotations: A Collection of Passages, Phrases, and Proverbs Traced to Their Sources in Ancient and Modern Literature</u>. Boston: Little, Brown, and Company: 16th ed. 1992.

Longyear, Rey M. <u>Nineteenth-Century Romanticism in Music</u>. Englewood Cliffs: Prentice Hall, 1988.

"Romanticism." <u>The New Encyclopaedia Britannica: Micropaedia</u>. 15th ed. 1998.

Wold, Milo, et al. <u>An Introduction to Music and Art in the Western World</u>. Dubuque: Brown and Benchmark, 1996.

Wordsworth, William. <u>Literary Ballads</u>. London: Routledge, 1991. <u>Favorite Quotations from William Wordsworth</u>. Comp. Thomas Gannon. 25 May 1995. Preface. University of South Dakota. 15 July 1998 <http://www.usd.edu/~tgannon/txts/wordquot.txt>.

"I thought it had a pretty good story and interesting characters, but I really didn't like the font."

COMPOSITION

Chapter 16 Research Paper Writing **507**

Chapter 17

Business Writing

● ● ● ● ● ● ● ● ● ● ● ● ● ● ●

17.1 WRITING A COVER LETTER

Often the first contact you have with a potential employer is the cover letter you include with your résumé. Many employers read the cover letter before they look at the résumé. It is important, therefore, that you make a good impression in the cover letter. One way to do this is to make sure your letter is completely free of errors. The tone of your letter should be more personal than that of the résumé. However, keep your letter clear and direct, because most employers don't have time to read long, rambling letters.

A résumé describes your background concisely and somewhat impersonally. A cover letter allows you to add details about your background in a more relaxed and personal way. Each time you submit a résumé, you should include a cover letter.

Résumés are written for specific positions, but not often for specific employers. A cover letter, on the other hand, allows you to point out how your qualifications will make you an asset to a specific employer's company. Although you might send a copy of the same résumé to several potential employers, each cover letter should be unique, written especially for that company.

Cover letters must include all the parts of a business letter: the heading, inside address, salutation, body, closing, your signature, and your typed name.

GATHERING INFORMATION

Before you start writing a cover letter, find out as much as you can about the employer and the position you're seeking. Many employers have Web pages that describe their organizations. You might find out that the company is developing a new product, upgrading its services, or facing a challenging competitor. Then you can use your cover letter to show you are familiar with the company and its goals. Potential employers will be impressed that you made an effort to learn about them.

If possible, you also need to find the name of the person at the company who will review your résumé and cover letter. You should address your cover letter to this person. He or she might be the supervisor of the human resources department or the manager of the department where you would work. To find out this person's name and title, call the company and ask. Be sure to get the correct spellings.

If you cannot find out the name of a specific person, use clues from the ad to write a salutation similar to one of these:

> Dear Human Resources Department:
> Dear Supervisor, Accounts Payable:
> Dear Manager of Support Services:
> Dear Hiring Coordinator:

ORGANIZING YOUR LETTER

Your cover letter should include about four paragraphs. In the first paragraph, state the specific job you are seeking and how you found out about it. Be sure to include the job title; writing "I am applying for the job you advertised in Sunday's newspaper" will not be sufficient if the company has advertised more than one job opening. By expecting the reader to guess which job you want, you are giving him or her a reason to eliminate you from consideration for any position.

The next two paragraphs are the heart of your letter. Here you will explain how you meet the requirements in the newspaper ad or Internet listing and why you are the person to hire for this opening.

Explain how you meet the job requirements. Study the position requirements carefully. Think about how your background and knowledge match those requirements. Your cover letter is an opportunity to sell yourself, so add details to show why you're qualified for this specific job. For example, if the job opening calls for an "articulate" person, describe your experience on the debate team or as a telephone surveyor for a volunteer group.

Emphasize ways you can contribute to the position, not what you expect to gain from the job. Avoid this type of statement: "I know this job could help me develop my abilities and lead to a challenging position in management." This comment suggests that you are more focused on what the company can do for you than on what you can offer the company.

Do not apologize for being unable to meet a requirement in an ad. Describe only the relevant experience, training, or abilities you do have. The requirements listed in ads describe ideal candidates for the job, but many companies are willing to be flexible if you can meet most of their needs.

Show you're the person for the job. You might also be a valuable employee because of special courses you have taken at school, your volunteer work, or your natural abilities. Use your cover letter to show that you are familiar with the employer and have these unique qualifications but be careful not to overstate your abilities. Employers are not eager to hire inexperienced applicants who believe they know everything.

In the last paragraph of your cover letter, ask for an interview and explain when you would be available for it. Then repeat your phone number, making it easy for the employer to call you.

If you are applying for a position in sales, where employees are expected to be somewhat aggressive, you might tell the employer that you will call in a few days to check on the status of your application. However, most employers don't welcome calls from job applicants, so it's usually best to wait for someone to call you.

COVER LETTER ESSENTIALS
• Write to a specific person.
• Name the title or number of the job you want.
• Explain how you meet the job requirements.
• Show why you're the person to hire.
• Ask for an interview.

WRITING THE LETTER

Getting Started

The next page shows a sample cover letter. Notice that it includes all the parts of a business letter.

754 Harbor View Drive
Wheaton, IL 98767
March 16, 2000

Joseph Simpkins, Personnel Director
Simpkins Publishing Company
72 Central Avenue
Wheaton, IL 98767

Dear Mr. Simpkins: < Write to a specific person.

Please consider me for the summer internship (Job number 132-I) described in your Web site.

> Name the job you want and how you know about it.

I am currently a senior at Robertson High School and plan to major in journalism at the University of Illinois this fall. I believe this makes me eligible for the internship. < Explain how you meet the job requirements.

This past year I served as editor of our high school's weekly newspaper and often incorporated information from your paper's "Facts and Figures" column into my articles. During my journalism class, we often analyzed the techniques your staff used in both news stories and features. I would really appreciate an opportunity to help your staff gather information for their stories, proofread, and perhaps write some short articles.

Show your knowledge of the employer.

Please call me for an interview any day after 3:00 P.M. I would be glad to bring my file of clippings from the school newspaper. I could begin the internship any time after graduation, which is on June 3. I look forward to hearing from you.

Ask for an interview.

> Explain specific ways you can contribute to the organization.

Sincerely,

Karen Carbone

Karen Carbone

Another Kind of Cover Letter

Many job openings are advertised, but most are not. Unadvertised jobs are called the "hidden job market." You find out about these openings through friends, family members, neighbors, and school staff. Just explain what type of position you want; then ask them to let you know if they hear about an opening that might suit you.

Your cover letter will change somewhat if you are seeking an unadvertised position. You may have to convince the reader to create a job for you, or, with some luck, your qualifications may fit a job position that is vacant but has not yet been advertised.

Frank and Ernest

© 1996 Thaves / Reprinted with permission. Newspaper dist. by NEA, Inc.

17.2 WRITING A RÉSUMÉ

As you enter the job market, sooner or later you will need a résumé. A résumé is a combination of carefully selected information about you, presented as concisely and neatly as possible, with the goal of convincing an employer to invite you for an interview.

To write an effective résumé, think about how it will be used. Employers may receive hundreds—even thousands—of résumés. The human resources department, sometimes just one person, has to eliminate most of the résumés and choose a few promising people to interview. On the first pass, this person may spend less than twenty seconds scanning each résumé.

What kinds of résumés get eliminated immediately?

- *The messy ones.* Some people submit résumés that are hand-written or coated with correction fluid. Type yours on a typewriter or use a personal computer. If you spot a mistake, type or print your résumé again.
- *The long ones.* While you're in high school, one page offers enough space to describe your accomplishments. After you've been working for ten or more years, you might need two pages.
- *The ones that are hard to read.* Narrow margins, tiny printing, and no white space discourage the résumé reader and often lead to rejection.
- *The flashy ones.* Unless you're applying to be a model or a performer, don't include a picture of yourself. Neon-colored paper or "cute" graphics will get noticed, but they won't usually get you an interview.

The résumé on the next page is simple and effective. You can place information in other positions, of course, as long as your résumé is still easy to skim. Make sure it looks neat, has plenty of white space, and is free of typing or spelling errors. The questions and answers following the sample résumé will help you further polish your own résumé.

Jeremy Jacobs
903 East Oak Street
Aurora, IL 98765
Phone: 312-555-2345
E-Mail: jjacobs@email.com

Include your full name, address, phone number, and e-mail address.

Objective   To obtain a position as Head Lifeguard

Qualification Summary

- Gained knowledge and skills as a lifeguard and as a supervisor during the past two summers

- Certified Water Safety Instructor

Experience

Summers, 2001 and 2000

HIGH LAKES POOLS, Aurora, Illinois
Lifeguard
In 2000, recognized by the city for saving a child's life. In 2001, supervised two other guards.

Be consistent. For example, if you type one company name in capital letters, type them all that way.

7/00-6/01

AURORA COMMUNITY CENTER, Aurora, Illinois
Swim Coach (volunteer position)
Coached a team of nine- and ten-year-olds to a city championship.

Line up the columns vertically.

Education   Completed my junior year at Westfield High School.
Selected for Honor Roll three of four grading periods.
Captain of school swim team

Certifications   Certified as a Water Safety Instructor and lifeguard; also certified in standard first aid and CPR.

Make your headings stand out and use any headings that make sense.

References Available

COMPOSITION

Do I have to include an objective?

An objective is often used to indicate the kind of job you are seeking. Some objectives are too vague, such as this one: "A challenging position with a progressive company that will allow me to advance in my field." Prospective employers will look for résumés from people who have a clearer idea of the job they want.

In place of an objective, you might start your résumé by simply naming your career field, or you could write a qualification summary. This short section at the beginning of your résumé sums up what you offer in several bullet points. Here you can point out your strengths, including those you developed as a volunteer, without tying them directly to a job you've held. A qualification summary can highlight the skills you have, even though you might not have much employment experience.

Should I put my education or my work experience next?

If you have taken courses that will help you on the job you're applying for, put your education first and list those courses. If you have some work experience in the field in which you're applying, put your employment history first.

How can I best describe my work experience?

Start with the job you have now or your most recent job and work backwards. Include the employer, its city and state, your job title, and the dates you worked there. Make it easy for the reader to see at a glance where you've worked and what you did there.

Under each position, don't just list the responsibilities anyone would have in that job. Explain what you did that made you a valuable employee. For example, if you work for a fast-food restaurant, the reader can guess that you take orders and cook burgers. Instead, name any promotions or awards you have received. Do you supervise other workers?

Are you responsible for opening or closing the restaurant? Mention any skills or knowledge you have gained that will help you do the job for which you're applying.

Subjects are not used in good job descriptions. Each statement starts with a verb, so choose a strong verb that will add strength to your résumé. For example:

Weak:	Was asked to balance the cash drawer
Strong:	Balanced the cash drawer
Weak:	Was a clown at children's parties
Strong:	Established my own company to provide entertainment at children's parties

"The nearest parking garage is six blocks away and our elevators are always broken. That's just part of our ongoing commitment to employee fitness!"

© 1998 Randy Glasbergen

Should I explain why I quit a job?

No! Leave that for the interview and don't bring it up then unless the interviewer asks.

Should I include my volunteer experience, hobbies, or interests?

No—if they are common and likely to appear on many of the résumés the employer receives. Yes—if they have helped prepare you for the new job or they show that you are a well-rounded person who contributes to the community. You can combine paid and unpaid work under a heading such as Experience; you can include hobbies and interests under the heading Personal.

Can I exaggerate a little?

No! If you didn't increase the sales where you work all by yourself, don't claim credit for it. Instead, you could say "Significantly contributed to a 10 percent increase in sales." If you don't actually supervise the other people on your team, don't say you do. Truth has a way of coming out, especially during job interviews. Exaggeration can cost you a job.

Should I list references on my résumé?

You can, if you are sure they will help you make a good impression on the employer. Alternatively, you can take a list of references with you to your interview. In any case, make sure you ask your references ahead of time for permission to list their names.

As you write your résumé, select information about your experience, education, and skills that will convince the résumé reader to call you to set up an interview.

17.3 MAKING A PRESENTATION

Most people are required to give an oral presentation at some point in their lives. You have probably already given several yourself, as book reports in English class or oral reports in social studies class. After you graduate, you might be asked to make oral presentations in college or other training programs. When you begin working, you might help a team prepare a presentation for another department or for a client. Confidence in giving oral presentations will get you noticed and appreciated in the workplace.

Knowing how to plan an effective oral presentation will give you this confidence. Here are the steps you will learn in this lesson:

COMPOSITION

1. Consider your topic and your purpose.
2. Analyze your audience.
3. Choose the form of your presentation.
4. Decide what to say.
5. Organize your presentation.
6. Create visuals for a multimedia presentation.
7. Practice giving your presentation.
8. Look professional and speak effectively.

CONSIDER YOUR TOPIC AND YOUR PURPOSE

First, find out what the audience needs to know about the topic. Is your goal to inform them? If so, you might need to narrow a topic that is too broad. Perhaps your purpose is to persuade the audience to change their opinions on your topic. To succeed, you must analyze the audience's needs and viewpoints so you can motivate them to act or, at least, to think differently about the topic.

If you're not thoroughly familiar with the topic, do some research. Look for information at the library and on the Internet. The more you know about your topic, the easier it will be to narrow it and to organize your presentation. You must feel confident and knowledgeable about your topic to make an effective presentation.

ANALYZE YOUR AUDIENCE

Consider how your audience might respond to your topic. Audience members who are familiar with the topic might already have strong opinions on it. You will need to respect their opinions, even if you intend to convince your audience to adopt a new point of view. If the audience have heard this topic many times before, you might have to think of a new approach to rekindle their interest.

If the topic is relatively new to this audience, consider the following:

COMPOSITION

- What, if anything, do the members of the audience already know about your topic?
- Can you use technical terms? If so, will you have to define them?
- What is the audience's educational level?
- What interests or experiences do they have that will help them relate to this unfamiliar topic?
- How can you show them that the topic is important in their everyday lives?

In a work setting, you will also need to know whether your audience will be mostly co-workers, mostly management, or a combination of the two. Are your listeners the decision-makers or the ones who carry out decisions? Will they accept your recommendations, or will you have to support your arguments with statistics and experts' opinions?

Answering these questions will help you decide what your presentation should include to meet the audience's needs and to accomplish your own goals.

CHOOSE THE FORM OF YOUR PRESENTATION

Will your audience play an active or a passive role in your presentation? Here are two possible forms you may choose for your presentation:

A traditional speech or lecture In this approach, you provide information on a topic and answer questions from the audience afterward. This approach is often used because it is a direct way to share information. However, the audience has only a passive role: sitting and listening.

An interactive presentation This approach is more like a conversation and is effective with a smaller audience. You provide basic information and then ask the audience questions. Here are some possible goals for this type of presentation:

- to get the audience's feedback on an issue
- to convince the audience to act on an issue
- to help a group work together to solve a problem
- to encourage the audience to ask questions that will help them explore and understand the topic
- to guide the audience to see how they can apply a certain concept or technique in their everyday lives

Interactive presentations get the audience more involved, but the presenter must be able to keep discussions on track and quickly adjust the questions to meet the audience's needs and interests.

DECIDE WHAT TO SAY

Learning more about your topic and analyzing your audience will help you decide what to include in your presentation. The length of your presentation will also help determine the amount of information you include. Instead of saying a little about many aspects of the topic, focus on two or three main points that will be meaningful to your audience. Your audience will not remember lots of facts and statistics, but they are likely to remember two or three points if you offer interesting examples and solid evidence to support them.

" 'How I spent my Summer vacation,' by Lilia Anya, all rights reserved, which includes the right to reproduce this essay or portions thereof in any form whatsoever, including, but not limited to, novel, screenplay, musical, television miniseries, home video, and interactive CD-ROM. "

COMPOSITION

ORGANIZE YOUR PRESENTATION

Plan an opening that will grab the audience's attention and introduce your topic. Here are some possibilities:

Tell a story You may want to begin with a true story about yourself or others but make sure it won't embarrass anyone. Instead you could tell a story that "sounds true" and helps you introduce your presentation. For example: "I had a friend once who was a slave. He was a slave to his anger. It controlled everything he did. . . ."

Ask a question Get the audience thinking about the topic by asking a question. For example, you might ask, "When was the last time you felt really angry?"

Offer a surprising fact Get the audience's attention with a fact that challenges their ideas. For example: "You make yourself angry. No one else can do it; only you have that power!"

Tell a joke Tell a joke only if you're good at it. Choose one that relates to your topic and make sure it does not insult any person or group of people. Most libraries have books of jokes written especially for speakers to use. After you choose a joke, try it on friends first to see if they think it's funny, doesn't insult anyone, and isn't too silly. Telling a joke can relax both the audience and you, but you do risk embarrassing yourself if the joke flops.

After deciding how to begin your presentation, make an outline that organizes your main points into a logical order. Be sure to include examples, quotations, or statistics to back up each point. Here are some organizational patterns:

- **Chronological:** Explain a series of events or steps in the order they occurred.

COMPOSITION

- **Priority:** Persuade your audience by arranging the reasons they should do something from least to most important.
- **Problem/Cause/Solution:** Describe a problem, explain why it happened (or will happen), and offer a solution (which usually involves some action by the audience).
- **Compare and Contrast:** Show how two events, people, or objects are similar and different; use this organization to help the audience understand an unfamiliar concept or to convince them that one course of action is better than another. A variation on this organization is the pro/con pattern, in which you give both the advantages and the disadvantages of a certain action.
- **Categories:** Divide the topic into categories and explain each one. For example, you might use this approach to explain several anger management techniques.

The ending of your presentation is as important as the beginning. Here are two effective endings:

- Summarize your main points and then go back to your opening statement. Finish your story, repeat your question, or refer to the fact or joke you used. Going back to the beginning gives the audience a sense of closure.
- Repeat your strongest point and then ask the audience to do something specific in response, such as trying a technique that same day.

After organizing your presentation into an outline, write the main points on separate note cards. On each note card, include any important details you want to mention, along with any quotations or statistics you think will be effective. Use words and phrases, not sentences. You are not going to read these cards aloud, just use them to remind yourself of what you planned to say. Number the cards so you can keep them in order during your presentation.

COMPOSITION

Four responses to anger
1. turning it inward – "It's my fault."
2. avoiding it – leaving the room
3. blaming others – "It's their fault."
4. resolving the problem – identifying what's wrong and making changes

CREATE VISUALS FOR A MULTIMEDIA PRESENTATION

Multimedia simply means "involving several media or channels of communication." Speaking is one channel of communication, and visuals are another. Some people prefer the auditory channel and like to listen to new information, while others prefer the visual channel and would rather read or view new information. This second group will certainly appreciate your use of visuals.

Visuals explain your points and help keep the audience interested. A series of visuals can serve as an outline for your presentation and reduce the number of note cards you need. Visuals have two other important benefits: they give the audience something to look at besides you, and they provide something for you to do with your hands! In addition, using visuals makes you look professional and well organized.

Visuals can be as simple as a list printed on poster board or as complex as animated computer graphics. Visuals can include charts, tables, graphs, maps, models, samples, videotapes, drawings, photographs, or diagrams. They can be presented on handouts, poster board, or overhead slides or transparencies. They might be created by hand or by computer.

When designing visuals

- Explain only one point per visual. Keep the visual simple so your audience can grasp the point right away. If necessary, explain a complicated point with a series of visuals or with overlays on a basic transparency.

- Give every visual an informative title that stresses the point you want to make. For example, instead of "Causes of Anger," you could use "Stress Is a Major Cause of Anger."

- Use a font with 14-point type or larger so your audience can read labels and explanations. Do not use all upper case. IT'S MUCH HARDER TO READ!

- Don't try to include every detail of your presentation in the visuals, just the main points.

- Avoid clutter, such as too many colors, fonts, clip art graphics, or borders. Three colors and two fonts are enough. Choose art that closely relates to your topic. You might use the same border on all your visuals to tie them together.

- Don't forget to proofread. Otherwise, a transparency might display a misspelled word or other error in three-inch letters.

Keep your visuals simple; use
- one idea for each visual
- no more than 5–7 lines of type per visual
- no more than 6–8 words per line
- no more than 35 words total

Using Computer Software

Many software packages have been developed to aid in school and business presentations. Several programs can create slides and transmit them directly from a computer to an overhead projector. They allow you to make words, paragraphs, or graphics appear and disappear on the slide. You can also add sound effects and fade the picture between slides. Using a chart or graph, you can make lines or bars "grow," or you can separate one bar into several bars.

Evaluate your visuals by looking at them from the audience's point of view. Are they
- easy to understand?
- interesting?
- relevant?
- neat and uncluttered?

Using some computer programs, you can design visuals that a service center, such as a camera store, can convert into 35-mm slides for use in a projector. You can also use computer programs to design overhead transparencies or handouts for the audience. Some programs allow you to write notes to use during your presentation, with the appropriate slide or overhead printed right on the page.

Using Visuals

- Before using the visuals you've prepared, check your equipment. Check it again just before the presentation to make sure it works. A program that worked at home may not work in another setting. A power surge may have scrambled the computer. The bulb on the overhead projector may have burned out. Be ready with another way to share the information in case of disaster.

- Don't show a visual until you're ready to talk about it. Then display it until you are ready for the next visual. Turning equipment on and off can annoy an audience. Glaring white screens can also be distracting.
- Face your audience and stand to one side of the visual. Do explain your visuals but don't read them to the audience.

PRACTICE GIVING YOUR PRESENTATION

Use your visuals as you rehearse your speech so that you will feel comfortable with them. After your opening, tell the audience the points you will cover to let them know what to expect. Practice making smooth transitions between your points so your presentation will flow well.

Ask a few friends or family members to listen to your presentation and give you feedback on both the content and your delivery. You might prefer to videotape yourself and do your own critique. Watch and listen for times when your words were difficult to understand or you didn't clearly explain what you meant. Were any points a little dry and boring? If so, find more interesting examples to liven them up.

Check your timing and make adjustments if your presentation is too long or short. Remember that you might speak more quickly in front of a larger audience. Be careful not to practice so many times that you memorize your presentation. You want it to be fresh and interesting for you and the audience.

LOOK PROFESSIONAL AND SPEAK EFFECTIVELY

As you know, a carefully planned presentation can be ruined by a panicked speaker. But if you feel nervous before speaking to a group, congratulations! You're just like ninety-nine percent of speakers. That doesn't mean you won't do well. Admit to yourself that you're feeling a little jittery and use that energy to do your best.

Getting Ready

Get a good night's sleep and arrive at the location at least a half hour ahead of time so you don't have to rush. To prevent hiccups, avoid carbonated beverages for several hours before your presentation. Also, don't drink any more caffeine than you usually do.

To help yourself relax just before the presentation, take several deep breaths. Next, tighten and relax your muscles, working from your toes to the top of your head. Then take a few more deep breaths for good measure. Finally, gather your notecards in your hand and take your place, with your visuals waiting for you. Pause and smile at the audience. Remember that they want you to do well. Don't apologize for being nervous. Begin!

Using Your Body Effectively

- Stand up straight, but in a relaxed way.
- Maintain eye contact with the audience. Pretend you are talking to just one person but focus on a different person in a different area of the audience every minute or so. (According to several studies, audiences believe that speakers who look at them are better informed, more experienced, friendlier, and more sincere than speakers who do not make eye contact.)
- Use gestures when they're appropriate. They help show your enthusiasm and interest in your topic.
- Move around. Unless you're standing on a stage or must stay close to a microphone, try walking among the audience members. It will bring you closer to them, physically and emotionally.

Using Your Voice Effectively

- Speak clearly and slowly. Let your voice rise and fall naturally, as if you were having a conversation. Try not to rush.
- Speak loudly enough to reach people in the back of the room. However, if you're using a microphone, let it carry your voice. Don't shout.
- Show enthusiasm in your voice. Get excited about your topic. Your audience will "catch" your excitement because enthusiasm is contagious.

PUTTING IT ALL TOGETHER

Now you know how to do well on your next presentation. If you still feel nervous about it, imagine the worst thing that could happen. Here are some disasters that might come to your mind:

- You'll forget what you were going to say. (No, you won't. Your notecards and your visuals will keep you on track.)
- You'll mispronounce a word. (If a word is giving you problems, check a dictionary, ask someone how to say it, or use another word.)
- Your presentation will be boring. (Not after all the thought you've put into it! You know your audience and your topic well. You're going to start with an interesting story, and you've found good examples to support your main points. You have also created excellent visuals.)

So when *is* your next presentation? Are you looking forward to it now? You will as soon as you follow the steps you just learned. Remember: If you have prepared and carefully considered your audience's needs, you will be an impressive, effective speaker.

COMPOSITION

Part Four

● ● ● ● ● ● ● ● ● ● ● ●

Resources

Knowledge is of two kinds: we know a subject ourselves, or we know where we can
find information on it.

—Samuel Johnson

Chapter 18

The Library
or Media Center

● ● ● ● ● ● ● ● ● ● ● ● ● ●

Although you've probably been in a library, you might not realize all the resources the library has to offer or how to find them. This chapter will guide you through the library and help you understand how and where to find what you need.

CIRCULATION DESK

At the circulation desk, you'll find a librarian who can answer your questions and check out your books. In addition to a circulation desk, some libraries have computers you can use to check out your own books. Larger libraries might station additional librarians in other sections of the library.

CATALOG

A computer or card catalog will tell you which books are available in the library and where to find them. You'll learn more about using both kinds of catalogs on pages 535–541.

STACKS

The stacks, or rows of book shelves, are called the "adult section" in some libraries, but you don't have to be an adult to use these books. The stacks are usually divided into sections for fiction (novels and short stories that are works of the imagination) and nonfiction (books based on fact about subjects such as history and science).

YOUNG ADULT AND CHILDREN'S SECTION

Young readers, including high school students, can find excellent resources in the young adult and children's section. Fiction, nonfiction, and biographies are usually grouped separately, with picture books for very young readers in their own section. All of these books are listed in the library's computer or card catalog.

REFERENCE AREA

The reference area might include encyclopedias, dictionaries, almanacs, yearbooks, atlases, and other reference materials. Books in this area can be used only in the library. By not allowing people to check out these books, the library ensures that all reference materials will always be available for anyone who needs to consult them.

NEWSPAPERS AND PERIODICALS

In the newspaper and periodical section, you can read local newspapers as well as papers from major cities in the United States and perhaps from other countries. You can also browse through periodicals, which include magazines and journals. You probably cannot check out the currrent issues, but you can usually take older issues home to read. The young adult and children's section might have its own periodicals area. You'll learn more about finding specific articles in newspapers and periodicals on pages 547–549.

AUDIO-VISUAL MATERIALS

The audio-visual section of the library may stock software programs, audiocassettes and compact discs (CDs) of your favorite music, books on tape, videos, and slides for you to borrow and enjoy at home.

COMPUTER AREA

Many of today's libraries offer the use of personal computers for research on the Internet or for writing reports and papers. You may have to reserve a computer ahead of time, and the library might set a time limit on your use of it. Many library computer areas also have software programs for you to use there, such as a résumé-writing program, an accounting program, or even a program to teach you how to type. For a small fee per page, you can usually print the articles you've located or the papers you've written.

STUDY AREAS

Many libraries now have desks or small rooms set aside for quiet study. You might need to reserve them ahead of time.

SPECIAL COLLECTIONS

Some libraries set aside a special room or section for collections of rare books, manuscripts, and items of local interest, including works by local students.

Using Print Resources

• • • • • • • • • • • • • • •

Imagine how frustrating it would be if you had to walk up and down the stacks in a library, looking for a book that might—or might not—be anywhere on the shelves! To make life easier, libraries use cataloging systems to keep track of what's available and arrange books on the shelves according to their content.

19.1 UNDERSTANDING CATALOGING SYSTEMS

Whether you want information on a particular subject, books by a certain author, or a specific book, the catalog will help you find what you're looking for. Many libraries now use computerized catalogs, but some still rely on paper card catalogs. You should be able to use both kinds of tools. Then no matter what library you enter, its catalog will be at your service.

COMPUTER CATALOGS

Computer systems vary, so before you use one for the first time, read the instructions posted beside the computer or printed on the screen. Most catalog programs begin by asking whether you want to search by author, title, or subject. If you use the author's name, type the last name first, followed by a comma and the first name, as in *Johnson, Samuel.* (Some systems will allow you to type *Samuel Johnson* or even just *Johnson*, although in the latter case you'll have to search through a list of all the authors named Johnson to find the one you want.) If you search by title, enter the title but start with the first important word, ignoring *A, An,* and *The.* For a subject search, you'll use a **keyword,** a word or phrase that describes your topic. Whenever you search a computer database, including the Internet, to find books, articles, or other media, the keyword you choose will greatly affect the results you get.

Search TIP

1. **Be specific.** A general keyword, such as *animal,* will get you a long list of sources, sometimes called **matches** or **hits.** However, few of them will be helpful to you. If you use a more specific keyword, such as *dachshund,* you won't have to read screen after screen of possible sources, trying to find a few that might be helpful.

2. **Use Boolean search techniques,** which offer different ways to combine words. You can use these techniques to look for books in a computer catalog, to find articles in magazine databases (described later), or to locate information on the Internet (also described later).

Named for George Boole, a nineteenth-century English mathematician, Boolean techniques use the words *and, or, not,* and sometimes *near* or *adj.*

and: If you combine two keywords with *and* (such as *genetics and disorders)*, the computer will list only sources that contain both words. This kind of search results in far fewer hits, but a much higher percentage of them will relate to your topic. (Some programs use + in place of *and: genetics + disorders.)*

or: If you want information on either one of two related topics, link them with *or,* as in *alligators or crocodiles.* This technique tells the computer to conduct two searches at once.

not: To eliminate a category of information from a search, use *not.* For example, if you want information about genetic disorders but not Down's Syndrome, you can enter *genetic and disorders not Down.*

near *or* adj: Some computer programs allow you to use *near* or *adj* (adjacent) to locate sources, usually articles, that have two keywords used near each other. For example, you might use *genetics near laboratory* as your keywords. One program may list only those sources in which the keywords are within eight words of each other. Another program might allow the keywords to be fifteen words apart. This search technique has

RESOURCES

an advantage over linking words with *and,* a method that can generate a long list of articles in which both words appear but never in connection with each other.

Not all computer programs recognize Boolean techniques; some will treat *and, or, not, near,* or *adj* as part of your keyword/phrase. For some other computer programs, you must begin a Boolean search with *b/,* as in *b/genetics and experiments.*

3. **Use quotation marks.** Enclosing a phrase in quotation marks (for instance, *"experimenting with DNA"*) tells the computer to find every book or article with exactly those words.

4. **Try truncating.** If you **truncate,** or shorten, your keyword by using an asterisk (*), the computer will search for all words that begin with the letters before the asterisk. For example, using *experiment** as a keyword will tell the computer to list books or articles containing such words as *experiment, experimental, experimented, experimenting,* and *experiments.* By truncating your keyword, you make sure the computer doesn't overlook various forms of the word.

   You can also truncate when you aren't sure how to spell a word. For example, you could use *Azer** as a keyword if you couldn't remember how to spell Azerbaijan, a country in southeastern Europe.

5. **Use a "wildcard"** by inserting a question mark *(?)* into certain words. For example, if you aren't sure whether to use *woman* or *women,* enter *wom?n.*

Now that you know how to choose keywords, here is an example of their use. To use a computer catalog, you type in the author's name, the book title, or a keyword or phrase, and the screen will list any related sources available at that library. Let's say you type the keywords *credit card safety*. The screen will then show you a list similar to the one below. If the catalog program is connected to a printer, you could print this list.

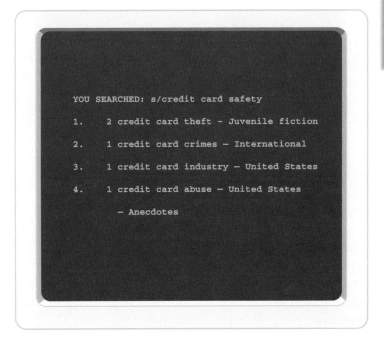

YOU SEARCHED: s/credit card safety

1.   2 credit card theft - Juvenile fiction

2.   1 credit card crimes — International

3.   1 credit card industry — United States

4.   1 credit card abuse — United States

        — Anecdotes

The first listing (1) tells you that the library has two books about credit card theft in the juvenile fiction category. Books listed in this category will be novels or collections of short stories that are appropriate for young readers. The second listing (2) tells you that the library has one book about international credit card crimes. This book isn't marked fiction, so it's nonfiction; it isn't marked juvenile, so it's for adults. To find out more about this book, enter the number of its listing, 2. The next screen might give you the following information.

```
        CALL NO: 364.163 DAV

        AUTHOR: Davisson, Judith

        MAIN TITLE: Identities for Rent: how

 international thieves can be you for a day

 / by Judith Davisson.

        PUBLISHER: New York: Atheneum Books, c1995

        LOCATION          STATUS          UNITS

 1.     ADULT NON-FICTION  Available  364.163 DAV
```

The status column indicates that no one has checked out this book, so it should be filed on a shelf. To find it, you would write down its call number, shown at the top of the listing. (**Call numbers** are numbers and letters used to classify books. They are explained on pages 541–546.) Then you would go to the location listed (the adult non-fiction stacks), find the shelf with call numbers between 360 and 370, and look down the rows for the book marked 364.163 DAV. The books are in numerical and alphabetical order.

If someone had checked out this book, the status column would state the date when it was due back at the library. If the library had several copies of the book, the status of each copy would be stated. Some catalog entries also include the number of pages in the book; whether it has illustrations, an index, a glossary, or a bibliography; and what kind of medium it is, such as a book or videotape. Many entries list additional headings you could enter into the catalog as keywords to find more information about the same topic.

The computer instructions will tell you how to move forward and backward as you search through the library's listings. For example, you might enter *ns* (next screen) or *f* (forward) to see more of a listing. To go backward, you might enter *ps* (previous screen) or *b* (backward).

CARD CATALOGS

Card catalogs are stored in long, narrow drawers. The drawers hold two or three small cards for every book in the library, arranged alphabetically. Fiction books have two cards each, one listing the book by its author and one listing it by its title. Nonfiction books have three cards each, listing the book by its author, title, and subject.

The cards list the same information as the computer catalog, although they don't, of course, tell you whether someone has checked out the book. A library may divide its card catalog into two categories: subject cards and author/title cards. Often cards are cross-referenced, listing other available books on the same subject or a related topic. A card catalog might also have separate cross-reference cards, filed alphabetically and listing related topics.

19.2 LOCATING BOOKS

The purpose of call numbers is to help you locate books. Most school and community libraries use call numbers based on the Dewey decimal system, while many college and university libraries use call numbers based on the Library of Congress system.

DEWEY DECIMAL SYSTEM

The Dewey decimal system, created in 1876 by a librarian named Melvil Dewey, divides nonfiction books into the ten categories listed below.

DEWEY DECIMAL CATEGORIES OF NONFICTION

NUMBERS	CATEGORY	EXAMPLES OF SUBCATEGORIES
000-099	General Works	encyclopedias, bibliographies, newspapers, periodicals
100-199	Philosophy	ethics, psychology, personality
200-299	Religion	theology, mythology, bibles
300-399	Social Sciences	sociology, education, government, law, economics
400-499	Language	dictionaries, foreign languages, grammar guides
500-599	Sciences	chemistry, astronomy, biology, mathematics
600-699	Technology	medicine, engineering, business
700-799	Arts	painting, music, theater, sports
800-899	Literature	poetry, plays, essays
900-999	History	ancient history, biography, geography, travel

Let's say you wanted to know more about Samuel Johnson, a seventeenth-century British author and dictionary writer. You would begin by entering his name as a keyword in a computer catalog or by looking under the *J*s in a card catalog.

The library might have many books about Johnson and his work, but the call numbers of these books could fall into different categories on the Dewey decimal chart, depending on their content. For example, one book listed by a computer catalog is *The Samuel Johnson Encyclopedia* by Pat Rogers. The 800 category, Literature, is broken down into subcategories; for example, 810 is American literature and 820 is English literature. Samuel Johnson was an English author, so this book has a call number of 820.

The more specific the topic, the more specific the call number. Some call numbers have decimals added to make them even more specific. We saw this earlier in *Identities for Rent*, which had a call number of 364.163 DAV.

Many libraries add the first three letters of the author's last name to the call number, in this case DAV for Davisson. Thus, in some libraries, the call number for *The Samuel Johnson Encyclopedia* would be 820 ROG (for Rogers).

Let's say our library also has a book titled *The Making of Johnson's Dictionary, 1746–1773* by Allen Reddick. Since this book is more about language than about Johnson, it's classified in the 400 category, Language, with a call number of 423. Another book is titled *Dr. Johnson's London*, by Dorothy Marshall. This historical account falls in the 900 category, History, so it has a call number of 942.1.

Research TIP

All libraries that use the Dewey decimal system use the same chart to assign call numbers to books. However, two librarians may put the same book into different categories. For this reason, the same book may have different call numbers in different libraries.

Biographies Our library has another book called *Everybody's Boswell: the Life of Samuel Johnson* by James Boswell. It has a call number of *B*, which stands for biography. Many libraries group their biographies together, with one biography section in the adult stacks and one in the young adult and children's section. Biographies are shelved alphabetically according to the last name of the subject of the book. *Everybody's Boswell: The Life of Samuel Johnson* will be in the *J* section of the biographies.

The library also has another biography of Johnson: *The Personal History of Samuel Johnson* by Christopher Hibbert. Two books about the same person will be shelved alphabetically by the author's last name. So Boswell's book will be before Hibbert's book in the *J* section of the biographies.

Fiction Most libraries that use the Dewey decimal system identify fiction with the call number *F* or *Fic.* The second line of the call number consists of the first three letters of the author's name or of the author's entire last name. Fiction is shelved alphabetically by the authors' last names. Books by the same author are shelved alphabetically by the first word in each title (not counting *A, An,* and *The*). Many public libraries have separate sections for some categories of fiction, such as mysteries or science fiction. In that case, usually a mark or label on the book's spine shows its inclusion on these special shelves. Within the mystery or science fiction section, books are shelved alphabetically by author's last name.

Reference Books Reference books, such as encyclopedias and current yearbooks, have an *R* or *Ref* preceding their call numbers. This label will alert you that you cannot check out these sources and must use them in the library. An *OV* or another symbol added to a call number indicates that the book is oversized and kept in a section of the library with taller shelves. (Ask the librarian where this section is.)

LIBRARY OF CONGRESS SYSTEM

The Library of Congress system divides books into twenty-one categories, each represented by a letter as shown in the chart below. Like the Dewey decimal system, the Library of Congress system has subcategories, which are identified by a second letter. For example, N is the category for fine arts. You would look under NA for books about architecture, NB for sculpture, ND for painting, and so on. Numbers added to the letter combinations identify more specific categories.

LIBRARY OF CONGRESS CATEGORIES

LETTER	CATEGORY	LETTER	CATEGORY
A	General Works	N	Fine Arts
B	Philosophy and Religion	P	Language and Literature
C–F	History	Q	Science
G	Geography and Anthropology	R	Medicine
H	Social Sciences	S	Agriculture
J	Political Science	T	Technology
K	Law	U	Military Science
L	Education	V	Naval Science
M	Music	Z	Bibliography and Library Science

In one library using the Library of Congress system, Pat Rogers' book, *The Samuel Johnson Encyclopedia,* has a call number of PR 3532.R64. *P* represents the general category of Literature, while *R* indicates a work by a British author.

The second *R* in the call number is from the author's name, Rogers.

Note that in the Library of Congress system, biographies are not filed separately but with the other books. Therefore, the call numbers of the biographies for Johnson begin with *PR*, indicating a British author.

FINDING INFORMATION IN NONFICTION BOOKS

Being familiar with the content and purpose of the parts of books will help you quickly determine whether a source will be useful to you. Not every book contains all the sections described below.

Information about a book

To find information about a book, check the following parts:

The **title page** contains the book title, author's name, and usually the publisher.

The **copyright page**, which is usually printed on the back of the title page, gives the publication or copyright date. Check the copyright date to determine how current the information is.

The **table of contents** lists the main topics covered to help you decide whether the book has the information you're seeking.

The **foreword**, **introduction**, or **preface**, which is written by the author or an expert in the same field, may explain the purpose of the book or the author's outlook on the subject.

Information in a book

To find information in a book, check the sections below:

The **index** lists alphabetically the people, places, events, and other significant topics mentioned in the book and gives the pages where you can find references to them.

The **glossary** lists terms in the book alphabetically and defines them, taking into account the intended readers. (Books for young children define basic terms; those for adults define terms that would be unfamiliar to most adult readers.)

The **bibliography** suggests additional research sources that are appropriate for the intended readers of the book. It may also include the sources of the information in the book.

The **appendix** contains additional information related to the book, such as maps, charts, illustrations, or graphs.

The **afterword** or **epilogue** is used by some authors to make a final statement about the book, discuss implications, or offer additional findings.

19.3 LOCATING ARTICLES IN NEWSPAPERS AND OTHER PERIODICALS

If you need current information from newspapers, magazines, or journals, the two tools described below may make your search easier.

COMPUTER DATABASES

Many libraries subscribe to databases holding collections of magazine, journal, and newspaper articles that you can access using the library computers. Most of these databases allow you to search by topic, by type of publication, or by specific publication. Some programs also allow you to select the years you want to search. You might choose to browse through all the magazines or all the newspapers in the database that cover a certain period of time, or you could narrow your search to a specific magazine or newspaper, such as the *New York Times.* Some databases allow you to review the table of contents of one issue of a magazine and read any of the articles that interest you.

If you enter a keyword that describes your topic, the database will list the title of each article on that topic along with the author, the publication, the date, and a short description of the article. You can select any titles that seem especially relevant and read either a short summary or the whole article on the computer screen. For a small fee, you can print a copy of articles that you want to take home with you.

What kinds of articles you will find depends on the database you use. If you search using the keywords *genetic disorders,* for example, one database might list articles on this subject from publications such as *Time, Newsday, Rocky Mountain Press,* and *USA Today.* If you enter the same keywords in a more academically oriented database, you might find articles from the *Journal of the National Cancer Institute* and *Biological Bulletin.* Don't check just one database and assume you've seen all the articles that are available.

READERS' GUIDE TO PERIODICAL LITERATURE

Not every library can afford to subscribe to computer databases, but nearly every library stocks the paper edition of *Readers' Guide to Periodical Literature.* This guide includes the titles of articles from nearly two hundred magazines and journals, with both subjects and authors listed alphabetically and cross-referenced. It's also available on a compact disc that you can search using a computer.

An update of the paper index is published every two weeks, and information about all the articles for the year is reprinted in a hardbound book at the end of the year. One index provided the following listing under *credit card crimes.*

> **CREDIT CARD CRIMES**
> *See also*
> Credit cards—Security measures
> Identity theft
> Are your theft fears overblown? S. Medintz. il
> *Money* v27 no6 p137-9 Je '98

If the article "Are Your Theft Fears Overblown?" in *Money* sounds interesting, you must locate the June 1998 issue of this magazine and turn to page 137. (The *il* indicates that the article is illustrated.)

Libraries often keep issues for the current year in their newspapers and periodicals section. Issues from the previous one to five years may be stored in a different area, and older issues may be on **microfilm** (a roll or reel of film) or **microfiche** (a sheet of film). Both types of film must be inserted into special projectors that enlarge the images so you can read them. You can usually make photocopies of these articles to take home.

Not every book or article in the library or on its databases offers unbiased, valuable, reliable information. The following steps will help you avoid sources that offer irrelevant, outdated information or biased opinions.

1. **Evaluate the author of each source of information** and read any biographical information about him or her. Consider whether the author is an expert in a certain field or simply someone who has opinions about it.

2. **Evaluate the information itself,** starting with whether it is directly related to your topic. If it's only loosely related and you try to include it in your report, your work may seem unorganized and disjointed.

3. **Evaluate the author's reasoning.** Are the "facts" in a source actually unsupported opinions or exaggerations? Does the author seem to make too many assumptions? Does he or she overgeneralize from one situation to another?

4. **Check the publication date.** Are certain statistics now out of date? Is it likely that the findings have been contradicted by more recent research? Information on many topics, such as Mark Twain's childhood, may be the same whether it was published last week or twenty years ago. However, you must use up-to-date information when discussing topics that are still being researched or debated.

5. **Gather information** on the same topic from several sources. This way, you'll be more likely to become familiar with different opinions on the issue or topic. Then compare and contrast facts from each source. If three sources agree and one disagrees, the latter source may be mistaken—unless it's more current than the other sources.

19.4 USING OTHER REFERENCE SOURCES

GENERAL REFERENCE SOURCES

General reference sources are easy to locate and easy to use. They also provide detailed information on thousands of topics. Following are some excellent examples of these sources.

TYPE OF REFERENCE	EXAMPLES
General Encyclopedias These encyclopedias usually consist of many volumes. Subjects are arranged alphabetically, with an index and cross-referencing to help you find related topics. Many encyclopedia publishers offer yearly updates.	*World Book Encyclopedia* *Encyclopædia Britannica* *Collier's Encyclopedia* *Grolier Encyclopedia* *Encarta Encyclopedia* (Some encyclopedias are also available on compact discs; *Encarta Encyclopedia* is available only on a CD-ROM. CD-ROMs are described in Accessing Electronic Resources, page 569.)
Specialized Encyclopedias Each of these references focuses on a certain subject. Most provide specialized information, while some, such as *Books in Print,* tell you where to look for the information you seek. You might be surprised at the number of specialized encyclopedias that are available.	*Encyclopedia of World Art* *Van Nostrand's Scientific Encyclopedia* *Encyclopedia of World Crime* *Encyclopedia of the Opera* *Encyclopedia of the Third Reich* *Encyclopedia of Vitamins, Minerals, and Supplements* *Encyclopedia of Western Movies* *Encyclopedia of the Geological Sciences* *Books in Print*
Almanacs and Yearbooks These references are published frequently to provide up-to-date facts and statistics.	*Information Please Almanac* *World Almanac and Book of Facts* *Guinness Book of Records* *Statistical Abstract of the United States*
Atlases Atlases can be historical or current; they contain maps and statistics about countries and continents, climates, exports and imports, and the spread of world cultures, among other topics.	*Hammond World Atlas* *Cambridge Atlas of Astronomy* *Historical Atlas of the United States* *Goode's World Atlas* *National Geographic Atlas of the World* *Atlas of World Cultures*

Literary and Other Biographical Works

These references include brief histories of notable people, living or dead, and are usually organized by fields instead of by names.

Contemporary Authors
American Authors 1600–1900
European Authors 1000–1900
Cyclopedia of Literary Characters
Webster's New Biographical Dictionary
Dictionary of American Biography
Current Biography
Biographical Dictionary of World War I (and II)
Biographical Dictionary of Scientists (by field)
Biographical Dictionary of Artists

Government Documents

Some large libraries hold the federal government documents that are available to the public. These pamphlets, journals, and reports offer information on agriculture, population, economics, and other topics.

Monthly Catalog of United States Government Publications
United States Government Publications Catalog
(both also available on compact discs and online)

Books of Quotations

The indexes of these references help you look up quotations by certain people and by subject. The quotation from Samuel Johnson at the beginning of Part Four was taken from *The Harper Book of Quotations*. It was included in the category titled "Knowledge."

Bartlett's *Familiar Quotations*
The Harper Book of Quotations
The Oxford Dictionary of Quotations
The International Thesaurus of Quotations

PLANNING LIBRARY RESEARCH

1. Start early. If you wait, other students may check out the sources you want to use.

2. Begin with the general reference sources rather than those that deal with specific fields or topics. A general source will offer an overview of your topic. It may provide all the information you need, or it may guide you to additional sources.

3. List the sources you want to check and mark each one off your list after you've examined it so you won't check the same source twice.

4. Take careful notes and include the title, author, publisher, publication date, and page number of each source. (See page 481 for more information about compiling note cards.)

5. Talk with the librarian about your project, its purpose, its length, and the kinds of sources you have been asked to use. Describe what you've done so far and be ready with specific questions you'd like answered. Librarians can often suggest valuable references you haven't considered and perhaps help you locate them.

19.5 MAKING THE MOST OF WORD RESOURCES

When you're visiting a library's reference department, your goal is to go right to the information you need. Hunting aimlessly through the shelves and finding only irrelevant information is a waste of your time, no matter how interesting the information might be. This section will show you the uses and benefits of the different reference books that are available.

KINDS OF DICTIONARIES

Maybe you never stopped to think about it, but there are many kinds of dictionaries. Most of the dictionaries you've seen at school and in public libraries are general dictionaries, each including words from general English for a general reader. Then there are specialized dictionaries that define only words used in a particular field or profession, art or craft.

General Dictionaries

General dictionaries fall into these three categories:

School dictionaries contain fewer than 90,000 entries. They focus on common words and offer easy-to-understand definitions.

College dictionaries have about 150,000 entries. These references are used in homes, schools, and businesses. They answer most questions about spelling and definitions.

Unabridged dictionaries contain more than 250,000 entries and often fill several volumes. They are generally located in libraries and include extensive definitions and word histories.

Specialized Dictionaries

Specialized dictionaries list words used in a particular field. Following are some examples of the many kinds of specialized dictionaries:

Dictionary of Sports Idioms
Dictionary of Inventions and Discoveries
Facts on File Dictionary of 20th-Century Allusions
Dictionary of Italian Literature
Dictionary of Occupational Titles
Dictionary of Medical Folklore
Dictionary of Historic Nicknames

WORD ENTRIES IN GENERAL DICTIONARIES

Any one page in a dictionary probably *contains* a few thousand words, but it probably *defines* only a few dozen. A word entry discusses the meanings and the various forms of the entry word or headword, which is the word in bold-faced type that begins the word entry. When you look up a word in a dictionary, you are looking for its word entry.

Finding Words

Words are listed alphabetically in dictionaries, usually with no regard to hyphenated words or open compounds, as in this example:

soften
soft-focus
soft pedal
softshell

Words beginning with the abbreviation *St.* are listed as if the abbreviation were spelled out. So *St. Louis encephalitis* comes before the word *saintly*.

As you search for a word, don't forget to use the guide words at the top of every page. Guide words are the first and last entry words on the page. If the word you seek doesn't fall between these words alphabetically, it won't be on that page.

Search TIP

When you can't find the word you're looking for, consider these possibilities:

1. The word might have silent consonants, such as the *k* in *knight,* the *b* in *doubt,* or the *gh* in *blight.*
2. A consonant in the word might have an unusual spelling. For example, the *k* sound can be spelled with a *k (kindness), c (concur, lecture), ck (mackerel),* or *ch (chrysanthemum, chrome).*
3. A vowel in the word might have an unusual spelling, such as the first vowel sound in *beautiful* and *eerie.*
4. Your dictionary might not be large enough. An unusual word might not be listed in a school dictionary, for example.

Understanding Word Entries

Let's analyze a sample word entry to see what kinds of information it offers.

A   B   C   D

glad[1] (glad) **glad•der, glad•est.** *adj.* **1.** feeling or expressing joy, pleasure, or satisfaction; happy. **2.** causing joy or pleasure; pleasing: glad tidings. **3.** very willing: *Tom will be glad to go with you.* [Old English *glæd* bright, cheerful.] —**glad′ly,** *adv.* — **glad′ness,** *n.*

F   E

G

H   **Syn.** *Glad, happy, delighted* mean expressing feelings of pleasure. **Glad** is generally used to convey a degree of pleasure ranging from pleased satisfaction to a feeling of elation: *The sailors were glad to see land on the horizon.* **Happy** suggests enjoyment brought about by the fulfillment of one's desires: *The child was happy pounding away at his new drum.* **Delighted** implies a quick and lively emotional reaction that is keenly felt and vividly expressed: *Ben uttered a delighted hurrah when he saw our guest.*

glad[2] (glad) *n. Informal.* gladiolus. [Latin *gladiolus* little sword, diminutive of *gladius* sword; referring to the plant's sword-shaped leaves.]

I   D J   E

A. The Entry Word: The boldfaced word at the beginning of the entry is the entry word. If this word can be divided at the end of a line, the divisions will be indicated by a raised dot. The word *explicate,* for example, is written ex•pli•cate; this means you can divide the word after *ex* or after *expli.* In the sample word entry, *glad* has only one syllable and therefore cannot be divided. The entry word also tells you when a compound word should be written as one word (as in *handbag*), when it should be hyphenated (as in *hand-me-down*), and when it should be written as two words (as in *hash brown*).

B. Pronunciation: The correct way to say the word is shown immediately after the entry word and indicated in three ways: accent marks, phonetic symbols, and diacritical marks. In entry words with more than one syllable, accent marks indicate which syllable should be stressed. To check the meaning of the other marks and symbols, look at the pronunciation key that is usually located at the bottom of the page.

C. Inflected Forms: Plural forms of nouns, adjective forms, and forms of verbs in other tenses are included in an entry. In this case, we see that the comparative and superlative forms of *glad* are *gladder* and *gladdest.*

   When two spellings are connected with *or,* they are equally acceptable. However, when they are joined with *also,* the first spelling is preferred. For example, the dictionary shows the plural of *alga* as "**algae** *also* **algas.**"

D. Parts of Speech: Abbreviations in italics indicate the part of speech of the entry word and other forms of the word. At the beginning of this entry, we see that *glad* is usually used as an adjective, but later we learn that the same spelling can be used as a noun.

E. Etymology: Many entries include the history of the word, or etymology. The entry for *glad¹* indicates that this word is based on an Old English word. The entry for *glad²* shows this word comes from Latin.

F. Definitions: If an entry has more than one meaning, each meaning is numbered. Definitions might be listed by frequency (starting with the one used most often) or chronologically (starting with the first definition given to that word). Example sentences using the entry word are often included in definitions to make meanings clearer.

G. *Derived words:* A definition may end with a variation of the entry word, preceded by a dash and followed by its part of speech. In the example, the derived words *gladly* and *gladness* are shown. When the meaning of the variation is taken from the entry word, the variation is not defined. If the pronunciation changes, it is given for each variation. Phrases that include the entry word are defined because their meanings tend to be different from that of the entry word by itself.

H. Synonyms: Many entries list words with similar meanings along with examples so you'll know when to use each word. Understanding small differences in meaning will keep you from using words incorrectly. Some dictionaries also include antonyms in entries.

I. Homographs: Homographs are words that are spelled the same but have different meanings and histories. Homograph entries are listed separately and are followed by small numbers. *Glad* has two homographs pronounced the same. (When homographs vary in pronunciation, their entries make that clear.) As you can see, the homographs of *glad* have quite different definitions and completely different etymologies.

J. **Usage Label:** Some entries also provide information on how words are used in different contexts. The entry *glad²* is labeled *Informal*. The following chart describes some usage guidelines you might encounter in a dictionary entry. Words that are often misused, such as *aggravate* and *complected,* may be followed by an entire paragraph explaining their usage.

TYPE OF INFORMATION	DESCRIPTION	EXAMPLE FROM AN ENTRY
Capitalization	indicates that a word should be capitalized under certain conditions	**pilgrim** . . . *n* . . . **3.** *cap:* one of the English colonists settling at Plymouth in 1620
Out-of-Date Usage	identifies meanings that are obsolete (no longer used) or used only in special contexts	**play**. . . *n* . . . **1.b** *archaic:* GAME, SPORT
Special Field Usage	uses a phrase or label to indicate a definition used only in a particular field	**break** . . . *n* . . . **5.d** *mining:* FAULT, DISLOCATION
Informal	advises that the word be avoided when speaking and writing formally	**bloom•ing** . . . *adj* . . . **3.** *Informal.* complete, utter: *a blooming idiot.*
Regional Usage	explains how a word is used in a certain geographical area	**pet•rol** . . . *n. British.* gasoline

TYPE OF INFORMATION	DESCRIPTION	EXAMPLE FROM AN ENTRY
Usage Note	offers general guidelines for using a word in a certain situation; often preceded by a dash and by the abbreviation *usu.* for *usually* or the words *called also.*	**fire away** *vi* . . . — usu. used as an imperative. **hun•dred•weight** *n* . . . —called also *long-hundredweight.*

OTHER KINDS OF INFORMATION IN GENERAL DICTIONARIES

When did Genghis Khan live? What does *de mal en pis* mean? You can find out by looking in the back of your dictionary.

Biographical Names

This section lists the spelling and pronunciation of the names of thousands of notable people. It also includes each person's birth and death dates, nationality, and field or title.

Geographical Names

In the geographical names section, you can find the correct spelling, pronunciation, and location of countries, regions, cities, mountains, rivers, and other geographical features.

Abbreviations and Symbols for Chemical Elements

Check this section if you are confused by the abbreviation *PAT* (point after touchdown) or want to learn that *Fe* is the chemical symbol for iron.

Foreign Words and Phrases

The foreign words and phrases section defines unusual phrases, such as *Ars longa, vita brevis* (Art is long; life is short). Commonly used foreign phrases, such as *déjà vu,* are listed with the regular word entries.

Signs and Symbols

This section provides the symbols used in astronomy, business, math, medicine, weather forecasting, and other fields.

Style Handbook

Use the style section to check your punctuation or capitalization and for help with documentation of sources and ways to address people in certain positions, such as government officials.

THESAURUSES

A thesaurus, one kind of specialized dictionary, lists synonyms. The synonyms can be arranged categorically (traditional style) or alphabetically (dictionary style).

Traditional Style

To use a thesaurus arranged in the traditional style, begin by looking in the index for the word for which you want a synonym. For example, if you looked in the index under *require,* you might find these choices:

require entail 76.4
necessitate 637.9
lack 660.6
demand 751.4
oblige 754.5
charge 844.14
obligate 960.11

Let's say that *demand* seems like a good word to replace *require* in the report you're writing. You could simply use *demand,* or you could look in the front of the book under 751.4 for more choices. Guide numbers at the top of each page, similar to a dictionary's guide words, help you find the number you want quickly. On the page with the guide numbers 748.16–751.7, you find that word 751 is *demand.* Under this word are numbered paragraphs, each with possible synonyms for *demand.* The most commonly used words are printed in boldface type. Because *demand* can be a noun or a verb, the synonyms are separated into those two categories. You locate paragraph 751.4:

> VERBS **4. demand, ask,** make a demand; **call for,** call on *or* upon one for, come upon one for, appeal to for; cry for, clamor for; **require, exact,** require at the hands of; **requisition,** make *or* put in requisition, lay under contribution.

You decide that *exact* is an even better choice than *demand,* but you also read the other entries under *demand,* as those words are closely related. You notice that the thesaurus also includes synonyms in other languages, such as French and Latin. Some synonyms are marked *[coll.],* meaning "colloquial" or "informal." A page in the front or back of the thesaurus explains the other abbreviations that are used.

Dictionary Style

Looking up a word in a thesaurus organized alphabetically is just like looking up a word in a dictionary. Using the guide words at the top of the page, you locate the entry for the word *require:*

REQUIRE
Verb. **1.** [To need] want, feel the necessity for, have need for; see NEED. **2.** [To demand] exact, insist upon, expect; see ASK.

For more choices, you check *ask*, one of the capitalized words:

ASK

Verb. request, query, question, interrogate, examine, cross-examine, demand, pose *or* raise *or* put a question, inquire, frame a question, order, command, challenge, pry into, scour, investigate, hunt for, quiz, grill, *needle, *sound out, *pump, *put through the third degree.

Antonym: see ANSWER, REFUTE, REJOIN.

Checking the front of the book, you learn that an asterisk (*) indicates that a term is colloquial or slang.

B.C.   by johnny hart

By permission of Johnny Hart & Creaters
Syndicate, Inc.

STYLE GUIDES

Should you capitalize a title when it follows a person's name? Should you write *87* or *eighty-seven*? You can find a number of style guides, such as *The Chicago Manual of Style*, that will answer these questions. Style guides are reference books with detailed indexes that allow you to look up specific questions. The answers in one style guide may contradict the answers in another guide, so everyone working on the same project should agree to use the same style guide. Perhaps some of your teachers have asked you to follow a certain style guide in your writing.

Chapter 20

Accessing Electronic Resources

● ● ● ● ● ● ● ● ● ● ● ● ● ● ●

The Internet is an increasingly important source of information for people of all ages worldwide, but CD-ROMs
and other electronic resources not connected to the Internet
also offer vast amounts of information.

20.1 USING THE INTERNET

The Internet is a computer-based, worldwide information
network. The Internet uses telephone and cable lines and
satellites to link personal computers worldwide. The World
Wide Web, or WWW, is a set of programs and rules that
determine how files are created and displayed on the
Internet. To understand the difference, try this analogy: if
the Internet were one computer, the WWW would be a program that runs on that computer. As you research a topic,
the Internet and World Wide Web allow you to identify,
retrieve, and study documents without leaving your home,
school, or library. You can also use electronic mail, or
e-mail, to communicate with others interested in a specific
topic or to experts on that topic.

GAINING ACCESS

Your library computers can probably link you directly to the Internet at no cost to you. If you are using a computer at home, you'll need a **modem,** a device that connects your computer to a telephone or cable line. You must also subscribe to an **Internet service provider.** This service will connect you to the Internet for a fee.

UNDERSTANDING ADDRESSES

The information on the Internet is organized by locations, or sites, each with its own address. A Web address is also called a **Uniform Resource Locator,** or URL. Most addresses begin with *http://,* which stands for "hypertext transfer protocol" and identifies a way in which information is exchanged among computers connected by the Internet. The last part of an address, or its suffix, indicates the type of site it is. Here are some of the suffixes in use:

SUFFIX	TYPE OF SITE
.com	commercial
.edu	educational
.gov	government
.mil	military
.net	network organization or Internet service provider
.org	organization

USING BROWSERS

Each Internet service provider uses a specific **browser,** a program that locates and displays Web pages. Some browsers display only the text, or words, on a Web page;

most will display both text and **graphics** (pictures, photos, and diagrams). Browsers also allow you to print or download part or all of a Web site. (**Downloading** means copying information from Internet files onto a computer hard drive or a diskette.) Browsers permit you to move from page to page within a site or to jump from one site to a related site. Names of current browsers include Netscape Navigator and Internet Explorer.

ACCESSING WEB SITES

Let's say you are now connected to the Internet. If you want to see the information offered at a certain site, you can enter the site's address on the computer screen and be transferred there. You can also access specific reference sources this way, such as the *New York Times* or *Encyclopædia Britannica*. Some of these sources are free, but to gain access to others, you must subscribe and pay a fee in addition to the cost of the online service. A screen will explain any extra charges that are involved and let you choose whether to continue.

USING SEARCH ENGINES AND SUBJECT DIRECTORIES

If you don't have a specific address in mind, you can search by keyword with the help of a search engine or a subject directory.

Technology Tip

Be sure to read the Search Tip on pages 536–538, which provides information about using keywords. A keyword that is too general may generate hundreds of thousands of possible Web sites. It will take you a long time to search them and find a few helpful sources.

"First, they do an on-line search"

Search Engines Search engines are a type of software that uses your keyword to compile lists of related Web sites. Internet service providers use certain search engines, but you can switch to a different one by entering its address. Many kinds of search engines are available, and they offer slightly different services. Some print the first sentence or two of the information offered at each Web site, while other search engines list only the site's title and address.

Subject Directories Subject directories are a kind of software that provides an excellent place to start a search for a specific topic. A subject directory first lists general topics. After you choose one, the directory offers a list of possible subtopics. The directory then offers several more lists of subtopics to help you further narrow your topic. Finally, it provides a page of links to Web sites that are related to the specific topic you have now chosen.

MOVING AROUND WEB SITES

Often a word or phrase within the text of a Web page or at the end of the file will provide a link to a related Web site. These special words or phrases are called **hyperlinks.** They may be underlined or printed in a different color to make them easy to spot. When you click your mouse on a hyperlink, you'll immediately be transferred to another Web site. To get back, you can click on the back arrow or a similar symbol at the top of the computer screen.

Many Web sites are not checked for accuracy, so you must evaluate each site yourself. Begin by reviewing the Evaluating Tip on pages 549–550; this tip applies to Internet sources too.

1. Determine whether a Web site actually relates to your topic. A search engine will use every possible meaning of your keyword or phrase to compile a list of hundreds or thousands of sites. You may find that your keyword is also the name of a computer game or a sports team.

2. Pay particular attention to the source of the information in a Web site. (You may have to press the "move back" key several times to identify the organization sponsoring a site.) If a site is a personal Web page or if you cannot figure out its source or author, be sure to find another source to verify the information you find.

3. Evaluate the accuracy and fairness of the information. Is it based on more than one source? Are dissenting opinions included? After doing some of your own research elsewhere, are you aware of important information that was omitted from the site? Does the site include a bibliography and links to other sites? The answers to these questions can help you decide whether to use that source.

20.2 USING CD-ROMS AND DVDS

Technological advances create new research opportunities every day, so any discussion of the resources available quickly becomes out-of-date. Still, two resources are likely to be used for many years to come: CD-ROMs (<u>C</u>ompact <u>D</u>isc-<u>R</u>ead-<u>O</u>nly <u>M</u>emory) and DVDs (<u>D</u>igital <u>V</u>ideo <u>D</u>iscs). They can be used with a personal computer at home, at school, or at a library.

CD-ROM databases store both visual and audio information, such as photographs, maps, samples of different kinds of music, sound clips of famous speeches, and bird calls. Some CD-ROMs offer short videos of historical events and animated, narrated sequences that explain, for example, how acid rain forms or how airplanes fly.

One CD-ROM can store the same information as seven hundred diskettes; therefore, many dictionaries, encyclopedias, and other reference sources are now available as CD-ROMs. Many manufacturers offer yearly or monthly updates. To read a CD-ROM, your computer must have a CD-ROM drive. To broadcast sound effects, it must have speakers and a sound card.

Similar to a CD-ROM, a DVD has a larger storage capacity, enough space to store a full-length movie. DVDs require a DVD drive, which can also read CD-ROMs. (CD-ROM drives, however, cannot read DVDs.)

Library computer catalogs are another example of electronic resources that are not part of the Internet. Some of the databases available at the library are actually on CD-ROMs purchased by the library; other databases accessible from library computers are part of the Internet.

Knowledge often means knowing how to find information. Now you have knowledge. You can use it to find out more about the world and to take your place in it.

Index

D